# *Lewises, Meriwethers and Their Kin*

"LOCUST HILL"—HOME OF WILLIAM LEWIS (SEE PAGE 504) FROM AN EARLY SKETCH

# LEWISES, MERIWETHERS AND THEIR KIN

---

LEWISES AND MERIWETHERS
WITH THEIR TRACINGS THROUGH THE FAMILIES
WHOSE RECORDS ARE HEREIN
CONTAINED

---

COMPILED FROM FAMILY PAPERS AND
FROM RELIABLE SOURCES BY

SARAH TRAVERS LEWIS (SCOTT) ANDERSON

---

*"Lest we forget"*

CLEARFIELD

Reprinted for
Clearfield Company by
Genealogical Publishing Co.
Baltimore, Maryland
2008

ISBN-13: 978-0-8063-1072-5
ISBN-10: 0-8063-1072-3

*Made in the United States of America*

Originally published: Richmond, Virginia, 1938
Reprinted by Genealogical Publishing Co., Inc.
Baltimore, 1984, 1995

Library of Congress Catalogue Card Number 84-80082

*Dedicated*

TO

MY SISTER

FRANCES GREENHOW SCOTT

# Preface

In following the wishes of others that my collection of genealogical notes be arranged in a form to be readily understood by persons inexperienced in such work, I offer an explanation of my necessary use of the research of others to incorporate with my own research work.

Since genealogy reaches through many generations up to the present time and is necessarily the work of successive authors, each chronicler has to build on the work of others for tracings and evidences, and if need be, correct what may have been proved erroneous or incomplete in previous genealogies.

Justice to former authors demands that their work be given due credit—both in honor to the compilers—as well as furnishing legal references for those seeking further information.

In my own researches extending over many years, I have accepted the work of others to incorporate with my own work which is based on family papers, family registers, court records and historical sources, to which is added information gained from accredited genealogies.

Some of these genealogists received full assistance from members of my connection as well as myself.

The many applications which are made to me for help by persons who seek the earlier generations of their descent causes me to insert some fragmentary genealogies which may be helpful to such investigators.

HISTORIAN AND GENEALOGIST FOR THE LEWIS ASSOCIATION OF AMERICA (INCORPORATED)

# Family Feelings

(CHARLES WAGNER, author of "The Simple Life")

Here we are talking of right family feeling, and nothing else in the world can take its place; for in it lie in germ all those fine and simple virtues which assure the strength and duration of social institutions. And the very base of family feeling is respect for the past; for the best possessions of a family are its common memories. An intangible, indivisible, inalienable capital, these souvenirs constitute a sacred fund that each member of a family ought to consider more precious than anything he possesses. They exist in dual form, in idea and in fact. They show themselves in language, habits of thought, sentiments, even instincts; and one sees them materialized in furniture, buildings, dress, songs.

To profane eyes they are nothing; to the eyes of those who know how to appreciate the things of the family they are relics with which one should not part at any price.

# Contents

Contents

*Lewis Family*

# The Twelve Leakages

Twelve—Royal persons—are ancestors from whom "the people" may derive descent, namely:

| | |
|---|---|
| King John | 1 child |
| King Henry III | 1 child |
| King Edward I | 5 children |
| King Edward III | 4 children |
| King Henry VII | 1 child |

Many Virginians have descended from some one of the above named persons.

| | |
|---|---|
| Diggs | Edward III |
| Carters | Henry III |
| Smiths of Shooters Hill | Edward I |
| Peytons and Randolphs | Edward I |
| Fairfaxes | Edward III |
| Meads and some of the Bollings | Edward III |
| Spottswoods | Alfred the Great |
| Skipwiths | Henry III |
| Wests | Henry III |
| Claibornes | Henry III |
| Reads, Rootses, Nelsons of Yorktown, Berkleys, Warners and Washingtons | Edward III |
| Lewises and Lightfoots | Edward III |
| Throckmortons | Edward I |

Number of Descendants of Said Kings:

| | |
|---|---|
| Edward III | 60,000 |
| King John | 20,000 |
| Henry II | 20,000 |
| Henry VII | 20,000 |
| Descendants of Alfred the Great | 1,000,000 |

These royal descents are found among all sorts and conditions of people.

Roger Stafford, heir to the Barony of Stafford, was too poor to assume this title. His sister, wife of a joiner, her son a cobbler. Roger and his sister Jane, great-grandchildren of Margaret, Countess of Salisbury, the last of the Plantagenets.

The Woodcocks of England (descended from Henry VII) have among them, a butcher, toll gate keeper, a game keeper, a tailor, a painter, a glass cutter, a private soldier and a sailor.

A plumber who traced his descent back eight hundred and fifty years, is descended from Edward II; and a cab driver descended from Edward I.

"In Virginia also descendants of these same heredities ofttimes have fallen to poverty which has forced them to lowly employment.

"Yet sometimes these impoverished ones smile at the borrowed crests, and pedigrees which add no luster to the equally borrowed *homes* of the *newly rich*."

# The Lewis Families in Virginia

We have knowledge of six Lewis families of different descents and time of emigration to Virginia. These different dates of arrival in Virginia preclude all thought of "the three brothers." And so far as is known, the earlier generations of these lines of Lewises did not claim to be kin, though in old deeds they sometimes referred to each other as executors in a ceremonious way.

1. Robert Lewis of Brecon, emigrated......1635
2. John Lewis of Hanover " ......1640
3. John Lewis of Henrico " ......1660
4. Zachary Lewis " ......1694
5. John Lewis of Donegal " ......1732
6. John Lewis of Shenandoah, Va., emigrated........................1737

whose third child was born in Shenandoah, Va.

From GENERAL ROBERT LEWIS of Brecon, Wales, descend the "Meriwether Lewises" with many other lines of the "Warner Hall Lewises."

JOHN LEWIS of Hanover, emigrated from Wales, 1640, died in Virginia 1726, will probated in Hanover—fifth child, David Lewis lived near or at "Birdwood", near Charlottesville; his descendants, the Piedmont Maurys, Barkesdales and Frys still live near their old home. These Lewises scattered widely and bore a wonderful Revolutionary record. This David Lewis died in Albemarle in 1779. His descendant, Maj. Micajah Lewis, commanded a company at Kings Mountain in which were twenty-three Lewises—all descended from this same David. This family was noted for longevity.

JOHN LEWIS of Henrico County appears 1660.

From him descended—

Major John Lewis of Goochland, who married Mildred, daughter of Robert Lewis and Jane Meriwether. This family intermarried with the "RoBards", Cocks, Moseleys, etc.

ZACHARY LEWIS I, born 1650, name of wife unknown, took up lands in Virginia on Dragon Swamp in what is now King William or King and Queen County. Two sons are definitely known, John, and Zachary II. Descendants of these are many and widely scattered. They intermarried largely with the Belvoir Lewises.

*Note:* "Planter John Lewis" of Albemarle near Scottsville seems a separate line, supposed to be descended from, or related to, Zachary Lewis. The will of this John Lewis is in Albemarle records, written July, 1786 codicil 1792-1794 probated June 6, 1800. This family intermarried with Gilmers, Gnautts and Pattersons.

JOHN LEWIS of Donegal settled at Staunton, Augusta County, 1732. His family, wonderful for Revolutionary record and for patriotism, is too generally known to require explanation; like the other Lewises, this family is widely scattered, has intermarried with other Lewises, and with other distinguished families. John Lewis himself was the founder of Augusta County, Va. Among his sons, Col. Charles Lewis was killed at the battle of Point Pleasant. Gen. Andrew Lewis who won that battle, and was later distinguished in the Revolution, lived in what is now Botetourt County. John Lewis' other sons had useful records and military service.

JOHN LEWIS of Shenandoah County, Va., born in Wales, m. Margaret ——. Issue nine children.

(*a*) Reese Lewis, born 1730.
(*b*) Susannah Lewis, born 1735.
(*c*) Amos Lewis, born 1737, m. Mollie Chrisman.
(*d*) Thomas Lewis, born 1739.
(*e*) Annie Lewis, born 1742.
(*f*) George Lewis, born 1744.
(*g*) Hannah Lewis, born 1746, died 1748.
(*h*) Evan Lewis, born 1749.
(*i*) Mordecai Lewis, born 1751, m. Mary Segler.

This Mordecai after the Revolution emigrated to Tennessee from Shenandoah carrying with him the old Welsh Bible brought from Wales. It is now in the possession of his descendants in Marion County, Tennessee. He left eight children.

REFERENCES:
*The Genealogy of the Lewis Family* by William Terrel Lewis.
*Lewises and Kindred Families* by John Meriwether McAllister and Mrs. Lula Tandy.

*Note:* I also find other Lewises, who claim their families came from Wales to Virginia, but they have not kept their records and do not appear to be of the six mentioned families.

## LEWISES

"The love of ancient ancestry is said to be laughably displayed by the Lewis family of England who are said to have in their possession a picture of the Ark with Noah emerging from it bearing a large trunk labelled, 'Papers belonging to the Lewis Family'."

Extract from "A Glimpse of an old Dutch Town."
*Harpers Magazine,* March 1881.

The Lewises have the Celtic love of genealogy, and have always kept record of themselves and ancestry, if possible, and have searched out latterly quite a number of long and indisputable tracings. And in spite of the many sources of other blood, this love for family history asserts itself in spite of all obstacles at some period in the life of each *Lewis;* for all claim that name who have a drop of Lewis blood, no matter how far they go back to trace it.

## THE "WARNER HALL" LEWISES

This branch of Lewises has several long tracings which can be more readily understood if reduced to chart form, so I have copied each extract and numbered each one as Charts I, II, III, and IV.

Since the descendants of the Warner Hall Lewises trace beyond Noah, his trunk could no longer hold the "Papers of the Lewis Family"; for their genealogies have spread out far and wide since the Flood.

Chart No. I taken from the chart of "Lineage of the Royal Family of Great Britain," runs down to Lionel and his daughter, Philippa.

Chart II does the same, also Chart III.

As Col. George Reade of England and Virginia traces directly back to these lines through Philippa Plantagenet, daughter of Lionel, all the families—Warner, Lee, Lewis, Washington, Reade, and others descending from Col. George Reade, have these long descents.

# ILLUSTRIOUS LINEAGE

*of the*

ROYAL HOUSE OF GREAT BRITAIN

## EXTRACT—CHART I

---

JUDAH<br>
Dardanus or Darius<br>
Erichthonius<br>
Tros or Troes

AUTHORITY:
Sanchoniatho in Tara Vindicata. The Ancient Icelandic Langfedgatal in Sharon Turner, Windsor Castle MS. Genealogy.

Ilus<br>
Laomedon<br>
Priam<br>
Daughter married Memnon<br>
Tror, their son, whom we call Thor<br>
Hloritha<br>
Einridi<br>
Vingethorr<br>
Vingener<br>
Moda<br>
Magi<br>
SCEAF (Anglo-Saxon Chronicle)<br>
Bedwig (Sharon Turner)<br>
Hwala<br>
Hadra or Athra<br>
Hermon or Itormann<br>
Heremad<br>
Sceldwea or Scealdna<br>
Beaw or Beaf<br>
Taetwa<br>
GEAT or Getha (Heralds' College MS.)<br>
Flocwal<br>
Flokwal<br>
Flocwaldus<br>
Flym<br>
Fredulfe

ODIN married FREA

AUTHORITY: (Anderson, Du Chaillu, Haigh, Sharon Turner.)

| | |
|---|---|
| Baeldaeg | Yngvi |
| Brand | Fiolner |
| Gewis | Svegdir |
| Elesa | Vanlandi |
| | Visbur |
| | Domaldi |
| | Domar |
| CERDIC | Dyggvi |
| | Dagr |
| Creoda | Agni |
| | Alrek |
| Cyneric | Yngvi |
| Ceawlin | Jorund |
| Cuthwine | Aun the Aged |
| | Egil |
| Cutha | Ottar |
| Ceolwald | Adils of Upsala |
| | Eystein |
| Coenraed | Yngvar |
| Ingild | Braut Onund |
| Eoppa | Ingiald the Cunning |
| | Olaf the Woodcutter |
| Eafa | Halfdan the Whitefoot |
| Ealmund | Eystein |
| | Halfdan the Meek |
| EGBERT | Gudrod the Magnanimous |
| Ethelwolf | Halfdan the Black |
| ALFRED the Great | HARALD FAIRHAIR |
| Edward | Rognwald |
| Edmund | ROLLO |
| Edgar | William |
| Ethelred | Richard "The Little Duke" |
| Edmond | Richard |
| Edward | Robert |
| St. Margaret Athelling who married Malcolm Canmore | William the Conqueror |

King of Scotland    Henry I.

Matilda married

Henry I.

Maud or Matilda m. Geoffrey Plantagenet who was descended from Melisenda, Heiress and Ancestress of the Kings of Jerusalem. (Logan)

Henry II

John

Henry III

Edward I

Edward II

Edward III

Lionel Duke of Clarence m. Lady Elizabeth de Burgh

Philippa m. Edmund Mortimer

Elizabeth Mortimer m. Henry Hotspur

Henry Percy Earl of Northumberland

Margaret Percy m. Sir Wm. Gascoigne

Elizabeth Gascoigne m. Sir George Talbois

Anne Talbois m. Sir Edward Dymoke, Hereditary Champion

Frances Dymoke m. Sir Thomas Windebank

Mildred Windebank m. Robert Reade

Col. George Reade m. Mil~~dred Martian~~ Elizabeth Martiau

Mildred Reade m. Col. Augustine Warner

Elizabeth Warner m. Col. John Lewis 2rd. of "Warner Hall"

AUTHORITY:

Battle Abbey Roll.
"The Royal Lineage" by Mrs. Watson.

END OF CHART I

## EXTRACT—CHART II

AUTHORITIES: Glover, Grimaldi, Tara Vindicata, Bede.

---

DAVID
Solomon
Rehoboam
Abijah
Asa
Jehosaphat
Jehoram
Ahaziah
Joash
Amaziah
Uzziah
Jotham
Ahaz
Hezekiah
Manasseh
Amon
Josiah
Zedekiah
Tea Tephi m. Eochaidh the HEREMON

*Note:* Tea Tephi, "Daughter of God's House", Princess of the House of David, came to Ireland 580 B. C. and brought with her a relic of immemorial antiquity said to be Jacob's Pillow, and to have been carried to and from Egypt with the Israelites. It was later called "The Stone of Scone". Her husband, Eochaidh, was descended from Judah. (Totten, Feilden.)

From Tea Tephi and Eochaidh the HEREMON descended:
Ungaine the Great
Angus the Prolific

| KINGS IN IRELAND | KINGS IN SCOTLAND |
|---|---|
| Enna | Fiachra or Ferchard |
| Labhra Luire | FERGUS I |
| Blathachta | Manius or Maine |

| | |
|---|---|
| Easamhuin | Dornadil or Arandil |
| Roignein | Reuthar |
| Finlocha | |
| Finn | Eders or Edersceol |
| Eochaidh Feidhlioch | |
| Brias Fineamhuas (A. D. commences) | |
| Lughaidh Riebdearg | |
| Crimthann | Conaire the Great |
| Fearadhach | Corbred I |
| Tuathal Teachtmar | Corbred II |
| Conn of the 100 Battles | Modha Lamha |
| Saraid ————married———— | Conaire II |

CORBRED DALRIADA or Reuda
Eochaidh or Etholdius
Athirco of Athirkiwr
Findachar
Thrinklind
Fincormach
Romaich
Angus
Eochaidh of Ethod
Erc, Erch, or Erth
FERGUS THE GREAT died A. D. 506
Dongard
Govran
Aydan
Eugene or Eochaid
Donald
Ethach
Ethdre
Ethafind or Ethfin
Ethas or Achaios
Alpin

KENNETH MACALPIN, 1st King of Scotland
Constantine
Donald VI
Malcolm
Kenneth II
Malcolm II
Beatrix
Duncan
Malcolm Canmore m. Margaret of England
Matilda married Henry I
Maud or Matilda m. Geoffrey Plantagenet
Henry II
John
Henry III
Edward I
Edward II
Edward III
Lionel m. Lady Elizabeth de Burgh
Philippa m. Sir Edward Mortimer
Elizabeth Mortimer m. Henry Hotspur
Henry Percy Earl of Northumberland
Henry Percy Earl of Northumberland
Margaret Percy m. Sir William Gascoigne
Elizabeth Gascoigne m. Sir George Talbois
Ann Talbois m. Sir Edward Dymoke
Frances Dymoke m. Sir Thomas Windebank
Mildred Windebank m. Robert Reade
Col. George Reade m. Mildred Martian
Mildred Reade m. Col. Augustine Warner 2nd
Elizabeth Warner m. Col. John Lewis 2nd of "Warner Hall", Gloucester County, Va.

AUTHORITIES:
"Some Notable Families of America."
"The Royal Lineage."
"Henning's Statues at Large."

END OF CHART II

## CHART III

Descent of

LEWIS OF "WARNER HALL"

*from*

CHARLEMANGE AND HIS 3RD WIFE, HILDEGARDE

(Died 783)

---

Pharamond King of the Franks A. D. 300
Clodis " " " " A. D. 390
Albro " " " "
Verbertus " " " "
Ausbert " " " "
Arnold " " " "
St. Arnolph, Bishop of Metz
Ancheons and Bezga, daughter of Pippen of Landin 600 A. D.
Pepin d'Heredat, Mayor of the Palace
Charles Martel, King of France
Pepin le Bref, King of France and Bertha da Leon
Charlemange, Emperor of the West and Hildegarde, daughter of Duke of Suabia, Childebrand
Louis I, King of France and Judith, Fair Maid of Bavaria.
Ludwig, Emperor of Germany
Charles II, Emperor of Germany and Rechedis
Princess Judith and Baldwin of Flanders (1st count)
Baldwin II, Count of Flanders and Ethelweda, daughter of Alfred the Great of England.
Arnolph the Great, Count of Flanders and Luxemburg, 1067 A.D. married 2nd, Madeline (daughter of Robert the Pious and his 2nd wife)
Baldwin III of Flanders and Matilda of Saxony
Arnolph II, Count of Flanders and Susanna, daughter of Berenger II, King of Italy
Baldwin IV, Count of Flanders and Ogive of Luxemburg
Baldwin V, Count of Flanders and Adela, daughter of Robert II of France
Maude of Flanders, and William the Conqueror, 15th in descent from Adelis the Great, King of Sweden.

Henry I, and Matilda of Scotland, 13th in descent from Ethafind, King of Scotland.

Maude of England, and Geoffrey Plantaganet who was the 8th in descent from Fulk I, Count of Anjou, 900 A. D.

Henry II of England and Eleanor of Guienne

John, King of England and Isabella of Angouleme

Henry III and Eleanor of Provence, 9th in descent from Armadeus of Provence

Edward I and Eleanor of Castile, 11th in descent from Sancho II, King of Navarre

Edward II and Isabella of France

Edward III and Philippa of Hainault

Lionel, Duke of Clarence and Elizabeth DeBurgh

Edward Mortimer, Earl of March, and Philippa Plantaganet

Elizabeth Mortimer and Henry Percy (Hotspur)

Henry Percy, Earl of Northumberland, and Eleanor DeNeville

Henry III, Earl of Northumberland, m. Lady Eleanor Poinings

Margaret Percy, m. Sir William Gascoigne

Elizabeth Gascoinge, m. Sir Geo. Talbois

Ann Talbois, m. Sir Edward Dymoke

Frances Dymoke, m. Sir Thomas Windebank

Mildred Windebank, m. Robert Reade

George Reade, m. Elizabeth Martian of Virginia (pronounced Marchen)

END OF CHART III

## CHART IV

### Descent of

### "WARNER HALL LEWISES" THROUGH EARLS OF DORSET

AUTHORITY: See "Burke's Peerage to Twenty-Six Generations"

---

Robert, Count of Anjou
Robert, Duke of France
Hugh, Grand Count of Anjou and Duke of France
Hugh Capet
Robert
Henry I, King of France
Philip I, King of France
Louis VI, King of France
Louis VII, King of France
Philip II, King of France
Louis VIII, King of France
Louis X, King of France
Philip III, King of France
Margaret m. Edward I of England
Thomas Plantagenet
Margaret Plantagenet m. Lord John Seagraves
Elizabeth Seagraves m. Sir John Mowbray
Thomas de Mowbray m. Elizabeth ——
Margaret de Mowbray m. Sir Robert Howard
Sir John Howard m. Catherine ——
Thomas II, Duke of Norfolk m. Elizabeth ——
Thomas III, Duke of Norfolk m. Elizabeth ——
Henry, Earl of S—— m. Frances ——
Thomas IV, Duke of Norfolk m. —— ——
Margaret m. Robert, Earl of Dorset
Ann m. Sir Edmund Lewis
Gen. Robert Lewis of Wales
Robert Lewis of Brecon, Wales came to Virginia

John Lewis m. Isabella Warner
John Lewis m. Elizabeth Warner (Warner Hall Lewises)
|
Catherine; Elizabeth; Col. John Lewis; Col. Charles Lewis; Col. Robert Lewis; Elizabeth; Isabella; and Ann were the eight children of this marriage whose names are preserved.

END OF CHART IV

## THE ROYAL CHAMPIONSHIP
OF
## MARMION AND DYMOKE

Sir Robert Marmyon "Dispensator" Sieur de Fontenay le-Marmyon (descended from Rolf the Granger, Hereditary Champion to the Duke of Normandy) came over with William I and was granted Scrivelsby and created Champion of England.

|

Sir Roger Marmyon, Knight
2nd Champion

|

Sir Robert
3rd Champion

|

Sir Robert
4th Champion

|

Sir Robert
5th Champion
Justiciary and Sheriff of Worcestershire

|

Sir Robert
6th Champion

|

Sir Philip Marmyon
7th Champion
Governor of Kenilworth
Lord of Tamworth, Scrivelsby, etc.

| Margaret | Joan |
|---|---|
| 1st daughter and heiress of Tamworth, married Sir Baldwin Freville, Knight claimed the | 2nd daughter and heiress of Scrivelsby and the Championship married Sir Thomas |

Championship but was disallowed by Court of Claims I, V.

(Richard 2, 1st Y.)

Ludlow, Knight and Dep't. Champion.

Thomas de Ludlow D. V. M.

Margaret Ludlow, daughter and heiress of Scrivelsby and the Championship; d. 2nd Henry 5, married Sir John Dymoke Kn't., Dep't. Champion at Coronation of Richard II (defeated Freville.) R. G. M. P. Line.

Sir Thomas Knt. K. B. Dep't Champion for his Mother for Henry IV and Henry V, d. 1422.

Sir Philip Knt. Champion to Henry VI

ARMS

*Crest*..........Crest is a Hare's head.
*Shield*..........On the shield are two Lions with a Crown over each one's head.
Shield is black.
Lions are silver.
Crowns are gold.
*Motto*.........."PRO REGE DIMICO".

---

## ROYAL LINEAGE (*Continued*)

Extract from "A Royal Lineage", by Annah Robinson Watson.

---

Edward III, m. Philipa of Hainault, 1312-1327.

Their 2nd son, Lionel, Duke of Clarence m. The Lady Elizabeth de Burg, 1368. She was daughter of William de Burg, Earl of Ulster.

She was descended from Charlemagne, from Henry III and from the Red Hand, King of Connaught.

Tradition says that three Vikings approaching Ireland agreed that he who first touched land should own it. Seeing himself outstripped by the others, the hindmost one cut off his left hand and flung it bleeding, and red, far ashore, thus making good his title as first to touch the land. War-like clans descended from him used the (*Red Hand*) on their crests, and shields. The Lewises have this crest—"a bloody hand in a dragon's mouth," and since they are lineally descended from this Red Handed King of Connaught this legend probably explains the crest.

Philipa Plantagenet, daughter of Lionel and Lady Elizabeth de Burg m. Edward Mortimer, Earl of March, who was descended from Llewellenap Lowerth and other distinguished Welsh chieftains.

Elizabeth Mortimer m. Henry Percy (Hotspur).

Henry Percy, 2nd Earl of Northumberland m. Lady Eleanor Neville (she was descended from John of Gaunt and his wife Catherine of Swynford.

Their son Henry Percy, 3rd Earl of Northumberland m. Lady Eleanor Poynings.

Lady Margaret Percy m. Sir William Gascoigne.

Lady Elizabeth Gascoigne m. Sir George Talbois.

Lady Anne Talbois m. Sir Edward Dymoke, Hereditary Champion of England, descended from Edward I and his 2nd wife through their son Thomas Plantagenet; also from Princess Joan d'Aines who m. Gilbert, called the Red Earl of Clare.

Lady Anne Talbois was descended from both John of Gaunt and Lionel Duke of Clarence (two sons of Edward III.)

Sir Edward Dymoke descended in the female line from Robert, Marmyon (Lord), cousin to William the Conqueror and hereditary Champion to the Dukes of Normandy through his descent from Rollo, the Dane. He fought at Hastings, and was hereditary Champion at the Coronation of William and Matilda at Winchester 1068, holding Tamworth Castle and Scrivelsby Court in England and Fontenaye in Normandy for this service.

The Dymokes still hold Scrivelsby under this tenure. The last exercise of this office was at the coronation of George IV when the Champion in full armor rode into the state dining hall, issued his challenge to any that might contest the King's right, drank the King's health out of a golden cup that he retained as a fee, then backed his horse out of the presence of the King.

Their daughter, Frances Dymoke m. in 1556, Sir Thomas Windebank (son of Sir Richard Windebank of Haines Hill, Parish of Hurst, Berkshire, England, and his wife Margaret, daughter of Griffith ap Henry.) He was clerk of the signet to Queen Elizabeth and her successor, James I. He died October 24, 1607.

Mildred Windebank m. Robert Reade (son of Andrew Reade, who died 1623, in his Manor of Linkinholt, Hampshire, England, and who m. Miss Cooke of Kent. His will was probated October 24, 1623.)

Their 5th son Col. George Reade born 1600, died 1671, came to Virginia in 1637. Married Elizabeth Martian, daughter of Capt. Nicholas Martian, a Frenchman, who came to Virginia and naturalized both himself and his name, which was originally spelled Martineu.

## NICHOLAS MARTIAN, (MARTIAU), (MARTINEU)

Nicholas Martian was the first owner of the land on which later Yorktown was established, was of French birth, a Protestant, a naturalized citizen of England, was in Virginia 1621 with a wife and two children, married second after 1625, Jane, widow of Lieutenant Berkley, married a third time, 1645, Isabella Beech, (colonial record given later), divided his estate between his daughters Elizabeth, wife of Col. George Reade; Mary, wife of Col. John Scasbrook; and Sarah, wife of William Fuller, Governor of Maryland. All three of these daughters were by Elizabeth, his first wife. Nicholas Martian's will is dated March 1, 1656 and is recorded in York County 1657.

## COL. GEORGE READE

Col. Reade came to America in 1637, was Secretary to the Colony of Virginia in 1640, then a Burgess, a Colonel of Militia, etc. (See Colonial Record). When he first came to the colony he stayed with Governor Harvey at Jamestown; after his marriage to Elizabeth Martian he is supposed to have lived on land he inherited from his father-in-law.

Issue: Twelve children, seven of whom are on record.

1. Robert Reade, m. Mary Lilly. (Ancestors of General Thomas Nelson and family of Anthony Robinson.)
2. Francis Reade, m. first, Jane Chisman. (Descendants are Davises and Watlingtons.)

3. Thomas Reade, m. Lucy Gwyn, daughter of Edmund Gwyn of Gloucester. (Descendants are Rootes, Dixons, Taliaferros, Throckmortons, and probably Col. Clement Reade of Charlotte County. Born January 1, 1707, m. 1730, Mary Hill.)
4. Mildred Reade, m. Col. Augustine Warner. (Descendants are Lewises, Washingtons, Taliaferros, Brookes, Seldens, etc.)
5. Benjamin Reade, m. Lucy ——, and had descendants.
6. George Reade, m. Dorothy ——, died without issue.
7. Elizabeth Reade, m. Capt. Thomas Chisman of York County, Virginia.

## NELSON

Margaret, daughter of Robert and Mary Lilly Reade, married Thomas Nelson, an emigrant from Scotland who came over in 1690. (In 1691 his brother-in-law, Benjamin Reade, consented for a part of his land to be surveyed for town lots by Major Lawrence Smith.) Thomas Nelson had a store there and doubtless inherited land through his wife, also. He had been in Virginia fifteen years before his marriage. He built first a wooden house on land opposite this present Nelson house. Later he built the brick house, the kitchen of which stands today at Yorktown, Virginia.

Issue:

1. William Nelson, President of the Colony. He built to the present Nelson House, which remained in the family until 1909. He married Betty Burwell of Carter's Creek. The Nelsons are the only Reade descendants that remained in Yorktown.
2. Thomas Nelson, Jr., Secretary of the Colony, m. Lucy Armistead. His children were:
   *a.* Col. William Nelson.
   *b.* Capt. Thomas Nelson.
   *c.* Major John Nelson.

   All these were gallant officers in the Revolution. The first two moved to Hanover County after the War. John moved to Mecklenburg County, Va.

3. Mary Nelson, married Col. Edmund Berkely of "Barn Elms".

---

Scotch Tom Nelson m. second a widow, Tucker of the Bermudas and had: Sally Nelson, who married Robin Burwell.

## WARNER

AUGUSTINE WARNER, first of the name to come to America came to Virginia before 1630 (*William and Mary Quarterly*). He was born November 28, 1610, died "Ye 26th of December 1674, aged 63 years, 2 mos. 26 days." (Epitaph at "Warner Hall"). Mary, his wife, born "Ye 15th of May 1614, died August 11th, 1660." Augustine Warner took up lands in 1654 and bequeathed them after his death to his son of the same name. His children were:

I. Sarah Warner m. Col. Lawrence Townley (ancestors of General Robert E. Lee.)

II. Isabella Warner wife of Maj. John Lewis of "Warner Hall".

III. Col. Augustine Warner (2) was born "ye 3rd of June 1642 and died ye 19th of June 1681". He matriculated at the Merchant Taylor School, London, England, at eleven years of age as eldest son of Augustine Warner, gent. Completing his education and returning to Virginia he married Mildred Reade, daughter of Col. George and Elizabeth Martian Reade.

He and his wife had issue:

A. Mildred Warner m. 1690, Lawrence Washington (1661-1697). Their son Augustine was father to Gen. George Washington.

B. Mary Warner born (?), died 1700, m. February 17, 1680, John Smith of Purton, Gloucester County.

C. Augustine Warner "born ye 17th of January 1666 or 67 and died ye 17th of March 1686 or 87".

D. Robert Warner died without issue.

E. George Warner died without issue.

F. Elizabeth Warner m. Col. John Lewis. They lived at "Warner Hall", and from them descend, so far as it is known, all entitled to this "Warner-Lewis" descent.

Tombstone at "Warner Hall"—"Elizabeth Warner born at Ches-ake Nov. 24th 1672, died aged 47 yrs. 2 mos. & 12 days. She was the Tender Mother of 14 children. She departed this life the 6th Day of Feb. 1719/20."

# Warner Hall Lewises

"These Lewises, coming through long lines of descent from many rulers, are remarkable for ability in civil affairs, though have a military record also. In Wales they were sheriffs, county lieutenants, justices and members of Parliament, from Brecknock, Pembroke, Glamorganshire and other Welsh counties; their abilities asserting themselves in many directions." (*Notable Families of America.*—Mrs. Watson.)

General tradition gives as the immediate ancestor of the Virginia Warner Hall Lewises in Wales—

Sir Edmond Lewis, Witny County, m. Lady Ann Dorset (daughter of Earl of Dorset, see Chart 4.) Among their issue was—

General Robert Lewis of Brecon, Wales, born 1574.

The latter's son, Gen. Robert Lewis, the emigrant, was born in Brecon, Wales 1607; came with his wife Elizabeth to America 1635 and settled in Gloucester County, Virginia. We have record of two children.

William Lewis of Chemokin, New Kent County died without issue. His estate was inherited by his brother Major John Lewis. (*Hennings Statutes at Large.*) 1769.

Major John Lewis I, born 1635, member of House of Burgesses 1653 and King's Council from Gloucester County 1658-59-60. Married Isabella Warner 1666 and he and his wife are said to have been the original settlers of "Warner Hall", the place being named in honor of Isabella Warner. Augustine Warner took up lands on Piankitank and later the tract on which Warner Hall stands in Robin's Neck, therefore through this marriage it seems probable that the Lewises acquired "Warner Hall". The house is said to have originally contained 40 rooms. Mr. Joseph Bryan of Richmond City and Eagle Point, Gloucester County, told me that this house, when burnt in 1849, was the oldest colonial house existing in Virginia. In this fire the center brick house was destroyed, leaving the smaller detached houses at either end intact. The Clarks who owned the place at the time of this fire (which Mr. Bryan remembered) placed a wooden house on the site of the original brick center part of the old house. This frame house was later removed, and a beautiful Colonial wooden building placed between the brick wings by Mr. R. P. Cheney, making an interior full of comfort and charm. The living room, and dining room, are baronial in size and furnishings, and the view from an upper room down a magnificent avenue of trees is after the order of an English country house. The house is set in a beautiful lawn, which falls to the Severn at the back and touches the main road in front, which road taps the highway from Gloucester Point and cuts Robin's Neck in two. Somewhat back of the house lies the old graveyard which was in good repair at the time of my visit—1907. Mr. Cheney thoughtfully had it mowed so that Mrs. Herdman and I might the more easily go over it in copying the inscriptions. Warner Hall remained in the possession of the Brookes (descendants in direct line of Warner Lewis I) until 1848, when it was sold by the heirs of Mrs. Matthew Brookes to a Colonel Tennant of Baltimore, whose daughter lived there for a time. Later it was purchased by Colin Clarke who with his interesting family lived there many years. Later it was rented by various people—then bought by Mr. Alfred Withers, who sold it to Mr. Cheney. Mr. Withers reserved the graveyard which contained the ashes of his wife's ancestors. He repaired it and presented it to the Association for the Preservation of Virginia Antiquities. During the time the place was rented it was the scene of frequent "surprise parties" the young people enjoying dancing on the hard slippery floors, and promenades down the avenue in the bright moonlight.

We were also guests of Mr. and Mrs. Joseph Bryan at Eagle Point. This plantation adjoining Warner Hall had formerly belonged to John Lewis, son of John and Frances Fielding Lewis who lived there in 1798 and called it "View de L'eau". Mr. Bryan took me into the old Lewis parlor, a high pitched room, with the old mouldings, and a heavy frieze.

Mr. Bryan's father bought the place before the Civil War, some of the Lewis slaves being included in the sale. Mr. Joseph Bryan was born there. As some eagles nested in a nearby group of tall trees, the Bryans changed the name of the place to "Eagle Point", the name it still bears.

Mr. Joseph Bryan had repurchased Eagle Point, which his

father had sold years before, and was living there at the time of my visit to Gloucester. His alterations of the original house were most happy and beautiful, fitting it as Warner Hall had been fitted to modern conditions. It is a beautiful location on the river's edge. The burial ground of the Bryan's is on an island out in the river, reminding one of descriptions of similarly situated graveyards in the Scottish Islands.

---

Councilor John Lewis II (son and only remaining child of John and Isabella Lewis) one of his Majesty's Honorable Council of this colony, was born ye 30th of November, 1669, died November 14, 1725 (member of Kings Council 1715). He m. Elizabeth Warner, born November 24, 1672 and died February 6, 1720. They had fourteen children—the names of eight only being preserved, the others are supposed to have died in childhood.

Children of Colonel John Lewis and Elizabeth Warner of Warner Hall:

1. Catherine born ——, baptized 1702.
2. Elizabeth born ——, baptized 1702.
3. Col. John Lewis III, born ——, baptized November 1702, married Frances Fielding, daughter of Henry Fielding of King and Queen County.
4. Col. Chas. Lewis of the Byrd, Goochland County, b. October 13, 1696, d. 1779, m. 1717, Mary Howell, daughter of John Howell, gentleman.
5. Col. Robert Lewis of Bel-voir, Albemarle County, baptized May 4, 1702, m. Jane Meriwether 1725, daughter of Nicholas Meriwether and Elizabeth Crawford, d. 1753.
   Robert Lewis m. 2nd, Mrs. Elizabeth Meriwether, d. 1765, widow of Thomas Meriwether.
6. Elizabeth, baptized March 7, 1706.
7. Isabella, baptized December 18, 1707, m. Dr. Thomas Clayton, July 14, 1720. She, her husband and infant child, Juliana are all buried at Warner Hall. Her and her bus-

band's tombstones have each the Clayton Arms, with different crests.

8. Ann, baptized February 14, 1712.

Col. John Lewis of Warner Hall, m. 2nd, Mrs. Priscilla Carter, daughter of Col. Wm. Churchill of Middlesex County, Va. No issue. His descendants through the three sons of his 1st marriage.

## COL. JOHN LEWIS III

Married Frances Fielding. He inherited Warner Hall and the historic Belle Farm.

Issue: Six children—

1. Warner Lewis, b. 1720, m. Eleanor Bowles Gooch, widow of Wm. Gooch, and daughter of Governor Bowles of Maryland. Their descendants retained possession of Warner Hall for many generations.
2. A second child whose name was illegible on an old church register.
3. Col. Fielding Lewis, born 1725.
4. Mildred, died in infancy.
5. Charles Lewis, born February 20, 1729.
6. John Lewis, born March 5, 1727, "View de L'eau."

The oldest son, Warner Lewis (5) inherited Warner Hall, married Eleanor Bowles Gooch and had issue:

1. Warner Lewis (6), who married 1st, Mary Chiswell, and 2nd, Mary Fleming.
2. Fielding Lewis (6) of Weyanoke, m. Agnes Harwood.
3. James Lewis (6), m. Mrs. Thornton.
4. John Lewis (6) (no record.)
5. Addison Lewis (6), m. Susan Fleming, sister of Mary.
6. Thomas Lewis (6), m. Nancy Harwood.
7. Rebecca Lewis (6), m. Dr. Robert Innis.

Warner Lewis (6) had by his 1st marriage to Mary Chiswell:

1. Warner Lewis (7), m. Courtnay Norton.
2. John Lewis (7), m. Ann Griffin.
3. Elizabeth Lewis (7) (never married.)
4. Eleanor Lewis (7) m. 1st, John Fox and 2nd, Augustine Olivier.

By his second marriage to Mary Fleming Warner Lewis (6) had:

5. Caroline Lewis, m. Charles Barnett or Barret.
6. Julia Lewis (7), m. Thomas Throckmorton.
7. John Lewis (7), m. his cousin Eleanor Lewis.
8. Philip Warner (7) (never married.)

Warner Lewis (7) and his wife Courtnay Norton had issue:

1. Mary C. Lewis (8), m. John Peyton and had:

   Rebecca Peyton (9), m. Ed. C. Marshall son of Chief Justice Marshall, died in Fauquier County, February 8, 1882.

2. Elizabeth Lewis (8), m. Mathew Brooke, M. D., and had issue:
   1. Elizabeth Brooke (9), born October 1813, m. May 16, Henry M. Marshall.
   2. Courtnay W. Brooke (9), m. Robert Selden 1834 and died 1922.
   3. Mary L. Brooke (9), m. Dr. S. P. Byrd.
   4. John Lewis Brooke (9), m. Maria Louisa Ashby, born 1828, died 1882.

Fielding Lewis (6) of Weyanoke (son of Warner Lewis (5) and his wife Eleanor Gooch), m. Agnes Harwood and had issue—four daughters:

1. Nancy Lewis (7).
2. Fanny F. Lewis (7), m. Archibald Taylor.
3. Margaret Lewis (7), born at Weyanoke in Charles City County, 1772, died at Oakhill, Fauquier County, 1829, m. October 19, 1809, Thomas Marshall, son of Chief Justice Marshall, born in Richmond, died in Baltimore 1835, and had—
   1. John Marshall (8), b. 1811, d. 1854, m. 1837, Annie E. Blackwell.
   2. Agnes H. Marshall (8), m. Gen. Alex. Taliaferro.
   3. Mary Marshall (8), m. William B. Archer.
   4. Fielding Marshall (8), m. first Rebecca Coke, second Mary V. Thomas.

5. Annie L. Marshall (8), m. James F. Jones.
6. Margaret Marshall (8), m. John Thomas Smith.
7. Col. Thomas Marshall (8), m. Maria Barton.

4. Eleanor W. Lewis (7), m. Robert Douthat and had issue:
   1. Robert Douthat (8), m. Mary A. Marshall.
   2. Jane Douthat (8), m. Dr. William Selden.
   3. Agnes Douthat (8), m. Robert Lewis McGuire.
   4. Fielding Lewis Douthat (8), m. Mary Willis Marshall.

Fannie Lewis (7), m. Archibald Taylor and had issue:
   1. Col. F. L. Taylor (8), m. E. L. Fauntleroy.
   2. Dr. Archibald Taylor (8), m. Martha Fauntleroy.
   3. Robert Taylor (8).
   4. Thomas Taylor (8).

James Lewis (6), son of Warner and Eleanor (Gooch) Lewis, lived at the old Brew House on the Severn River near Warner Hall. He married Mrs. Sarah Thurston Thornton. She married three times, 1st: Thornton, 2nd: Lewis, 3rd: Tabb. The Lewis children were Eleanor, who married her cousin John Lewis, no issue, and Sally who married Dr. Samuel Griffin. His parents were Cyrus Griffin, President of the Continental Congress and Lady Christina Stuart of Traquar's Castle, Scotland.

Children of Sally (7) and Dr. Griffin were:
   1. James Griffin (8), no issue.
   2. Cyrus Griffin (8), died unmarried.
   3. Louisa Griffin (8), m. Dr. Wright and had—
      1. Sally Wright (9), m. Dr. Ball.

Addison, son of Warner and Eleanor (Gooch) Lewis, married Susan Fleming and had issue:
   1. Susan Lewis, b. 1782, d. November 12, 1865, m. William P. Byrd of Westover and had issue:
      1. Addison Byrd (8), m. Sue Coke.
      2. Mary Willing Byrd (8), m. Richard W. Coke.
      3. Jane Otway Byrd (8), m. G. W. MacCandish.
      4. Samuel P. Byrd (8), m. 1st: Catherine C. Corbin, 2nd: Mary Lewis Brooke.

Eleanor Lewis (7), daughter of Warner and Mary Chiswell Lewis, married first: John Fox; second: Augustine Olivier.

Children:

1. John W. Fox (8), married Mary F. Ball, died in Gloucester County, Va.
2. Eleanor Lewis Fox (8), married Dr. George Daniel Baylor, New Market, Caroline County. Their daughter, Frances Courtenay Baylor married Charles William Pollard, and their daughter, Katharine Roy Pollard married G. W. Olivier.
3. Warner Lewis Olivier (8), married Frances Fox.
4. Margaret P. Olivier (8), died unmarried.
5. Mary Olivier (8), married John Fox Whiting.

Warner Lewis Olivier (8) and Frances Ann Fox had:

a. Fannie W. Oliver (9), never married.
b. Louisa Olivier (9), married Mr. Parham, no issue.
c. Bettie C. Olivier (9), living in 1937.
d. Ann Olivier (9), never married.
e. Warner Lewis Olivier (9), married Mattie Statton and had:
    1. Warner Lewis Olivier (10), married Elizabeth Gratton and has, Warner (11).
    2. Fielding Lewis Olivier (10).
    3. Stuart Olivier (10).
    4. Courtenay Olivier (10).
f. George Wythe Olivier (9), married Katharine Roy Pollard.
g. Fielding Oliver (9), never married.

George Wythe Olivier (9) and Katharine Pollard had:

1. Charles Pollard Olivier (10), married 1919, Mary Frances Pender (1896-1934); married second: Miss Seymour.

    Children:

    a. Alice Dorsey Olivier (11), born 1920.
    b. Elise Pender Olivier (11), born 1925.

2. Katharine Roy Olivier married H. C. Maddux and has:
    a. Henry Cabell Maddux (11), born 1916.

Later tracings of this Lewis line can be found in *Lewises and Kindred Families*, also in *Genealogies of the Lewis Family* by

William T. Lewis. Their descendants include the Seldens of Sherwood, Byrds of White Hall, Judge Fielding Taylor of Rosewell, and William Taylor of "Belle Farm" and "Fielding House."

John Lewis (5), son of John and Frances Fielding Lewis of Warner Hall had no children. He lived near Warner Hall, his place called "View de L'eau", later called "Eagle Point." Many interesting stories are told about his wife who was called "Aunt Nancie." Mrs. George Olivier of Charlottesville inherited the handsome miniature of this John Lewis.

## COL. FIELDING LEWIS

Col. Fielding Lewis, son of John Lewis and Frances Fielding was born 1725, m. 1st, Catherine Washington, daughter of John and Catherine (Whiting) Washington. He married 2nd, her first cousin, Betty Washington, daughter of Augustine Washington and his wife Mary Ball. He lived first in Gloucester, then at "Pine Grove" Stafford County and at "Kenmore", Fredericksburg, was an officer in the Revolutionary War, manufactured arms at Fredericksburg for the Americans, sacrificed thousands of dollars of his private means in this work for which he was never repaid by the Government; and died insolvent, "Kenmore" being sold to pay his debts. First marriage to Catherine Washington 1746, second marriage to Betty Washington 1750. He had only one surviving child by his first wife, John Lewis, b. July 22, 1747 who married five times. Died November 23, 1825.

1st, Lucy Thornton, daughter of Col. John Thornton and granddaughter of his grandaunt, Mildred (Washington) Gregory.

2nd, married Elizabeth Thornton, daughter of Col. Thomas Thornton, double cousin of his first wife, no issue.

3rd, married Elizabeth Jones, daughter of Gabriel Jones, distinguished lawyer.

4th, Mrs. Mary Ann Armistead (*nee* Fountaine).

5th, Mildred Carter, daughter of Landon Carter and widow of Robert Mercer, son of Gen. Hugh Mercer, she was a granddaughter of Mrs. Roger Gregory and Col. Henry Willis.

John Lewis (6) by his first marriage to Lucy Thornton had one daughter—

Mildred Lewis (7), m. Col. William Minor and had three children (Warner, Lucy and Elizabeth).

1. Warner Minor (8), m. Maria Timberlake and had issue:
   a. Lewis Minor, m. and left children in Texas.
   b. Mary Ann Minor, m. Mr. Swan of Georgia.
   c. Virginia Minor, m. Dabney Minor. No issue.
2. Lucy Minor (8) (second child and oldest daughter of William Minor and Mildred Lewis), m. James Byars and had issue: William, James, Elizabeth Minor and Warner. (James married Mary Vincent and had a son, James Vincent Byars on the staff of the New York *Herald*.)
3. Elizabeth Minor (8), youngest daughter of Col. William Minor and Mildred Lewis, m. Col. Wm. Campbell and left children.

John Lewis (6) and his third wife, Elizabeth Jones had: 1. Warner, died young and, 2. Fielding, died young and, 3. Gabriel Lewis, born September 16, 1775, m. November 24, 1807, Mary Bibb and had issue:

1. John Lewis (8), m. Mary Martin—had issue.
2. Fielding (8), left no issue.
3. Mary (8) left no issue.
4. Elizabeth Lewis (8), born Nov. 11, 1813, m. Sept. 29, 1831, Col. Samuel McDowell Starling—had issue:
   1. Mary Starling (9), m. W. R. Payne was a noted genealogist—no children. Died 1896.
   2. —— Starling, son of Elizabeth Lewis and Col. S. McD. Starling, m. Nanny Killebrew and left five children:
      *a.* Ellis (10), *b.* Nanny (10), *c.* Lizzie (10), *d.* Lewis (10), *e.* Kate (10), who m. Harvey Brithell.

Fourth wife of John Lewis, Mrs. Mary Ann Armistead, widow of Boyles Armistead.

Fifth wife of John Lewis, Mildred Carter, daughter of Landon Carter and widow of Robert Mercer, son of Gen. Hugh Mercer. She was a granddaughter of Mrs. Roger Gregory.

*Note.*—Mildred Washington Gregory and Roger Gregory had three daughters who married the three Thornton brothers:

John Thornton, m. Mildred Gregory.
Francis Thornton, m. Frances Gregory.
Reuben Thornton, m. Elizabeth Gregory.

Mrs. Mildred Washington Gregory later became the fourth or fifth wife of Col. Henry Willis, and had issue.

Col. Fielding Lewis (5), married second, Betty Washington, daughter of Augustine Washington and Mary Ball, and had:

1. Fielding Lewis (6), b. February 14, 1751.
2. Augustine Lewis (6), b. January 22, 1752.
3. Warner Lewis (6), b. June 24, 1755.
4. George Lewis (6), b. March 14, 1757.
5. Charles Lewis (6), b. October 3, 1760.
6. Samuel Lewis (6), b. May 14, 1763.
7. Mary Lewis (6), died in infancy.
8. Betty Lewis (6), b. February 23, 1765.
9. Lawrence Lewis (6), b. April 4, 1767.
10. Robert Lewis (6), b. June 25, 1769.
11. Howell Lewis (6), b. December 12, 1771.

Fielding Lewis, Jr., m. Ann Alexander of Fairfax County, and had five children:

1. Charles Lewis (7), b. Nov. 15, 1775, Fairfax County. Appointed Lieutenant in the Army by his great-uncle, General George Washington, and served in the War of 1812. He married Ann Davidson, died Aug. 9, 1829. His children were:
    a. George W. Lewis.
    b. John C. Lewis.

    Both merchants in St. Louis.

2. John Augustine Lewis M. D. (7), m. Rebecca Ann Latimer, and had:
    a. Mary Mildred Lewis (8), m. Hon. Beader Proctor.
    b. Ann Elizabeth Lewis (8).
    c. Fielding Lewis (8).

d. Addison Lewis (8).
e. Alexander Lewis (8).
f. William Lewis (8).
g. Robert Lewis (8).

3. George Lewis (7).
4. Catherine Lewis (7), m. Henry Chew Dade.
5. A daughter (7), said to have m. a Spottswood.

Capt. George Lewis (6), son of Fielding and Betty Lewis, m. Kate Dangerfield, and had issue:

1. Dangerfield Lewis (7), m. ——, and had issue:
   Lucy Lewis, m. Michael Wallace, son of Gustavus Wallace and Frances Lurty. Issue:
   a. Gustavus Brown Wallace (9), b. at "Marmion", King George County.
   b. Mary Boyd Wallace, m. 1st, a Taylor; 2nd, a Taliaferro.
2. Samuel Lewis (7), m. and had:
   a. Alloway (8), m. John Putnam.
   b. Henry Howell Lewis (8).
   c. Mary Lewis (8) of Mansfield, Kentucky, m. John Casey.
   d. George Lewis (8).
   e. Thomas Lewis (8).
   f. John Lewis (8).
3. Mary Lewis (7), m. Byrd Willis, and had:
   1. Fanny Willis (8), b. 1805, d. 1867, lived in Florida, and m. Archibald Murat, son of Caroline Bonaparte and received a pension from Napoleon III.

Betty Lewis (6), daughter of Fielding and Betty Lewis, m. Charles Carter of Culpeper County, and had:

1. Maria Carter (7), m. Prof. George Tucker, and had:
   1. George Tucker (8), left no issue.
   2. Lelia Tucker (8).
   3. Maria Tucker (8), m. George Rives. Issue:
      a. Tucker Rives (9).
      b. Rosalie Rives (9).
      c. Edward Rives (9).
      d. Alexander Rives (9).

4. Elisa Tucker (8), m. Gesner Harrison. Issue:
   a. Maria Harrison (9), m. John A. Broaddus.
   b. Mary Harrison (9), m. Prof. Frank Smith.
   c. George Harrison (9), m. Lelia Edwards.
   d. Peachy Harrison (9).
   e. Robert Harrison (9).
   f. Rosalie Harrison (9), m. Professor Wm. M. Thornton, University, Va.

2. Sarah Carter (7), daughter of Betty Lewis and Charles Carter, m. Sir John Peyton.
3. Eleanore Carter (7), m. Henry Brown.
4. Farley Carter (7), m. Elisa. A. Conn of Kentucky (had issue).
5. George Washington Carter (7), m. Mary Wormley (had issue).
6. Otway Ann Carter (7), m. Dr. Owens of Lynchburg.
7. Fielding Carter (7), m. Miss Smith of Arkansas.

Lawrence Lewis (6), b. April 4, 1767, was aid to General Morgan 1796, and m. Feb. 22, 1799, Eleanore Park Custis, granddaughter of Mrs. Martha Washington. Issue:

1. Eleanore Park Lewis (7), b. Dec. 1, 1799, m. Col. E. G. Butler.
2. Angela Lewis (7), b. 1801, m. Charles Conrad of New Orleans.
3. Lorenza Lewis (7), b. 1803, d. 1826, m. Esther Maria Cox, daughter of John B. Cox, of Philadelphia.

Robert Lewis (6), b. Jan. 25, 1769, private secretary to General Washington, m. Judith Brown, daughter of William Barret Brown and Judith Carter. Issue:

1. Betty Lewis (7), m. George W. Barret of Hanover Co.
2. Judith Lewis (7), m. Rev. John McGuire, had issue:
   a. Rev. E. C. McGuire (8), m. 1st, Miss Murphy; 2nd, Miss Fitzhugh.
   b. Dr. Robert McGuire (8), m. Agnes Douthat.
   c. William McGuire (8), m. Miss Alexander.
   d. Betty Burnet McGuire (8), b. April 23, 1827, d. April 29, 1856, m. July 29, 1851, Rev. Charles Ambler.

Howell Lewis (6), b. Dec. 12, 1771, m. Ellen Hackney Pollard of Culpeper County and moved to Kanawha, West Virginia, and died Dec. 26, 1822, had issue:

1. Betty Washington Lewis (7).
2. Robert Pollard Lewis (7).
3. George Richard Lewis (7).
4. Ellen Gooch Lewis (7).
5. Frances Fielding Lewis (7), m. Humphry Brooke Gwathmey.
6. Virginia Lewis (7).
7. Howell Lewis (7).
8. Mary Ball Lewis (7).
9. John Edward Lewis (7).
10. Lawrence Lewis (7).
11. Henry Dangerfield Lewis (7).

Frances Fielding Lewis (7), fifth child of Howell Lewis and Ellen Pollard, married Humphry Brooke Gwathmey.

Had:

1. Ellen Gael Gwathmey (8), married James R. Caskie of Richmond, and had issue:

    Norvel Caskie (9), married A. Seddon Jones, son of Philip B. Jones and Elizabeth Taylor Sutton (of Hanover and Orange Counties).

    Issue of Norvel Caskie (9) and A. Seddon Jones of Rapidan, Virginia:

    a. Nanny H. Jones (10).
    b. Seddon Jones, Jr. (10), married Clair Tinsley.
    c. Matilda Jones (10).
    d. Sutton Jones (10), married Miss Steele.
    e. Phillis Jones (10).

2. Gaston Gwathmey (8) (lived in Albemarle), married Fanny Minge.

    Their daughters—

    a. Fanny Gwathmey (9), married Frank Byrd Jackson of Richmond.
    b. Elvira Gwathmey (9), married Robert Jackson of Birmingham, Ala.

3. Matilda Gwathmey (8), married Moore of Richmond, Va. and had, Vernon Moore (9).
4. Theodore Gwathmey, died unmarried in Richmond.
5. Virginia Gwathmey (8), married Empie of Wilmington, N. C., and had:
    1. Fannie Empie (9), who married several times.
    2. Alden Empie (9), and others.
6. Fanny Gwathmey (8), married Andrew Reid, and lived in Baltimore, Md., and had:
    1. Ellen Reid (9), married Dr. Henry Van Dyke.
    2. Harry Reid (9).
    3. Andrew Reid (9).
    4. Brooke Reid (9).
    5. Fanny Reid (9), married Browning.
    6. Imogen Reid (9), married Byrd.

Record supplied by Miss Sarah M. Gwathmey.

END DESCENDANTS OF COL. FIELDING LEWIS.

## KENMORE

### BUILT PRESUMABLY 1750-52

Was the home of Col. Fielding Lewis after his second marriage to Bettie Washington. They are said to have lived for a time at Pine Grove, Stafford County, possibly while Kenmore was being built.

Col. Fielding Lewis and his brother Warner Lewis, of Warner Hall, Gloucester County, are said to have been mutual owners of land in or on the edges of Fredericksburg. Kenmore was probably built on some of the same land.

It has always been said the beautiful fresco work on the ceilings of the lower rooms of Kenmore House, was done by two experts in this art, who were to be liberated for its execution. Conflicting traditions leave a doubt as to who these men were—if *indentured* servants at the time Kenmore was built, or Hessians of those captured at Princeton who were in prison camp at Dumfries. This would place this work many years after the building of Kenmore. The design over the drawing-room mantlepiece illustrative of three Fables is said to have been chosen by Mrs. Lewis's brother, George Washington.

The recent fresco work on the front hall is by Mr. Howard, whose ingenuity and perseverance is in evidence. Many years later when he also repaired the original work of the other rooms which had become broken and parts of the design missing.

Fielding Lewis served in the House of Burgesses repeatedly. July, 1775, he was appointed by the Virginia Assembly to establish in Fredericksburg a manufactory of small arms (this being the first in the country) the same year it was in operation, turning out arms and ammunition, and continued to do so during the Revolution. The government failing to meet this expense, Fielding sacrificed his whole fortune and was never repaid. After his death, Kenmore was sold to satisfy his creditors. He is buried beneath the steps of St. George's Church in Fredericksburg.

His wife went to live with her daughter, Mrs. Carter, at West View, Culpeper County, where she died and was buried.

Kenmore Farm in 1858 was yet open cultivated fields, no houses nearer than those forming Prince Edward Street. Lewis Street was then a farm lane, with a farm gate on a line with a fence at the back of Kenmore garden, this gate giving entrance to Prince Edward Street. The Kenmore garden extended down to the shallow lots of the back of the houses fronting on Prince Edward Street, being separated from them by a board fence.

At each end of the main house were two detached brick houses, their floors on a lower level than those of the main house, each with two rooms below, and two above, these latter with dormer windows. The one at the far end of the house contained kitchen and servants' quarters; the other towards the yard gate leading out to the lane, (the present Lewis Street) was the usual "office" used as quarters by the gentlemen.

After the War Between the States this "office" was used for school rooms by Judge Coleman who rented Kenmore, and taught a classical school there for some years. This building was later removed, also the one that formed the kitchen changed, and doubtless the surplus bricks were used in the new work at the end of the main house, which is now joined to the kitchen.

The hood over Kenmore door has been added in recent years.

The old garden and the farm lands are now traversed by well-built streets.

The women of America have marked the grave of Mrs. Lewis's mother, Mary Washington, with a memorial shaft.

And the Kenmore Association, who has bought Kenmore to save it from further desecration, is doing a noble work in the restoration and preservation of this home of Col. Fielding Lewis.

(*The Revolutionary Patriot*).

## COL. CHARLES LEWIS OF CEDAR CREEK

Col. Charles Lewis (5) of Cedar Creek, b. 1729, youngest son of John Lewis and Frances (Fielding) Lewis, m. Lucy Taliaferro, daughter of John Taliaferro and Mary Catlett of "Snow Creek."

Issue:

I. Dr. John Taliaferro Lewis (6).

II. Charles Augustine Lewis (6). (See page 40.)

III. Mary Warner Lewis (6). (See page 41.)

The first son, Dr. John T. Lewis settled "Mulberry Green", Culpeper County and m. 1st, Hannah Green; 2nd, Susannah Waring. And had by his first wife:

A. Augustine Lightfoot Lewis (7), m. Mary Warner Lewis, (daughter of Charles Augustine Lewis and Catherine Battaile). They had:

1. Hannah Lewis (8).
2. Arthur Lewis (8).
3. Rebecca Lewis (8).
4. Thomas Lewis (8).
5. Fielding Lewis (8).
6. Patsy Lewis (8).

Second marriage of Dr. John T. Lewis, issue:

B. Lucy Lewis (7), b. Sept. 5th, 1783, m. Col. John Thom of Berry Hill, Culpeper County, and had issue:

1. Warner Lewis Thom (8).
2. Lucy Lewis Thom (8), m. Col. William Taylor. No issue.
3. John Catesby Thom (8), m. Ada Downman, and had:
    a. Prof. William Taylor Thom (9) (Hollins Institute).

C. John Lewis (7), son of Dr. John T. Lewis and Susannah Waring, b. July 18, 1785, m. his cousin, Fanny Tasker Ball, daughter of Col. Spencer Ball of "Potici" and Betty Landon Carter. They had:

1. John Taliaferro Lewis (8), m. Rebecca Lewis, daughter of Capt. Charles Augustine Lewis. No issue.
2. Elizabeth Lewis (8), m. Dr. Brown, and had issue.
3. Robert Mottram Lewis (8), m. ——.
4. Frank Waring Lewis (8), m. Fanny Stuart, and had:
   a. Robert L. Lewis (9), m. Miss Carter, and has:
      1. Robert Lewis, Jr. (10).
      2. Janai Lewis (10), m. Harold Morris McCall, U. S. N., of the McDonald Clan of Scotland.
   b. Warner Lewis (9).
   c. Rose Lewis (9).

D. Joseph Jones Lewis (7), son of Dr. John T. Lewis and Susannah Waring, was b. Sept. 16, 1788. He lived in Culpeper County, d. 1824. He was a man of brilliant parts. Never married.

E. Warner Lewis (7), of "Lewis Level".

## WARNER LEWIS (7) OF "LEWIS LEVEL"

Warner Lewis (7) of "Lewis Level", son of Dr. John Taliaferro Lewis and Susannah Waring, m. first, March 10, 1810, Ann Susannah, daughter of William Latané of Essex, and had issue:

1. Thomas Waring Lewis (8), b. Aug. 15, 1815, m. 1842, Ann Misula Latané, daughter of Henry Waring Latané.
2. William Latané Lewis (8), b. Dec. 29, 1847, d. unmarried.
3. John Latané Lewis (8), b. Jan. 17, 1820, m. Barbara Winston, daughter of Philip Winston, Clerk of Hanover County.
4. Joseph Henry Lewis (8), b. June 27, 1822, d. Nov. 25, 1850, m. Lucy Robertson, daughter of Thomas Lewis Latané and Mary Berkley of Essex. Issue:
   Mary Josephine, m. Dr. Wm. M. Kirk.

Warner Lewis of Lewis Level, m. second, December 4, 1823, Catherine Butler, daughter of Col. Rubin Butler of Revolutionary War, and had issue:

5. Col. Meriwether Lewis (8), b. 1827, d. 1883, m. Julia Ann Sanders, Lancaster County.
6. Robert Lewis (8), son of Warner and Catherine Butler Lewis, died unmarried.
7. Ann Susannah Lewis (8), b. Feb. 1830, m. Robert Munday.
8. Warner Lewis (8), b. June 24, 1835, m. Louisa H. Noel, daughter of Edmund Noel of Essex County.

Warner Lewis of Lewis Level, m. a third time, Aug. 4, 1836, Maria Isabella Shore, daughter of Henry S. Shore of Richmond, and had:

9. Catherine Winston Lewis (8), b. April 1837, m. Dr. Archie R. Rowzie.
10. Hannah Shore Lewis (8), b. 1839, m. 1865, Captain Robert Meriwether Anderson of the Richmond Howitzers (son of William Lewis Anderson and Miss Webb, and great nephew of Meriwether Lewis, the head of the Lewis and Clark Expedition), and had issue:
    a. Philip Lewis Anderson (9).
    b. Warner Meriwether Anderson (9).
    c. Henry Temple Anderson (9).
    d. Robert Mandeville Anderson (9).
    e. Henry Webb Anderson (9).
11. Philip Winston Lewis (8), b. June 24, 1841, fell fighting gallantly in a charge of cavalry at Manassas, 1863.
12. Lucy Temple Lewis (8), b. Sept. 13, 1844.
13. Catesby Latané Lewis (8), b. July 1840, m. Lucy, daughter of Rev. Henry Waring Latané Temple.
14. Fielding Lewis (8), b. Nov. 21, 1847.

## CHARLES AUGUSTINE LEWIS (6)

Charles Augustine Lewis (6), second son of Charles Lewis (5) and Lucy Taliaferro, a gallant officer in the War of 1812, m. Catherine Battaile, and had issue:

1. Mary Warner Lewis (7), m. Augustine Lightfoot Lewis (see record of Dr. J. T. Lewis and Hannah Green).
2. Charles Augustine Lightfoot Lewis (7), was Principal of Rappahannock Academy, m. widow of Catesby Woodford of Caroline County, Elizabeth Goodwin, and had issue:
   a. Betty Meriwether Lewis (8), m. Prof. Rodes Massie.
3. Hannah Green Lewis (7).
4. Arthur Lewis (7), Captain U. S. N., died unmarried.
5. Lawrence Battaile Lewis (7), m. Miss Coleman.
6. Rebecca Lewis (7), m. Dr. John Taliaferro Lewis, her cousin.
7. Elizabeth Battaile Lewis (7), died unmarried.

## MARY WARNER LEWIS

Col. Charles Lewis of Cedar Creek and Lucy Taliaferro, had one daughter:

Mary Warner Lewis (6), m. first, Philip Lightfoot of Sandy Point on the James River and lived at Cedar Creek, and had one son:

1. Philip Lightfoot (7), m. Sally Bernard, daughter of Wm. Bernard of Mansfield, near Fredericksburg, and had:
   1. Fannie Lightfoot (8), m. Capt. Gilchrist Robb, U.S.N.
   2. Philip Lewis Lightfoot (8), m. first, Miss Mary Virginia Smith of Falmouth. Second Miss Drumond of Mississippi.
   3. John Bernard Lightfoot (8), m. Harriet Field of Gloucester County, and lived at Port Royal.
   4. Wm. Bernard Lightfoot (8), m. first, Roberta, daughter of Col. Robert Beverly of Blandfield, Essex, m. second, Sarah Ross of Mobile, Ala.
   5. Ellen Bankhead Lightfoot (8), m. Dr. Carter Warner Wormley of King William County.
   6. Rosalie Virginia Lightfoot (8), m. Dr. Hugh Mason of Stafford County.

Mrs. Mary Warner (Lewis) Lightfoot, m. second, Dr. John Bankhead, a nephew of President Monroe. He was a graduate of Edinburg. They lived at "Spring Grove", Caroline County, and had issue: three sons, Charles, John, and William.

2. Charles Lewis Bankhead (7), b. May 3, 1788, d. Sept. 17, 1808, m. first, Ann Cary Randolph, daughter Col. Thomas Mann Randolph and granddaughter of President Jefferson, and had issue:

a. John Warner Bankhead (8), b. Dec. 1810.
b. Ellen Monroe Bankhead (8), b. Sept. 5, 1813, m. Mr. Carter of Albemarle, and left issue.
c. Thomas Mann Randolph (8), b. Dec. 30, 1815, moved to Arkansas.

Charles Lewis Bankhead, m. second, Mary A. Carthrae, granddaughter of Thomas Lewis, son of John Lewis and Margaret Lynn Lewis, and had one son:

d. Charles Lewis Bankhead (8) of Orange, m. Mary Warner Bankhead—no issue. (Thus uniting the Gloucester and Staunton Lewises.)

3. John Bankhead (7), m. Ann Eliza Stuart, Sept. 26, 1816, and had issue:

a. Mary Eliza (8), b. July 16, 1817, m. Mr. Wallace of Fauquier County.
b. Rosalie (8), b. Dec. 1, 1818, m. Lucian Dade.

4. Dr. Wm. Bankhead (7) inherited "Spring Grove", and m. Dorothea Bayne Minor, daughter Garret Minor of Fredericksburg, October 15, 1829, and had issue:

1. Georgiana Bankhead, m. Wm. Moncure of "Somerset", Stafford County, and left a large family.
2. Mary Warner Bankhead (8), m. her cousin, Charles Lewis Bankhead of Orange County.
3. John Taliaferro Bankhead (8), b. July 18, 1833.
4. Eliza Garret Bankhead (8), b. Jan. 22, 1835, m. Mr. Bickerton Winston of Hanover County.
5. Rosalie Stuart Bankhead (8), b. Oct. 28, 1836, m. first, Richard Morris Winston; second, Mr. Selden.
6. Ellen Bayne Bankhead (8), b. May 7, 1838, m. Rev. Mr. Meridith, and had issue.
7. Leanora D. Bankhead (8), b. Feb. 9, 1840, m. Major John Lee, brother of General Fitzhugh Lee, and left issue.

Col. Charles Lewis of Cedar Creek was in Braddock's defeat, July 9, 1755, a year in which an army was organized by the colonists to resist the Indians. He accompanied this force as Captain and his journal gives in detail the incidents on the march from Fredericksburg to Fort Cumberland. Thomas W. Lewis of Essex has a copy of this journal.

END DESCENDANTS OF COL. JOHN LEWIS AND FRANCES FIELDING.

## COL. CHARLES LEWIS OF "THE BYRD"

Col. Charles Lewis of the "Byrd Plantation", Goochland County, (second son of John Lewis and Elizabeth Warner) was born October 13, 1696, died 1779. He married May 28, 1717, Mary Howell (daughter of John Howell, gentleman). He took up the Byrd Plantation in 1733, was an officer in the French and Indian Wars, and a member of the Council. His children were:

I. John Lewis (5), b. Oct. 8, 1720, d. 1791, m. Jane Lewis.
II. Charles Lewis of Buckeyeland, m. Mary Randolph.
III. Elizabeth Lewis (5), m. William Kennon. (See page 54.)
IV. James Lewis (5), m. Elizabeth Taylor. (See page 54.)
V. Mary Lewis, died young.
VI. Howell Lewis (5), m. daughter of Henry Willis. (See page 55.)
VII. Ann Lewis (5), m. Edmond Taylor.
VIII. Mary Lewis (5), died young.
IX. Robert Lewis (5), m. Jane Woodson. (See page 59.)
X. Frances Lewis (5), m. Robert Lewis, Jr. of Belvoir.

John Lewis (5) of the Byrd obtained permission from the House of Burgesses to dispose of this property, the Byrd plantation and reinvest the money in land on Dan River in Pittsylvania County and Halifax County. His home was in Pittsylvania County. The date of his removal is not known, but it was before the Revolutionary War. He was born October 8, 1720, d. 1791, m. his first cousin, Jane (daughter of Robert and Jane Meriwether Lewis of "Belvoir", and the widow of Thomas Meriwether by whom she also had issue.—See Meriwether Line).

The children of John and Jane Lewis were:

A. John Lewis (6), never married.
B. Charles Lewis (6), married three times. His last wife was Mrs. Garthrey Glover Johns, widow of Jacob Johns, of Pittsylvania County.
C. Robert Lewis (6), married Ann Ragland, and had issue.
D. Mary Lewis (6), married William Williams of Halifax County, and had issue.
E. Jane Lewis (6), married Jonathan Reade, and had issue.
F. Elizabeth Lewis (6), married Mr. Hobson, no issue.

Children of Charles Lewis and Mrs. Garthrey Lewis:

1. Nicholas Meriwether Lewis (7), married Lucy Bullock of Granville County, North Carolina. No issue.
2. Lucy Meriwether Lewis (7) (1804-1874), married in 1820, Ajax Walker, M. D. (1794-1850). Their home was in Milton, N. C. They had nine children.

The children of Lucy Meriwether Lewis and Dr. Ajax Walker were:

1. Robert Walker (8), died in infancy.
2. Mary Francis Walker, died in infancy.
3. Lucy Lewis Walker, died in infancy.
4. Sallie Rose Walker, died in infancy.
5. Charles Baylor Walker, died in infancy.
6. Eliza Ann Walker, married Dr. Thomas Stamps, and had no children.
7. Nicholas Lewis Walker (8), born in Amherst County, Virginia, in 1826, married Emily F. Hunt, and left issue.
8. Henry Ajax Walker (8), born in Milton, N. C. in 1841, married Mary McCotta Owens of Tarboro, N. C. in 1874, and had one son, John Owens Walker, now living in Memphis, Tenn.
9. Fielding Lewis Walker (8), born in Milton, N. C., July 4, 1843, died 1924, married Penelope Campbell Wilson of Milton, N. C. in 1866. His wife died in 1915. She was the daughter of John Wilson of Milton, N. C., formerly of Norfolk, Va. and his wife, Penelope Campbell, formerly of Edinburg, Scotland. Fielding Lewis Walker lived in Danville, Va.

The children of Fielding Lewis Walker and Penelope Campbell Walker are as follows:

1. Henry Ajax Walker (9), born in Milton, N. C., now living in Louisville, Ky. He married Ida Thames of Mobile, Ala. Their children are: 1. Mary Ellis Walker (10), married Robert Adams of Indianapolis, Ind., where they now live; 2. Ida Thames Walker (10) and, 3. Henry Ajax Walker, Jr. (10).
2. Maitland Walker (9) of Danville, Va.
3. Mary Wilson Walker of Danville, Va.
4. Agnes Campbell Walker of Danville, Va.
5. Lucy Meriwether Lewis Walker, married Lovick P. Morgan of Danville, Va. Their children are: 1. Penelope Campbell Morgan (10); 2. Fielding Lewis Morgan; 3. Lucy Meriwether Lewis Morgan and, 4. Lovick P. Morgan, Jr.
6. Penelope Wilson Walker, married William Humphries Jones of Danville, Va. Their children are: 1. Charlotte Townes Jones (10) and, 2. Meriwether Lewis Jones.
7. Fielding Lewis Walker, married Mary Dowd of Durham, N. C. and now lives in Durham, N. C. Their children are: 1. Fielding Lewis Walker, III (10) and, 2. Mary Lipscomb Walker (10).
8. Annie Louise Walker of Danville, Va.
9. Lewis Meriwether Walker, married Julia Gordon Willis of Buena Vista, and now lives in Petersburg, Va. Their children are: 1. Lewis Meriwether Walker, Jr. (10), 2. Gordon Willis Walker and, 3. Mary Churchill Walker.
10. Charles Baylor Walker (9), married Nell Lamon Walker of Blacksburg, Va. They have no children. Home in Pittsburgh, Penn.

Children of Nicholas Lewis Walker (8) and Emily Hunt of Milton, N. C. were:

1. Lewis Walker (9), married Sue Somerville Cunningham, Person County, N. C. Now living in Milton, N. C. No living issue.

2. Robert Lewis Walker (9), married Cornelia Stevenson Wilson of Milton, N. C. They had one child, Margaret Walker, who married Dr. Perry Watson Miles. Residence in Danville, Va.
3. Lucy Lewis Walker (9). Never married.
4. Leonard Hunt Walker, married Lockie White of Henderson, Ky. No children.
5. William Hunt Walker, married Kate Mieuse Dibrell of Richmond, Va. Their children are:
    1. Alphonso Dibrell Walker (10), unmarried.
    2. Emily Hunt Walker (10), unmarried.
    3. Nicholas Lewis Walker (10), married Elise Mims, lives in Raleigh, N. C. They have five children:
        1. William Mims Walker (11).
        2. Lewis Dibrell Walker (11).
        3. Edwin Mims Walker (11).
        4. James Hunt Walker (11).
        5. Cornelia Williamson Walker (11).
    4. Kate Dibrell Walker (10), married Dr. Thomas Stamps of Lumber Bridge, N. C., and have one son.
    5. Elizabeth LeGrand Walker (10), unmarried.
6. Nicholas Lewis Walker (9), married Jean Renbert of Missouri. No issue.

(Furnished by Fielding Lewis Walker of Danville, Va.)

Mary Lewis (6), daughter of John Lewis and Mrs. Jane (Lewis) Meriwether, married William Williams, and had:

1. William Lilburn Williams (7), married and had Mary, who married Albert Wheatly and, had two sons and four daughters.
2. Robert Williams (7).
3. Howell Williams (7).
4. Warner Williams (7).
5. Fielding L. Williams (7).
6. Charles Williams (7).
7. Coleman Williams (7).
8. Mildred Williams, m. Dr. James Wheatly and, had James (8) and Elvira (8). James H. Wheatly, m. Ella B. Bowen, and had James (9).

Fielding Lewis Williams (7), m. Frances Pemberton Boyd, and had:

a. William Boyd Williams (8).
b. Mary Frances Williams (8), died in 1886.
c. Mildred Lewis Williams (8).
d. Fielding Lewis Williams (8), m. Abby Louisa Miller, daughter of Augustus N. Miller and his wife, Harriet J. Waldron, residing at Bristol, Rhode Island, and had issue:
    1. Mildred Lewis Williams (9), married Dr. W. Fred Williams. No issue.
    2. Fielding Lewis Williams, Jr. (9).
    3. Louisa Williams (9), married John Taylor Lewis (fourth). (See record of James Lewis).

Coleman Williams (7), married first, Mary B. Wheatley. Married second, Sarah M. Floyd Jones, and had issue:

1. Robert F. Williams, died unmarried.
2. Mary Williams (8), m. John Gandy, and had Mary (9) and William (9).
3. Mildred Williams (8), died unmarried.
4. Howell L. Williams (8), died unmarried.
5. Leonidas P. Williams, m. Mary Roberts, and had Fanny (9) and Leonidas, Jr. (9).
6. Harriet E. Williams, m. James S. Brownson, and left seven children.

Jane Lewis (6), daughter of John Lewis and Mrs. Jane (Lewis) Meriwether, married Johnathan Reade, and had issue:

1. Margaret Reade (7), married Harrison.
2. Thomas Reade (7), married Miss Panel.
3. Eliza Reade (7), married Hobson, and had Howell (8) and George (8).
4. Mary Reade (7), no record.
5. Howell Reade (7), married Eliza T. Boyd.
6. Charles Lewis Reade (7), born 1795, died December 20, 1869.

These Reades intermarried with Mortons, Daniels, Sherrills, Bonds and Barbees and other families. The descendants found more fully in *Lewis and Kindred Families* by J. M. McAlister and Lula Tandy.

## DESCENT OF MARY RANDOLPH

William Isham traces through Ishams of Pytchely 1424, also to Plantagenet Kings.

Henry Isham, son of William, emigrated to Virginia, m. Catherine, widow of James Royall of Henrico County, d. about 1675. Issue:

1. Henry Isham, died unmarried.
2. Anne Fitzhugh Isham, m. Col. Francis Epps of Henrico County.
3. Mary Isham, m. William Randolph of Turkey Island, and had:
    - a. Isham Randolph of Goochland, m. Jane Rogers of London: They had:
        - 1. Mary Randolph, m. Charles Lewis.
            - a. Charles Lilburn Lewis.
            - b. Isham Lewis, unmarried.
            - c. Mary Lewis, m. Col. Charles Lewis.
            - d. Jane Lewis, m. John Hudson.
            - e. Elizabeth Lewis, m. B. Henderson.
            - f. Ann Lewis, m. Randolph Jefferson.
            - g. Frances Lewis, m. John Thomas.
            - h. Mildred Lewis, m. Edward Moore.

John Lilburn (1) of Thickley Punchedon Durham County, England.

George Lilburn (2), m. Jane Chambers.

William Lilburn (3), m. Elizabeth Nicholson.

Jane Lilburn (4), m. Charles Rogers.

Jane Rogers (5), m. Isham Randolph.

John Lilburn, "the leveler" and Robert Lilburn, the regicide, were nephews of George Lilburn. Robert was a member of Cromwell's Parliament 1654-1656.

## CHARLES LEWIS (5) OF BUCKEYELAND

Charles Lewis of Buckeyeland, second son of Charles Lewis and Mary Howell, was born May 14, 1722. Died May, 1782. Married Mary Randolph, sister of President Thomas Jefferson's mother, and daughter of Isham Randolph and Jane Rogers of Dungeness. They had issue: Eight children.

1. Charles Lilburn Lewis (6), married Lucy Jefferson (sister of President Jefferson). They went West in later life, had issue: Randolph (7), Isham, Lilburn, Jane, Mary, Lucy, Martha, and Ann. (*History of Albemarle*).
    a. Randolph Lewis (7), married Mary Lewis, daughter of Robert Lewis of "The Byrd" and Jane Woodson. Issue:
        a. Isham Lewis (8).
        b. Tucker Woodson Lewis (8).
        c. Randolph Lewis, Jr. (8).
        d. Howell Lewis (8), married first, Virginia Lee. His daughter, Virginia Lee Lewis, married Augustus Marion Hamilton, and had one son, John Marion Hamilton (10).
        e. Warner Lewis (8), died unmarried.
        f. Mary Lewis (8), married Charles Palmer of Richmond.
        g. Lucy Jefferson Lewis (8), no record.
        h. Susan Harrison Lewis (8), married Mr. Douthat of Botetourt County, and had:
            1. Mary Howell Douthat (9), married Mr. Royall, lived on James River near Westover, and had Alice and others.
            2. Warner Douthat (9).
            3. Robert Douthat (9), emigrated to California.
2. Isham Lewis (6), unmarried. His estate heired by his nephews, John Lewis Moore and Charles Lewis Thomas.
3. Mary Lewis (6), married Col. Charles Lewis, son of Robert Lewis of Bel-voir and Jane Meriwether. (See Bel-voir record for issue.)
4. Jane Lewis (6), wife of John Hudson, among other issue had Elizabeth Hudson, who married Charles A. Scott of

"Retirement", son of John Scott and Margaret Fry, daughter of Joshua Fry and Peachy Walker.

5. Elizabeth Lewis (6), married Bennett Henderson, and had twelve children:
   1. William Henderson (7).
   2. Sarah Henderson (7), married John R. Kerr.
   3. James Henderson (7).
   4. Charles Henderson (7).
   5. Isham Henderson (7).
   6. Bennett Henderson (7).
   7. Hillsborough Henderson (7).
   8. Eliza Henderson (7), wife of John H. Bullock.
   9. Frances Henderson (7), married Thomas Hornsby.
   10. Lucy Henderson (7), wife of John Wood.
   11. Nancy Clawford Bennett (7), m. Matthew Nelson.
   12. John Henderson (7), who married Ann B. Hudson, sister of his cousin William's wife.

Bennett Henderson lived at Milton, Albemarle County, was a man of much consideration in that vicinity, owned a large flour mill and warehouse at Milton which was a station for flat boat traffic to the James River and to Richmond markets. He died in 1793. His widow and children removed to Kentucky.

6. Ann Lewis (6), in 1781, married Randolph Jefferson, brother of Thomas Jefferson, and had:
   1. Thomas Jefferson, who married first, Mary, daughter of Charles L. Lewis. Married second, Mrs. Elizabeth Barker.
   2. Isham Jefferson.

7. Frances Lewis (6), born January 24, 1759, died Dec. 28, 1834. Second wife of Captain John Thomas, born April 1757, d. 1847, of Amherst and Albemarle Counties, who had issue by her:

*Note.*—Captain John Thomas, married first, Frances Henderson, had: Warner, Norbonne, Elizabeth, m. Mr. Wood, Lucy, m. James Lewis.

   1. Charles Lewis Thomas (7), who married Margaret, daughter of Nicholas and Mary Walker Lewis. (See page 52.)
   2. John L. Thomas (7), died unmarried 1846.
   3. Virginia Thomas (7).

4. Margaret Thomas (7), married first, Julius Clarkson, who died 1835. She married second, 1838, Robert Cashmere.

5. James Wilton Thomas (7), born Jan. 12, 1795 at "Red Hill, died Oct. 4, 1845 on bend at Big River, Jefferson County, Missouri. He married Eliza Ann Johnson, daughter of Benjamin Johnson and Sarah Clarkson, daughter of James Clarkson of Hardware Creek and his wife, Elizabeth Nash. James Wilton Thomas and family emigrated to Missouri in 1826. Had issue:

    1. Virginia Ann Mildred Thomas (8), married Walter Bowdoin Trumbull and among others born to them was:
        a. Frank Trumbull (9), born Nov. 7, 1858. Married first, Anna Cora Hale; married second, Mary A. Sisson, and had:
            1. Roscoe Hale Trumbull (10).
    2. Mary Lewis Thomas (8), married William T. Senter.
    3. James Avis Thomas (8).
    4. Sophia B. Thomas, m. Philip Pipkin.
    5. Sarah Frances Thomas (8), m. Ewing Young Mitchell.
    6. Judge John Lilburn Thomas (8), born Sept. 16, 1833, married Dec. 25, 1856, Sarah Ellen Pipkin, born Sept. 8, 1837, died April 17, 1916, daughter of Philip Pipkin by his first wife. Had issue, four children:
        a. Mary Viola Thomas (9), born Nov. 12, 1858, died Dec. 28, 1863.
        b. James P. Thomas (9), born Mar. 27, 1860, died Nov. 13, 1860.
        c. Fanny S. Thomas (9), born May 10, 1861, died July 3, 1862.
        d. Kora Susan Thomas (9), born Jan. 30, 1863, married to James Walter Evens, Nov. 4, 1885.

7. Julius Clarkson Thomas (8).
8. William Henry Harrison Thomas (8), married Rebecca A. Brill.

(Record furnished from "Descendants of James Wilton Thomas and Eliza A. Johnson" by John Lilburn Thomas.)

*Note.*—This Judge John Lilburn Thomas is a distinguished lawyer and has filled many places of public trust in the Legislature of Missouri, 1870—as circuit Judge 1880, Judge of Missouri Supreme Court 1890 (by Gov. Francis). In 1881 he organized the circuit judges for the purpose of reforming the State laws—was its president for eleven years till his retirement from the bench, May 1893. Was appointed Assistant Attorney General for the Post Office Department where he instituted many reforms. His entire career in public and private life furnished a true exemplification of American citizenship based on the principles of "Christian Ideals".—Extract from a biographical notice.

When last heard of he was living in Washington, D. C., largely in the eighties, his mind bright and alert in genealogical researches. It was my privilege to meet him and his wife repeatedly at Ivy and at Charlottesville when he was doing research work in the court records and county. He was instrumental in having a monument placed in the old Thomas cemetery near Red Hill. *S. T. L. A.*

Margaret Lewis, daughter of Nicholas Lewis and Mary Walker, married Charles L. Thomas (7). Issue, six children:

1. Charles L. Thomas, Jr. (8), married Anne Hull. Issue:
    - a. Jane Herndon Thomas (9), married Andrew Jackson.
    - b. Margaret L. Thomas (9).
    - c. Elizabeth Thomas (9).
    - d. Mary Walker Thomas (9), m. Mr. Townes. Issue:
        - 1. Charles Lewis Townes.
    - e. Virginia Thomas, married Dr. Townes.
2. Nicholas Thomas (8), married Ellen Carter. Issue:
    - a. Gilman Thomas
    - b. Mary Carter Thomas, died very young.
3. Mary Walker Thomas (8), married Judge A. M. Clayton of Mississippi. Issue:

a. Arthur Clayton (9), died unmarried.
b. Mary Lewis Clayton (9), m. William Hull: Issue:
 1. Mosby Hull (10).
 2. Lucy Minor Hull (10).
 3. Dabney Hull (10).
 4. Mary Walker Hull (10).
 5. Clayton Hull (10).

4. Robert Warner Thomas (8), married Araminta Hardin. Issue:
 a. Ben Hardin Thomas (9).
 b. Elizabeth Thomas (9), married Mr. Cummings. Issue:
  1. Robert W. Cummings.
  2. George Cummings.
 c. Lucy Thomas (9).
 d. Robert Thomas (9).
 e. John N. Thomas.
 f. Ellen Thomas.
 g. Charles L. Thomas.
 h. Fannie M. Thomas.
 i. Mary Walker Thomas (9), married James Minor Quarles. Issue:
  1.Robert W. Quarles (10).
  2. Bettie Quarles (10).
  3. Ellen Quarles (10).
  4. Lucy Quarles (10).
  5. James M. Quarles (10).
  6. Mary W. Quarles (10).
  7. Evalina Quarles (10).

5. Frances E. Thomas (8), married first, Dr. Charles Hunter Meriwether. (See Nicholas and Margaret Douglas Meriwether Record). Married second, Mr. James Hart. No issue.

6. John L. Thomas (8), married first, Lucy M. Quarles. Issue:
 a. Lewis Minor Thomas (9), died unmarried.
 b. John Quarles Thomas (9), died unmarried.

Married second, Kate Pendleton. Issue:

a. Pendleton Thomas (9).

b. Kate Thomas (9).

8. Mildred Lewis (6), daughter of Charles Lewis and Mary Randolph married Edward Moore, and had:

   a. John Lewis Moore, who inherited one thousand acres of land from his uncle, Isham Lewis.

   b. Ann Moore.

   c. Charles Moore.

END OF RECORD OF CHARLES LEWIS OF BUCKEYELAND

---

Elizabeth Lewis (5), oldest daughter and third child of Col. Charles Lewis and Mary Howell of the *Byrd Plantation,* born April 23, 1724, married May 3, 1744, William Kennon of Chesterfield County, son of William Kennon and Ann Epps, and grandson of Richard Kennon and Elizabeth Washam.

Their son:

1. John Kennon (6), married in 1779, Elizabeth Woodson, daughter of John Woodson and Elizabeth Hughes.
2. Elizabeth Kennon (6), in 1809, married D. L. White, son of David L. White and Mary Lyne, had Pleasant Woodson White, who married in 1848, Emily Gibson, daughter of Edward R. and Jeanette (Tilton) Gibson. Emily White died in 1902. Woodson Tilton White, their son, born July 26, 1849, is now a resident of Waco, Texas.

## JAMES LEWIS

James Lewis (5), fourth child of Col. Charles Lewis and Mary Howell, born October 6, 1726, died May 1, 1764, married Elizabeth or Isabella Taylor, daughter of John Taylor of Granville, N. C., and had issue:

1. Charles Lewis (6), in 1779, m. Mary Anderson, and had:
   a. Thomas B. Lewis, who married Elizabeth Cobb, and had issue, six children, of whom were:
      1. Willis Lewis (8).

2. Charles Ridley Lewis (8), who married Eloise Harris, and had:
   a. Charles Lafayette Lewis (9), who married Lucy Gregory, and had:
      1. Archibald Gregory Lewis (10).

2. John Taylor Lewis (6), Brunswick County, Va., 1793, married Lucy Maclin, and had:
   a. Col. John Taylor Lewis, 1794-1866, who married first, Sally Taylor. Married second, Mrs. Frances Hodge Boyd or Lyne and whose son,
      1. John Taylor Lewis III, married Lucy Townes. Their son:
         a. John Taylor Lewis IV, married first, Louise Williams, daughter of Fielding Lewis Williams and Louise Miller, of Philadelphia, Pa. and Bristol, R. I., and had:
            1. John Taylor Lewis V, born September 28, 1900, (Jack) married Hilda ——.

         John Taylor IV, married second, Elizabeth N. Wardwell, and had:
            1. William Wardwell Lewis (10).
            2. Elizabeth Frances Lewis.
            3. Ellen Townes Lewis.
            4. Louise Lewis.
            5. Meriwether Fielding Lewis.
            6. Wilbur Marsh Lewis.
            7. Lawrence Glading Lewis, formerly of Mecklenburg County, Va., but now of Ashland, Va.

3. Elizabeth Lewis (6), married Dr. James Ridley, born 1776.

4. Joseph Lewis (6).

Howell Lewis (5), sixth child of Charles Lewis and Mary Howell of "The Byrd", born in Goochland County, Va. 1731, will probated 1814 in Granville County, N. C., married Mary Isabella Willis, daughter of Col. Henry Willis of Fredericksburg.

(Not certain if child of second or third wife, who was Mrs. Mildred Washington Gregory Willis.) Issue:

1. Charles Lewis (6).
2. Willis Lewis (6), Captain in Revolutionary War.
3. Isabella Lewis (6), married Jeffries.
4. Ann Lewis (6), married Morton.
5. Francis Lewis (6), married Bugg.
6. Jane Lewis (6), m. David Hinton, Wake County, N. C.
   Major Charles Lewis Hinton (7), married Anne Perry.
   Major David Hinton (8), married Mary Coen, and had Mary Hilliard Hinton (9), and others.
7. Mary Lewis (6), married Kennon.
8. Elizabeth Lewis (6), married William Ridley of Granville, County, had issue:
   a. Dr. Robert Ridley of Atlanta, Georgia, whose first wife was a daughter of the "great Ben Hill", is one of her descendants.
9. Howell Lewis (6), born April 2, 1757, married Betsy Coleman, daughter of Robert Coleman of Goochland County.
10. Mildred Lewis (6), married John Cobbs of Goochland County, Va., Granville County, N. C. and Georgia, had issue:
    a. Howell Cobbs (7), born 1771, married Martha Jacquiline Roots. No issue.
       He was appointed an officer in U. S. Army during General Washington's administration. Resigned after he married, and lived on his plantation. Was in Congress from 1807 to 1812. Resigned his seat to serve as captain in War of 1812. Then resigned his commission.
    b. John Addison Cobbs (7), married Sarah Robinson Roots of Fredericksburg, and had issue:
       1. Howell Cobbs (8), born 1815 at Cherry Hill, Ga., married Miss Lamar of Georgia. Entered Congress 1843 and served continuously till 1851, when elected Governor of Georgia. Secretary of Treasury under President Buchanan and served

till resigning to serve the Confederacy. Married, and had issue:

a. Judge Howell Cobb of Athens Circuit, Ga.
b. Judge Andrew Cobb of the Supreme Court of Georgia.
c. John R. Cobb, and others.
d. Mrs. Tinsley Barber Rucker.

2. General Thomas R. R. Cobb (8), a lawyer and never in political life. In the War Between the States he went to the front as Brigadier-General and was killed December 12, 1862 at Fredericksburg by a cannon ball fired under the window of his mother—Sarah Roots'—old home, "Federal Hill", the window of the room in which his mother was married. A slab marks the place he fell. Married Miss Lumpkins, and had:

   a. Mrs. Hoke Smith.
   b. Mrs. Hull of Athens, Ga.
   c. Mrs. Henry Jackson.

3. Mildred Lewis Cobb (8), daughter of John Addison Cobb, married Col. Lucien Glenn, and had issue:

   1. Sally Glenn, married Mr. McBride, and had issue:

      1. Glenn McBride.
      2. William McBride.
      3. Sally McBride, married George Adair.

   2. Howell Glenn (9), a lawyer went to New York and died there.

   3. Col. John Thomas Glenn (9), distinguished lawyer, who held many positions of trust and honor, died in 1900 very suddenly in the prime of life. He married Miss Garrard of Columbus, Ga., and had:

      a. Isa Urquhart Glenn (10), married Gen. John Bayard Shindel, who died in 1920, of U. S. Army. Had issue:

1. Bayard Shindel.

Gen. Shindel was the youngest General in the U. S. Army. His wife is a talented writer and lives in New York City, and is President-General of the "Order of the Crown", the most exclusive of the historical societies.

b. William Glenn (10).

c. Garrard Glenn (10), lawyer in New York City, married Rosa Aubrey Wood, daughter of Charles Wood of Albemarle County, Va. and Cally (Hargraves) Wood of Georgia. Had issue:

1. Garrard Glenn (11).
2. John Forsythe Cobb Glenn (11).

d. Mrs. Gordon Ellyson (10), whose husband is a Naval officer has two daughters.

4. Mary Willis Cobb (8), daughter of John Addison Cobb, married first, Mr. Erwin, and had issue:

a. Howell Cobb Erwin (9).

b. Lucy Erwin (9), married Mr. Wilborn Hill. Married second, Dr. J. M. Johnson, and had issue:

1. James Johnson (10).
2. Sarah Cobb Johnson (10), married first, Dr. Hagan of Richmond, and had issue:

1. Hugh Hagan (11).
2. Willis Cobb Hagan (11).

Married second, Mr. Lucian Cocke of Roanoke, Virginia.

5. Sarah Martha Cobb (8), daughter of John

Addison Cobb, married John C. Whitner, and had issue:

a. John A. (9), married Lidie Farrow. Issue, eight children.
b. Thomas Cobb (9), married Emily L. Tichenor. Has two children.
c. Charles F. (9), married Margaret Badger. Issue, two children.
d. Eliza S. (9).
e. Sarah (9), married Warren Howard, and had two children.
f. Mary A. (9), married B. C. Milner, and had four children.
g. Matty Mildred (9), married Willis J. Milner, and had six children.

Robert Lewis (5), the youngest son of Charles Lewis and Mary Howell, born May 29, 1739, died January 10, 1803. He was Colonel of Goochland County militia in 1779. He married February 26, 1760, Jane Woodson, daughter of Tucker Woodson, and had issue:

1. Howell Lewis (6), born November 18, 1760.
2. Charles Lewis (6), born June 25, 1765.
3. Robert Lewis (6), born March 26, 1763, m. Mary Gilchrist.
4. James Lewis (6), born June 6, 1768.
5. John Woodson Lewis, born May 21, 1770.
6. Sarah Lewis, born June 8, 1772.
7. Mary Howell Lewis (6), born December 25, 1774.
8. Elizabeth Lewis, born August 14, 1779.
9. Warner Lewis (6), born May 2, 1777, died October 6, 1820, married June 11, 1798, Sarah Pleasant Woodson.
10. A daughter (6), born July 24, 1784.
11. Fielding Lewis (6), born October 20, 1782.

Warner Lewis and Sarah Pleasant (Woodson) Lewis went to St. Louis County, Mo., had issue:

1. Robert Lewis (7), born May 1799.
2. Charles Lewis (7), born February 4, 1801.
3. Samuel Lewis (7), born February 28, 1803, married Miss Bates of Iowa.

4. Warner Lewis (7), born November 28, 1804, settled in Dubuque.
5. Sarah P. Lewis (7), born August 8, 1806.
6. Robert Lewis (7), born March 8, 1808, died July 8, 1875. December 21, 1829, married Lucy Bacon of St. Louis, moved to Cass County, Mo., (She died Aug. 13, 1903) then Henry County, Mo., 1862.
7. James Howell Lewis (7), born 1809.
8. Jane Lewis (7), born November 20, 1811, married first, Furgerson. Married second, Col. William Talbot of Loutre Island, Mo.
9. John Lewis (7), born July 4, 1813.
10. Ann Lewis, born May 11, 1818.
11. Elizabeth Lewis (7), born July 1, 1814, married Capt. Robert Freeland.
12. William Price Lewis (7), born June 4, 1816.
13. John Pleasant Lewis (7), born August 27, 1819.

Robert Lewis, son of Warner Lewis and Sarah P. Woodson, married December 21, 1829, Lucy Bacon of St. Louis, Mo., and had issue:

1. Elvira Furgerson Lewis (8), who married first, James Orr. Married second, Jeptha D. Elliston, and had one son, James Lee Elliston.
2. Warner Lewis (8), Col. C. S. A., married first, Sarah Griffith in 1855. Married second, Mary Morrison Glenn in 1882, and had Robert Edgar Lewis, (Judge at Colorado Springs) born April 3, 1857, married Ella Avery of Clinton, Missouri, daughter of James Avery and Sally Woolfolk, and had issue:
   a. Mason Lewis (9).
   b. A daughter (9).
3. Anne Lewis (8), died young.
4. James Lewis (8), died young.
5. Ann E. Freeland Lewis (8), married Dr. John H. Britts, November 1, 1865.
6. Garland Bacon Lewis (8), C. S. A., killed at siege of Vicksburg.

7. Sarah L. Lewis (8), married Dr. T. T. Thornton, Hartwell, Missouri.
8. Lucy B. Lewis (8), married Robert W. Covington of Garland, Missouri.
9. Robert Lewis (8), died young.
10. Louisa Lewis (8), married William Covington.
11. Samuel Woodson Lewis (8), married Sterling Price Covington, and had issue:
    a. Annie Lewis (9).
    b. Kate Lewis (9).

Robert Lewis (6), son of Robert and Jane Woodson Lewis, m. May 11, 1786, Mary Gilchrist. Their youngest son, William (7), b. December 26, 1799, d. 1865, married Harriet Malvina Miller. They had seven children, one of whom was Robert Eston Lewis (8), who was born at the "Byrd", married Miss Martin of Goochland County, and had ten children. One of them, Ann Elizabeth Lewis (9), married her cousin, John M. Hamilton. Issue:

1. John Hamilton (10).
2. Ruby Pearl Hamilton (10).
3. Louise Hamilton (10).
4. Mercedes Christie Hamilton (10).
5. Augustus Hamilton (10).
6. Richard M. Hamilton (10).
7. Mrs. Ann Lewis (Hamilton) Jack (10).
8. Mrs. Ora Lee (Hamilton) Hargrave (10), Stony Creek, Va.
9. Mrs. Virginia Todd (Hamilton) Gayle (10).

END OF THE DESCENDANTS OF CHARLES LEWIS OF THE "BYRD".

---

## ROBERT LEWIS OF "BELVOIR"

Col. Robert Lewis (4) of "Belvoir" was the third son of Col. John Lewis and Elizabeth Warner. He was born at Warner Hall in Gloucester County in 1702, that being the date given for his baptism and also in old register.

He had land in Gloucester, which later he seems to have given to his oldest son, John Lewis of "Halifax" County.

But Robert Lewis, as well as his father-in-law, Nicholas Meriwether, pushed out to hitherto unoccupied lands in Piedmont, Virginia. Both took out grants for themselves of thousands of acres, being good judges of fertile, well watered selections.

In 1736 Robert Lewis located four thousand acres of land in North Garden on Hardware River.

In 1740 he took a grant of six thousand five hundred acres on Ivy Creek near Ivy Depot.

These grants were located in that part of Goochland County which later became Albemarle County.

These and other grants which he took up enabled him to divide among his children 21,660 acres of land in Albemarle and Orange Counties. Also an interest in one hundred thousand acres in Greenbrier County.

He founded his new home "Belvoir" in that part of Louisa County which was later added to Albemarle in 1761. He died 1765 (will probated 1766).

He served in House of Burgesses 1744-1746, was County Lieutenant for Louisa County. He married 1725, Jane Meriwether, daughter of Nicholas Meriwether and Elizabeth Crawford, and had eleven children, all of whom lived to be grown. His children:

1. John Lewis (5) of Halifax, married Catherine Fauntleroy.
2. Nicholas Lewis of "The Farm", married Mary Walker.
3. William Lewis of Locust Hill, married Lucy Meriwether.
4. Jane Lewis, married first, Mr. Meriwether; second, John Lewis of the Byrd.
5. Mary Lewis, married first, Samuel Cobbs; second, Waddy Thomson.
6. Mildred Lewis, married Major John Lewis of Goochland County.
7. Anne Lewis, married John Lewis of Spotsylvania County.
8. Charles Lewis of North Garden, married Mary Lewis.
9. Elizabeth Lewis, married Rev. Robert Barrett. Died 1747.
10. Sarah Lewis, married Waller Lewis of Spotsylvania County.
11. Robert Lewis of Halifax County, married Frances Lewis of the Byrd.

*Note.*—The original house at "Belvoir" of log—the usual pioneer type—was later replaced by John Walker with a more pretentious one, and this building—moved by Francis Walker to Milton—was again moved to the place given by Mr. James Terrell to his wife's niece Sarah Stanford, wife of James Howell Lewis. Its quaint beauty has saved it from alteration, though the present owner, Mr. McVeigh has changed the name from "Glenn Castle" to "Maxfield." The old Lewis graveyard is nearer the mountain than was the site of the house built by John Walker at "Belvoir."

## JOHN LEWIS (5) OF "HALIFAX"

John Lewis (5) of "Halifax", born 1726, d. 1787, inherited his father's estate in Gloucester County, later moved to Albemarle, then to "Dan River Settlement" about five miles east of Danville. He married Catherine Fauntleroy, daughter of Col. William Fauntleroy of Richmond and his wife Aphia Bushrod, and had issue:

a. John Lewis (6), b. Aug. 31, 1753, d. Sept. 29, 1871.
b. Francis Lewis (6), b. 1755.
c. Apphia Lewis (6), m. David Allen.
d. Sally Lewis (6), b. May 29, 1760, m. Philip Taylor.

John Lewis (6), oldest son of John and Catherine (Fauntleroy) Lewis, born August 31, 1753, Feb. 8, 1776 married Elizabeth Kennon, born Nov. 13, 1754, granddaughter of Charles Lewis and Mary Howell, and had eleven children:

a. John Lewis (7), born Dec. 28, 1776.
b. William Lewis, born Dec. 7, 1778.
c. Elizabeth Lewis, born Dec. 28, 1780, married —— Sturgis, and had issue:
    1. Elizabeth Sturgis (8), who married Richard Hines.
d. Augustine Lewis (7), b. Nov. 3, 1784, m. Louise Brooking.
e. Jane Lewis (7), b. Oct. 1786, m. Capt. William Kennon, and had issue.
    1. Woodson Kennon (8).
    2. Mary Kennon (8).
    3. Apphia Kennon (8).

f. Catherine Lewis (7), married Major William Dowsling, and had issue:
   1. Elizabeth Dowsling (8).
   2. William Dowsling (8).
   3. James Dowsling (8).
   4. Mary Dowsling (8).
   5. Martha Dowsling (8).
   6. Caroline Dowsling (8).
   7. Fielding Dowsling (8).
   Several others, names unknown.

g. Fielding Lewis (7), born July 1788, died September 15, 1857, married February 2, 1827, Elizabeth A. Berryman, and had issue:
   1. Americus Washington Lewis (8), b. Nov. 2, 1827.
   2. John Fielding Lewis, b. Jan. 10, 1831.
   3. Thomas Jefferson Lewis (8), b. Nov. 12, 1833.
   4. Catherine Lewis (8), b. May 22, 1838.
   5. Mary Jane Lewis (8), b. May 15, 1842.

h. Charles Lewis (7), born April 24, 1790.

i. Ulysses Lewis (7), first mayor of Columbus, Ga., also Judge of Russell County, Ala., married in 1824, Miss Ambercromby, and had issue:
   1. John A. Lewis (8).
   2. Thomas I. Lewis (8).
   3. Elizabeth Lewis (8).
   4. Claudia Lewis (8).
   5. Sarah E. Lewis (8).
   6. Martha G. Lewis (8).
   7. Jane H. Lewis (8).
   8. Joseph H. Lewis (8).
   9. Ulysses Lewis (8), born Feb. 27, 1845, married Frances Stuart.

j. Fauntleroy Lewis (7), youngest son of John and Elizabeth Lewis, born February 7, 1796, married Lucy Garland, and had issue:
   1. Edward Garland Lewis (8).
   2. Eliza Lewis (8).

3. Margaret Lewis (8).
4. Lucy Lewis (8).
5. Fannie Lewis (8).
6. Fauntleroy Lewis (8).
7. Celestine Lewis (8).
8. Mildred Lewis (8).

k. Elizabeth Lewis (7) (youngest of all), born 1800, married Col. William Stone, and had issue:
   1. Mary Stone (8), married James Sorley, banker of Galveston, Texas, and had issue:
      a. Lewis Stone Sorley (9), had Merrow E. Sorley (10).

Augustine Lewis (7), born November 3, 1784, son of John and Elizabeth Kennon Lewis, married July 13, 1809, Louisa Brooking. Among other issue was:

1. Dr. Francis B. Lewis (8), b. Oct. 3, 1825, d. Oct. 5, 1890, m. Feb. 25, 1866, Elizabeth B. Mann, and had issue: among others Vivian Marie Lewis (9), who married Martin L. Sigmon and has Frances Lewis Sigmon (10).

END JOHN AND ELIZABETH KENNON.

---

Francis Lewis (6), son of John Lewis and Catherine Fauntleroy, born 1755, married and left sons and daughters. He settled in Georgia. Many descendants moved to Alabama, one of whom Hon. Dixon Lewis of U. S. Senate was a man of ability and rare personality and most striking figure. His size gigantic, his weight five hundred pounds. He always paid double fare on the stage coach.

Mary Lewis (7), daughter of Francis and ——, married Mr. Glenn, and had issue:

1. Mary Glenn (8), married Judge Brickel, Chief Justice of the Supreme Court of Alabama, one of the most distinguished jurists of his day, whose opinions are accepted as authority throughout the United States.

Apphia Fauntleroy Lewis (6), daughter of John Lewis of

Halifax and Catherine Fauntleroy, married David Allen, lived in Pittsylvania County, and had issue:

1. Mary Meriwether Allen (7), m. John Ross, and had issue:
   a. Sarah Allen (8), married ——.
   b. Lizzie Allen Ross (8), married Mr. Turpin, and had Willy Turpin (9).
   c. Kate Apphia Ross (8), married William Patton.
2. Lewis Buckner Allen (7), born 1783, married Mary Catherine Jones, daughter of Richard Jones and Elizabeth Crawley Ward.
3. Sally Fauntleroy Allen (7), married Joseph Woodson.
4. Julius Allen (7), unmarried.
5. Fauntleroy Allen (7), married ——.
6. Felise Allen (7), married Margaret Allen White.
7. Christian Allen (7), married Sally Fortson.
8. David Bushrod Allen (7), married ——.

Lewis Buckner Allen (7) and Mary Catherine Jones family record:

a. Richard Allen (8).
b. Elizabeth Crawley Allen (8), born 1817, died 1848, married Clinton Heslip (1810-1896), and had four sons and Mary Cornelia.
c. Apphia Lewis Allen (8), married John Hightower.
d. William Ward Allen (8), married Martha Burroughs.
e. Ann Catherine Allen (8), married John Donelson.
f. John Lewis Allen, married Josephine Middlebrook.

Lewis Buckner Heslip, Jr., married Grizelda Seal, had two sons and a daughter, Mrs. Robert Hogam, all of St. Louis, Mo.

Mary Cornelia Heslip (9), married John Murray Hood, and had:

a. James Hood (10..
b. Elizabeth Allen Hood (10), married Richard Harris.
c. Ronald Chalmers Hood, married Carrie Morgan.
d. Lt. John Hood (10), U. S. Navy, married Rosalie Coswell. He was on the "Maine" when it was blown up and barely escaped with his life.
e. Joseph Heslip Hood (10), married ——.

f. Christian Heslip Hood (10).
g. Colman Foster Hood (10).
h. Mary Chalmers Hood (10).

Children of Apphia Lewis Allen (8) and John Hightower:

1. Judge Lewis Buckner Hightower (9), married and lives in Cleveland, Texas.
2. Mary Hightower (9), married Mr. Wiley and has Ervin Wiley and a daughter, Mrs. Wiley of Huntsville, Texas.

William Ward Allen (8) and Martha Burroughs have:

1. Louis Buckner Allen (9).
2. William Allen (9) and also several married daughters. All live in San Antonio, Texas.

END OF CHART FROM MISS M. C. HOOD.

---

Sally Lewis (6), daughter of John Lewis of Halifax and Catherine Fauntleroy, born May 29, 1760, married August 10, 1781, Philip Taylor, born March 25, 1759, son of Philip Taylor and Mary Anderson of Chatham County, N. C., and had issue:

1. Iphigenia Taylor (7), born August 21, 1781.
2. Apphia Taylor (7), born March 10, 1783.
3. Philip Taylor (7), born October 7, 1784.
4. John Taylor (7), born October 7, 1786.
5. Polly Walker Taylor (7), born April 10, 1788, married Charles Judson Williams, son of John and Philadelphia Williams, son of John A. Williams of Asheville, N. C.
6. James Taylor (7), born July 30, 1791, died 1793.

END OF JOHN LEWIS OF HALIFAX AND CATHERINE FAUNTLEROY.

---

## NICHOLAS LEWIS (5)

Nicholas Lewis (5), second son of Robert Lewis of "Belvoir" and Jane Meriwether, was a colonial and Revolutionary officer. He was born in 1728. He married Mary Walker, born July 24, 1742, daughter of Dr. Thomas Walker and Mildred (Thornton) Meriwether of "Castle Hill."

They lived on "The Farm", just on the edge of Charlottesville, which was inherited by Nicholas from his grandfather, Nicholas Meriwether. Had issue twelve children:

1. Jane W. Lewis (6), born 1759, married Hudson Martin.
2. Mildred W. Lewis (6), born 1761, married David Wood.
3. Thomas Walker Lewis (6), born 1763, married Elizabeth Meriwether.
4. Mary Lewis (6), born 1765, married Isaac Miller.
5. Nicholas Meriwether Lewis (6), born 1767, married Mildred Hornsby.
6. Elizabeth Lewis (6), born 1769, married William Douglas Meriwether. (Issue given in Nicholas and Margaret Meriwether line.)
7. Robert Warner Wood Lewis (6), born 1774, married Elizabeth Wood.
8. Alice Thornton Lewis (6), died young.
9. John P. Lewis (6), died young.
10. Charles Lewis (6), died young.
11. Frances Lewis (6), died young.
12. Margaret Lewis (6), born 1785, married Charles L. Thomas, son of John Thomas and his second wife, Frances Lewis, daughter of Charles Lewis and Mary Randolph. Issue given in Thomas family, page 52.

Jane W. Lewis (6) and Hudson Martin had issue, eight children:

1. Mary Martin (7), married Mr. Dickinson, and had issue:
   a. Mildred Dickinson (8), married Mr. Rhodes.
   b. Frances Dickinson (8), married Mr. Duggins.
   c. —— Dickinson (8), married Mr. Southerland.
   d. Hudson Martin Dickinson (8), married, and had eleven children:
      1. Ellen Dickinson (9).
      2. Araminta Dickinson (9).
      3. Jane Warner Dickinson (9).
      4. Henry Dickinson (9).
      5. William Dickinson (9).
      6. Walker Dickinson (9).

7. Annie Dickinson (9).
8. Sallie Dickinson (9).
9. Angie Dickinson (9).
10. Rose Dickinson (9).
11. Hudson Dickinson (9).

2. Nicholas Martin (7) and his wife, Miss Dickinson had nine children:
    1. Jane Lewis Martin (8), married James Brown.
    2. Hudson Martin (8).
    3. Henry Washington Martin (8).
    4. Thomas Walker Martin (8).
    5. William N. Martin (8).
    6. Charles L. Martin (8).
    7. Robert T. Martin (8).
    8. Mildred R. Martin (8).
    9. John N. Martin (8).

    Jane L. Martin (8) and her husband, James Brown, had issue, nine children:
    1. William N. Brown (9).
    2. Laurie J. Brown (9).
    3. J. Walter Brown (9).
    4. Charles T. Brown (9).
    5. Edgar S. Brown (9).
    6. Julian P. Brown (9).
    7. Howard Brown (9).
    8. Rosa Brown (9).
    9. J. Russell Brown (9).

3. Hudson Martin II (7) and his wife, had seven children:
    1. Eloise Martin (8), married Crenshaw. Issue:
        a. Gertrude Crenshaw.
    2. Virginia Martin (8), married Mr. Radford. Issue:
        a. Eloise Radford (9).
        b. William Radford (9).
    3. Walker Martin (8).
    4. Mary Martin (8), married Mr. Trigg. Issue:
        a. Eliza Trigg (9).
        b. William Trigg (9).

c. Hawkins Trigg (9).
d. Allison Trigg (9).

5. Edmund Martin (8), married ——. Issue:
   a. Massie (9).
   b. Mary (9).
   c. Kossuth (9).
   d. William (9).
   e. Clara (9).
   f. Cora (9).
6. Jane Martin (8), married Mr. Hawkins. Issue:
   a. John Hawkins (9).
   b. Betty T. Hawkins (9).
7. Hudson Martin (8), married Mildred Minor, daughter of Dabney Minor and went to Arkansas. Issue:
   a. Sarah Martin (9).
   b. Hudson Martin (9).
   c. Alice Martin (9).

4. Mildred Martin (7), married Mr. Carr. Issue:
   1. John H. Carr (8).
5. George W. Martin (7), married ——. Issue:
   1. Jane (8).
   2. Emmet (8).
   3. George Martin, Jr. (8).
6. John M. Martin (7). No record.
7. Henry B. Martin (7). No record.
8. Jane W. Martin (7), married Mr. Farber. No issue.

The family of Jane W. Lewis, and her husband, Hudson Martin, settled southwest of Charlottesville, Va., in the counties of Albemarle and Nelson, near Rockfish Gap and River. Some of the grandchildren are still living on and near the old homestead, and others are scattered south and west.

Hudson Martin was a Second Lieutenant in the Ninth Virginia, during the Revolution. For a number of years he was deputy clerk of the county, and subsequently a magistrate. He married Jane, the eldest daughter of Nicholas Lewis. Near the beginning of the century he removed to Amherst, in the vicinity of Faber's Mills, where his descendants still live. In 1834 Captain John

Thomas testified before the County Court in behalf of his heirs, to the fact of his having served in the Revolutionary army. A son, John M. Martin became a member of the Albemarle bar in 1809.—*History of Albemarle.*

END JANE AND HUDSON MARTIN.

---

Mildred W. Lewis, daughter of Nicholas and Mary Walker, married David Wood, son of Josiah Wood of Bush Mountain Creek and patentee in Albemarle 1741, and had issue, eight children:

1. Maria Wood (7), married Mr. Clarkson, removed to Kanawha, and had issue:
   - a. Mary W. Clarkson (8).
   - b. John Clarkson (8).
   - c. David Clarkson (8).
   - d. Margaret Clarkson (8).
   - e. Eliza Clarkson (8).
2. Thomas Walker Wood (7), Col. 88th Regiment 1814, died 1831. Married Miss Susan Irving. (She married second, a Mr. Fray), and had issue:
   - a. Mildred Wood (8), married Jerry Early, and had issue:
     1. Eugene Early (9), married Patty McIntire.
     2. Thomas Lewis Early (9), married ——. Lives in Brown's Cove.
     3. Alfred Cole Early (9).
     4. Ida Early (9).
     5. Maggy Early (9), married Edward Powers. Issue: a. Mildred (10), and others.
     6. Jerre Early (9).
     7. Minnie Early (9).
   - b. John Wood (8), died unmarried.
   - c. Mary Ann Wood (8), died unmarried.
   - d. Thomas Walker Wood (8).
   - e. Dr. Alfred Wood (8), married Martha Rogers, and had issue:
     1. Charles Hunter Wood (9) of Hopkinsville, Ky.

2. James Wood (9).
3. Alfred Wood (9), married Ella Rogers.

3. William Wood (7), married Miss Dickinson, emigrated to Missouri, and had issue:
   a. Cornelia Wood (8).
   b. David Wood (8).
4. John Wood (7), married Miss Harris, removed to Richmond, Va., and had issue:
   a. William Wood (8).
   b. John Wood (8).
   c. Webster Wood (8).
5. Robert Warner Wood (7), married Mary Ann Miller (of England), and had issue:
   a. David J. Wood (8), died young.
   b. Lucilla Wood (8), died unmarried.
   c. Robert Warner Wood (8) (inherited "Farmington" from his mother), married Margaret Lynn Woods, daughter of Dr. John R. Woods of Holkham, Ivy Depot, Albemarle and his wife, Sabina (Crea) Woods. Had issue:
      1. Robert Warner Wood (9), married June 28, 1922, Mathilde Warner Lewis, daughter of Howell C. Lewis and Bessie Smith of "Clay Hill."
      2. Joseph Miller Wood (9), married ——.
      3. William Wood (9), married Miss Gamble of Texas, and has one child.
      4. Mary Miller Wood (9), married Stephen Philip Holt.
      5. David Wood (9), married Miss Johns of Richmond, and has issue.
6. Nicholas Wood (7), married Miss Key, and had issue:
   a. John Wood (8).
   b. Nicholas Wood (8).

7. Margaret Lewis Wood (7), married Dr. Rogers, and had issue:
   a. Dr. William Rogers (8), married Marion Wood, daughter of Ben Wood and Ann Anderson (See Wood note), and had issue:
      1. Jane Rogers (9).
      2. Maggie Rogers (9).
      3. Ella Rogers (9), married Alfred Wood of Hopkinsville, Ky., and has issue, one daughter.
      4. Ben Wood Rogers (9).
      5. William B. Rogers, Jr. (9).
   b. Margaret Rogers (8), married William Overton Terrell.
   c. Martha Rogers (8), married Dr. Alfred C. Wood. Issue:
      1. Charles Hunter (9).
      2. James (9).
      3. Alfred (9), married Ella Rogers.
   d. Marion Rogers (8), died unmarried.
   e. Ella Rogers (8), died unmarried.
   f. James Rogers (8).
   g. Simon B. Rogers (8).
8. David Wood (7), died unmarried.

Thomas Walker Lewis (6), son of Nicholas and Mary Walker Lewis, born 1763, d. ——. Married Elizabeth Meriwether 1788, born February 24, 1771, died March 27, 1851. She was the daughter of Nicholas Meriwether V and Margaret Douglas. They had ten children.

I. Nicholas Hunter Lewis (7), born October 7, 1789, married November 9, 1812, Ann Terrell Meriwether, daughter of Nicholas Hunter Meriwether and Rebecca Terrell. Issue:
   1. Susan H. Lewis (8), born 1814.
   2. Margaret Douglas Lewis (8).
   3. Lydia Laurie Lewis (8).
   4. Mary Lewis (8).
   5. James H. Lewis (8).
   6. Nicholas H. Lewis (8).

7. Susan H. Lewis (8), married N. P. Minor December 2, 1848, and died October 14, 1859. Issue:
    1. Florence Minor (9).
    2. Richard Minor (9).
    3. Peter Carr Minor (9).
    4. Nicholas Lewis Minor (9).
8. Eliza Lewis (8), married Mr. Buchhanon and had Flora.
9. Lydia Laurie Lewis (8), died 1864, in Kentucky. Married first, Peter Carr, second, William Vaughan. No issue.
10. Thomas Walker Lewis (8).

II. Margaret Douglas Lewis (7), born July 9, 1791, married Major James Clark. Had issue:

a. Ann M. Clark (8), married Richard Watson, and had issue:
   1. Jane M. Watson, married William H. Fry, and had issue, nine children.
   2. Frances E. Watson (9), married V. E. Shepherd, and had issue:
      a. William Shepherd (10).
      b. Fannie Shepherd (10).
      c. James C. Shepherd (10).
   3. Susan T. Watson (9), married Col. Harris of Mississippi. Issue not known.
   4. Virginia Watson (9), married Mr. Byers. Issue unknown.
   5. Nancy Watson (9), died young.
   6. John Watson (9), died in C. S. A. Service.
   7. Dr. James Clark Watson (9), married Miss Butler.

b. Ellen Clark daughter of Margaret D. Lewis and James Clark, married first, Edward B. Hull. Issue:
   1. Col. E. B. Hull (9), C. S. A., married Lizzie Chambers. Issue:
      a. Nelly Hull (10).
      b. Edward B. Hull (10).
      c. Bessie Hull (10).

   Mrs. Ellen C. Hull, married second, Andrew Cockran, and had issue:

a. Margaret D. Cochran (9), married Frank E. Block, had issue:

1. Francis Cochran Block, married Ellen Orme. Had issue:

a. Margaret Douglas Orme Block (11).

2. Ellen Douglas Block (10), married Augustus Hugh Bancher.

3. Edward Bates Block, M. D. (10).

4. Lucretia Parker Block (10).

5. Isabel Margaret Block (10), married Brooks Sanderson Morgan, and has issue:

a. Margaret D. Morgan (11).

6. Hamilton Block (10).

b. Kate Cochran (9), married Mr. Waters.

c. Sally Cochran (9), married Dr. Knox.

d. Ellen Cochran (9), married Mr. Campbell, and had:

e. Eliza Cochran (9), married Dr. Weems.

c. Eliza Clark (8), married first, Thomas W. Minor, died 1838. Married second, Judge Aylette Buckner. Issue:

a. James C. Buckner (9), married Nannie Hyde, and had: Mittie (10).

b. Mildred Buckner (9), married Mr. Whiting. Issue:

a. Aylette Whiting (10).

b. Edgar Whiting (10).

c. Mildred Whiting (10).

c. Richard Buckner (9), died ——.

d. Charles Buckner (9), married Miss Adams.

e. "Stonewall" Buckner (9), married Miss Rudolph, and has:

1. Ralph Buckner (10).

2. Aylette, Buckner, Jr. (10).

d. Dr. Micajah Clark (8), married Margaret Sampson. Issue:

A. James Price Clark (9), killed C. S. A.

B. Richard A. Clark (9), married Miss Hardin, and has:
 1. Etta Clark (10).
 2. Sally Clark (10).
C. Etta Clark (9), married Mr. Nicklin, and has:
 1. Gordon Nicklin (10).
 2. Lewis Nicklin (10).
 3. Margaret Nicklin (10).
 4. "Hun" Nicklin (10).
D. Thornton Clark (9), married Sally Pollard. Issue:
 1. John Clark (10).
 2. Edward Clark (10).
E. Charles Clark (9), married Mary Dillard. No issue.
F. Robert Francis Clark ("Tuggie") (9), died 1887, married Jennie Turner, and has issue:
 1. Price Clark (10).
 2. Harry Clark (10).
 3. Leeta Clark (10).

e. Margaret D. Clark (8), married Dr. Richard Anderson. Issue.
 A. David M. Anderson (9), married Nancy E. Anderson. Issue:
  1. John McMurdo Anderson (10).
 B. Maggie D. Anderson (9), married Mr. Stonebreaker, and has one child.

f. Charles J. Clark (8), married Miss Roberts. Issue:
 A. Anna Clark (9), married Mr. Williams. Issue:
  1. Mattie Williams (10).
  2. Maria Williams (10).
  And others (10).
 B. Lizzie (9), married Emmett M. Meriwether, and has:
  1. Mary Christian Meriwether (10).
  2. Maria Louisa Meriwether (10).
  3. Bessie Meriwether (10).
 Charles J. Clark (8), married second, Mrs. ——, and died in Confederate service.

III. Mary Walker Lewis (7), born in Charlottesville, Va., March 25, 1793, died at "Pantops", June 21, 1872. She was the daughter of Thomas Walker Lewis and Elizabeth Meriwether. Married first, James Leitch, and had issue:

A. John Leitch (8), died young.

B. Thomas Leitch (8), died young.

C. Eliza Leitch (8), born August 23, 1815, died 1866, married in 1831, Meriwether Lewis Anderson, who died on October 6, 1872.

Mary Walker Lewis Leitch married second, David Anderson of "Pantops". No issue. Her descendants given in the Anderson family since the only child, Eliza Leitch, married her mother's stepson, Meriwether Lewis Anderson of "Pantops."

IV. Lydia Laurie Lewis (7), b. February 15, 1795, d. August 8, 1833, daughter of Thomas Walker Lewis and Elizabeth Meriwether, married Samuel Overton Minor, son of Col. Garrett Minor and Mary O. Terrell of "Sunning Hill", Louisa County. He died in Missouri, August 30, 1838. Issue:

A. Mary Overton Minor (8), born December 4, 1812, in 1838, married Samuel D. Eastin. Issue:

1. Samuel O. Eastin (9), married Annie M. Gilmer. Married second, Evaline Marmaduke.
2. Lydia Laurie Eastin (9), married Heath J. Meriwether, and had issue.
3. Nannie Eastin (9).

B. Thomas Walker Lewis Minor (8), born April 4, 1814, died 1838. Married November 9, 1837. He was first husband of Eliza Clark. No issue.

C. Garrett Minor (8), born November 15, 1815, in 1843 married Hettie M. McClanahan. Issue:

1. Bettie Minor (9).
2. Ada Minor (9), married S. O. Minor.
3. Nannie O. Minor (9), married Mr. Spurlark.
4. Maria Louisa Minor (9), married Hardin Stark.
5. Lewis Garrett Minor (9).

Garrett Minor, Sr. married second, his cousin, Mrs. Marianne Hallam. No issue.

D. William Woolfolk Minor (8), born March 10, 1817, died in Pike County, Missouri, May 3, 1885. He married first, Susan Walton Pepper; married second in 1852, Samara F. Fortune, born November 3, 1826, died November 24, 1882 in Texas.

Issue by first marriage:

1. Laurie Ann Minor (9), married Thomas Hutchison, and left issue.
2. Susan Elizabeth Minor (9), married James Reynolds.
3. Samuel O. Minor (9), married Adah M. Minor.
4. Edna McCord Minor (9), married Charles E. Carter.

Issue by second marriage:

5. Richard L. Minor (9), married Lizzie Marmaduke.
6. Peter Minor (9).
7. William W. Minor (9).
8. Mary M. Minor (9).

E. Dr. James Hunter Minor (8), born November 15, 1818, married December 22, 1843, Mary W. Morris, lived at "Music Hall", Albemarle County, left him by his great uncle, Mr. Jimmie Terrell. Issue, six children:

1. James H. Minor (9), married Ida Lake, and had issue, six children:
   a. Mary Minor (10).
2. Lizzie Minor (9), married Robert W. Lewis, and had issue:
   a. Annie Laurie Lewis (10), married 1890, Sylvanus Morris.
   b. Laurie Lewis (10).
   c. Hunter Lewis (10).
   d. Mary Minor Lewis (10), and others.
3. William Overton Minor (9), Circuit Judge in California, married Miss Clarke, and has issue:

a. Mary Constance Minor (10).
b. Lula Minor (10).

4. Thomas S. Minor (9), unmarried.
5. Richard C. Minor (9).
6. Annie Laurie Minor (9), died in childhood.

F. Samuel Overton Minor (8), born May 12, 1820, died March 24, 1880, married March 4, 1841, Elizabeth W. Carter. Had issue:

1. Lydia O. Minor (9), married Albert M. Weir.
2. Alice D. Minor (9), married C. D. Fry.
3. Jessie Minor (9), married D. A. Ball. No. issue.
4. John L. Minor (9), married Miss Hobbs.
5. Peter Carr Minor (9), married Catherine Valleray, and had:
   a. Overton L. Minor (10).
6. Augusta Cordelia Minor (9), married Mr. Dorrington, and had:
   a. Helen M. Dorrington (10).

G. Nicholas Peter Minor (8), Judge of Probate Court of Pike County, Missouri, born August 25, 1822, married first, Susan H. Lewis, and had issue:

1. Florence Minor (9).
2. Richard Minor (9).
3. Peter Carr Minor (9).
4. Nicholas Lewis Minor (9).

Judge Nicholas P. Minor married second, Lizzie Roots. Issue:

5. Fontaine Meriwether Minor (9).

H. Lydia Laurie Minor (8), born December 28, 1827, died June 11, 1851, married Dr. S. McKay. Issue:

1. Maggie D. McKay (9).
2. Richard McKay (9).
3. Overton McKay (9).

I. Sally Watson Minor (8), born January 3, 1829, died March 1873, married Dr. Edward Lee.

J. Louisa H. A. Minor (8), born April 13, 1833. She lived to be over eighty years old, her youth spent largely at "Pantops", Albemarle County. Here she collected and put in form material for her work, "The Meriwethers." Later she lived in Missouri and died near Eolia, Pike County, Mo. I have heard she was most interesting as a conversationalist. (We have a complimentary copy of her book, "The Meriwethers.")

K. Betty Lewis Minor (8), born September 12, 1825. July 18, 1843, married Andrew J. Brown. Issue:

1. Betty O. Brown (9), m. Dr. S. D. Moses. Had issue.
2. Susan T. Brown (9), b. December 26, 1845, m. George A. Staley of Savannah, Ga., May 25, 1869.
3. Lydia L. Brown (9), b. June 10, 1847, m. Rev. Frank Moore, and has issue.
4. James Hunter Brown (9), m. ——. Has issue.
5. Louis Minor Brown (9), b. 1851, d. July 12, 1869.
6. Margaret D. Brown, m. Mr. Huck of Texas. Issue three children.
7. Andrew Laurie Brown (9), m. Miss Dora Dean of Texas.
8. Charles Augustine Warner Brown (9).
9. Cornelia Brown (9).
10. Willy Timberlake Brown (9), m. Dr. Dodd of New York.

This family raised in and around Charlottesville is now scattered south and west.

V. Thomas Meriwether Lewis (7), born May 7, 1797, son of Elizabeth Meriwether and her husband, Thomas Walker Lewis, married 1820, Emeline Weimer. Issue:

A. Marianne Lewis (8), married first, Mr. Hallam, and had issue:

1. Thomas Hallam (9).
2. Alexander Hallam (9).
3. May Hallam (9), married Mr. Bryan.

4. Emma Hallam (9), married first, Mr. Gillum. Married second, Mr. Bryan. Issue:
   a. Etta Bryan (10).
   b. Loyde Bryan (10).
   c. Justice Bryan (10).
   d. Eugenia Bryan (10).

Mrs. Marianne Hallam (8), married second, Judge Garrett Minor. No issue.

B. William J. Lewis (8), born 1824, married first, Nannie L. Meriwether, and had issue:
   1. Hunter Lewis (9).
   2. Adeline Fontaine Lewis (9), married first, Edwin Davis, and had issue. Married second, George Akers. No issue.

William J. Lewis (8), married second, Helen Woolfolk, and had issue:
   3. George Lewis (9).
   4. Richard Lewis (9).
   5. Thomas W. Lewis (9).
   6. Callie Lewis (9), married Mr. Magruder in 1890.
   7. Chapleigh Lewis (9).
   8. Austin Lewis (9).
   9. Belle Lewis (9).
   10. Bessie Lewis (9).

C. Thomas Walker Lewis (8), born 1827, married Isabella Gilmer, and had issue:
   1. Henry Lewis (9).
   2. Annie L. Lewis (9).
   3. William W. Lewis (9).
   4. Mary Alice Lewis (9).

D. Robert W. Lewis (8), born 1829, died 1861, married in 1855, Jane Coffey, and had issue:
   1. Emma Lewis (9), married Mr. Basey, and had several children.
   2. William Lewis (9), born and died 1857.
   3. Robert Lewis (9), born 1858, married ——.

E. Henrietta B. Lewis (8), born 1833. 1854 married Eugene Bonfils. Issue:
   1. Thomas L. Bonfils (9).
   2. Eugene N. Bonfils (9).
   3. William D. Bonfils (9), born 1858, married Miss Sedlicke.
   4. Frederick Bonfils (9), born 1860, married Miss Barton.
   5. Henrietta L. Bonfils (9), married Mr. Walker.
   6. Nelly Bonfils (9), married.

VI. Charles Thornton Lewis (7), son of Thomas W. and Elizabeth Meriwether Lewis, born July 29, 1799, married Mary Quarles, born 1803 in Louisa, died 1888 in St. Joseph, Mo. Issue:

A. Eliza Lewis (8), married first, Mr. Forsythe. Married second, Mr. Williams. Issue:
   1. Ann Williams (9), married Mr. Geltreth.
   2. Thornton Williams (9), married Miss Laurence.
   3. Bertha Williams (9), married Mr. Kenckleham.
   4. Nettie Williams (9), married Mr. Teel.
   5. James W. Williams (9), married Miss Rogers.
   6. Lizzie Williams (9), married Mr. Simmons.
   7. Hattie Williams (9).
   8. Donnie Williams (9).

B. Meriwether Lewis (8), married Miss Mack.

C. Susan Lewis (8), married Mr. Mills. Issue:
   1. Charles Mills (9), married Miss Broclus.
   2. Bettie Mills (9), married Mr. Maxwell.
   3. James Mills (9), married Miss Maxwell.
   4. Hunter Mills (9), married Miss Thomas.
   5. William Mills (9), married Miss Craig.
   6. Lena Mills (9), married Mr. Elliott.
   7. Carrie Mills (9), married Mr. Potts.
   8. Earle Mills (9), married Mr. Tucker.
   9. Flora Mills (9), married Mr. Byles.
   10. Mary Mills (9).
   11. Walker Mills (9).

12. Addison Mills (9).
13. Kenckleham Mills (9).

D. Charles Lewis (8), married Miss Gooch. Issue:
1. Littie Lewis (9), married Mr. Miller.
2. Ada Lewis (9), married Mr. Tucker.
3. Mamie Lewis (9), married Williamson.
4. Lizzie Lewis (9), married Mr. Tucker.
5. Charles Lewis (9), married Miss Leah.

E. Nicholas Lewis (8), married Miss Thompson. Issue:
1. Hunter Lewis (9), married Miss Holmes.
2. Vivian Lewis (9).

F. John R. Lewis (8), married Miss Johnson, and had issue:
1. Charles Lewis (9), married Miss Wallace.
2. Ellis Lewis (9).
3. Mary Lewis (9).
4. John Lewis (9), married Miss Quarles.
5. Emslie Lewis (9), married, and has issue.
6. Annie Lewis (9).

G. James H. Lewis (8), married Miss Hackett. Issue:
1. William Lewis (9), married Miss Robidoux.
2. May Lewis (9), married —— Connelly.
3. Henry Lewis (9).
4. Charles Lewis (9).
5. Emma Lewis (9).
6. Louisa Lewis (9).

H. Emma Lewis (8), married Thomas H. Davis, and had issue:
1. Meriwether Davis (9), married Miss Nichols, and had issue: Thomas (10).
2. Thomas Davis (9).
3. Gilmer Davis (9).
4. Lewis Davis (9).

I. Helen Lewis (8), married Mr. Mills, and had:
1. Thadeus Mills (9).
2. Joseph Mills (9).

3. Louisa Mills (9).
4. Hallie Mills (9).
5. Robert Mills (9).
6. John Mills (9).

J. Louisa V. Lewis (8), married Mr. Wallace.

Charles Thornton Lewis (7) went with his young family to Cooper County, Mo., where he died.

*Note.*—I met Emslie Lewis and his wife and child and a brother of his at the St. Louis World's Fair in 1904.—S. T. L. A.

VII. Elizabeth Lewis (7), born December 2, 1801, daughter of Thomas W. and Elizabeth (Meriwether) Lewis, married John Wells and died in Lincoln County, Missouri. Issue:

A. Thomas Lewis Wells (8), died on "The Plains" on his way to California, June 4, 1849.

B. George N. Wells (8), married Miss Roberts and was killed by lightning in Lincoln County, Mo., June 14, 1849.

C. Anne Wells (8), married G. D. Meriwether, died March 26, 1852.

D. Henry F. Wells (8), married Miss Gilmer. (See Dr. Frederick Gilmer's record).

E. Lydia L. Wells (8), married Charles G. Meriwether. Issue:

1. Betty G. Meriwether (9), married David Crank, and had issue: James L. (10) and Charles Meriwether Crank (10).
2. Charles J. F. Meriwether (9), married Julia Brown, and had issue: Lydia Laurie (10) and Wm. Grover Brown (10).
3. George W. Meriwether (9).
4. Jane Meriwether (9).
5. Adeline Meriwether (9).
6. Thomas W. Meriwether (9).
7. Fred G. Meriwether (9).
8. John Lewis Meriwether (9).
9. Annie W. Meriwether (9).

Several others who died young.

F. Bettie M. Wells (8).

G. John Wells (8).

H. Jane Wells (8).

VIII. Alice Thornton Lewis (7), daughter of Thomas W. Lewis and Elizabeth Meriwether, born January 12, 1804, married first, George D. Meriwether of Bedford County, Va. Issue:
George D. Meriwether (8), who died young.

Married John W. Davis second. Issue:

A. John W. Davis (8), married Miss Pruett.

B. Thomas H. Davis (8), married Emma Lewis. (See Charles T. Lewis' record).

C. Walker Davis (8), married Jennie Roberts. Issue:
1. Winn Davis (9), married Ada Brown, and had issue.
2. Lizzie Davis (9), married Joe Brown, and has two children.

D. Dr. James D. Davis (8), married Julia Coalter, and has issue, five children.

E. Mary E. Davis (8), married William N. Meriwether, and has issue, nine children.

F. Willy Davis (8), died in Confederate Service.

G. Edwin Davis (8), married Adeline Fontaine Lewis, and had issue:
1. Lutie Winn Davis (9).
2. Nicholas Davis (9).
3. James Davis (9).
4. Alice Davis (9).

IX. Jane Warner Lewis (7), born January 25, 1806. November 28, 1822, married first, Walker G. Meriwether, (second wife) son of Nicholas Hunter Meriwether and Rebecca Terrell. Issue:

A. Elizabeth Mary Douglas Meriwether (8), born June 19, 1824, died March 27, 1852, married October 2, 1845, Dr. George Wilson. No issue.

B. George Douglas Meriwether (8), born December 9, 1826, died 1874 in Missouri. May 23, 1848 married first, Anne W. Wells. She died 1852. Married second, November 4, 1852, Betty J. Meriwether, died February 5, 1855. Issue:
   1. Walker Gilmer Meriwether (9), m. Anne M'Cravey. Issue:
      a. Alice C. Meriwether (10).
      b. George Meriwether (10).
      c. Fontaine C. Meriwether (10).

   George Douglas Meriwether married third, Elizabeth M. Anderson, died June 6, 1872. No issue.
   He married fourth, Lizzie Miller. No issue.

C. Thomas L. Meriwether (8), born May 21, 1829, died December 23, 1829.

D. Franklin Montgomery Meriwether (8), born March 14, 1831, died September 10, 1856. Married Mary C. Meriwether, and left no issue.

E. Alice V. Meriwether (8), born November 10, 1834, died October 1837.

F. Alice V. Meriwether (8), born June 18, 1838, married Henry V. P. Block. Issue given under Nicholas Hunter Meriwether and Rebecca Terrell descendants through Walker Gilmer Meriwether and second wife, Jane Warner Lewis.

Jane Warner Lewis (7), married second, Dr. Richard Anderson. No issue. She died at her home "Aberdeen", Pike County, Mo., June 7, 1871. Dr. Anderson died there 1858.

X. Robert Walker Lewis (7), son of Thomas Walker Lewis and Elizabeth Meriwether, was born January 27, 1808, married Sarah A. Craven, March 15, 1831. Issue:

A. George N. Lewis (8), born January 14, 1835.

B. Elizabeth D. Lewis (8), born March 2, 1837, married William Hamilton. No issue.

C. Robert W. Lewis (8), born August 3, 1839, married Lizzie M. Minor, 1864. Issue given under Lydia Laurie Lewis and Samuel Overton Minor, Sr.

D. Alice Lucretia Lewis (8), born May 18, 1842, married James Terrell Lewis, 1862. Issue given under Col. Charles Lewis of "North Garden" and his wife, Mary Lewis, daughter of Charles Lewis of "Buckeyeland", and his wife Mary Randolph.

E. Ellen Overton Lewis (8), married Mr. Andrew Jackson Smith of Fauquier County, and left issue as follows:

1. Walter Smith (9), married Jenny Lewis, first cousins. Issue given under Charles Lewis of "North Garden."
2. Mrs. Evelyn (Smith) Jones, (married first, Mr. King. Married second, Mr. William P. Jones). No issue.
3. Phillip Smith (9), married Helen ——. No issue.
4. Elizabeth Smith (9), married and lives in Augusta County, Va., and has issue.
5. Eleanor Smith (9), married ——. Lives at Manassas.

F. Mary Thornton Lewis (8), died young.

G. John C. Lewis (8), born October 8, 1846, married Miss Lucy Austen. Died January 1923. Issue:

1. Edna Lewis (9), married Mr. Railey.
2. John Lewis, Jr. (9).

Others. Names unknown.

H. Thomas Walker Lewis (8), born July 10, 1850, died April 7, 1917. Married Jane Walker Page, born September 22, 1851, in January 1875 at Grace Church, Albemarle County, Virginia. She was daughter of Frederick W. Page and Ann K. Meriwether. Issue:

1. Frederick Page Lewis, born November 1875, drowned July 1893.
2. Archibald Cary Lewis (9), born July 1877. He married June 1914, Ruth Hastin of Memphis, Tenn. No issue.
3. Alice Douglas Lewis (9), born July 1879, married October 1903, Ashton Blair Jones of Virginia. Issue:
   a. Alice Page Jones (10), born February 1905.
   b. Ashton Blair Jones, born December 1906.
   c. Walker Lewis Jones (10), born August 1911.
   d. Archibald Cary Jones, born June 1914.

4. Thomas Walker Lewis II (9), born August 1881. Married Agnes Thomas of Memphis, Tenn. in 1912, and has issue:
    a. Thomas Walker Lewis III (10), born Sept. 1914.
    b. Francis Nelson Lewis (10), born April 1923.
5. Isabel Money Lewis (9), born September 1883. Married Albert Dexter Davis of Tennessee, in 1911. Issue:
    a. Mildred Page Davis (10), born September 1912.
    b. Archibald Dexter Davis (10), born March 1918.
6. Jane Page Lewis (9), born September 1885, died in 1886.
7. Anne Kinloch Lewis (9), born August 1887. Married Roger Scott Warren of Virginia in 1921. Issue:
    a. Annette Page Warren (10), born January 1924.
8. Francis Nelson Lewis (9), born June 1890. Died in France January 1919, from wounds received in the Argonne. Unmarried.
9. Mildred Nelson Page Lewis (9), born November 1893. Married Osten Everett Duling of West Virginia, 1916. Issue:
    a. Anne Nelson Duling (10), born May 1918 in Massachusetts.
    b. Jane Page Duling (10), born October 1920 in Pittsburgh, Pa.
    c. Osten Everett Duling II (10), born May 1922 in California.
10. Philip Meriwether Lewis (9), born 1898.

I. Margaret D. Lewis (8), born May 21, 1853, married Eugene Sampson. Issue:
1. Alice Gordon Sampson (9), married John Zachary Holladay, Jr., and had issue:
    a. Alice Gordon Sampson Holladay (10).
2. William Campbell Sampson (9), married May Ralston. Issue:
    a. Thelma Jean Sampson (10).
    b. William Campbell Sampson, Jr. (10).

3. Douglas Stuart Sampson (9), married Hazel McNutt. Issue:
   a. Douglas Stuart Sampson, Jr. (10).
   b. Jean Page Sampson (10).
   c. Barbara Lee Sampson (10).
4. Jean Sampson (9).

J. Lydia Laurie Lewis (8), born April 17, 1858, married Henry Lewis Smith. Has issue, six children:
1. Robert Alexander Smith (9), married Cornelia E. Scott. No children.
2. Ernle Gordon Smith (9), married Lucille Taylor. Issue, three children:
   a. Ernle Gordon Smith, Jr. (10).
   b. Nancy Marion Smith (10).
   c. Lydia Lewis Smith (10).
3. Henry Laurie Smith, married Mary Hawes Tyler. Three children:
   a. Mary Laurie Smith (10).
   b. Keith Marshall Smith (10).
   c. Lydia Lewis Smith (10).
4. Marion Douglas Smith (9). Unmarried.
5. Mary Worthington Smith (9), married Bernard L. Mastin, and has issue:
   a. Margaret Douglas Mastin (10).
6. Meriwether Lewis Walker Smith. Unmarried.

END OF DESCENDANTS OF THOMAS WALKER LEWIS AND HIS WIFE, ELIZABETH MERIWETHER.

---

Mary Lewis (6), daughter of Nicholas Lewis and Mary Walker, married Isaac Miller, and had issue.

1. Robert N. Miller (7), married first, Juliette Holloway, and had four children:

A. Emily Miller (8), married Dr. Thomas B. Bohannan, and had issue:
   1. Juliette Bohannan (9).
   2. Louisiana Bohannan (9).

3. Martha Bohannan (9).
4. Lucy Bohannan (9).
5. Robert N. Bohannan (9).
6. Mary H. Bohannan (9), married John M. Anderson. Issue:
    a. Annie Anderson (10).
7. Richard Bohannan (9).
8. Eliza Bohannan (9).
9. Hough Bohannan (9).

B. Dr. Isaac Miller (8), married Annie Miller, and had issue:
1. Isaac Miller, Jr. (9).
2. Florence Miller (9).
3. Robert Miller (9).
4. Alice Miller (9).

C. Robert Miller (8), married Mary L. Howard, and had issue:
1. Howard Miller (9), married Medora Griffin, and had issue:
    a. Mora Miller (10).
    b. Thomas B. Miller (10).
    c. Mary Howard Miller (10).
    d. Annie Miller (10), and others.

D. Madison L. Miller (8), married ——.

2. Warwick Miller (7), married Martha Meriwether Prather, and had issue, six children:

A. John T. Miller (8), married Miss Beckham.

B. Mary Frances Miller (8), married Rev. Mr. Cowgill.

C. Robert D. Miller (8), married Annie Reay.

D. Dr. Warwick N. Miller (8), married Maria Carr, and had issue:
1. Clara Winston Miller (9), married John Dabney.
2. Louisiana Miller (9), married Dr. Thum.

3. Annie Miller (9), first married Dr. Isaac P. Miller, and has issue:
   a. Isaac P. Miller, Jr. (10).
   b. Florence Miller (10).
   c. Robert D. Miller (10).
   d. Alice D. Miller (10).

Nicholas M. Lewis (6), son of Nicholas and Mary Walker Lewis, born 1767, married Mildred Hornsby. He died September 22, 1818. Issue, two children: Joseph (died young) and Annah Hornsby.

1. Annah Hornsby Lewis (7), married Hancock Taylor, brother to General Zachary Taylor. Issue, ten children:

A. Nicholas L. Taylor (8).

B. Eliza Taylor (8), married Mr. Spillman.

C. Mildred Taylor (8), married John McLane. Issue:
   1. Hancock McLane (9).
   2. John McLane (9).
   3. Nathaniel McLane (9).

D. Mary Louise Taylor (8), married Archibald Magill Robinson, and had issue, eleven children, among whom are:
   1. Richard Goldsborough Robinson (9), married Laura Picket Thomas.
   2. Lewis Magill Robinson (9).
   3. John Hancock Robinson (9), married Frances Scruggs.
   4. Anna Walker Robinson (9), married October 5, 1870, James Henry Watson. She is authoress of "A Royal Lineage" and "Some Notable Families of America." They live in Memphis, Tenn. Issue:
      a. Archibald Watson (10).
      b. James Henry Watson (10), married June 12, 1900, Miss Katherine Julia Black.
      c. Katherine Davis Watson (10).
      d. Elizabeth Lee Watson (10).

E. Joseph Taylor (8), married first, Lucy Bates. Married second, Ellen Bates.

F. Annie Taylor (8), married Theodore Hawes.

G. Edward Taylor (8), married Louisa Barker, and had issue:

1. Alexander Taylor (9).
2. Edward Taylor (9).
3. Lewis Taylor (9).
4. Robert Taylor (9), died young.

H. Robert Taylor (8).

I. Zachary Taylor (8).

J. Samuel Taylor (8).

Robert Warner Lewis (6), eighth child of Nicholas and Mary Walker Lewis, and his wife, Elizabeth Wood. He was born 1774. Issue:

1. John Nicholas Lewis (7), married first, Elizabeth Clarke. Married second, Rachel Clarke. Issue:

A. Ann Eliza Lewis (8), married Charles Dorsey. Issue:
1. Mary Comfort Dorsey (9).

B. Louisiana Walker Lewis (8).

C. Mary Virginia Lewis (8), married John Emmett.

D. Charles Warner Lewis (8).

E. William T. Lewis (8).

F. Herman Lewis (8).

G. John N. Lewis (8).

H. Warwick M. Lewis (8).

I. Mildred C. Lewis (8).

2. Robert Warner Lewis, Jr. (7), married Olivia Allston, and had:

1. Susan Mary Lewis (8).
2. Robert Warner Lewis, III (8).

3. Mary Elizabeth Lewis (7), died unmarried.

END RECORD OF NICHOLAS AND MARY W. LEWIS.

## COL. CHARLES LEWIS (5) OF "NORTH GARDEN"

Col. Charles Lewis (5) of "North Garden", third son of Robert Lewis of "Belvoir" and Jane Meriwether, married Mary Lewis, who died 1807, daughter of Charles Lewis of Buckeyeland and Mary Randolph. He was one of the first to offer his services on the outbreak of the Revolution. Was Captain of First Company of Volunteers raised in Albemarle. Lieutenant-Colonel of First Volunteer Regiment formed in Albemarle and adjoining counties; afterwards Colonel of 14th Virginia Regiment.

Died 1779, while in command of guards at "The Barracks" near Charlottesville (camp of Hessian prisoners). His health had failed—thus given a post. Will written 1766, probated 1779.

His children as given in *History of Albemarle:*

1. Howell Lewis (6), died 1841, married Mary Carr.
2. Charles Warner Lewis (6), died young.
3. Mary Randolph Lewis (6), married Edward Carter.
4. Jane Lewis (6), married John Carr.
5. Sarah E. W. Lewis (6), married Benjamin Brown.
6. Ann Lewis (6), wife of Mathew Brown lived in Amherst (grandparents of Judge Thomas Brown of Amherst).
7. Susan Lewis (6), wife of Joel Franklin, descendants emigrated South, some to Alabama.

His widow, Mrs. Mary Lewis, married second, Mr. Charles Wingfield, Jr. She died 1807.

Sarah Elizabeth Willis Lewis (6), (died December 2, 1836) oldest child of Col. Charles Lewis of North Garden and his wife and cousin Mary Lewis, (who was a daughter of Charles Lewis of Buckeyeland, and his wife Mary Randolph, daughter of Isham Randolph of Dungeness.)

Charles Lewis of Buckeyeland was second son of "Charles of the Byrd" and his wife, Mary Howell. Charles of the Byrd was second son of Councilor John Lewis and his wife, Elizabeth Warner.

Sarah Elizabeth Willis Lewis, married November 9, 1795, Benjamin Brown, lawyer, of Moresbrook, Albemarle County, Va., who died in 1851. They moved about 1813 to Amherst County,

Va., and their home was called "Berry Hill", a plantation near the village of Amherst, Va. Ten children.

I. Charles Lewis Brown (7), born October 25, 1796, died May 30, 1884 in Amherst County, Va. (he was the oldest child of Sarah Elizabeth Willis Lewis and Benjamin Brown). He married first, his cousin, Ann Carr (no issue). Married second, December 8, 1847, Sarah Ann Mountiply, who was born September 1, 1817 and died May 13, 1890, Amherst, Va. She was a daughter of William Mountiply, who emigrated from Scotland about 1770 and settled in Amherst County, Va., where he owned a large estate, and many slaves. His home was called "Woodlawn."

1. Sallie Lewis Brown (8), oldest child of Charles Lewis Brown and Sarah Ann Mountiply, born January 8, 1849 at "Pleasant View", Amherst County, Va., died January 23, 1918 at 392 Woodlawn Ave., Lynchburg, Virginia. Married January 24, 1874, William Thomas Royster, who was born at "Locust Grove", Amherst County, Virginia, June 24, 1849, and was the only son of Thomas Bannister Royster, who was a large land and slave owner, and his wife, Nancy Higginbotham. William Thomas Royster was a descendant of Jacob Royster who came from England and settled in Clarksville, Mecklenburg County, Va. in 1760.

Their children and grandchildren:

1. Thomas Brown Royster (9), born January 28, 1877, Amherst, Va., married September 14, 1904, Carrie Cordelia Hopkins, daughter of Samuel I. Hopkins, a Methodist minister (born in Maryland) and his wife Constance Gannaway of Lynchburg, Va.

Children:

Thomas Duval Royster (10), born June 27, 1905.

Catherine Randolph Royster (10), born August 23, 1911, Lynchburg, Virginia.

2. Charles Lewis Royster (9), born at "Locust Grove", December 23, 1878, married June 11, 1902, Mary Eva Saunders, of Nelson County. Second daughter of John L. Saunders and his wife Josephine Massie.

Their children:

Randolph Lewis Royster (10), born April 24, 1903.

Lucile Massie Royster (10), born June 27, 1905.

Lee Myers Royster (10), born November 24, 1907.
William Saunders Royster (10), born March 2, 1914.
All born at Amherst, Va.

3. Percy Claire Royster (9), born at "Locust Grove", December 5, 1880, married June 15, 1909, Ida Virginia Megginson, oldest daughter of James Benjamin Megginson and his wife, Betty Lewis of Appomattox County, Virginia.

Children:

Elizabeth Lewis Royster (10), born in Lynchburg, July 21, 1910.
Virginia Claire Royster (10), born July 24, 1912.

4. Claudia Randolph Royster (9), born at "Locust Grove", December 11, 1882, married January 14, 1911, Bently Mountiply (cousin), oldest son of Robert H. Mountiply and his wife, Alma Harris, who is a great-grandson of Doctor Littlebery N. Ligon of Nelson County, Va., and his wife, Elizabeth Kimbrough, and a descendant of John Crawford who emigrated from Scotland before the middle of the seventeenth century and settled in Virginia.

Their children:

William Robert Mountiply (10), born January 19, 1913.
Mary Louise Mountiply (10), born November 27, 1916.
Edward Bently Mountiply (10), born November 6, 1921.
All born at Amherst, Virginia.

5. Sue Royster (9), born at "Locust Grove", January 11, 1887. Married at "Locust Grove", Amherst County, Virginia, November 2, 1910, John Beardsworth, youngest son of Professor William Henry Beardsworth and his wife, Susannah Mary Driver of Blackburn, England. John Beardsworth was born December 20, 1882 at Atherton, England. His father with his family came to Philadelphia in 1887 and later was head of the music department of Southern Seminary, Buena Vista, Virginia.

Their children:

Margaret Lewis Beardsworth (10), born October 29, 1912.
John Beardsworth, Jr. (10), born April 8, 1918.
Carolyn Sue Beardsworth (10), born November 15, 1921.
All born in Lynchburg, Virginia.

2. Susan Marion Brown (8), second child of Charles Lewis

Brown and Sarah Ann Mountiply, was born March 4, 1851, married July 30, 1878, Peter Clarkson Hill, and had:

1. John William Hill (9), born September 10, 1882, married September 13, 1905, Susan Ella Gleeson, daughter of Rev. Robert Gleeson of Nelson County, Va., and had:

   1. Robert Clarkson Hill (10), born June 11, 1906.
   2. Wm. Austin Hill (10), born August 29, 1907.
   3. Catherine Louise Hill (10), born July 19, 1910.
   4. Peter Crawford Hill (10), born May 6, 1909.
   5. Harry St. George Tucker Hill (10), born November 9, 1911.
   6. Charlotte Gleeson Hill (10), born July 5, 1913.

2. Walter Lemon Hill (9), second child of Susan Marion Brown and Peter Clarkson Hill, was born April 7, 1885, died unmarried.

3. Sally Lewis Hill (9), born December 5, 1891, married March 6, 1920, Robie Atkins of Pittsylvania County, Va., and lives in Norfolk, Virginia.

II. Second child of Sarah E. W. Lewis and Benjamin Brown was Mary Ann Randolph Brown (7), born June 24, 1798, married November 21, 1816, Captain Samuel Wyatt. No issue.

III. Caroline Elizabeth Brown (7), born September 23, 1802, died June 1853, married November 20, 1821, John Thompson, a lawyer, Amherst, Virginia. No issue.

IV. Susannah Meriwether Brown, born November 24, 1804, married December 17, 1822, Arthur B. Davies, Clerk of Court, Amherst County, Virginia. No issue.

V. Sallie Overton Brown (7), born January 11, 1807, married March 1824, James Watson Dibrell. No issue.

VI. Mildred Warner Brown (7), married Julius or Phillip Adolphus Peticolas, a Frenchman in 1828, and had Jane Randolph Petticolas, married Joseph Parker, and had Mildred H. Parker, born February 21, 1869 in Amherst. Married June 13, 1900, Samuel Robbins Church of Washington. Issue:

   1. Alphonso Church (10), born June 14, 1903. Sophomore at Princeton, 1922.

2. Randolph Warner Church (10), born March 9, 1907 in Lynchburg, Virginia.

VII. Benjamin Franklin Brown (7), born May 29, 1812, died 1855. Married December 18, 1838, Mary Elizabeth Pierce, who was born October 1818, died July 23, 1905. They lived at "Berry Hill", near Amherst, Va. She died at the home of her daughter Mrs. George W. Dearborn, Amherst, Va.

Ten children, twenty-four grandchildren and eighteen great-grandchildren:

1. Mary Ann Randolph Brown (8), born August 24, 1839, married December 11, 1860, George H. Vaughan (lawyer), who died July 1863 in Confederate Army. No issue.
   Mary Randolph Brown Vaughan, married second, September 1, 1869, Alfred William Lucas (druggist), Hagerstown, Md. She died May 23, 1883. Children:
   A. Caroline Thompson Lucas (9), born June 10, 1871, married first, Frederick Maheer Thomas, January 1, 1896. No issue. Married second, June 6, 1908, Dr. William Henry Harrison Bixler. No issue.
   B. Jean Williams Lucas (9), born August 5, 1873, (unmarried) artist, Hagerstown, Md.
   C. Edward Bristol Lucas (9), born October 2, 1877, married June 2, 1909, Anne Reichard Buck. No issue.
2. Sallie Lewis Brown (8), born December 8, 1840, died young.
3. Benjamin Brown (8), born March 25, 1842, died May 29, 1920. Captain in Confederate Army and buried at Arlington. He was also a merchant at Amherst, Va., and afterwards Washington, D. C. Married March 19, 1867, Sarah Penn Brown, born July 4, 1844. Children:
   A. Mary Elizabeth Brown (9), born January 1, 1872, married November 26, 1900, J. G. Holcombe (civil engineer). She died May 20, 1915. Children:
      a. Walton Holcombe (10) (deceased). Married, and had several children.
      b. Benjamin Holcombe (10), Lieutenant in Navy.
      c. Gales Holcombe (10).

d. Elizabeth Holcombe (10), trained nurse, New York City.

B. Hugh Brown (9), born September 12, 1874, died March 3, 1910. Unmarried.

C. Benjamin Brown, Jr. (9), born December 24, 1877, died November 14, 1920, married Celestine Green. No issue.

4. Cornelia Pierce Brown (8), born August 17, 1843, died young.

5. Mildred Warner Brown (8), born August 16, 1845. Married B. T. Blew, druggist, Hagerstown, Md. No issue.

6. Caroline Thompson Brown (8), born March 31, 1847, died February 3, 1914. Married December 17, 1867, James Morgan Patteson. Their children and grandchildren:

A. Mary Grace Patteson (9), born 1868, married June 25, 1902, Ashby Perry. Their children:

a. Grace Elizabeth Perry (10), born August 1, 1903.
b. Ashby Patteson Perry (10), born October 25, 1907.
c. Virginia Randolph Perry, born April 25, 1910.

B. James Patteson (9), died in infancy.

C. Caroline Brown Patteson, born March 11, 1872.

D. Macon Patteson (9), born March 11, 1872, twins. Macon died in infancy.
Caroline Brown Patteson (9), married August 18, 1897, Dr. Wallace Hill Gilkyson, who died December 1921. No issue.

E. Ida Thompson Patteson (9), born November 11, 1876, married December 15, 1909, Austin Edward Bellew. Children, one:

a. Ruth Patteson Bellew (10), born October 28, 1910.

F. E. Virginia Patteson (9), born February 13, 1879.

G. Elizabeth Warner Patteson (9), born July 1882. Unmarried.

H. Benjamin Hunt Patteson (9), born June 5, 1884. Unmarried.

I. James Macon Patteson (9), born November 5, 1885. Married August 27, 1913, Helen St. Clair Woodward. Children:
  a. James Bryant Patteson (10), born Feb. 14, 1916.
  b. Eugene Randolph (10), born May 10, 1918.
  c. Macon Woodward Patteson (10), born October 25, 1919.

J. Randolph Lewis Patteson (9), born May 14, 1892. Unmarried.

7. Henry Davis Brown (8), born May 4, 1849, died ——.
8. Arthur Davis Brown (8), born April 1851, died July 1852.
9. Louisa Anne Brown (8), born December 15, 1854. Married February 20, 1878, George Washington Dearborn, who was for many years Agent Southern Railway at Amherst, Va. He died in 1920. Their children:

A. Peyton Brown Dearborn (9) (jeweler), born November 27, 1878, died July 1, 1906. Married September 17, 1902, Mary Gertrude Hichey. One child:
  a. George Townshend Dearborn (10), born September 20, 1903.

B. George Benjamin Dearborn (9) (railway dispatcher), born January 20, 1880, died October 1908. Married June 20, 1906, Fay Elizabeth Adams Kone. One child:
  a. Dorothy Dearborn (10), born April 14, 1907.

C. Mary Louise Dearborn (9), born May 22, 1881, married November 24, 1917, Howard McKinnon (banker). Their children:
  a. Luther McKinnon (10), born April 14, 1919.
  b. George Dearborn McKinnon (10), born February 20, 1921.

D. Sarah Virginia Dearborn (9), born December 25, 1882, died October 22, 1918. Married April 27, 1907, Dr. Edward Sandidge, (physician). Residence, Amherst, Va. One child:
  a. Louise Caroline Sandidge (10), born June 3, 1908.

E. Randolph Lucas (9) and Effie Blew Dearborn (twins), born June 6, 1885. Randolph Lucas died Feb. 2, 1886.

Effie Blew Dearborn, married S. M. G. Wills, druggist, April 11, 1908. Residence, Amherst, Va. No issue.

F. Nell Thompson Dearborn (9), born December 19, 1887, married June 5, 1912, W. P. Reed (banker). Children:

a. Nell Dearborn Reed (10), born March 25, 1913.

b. Marion Clarke Reed (10), born June 3, 1914.

G. Marion Hopkins Dearborn (9), born March 2, 1890. (Ticket agent, Amherst, Va.).

H. Gordon Jones Dearborn (9), born December 3, 1892. (Banker, Victoria, Va.). Unmarried.

10. Eliza Tinsley Brown (8), born January 3, 1855, unmarried. (Trained nurse, Washington, D. C.).

VIII. Robert Meriwether Brown (7), born July 25, 1814, died November 1, 1894, married December 14, 1840, Sarah Ann Whitehead, daughter of John Whitehead. Robert Meriwether Brown was a lawyer and lived all his life at Amherst, Va. Children: Five sons and one daughter, six grandchildren and three great-grandchildren, as follows:

1. John Whitehead Brown (8), born February 14, 1843, killed May 10, 1864, in the Civil War, at the battle of Beaver Dam, Va. "A gallant lad", is the mention of him in General J. E. B. Stuart's Biography.

2. Robert Meriwether Brown, Jr. (8), born December 24, 1845, died at Wharton, Texas, May 10, 1917. Married Nina Warren of Mississippi. Their several children died in infancy. Have no data.

3. Thomas Lewis Brown (8), born June 1848, died January 1875. Married Mamie Archer. No issue.

4. Annie Thompson Brown (8), born July 12, 1851, married Nathan Francis Gorsuch of Maryland, July 15, 1868. Children:

A. Sarah Elizabeth Gorsuch (9), born July 13, 1869, died January 28, 1870.

B. William Pierce Gorsuch (9), born October 2, 1871. Married June 20, 1900, Augusta Willoughby Tunnicliff of Illinois. No issue.
William Pierce Gorsuch is a professor in the University of Washington. Residence, Seattle, Washington.

C. Robert Meriwether Brown Gorsuch (9), born March 27, 1875, died at Wharton, Tex., May 26, 1896, unmarried.

Nathan Francis Gorsuch, died April 12, 1875, and his widow, Annie Thompson Brown Gorsuch married second, December 14, 1881, Rev. Colin Stokes, Presbyterian minister. Residence, Amherst, Va., and Covington, Virginia.

Children:

A. Richard Cralle Stokes (9), born December 10, 1882, married Lulu May Rinehart. Children:
   a. Bessie Rinehart Stokes, born June 10, 1908.
   b. Anna Lewis Stokes (10), born May 8, 1913.

B. Felde Warren Stokes, born December 28, 1885, died October 4, 1892.

C. Colin Stokes, Jr. (9), born February 11, 1887. Married Douglas Galloway. One child:
   Virginia Allison Stokes (10), born Sept. 17, 1916.

5. Arthur Davis Brown (8), born July 1856. Unmarried.

6. Benjamin Willis Brown (8), born April 1861, married first, Marion Black. No issue. Marion Black Brown, died December 1916. Benjamin Willis Brown married second, Lizzie Faison. No issue. He is a physician and surgeon.

IX. Jane Carr Brown (7), b. December 10, 1816, d. ——. Married March 2, 1836, William Erastus Coleman (farmer). They lived near Amherst, Virginia. Seven children, thirteen grandchildren and sixteen great-grandchildren:

1. Sarah Elizabeth Brown Coleman (8), born January 25, 1839, married Doctor Gustavus Adolphus Rose Tucker, November 26, 1857. She died in Chattanooga, Tenn., January 13, 1897. Their children:

A. Susie Meriwether Tucker (9), born April 6, 1860, died in Chattanooga, Tenn., July 28, 1911. Married September 5, 1888, Oswald August Dietz (Civil Engineer). Their children:

a. Mary Augusta Dietz (10), born January 11, 1890, died July 21, 1891.

b. Lawrence August Dietz (10), born August 8, 1895, married April 2, 1922, at the church of the Palace, Coblenz, Germany, Isabelle Jeannette Taylor, daughter of Mr. and Mrs. James Monroe Taylor, of Chicago. He was with the Army of Occupation, Coblenz.

c. Katherine Coleman Dietz (10), born October 17, 1897. Died in Chattanooga, Tenn., Jan. 16, 1918.

d. Julian Oswald Dietz (10), born September 25, 1899, died March 15, 1900.

B. William Laurence Tucker (9), born October 19, 1862, died in Colorado August 1, 1894. Unmarried.

C. Gustavus Adolphus Rose Tucker, Jr. (9), born November 15, 1866, married Katie Hulse January 23, 1889. Died in Chattanooga, Tenn., June 21, 1899. No issue.

D. Jennie Marie Tucker, born April 16, 1870. Teacher. Residence, Chattanooga, Tenn.

E. Erastus Coleman Tucker (9), born October 31, 1872. Unmarried. Residence, Chattanooga, Tenn.

F. John Randolph Tucker (9), born July 19, 1875. Died in Chattanooga, Tenn., August 26, 1899. Unmarried.

G. Roger Taliaferro Tucker (9), born December 9, 1878. Died in Chattanooga, Tenn., December 28, 1906. Married June 1, 1902, Myrtle Williams. Their children:

a. Susie Vivian Tucker (10), born March 3, 1903. Died in Chattanooga, December 28, 1906.

b. Virginia Estelle Tucker (10), born Nov. 23, 1905.

2. William Arthur Coleman (8), born February 1, 1843, died in South Carolina, 1890. Unmarried.

3. Alfred Lewis Coleman (8), born ——. Accidentally killed when a young boy.

4. John Thompson Coleman (8), born ——. Died in Georgia 1875. Unmarried.
5. Lindsay Taliaferro Coleman (8), born ——, married in 1884. Died in Virginia 1891. One child:
   A. Josephine Coleman (9).
6. Nancy Taliaferro Coleman (8), born August 15, 1853, died in Washington, D. C., May 1914. Married November 14, 1878, George Yellott Worthington. Residence, Seminary Hill, near Alexandria, Va., and afterwards, Georgetown, D. C. (Real Estate and Insurance). Their children:
   A. Hugh Skipwith Worthington (9), born ——. Married September 3, 1908, Helen Mill Coale. Their children:
      a. Nancy Coale Worthington (10), b. Oct. 13, 1909.
      b. Hugh Skipwith Worthington, Jr. (10), born October 27, 1912.
      c. Helen Parker Worthington (10), born September 12, 1914.
      d. William Coale Worthington (10), born July 20, 1917.

   Residence, Sweet Briar, Va. Hugh S. Worthington, Sr., is Professor of Romance Languages at Sweet Briar.
   B. William Coleman Worthington (9), born ——. Married at Ossining, N. Y., December 27, 1905, Margaret Page Dame. Residence, 1418 Eye Street, N. W., Washington, D. C. General Manager National Life Insurance Company of Vermont. Children:
      a. Mary Coleman Worthington (10), born October 3, 1906.
      b. Nelson Page Worthington (10), b. May 30, 1911.
      c. Margaret Dame Worthington (10), born April 22, 1913.
      d. William Coleman Worthington, Jr. (10), born April 30, 1910. Died June 14, 1910.

   Margaret Page (Dame) Worthington is the daughter of Rev. Mr. and Mrs. Nelson Page Dame, 2300 Park

Avenue, Richmond, Va. Mrs. Dame was Miss Mary Nimmo Walker, daughter of Rev. Cornelius Walker. Mr. William Coleman Worthington writes, "You might record that our marriage has been a living example that there are still supremely happy marriages in spite of the scoffers and the 'modern ideas'. We are agreed that we have grown happier as the years have passed."

C. Elizabeth Lewis Worthington (9), born ——. Died a few years ago. Married Angus McDonald Crawford. No issue.

D. George Yellott Worthington, Jr. (9), married October 20, 1914, Adele Kingsbury Waterman of St. Louis, Mo. Their children:

a. George Yellott Worthington III (10), born August 9, 1915.

b. Julia Turner Worthington (10), born March 20, 1917.

c. Mary Kingsbury Worthington (10), born November 9, 1919.

(Real Estate and Insurance, Woodward Building, Washington, D. C.).

E. Gustav T. Worthington (9), married Glenn Scanling of San Antonio, Texas. Died and left three children. Mrs. Glenn Scanling Worthington married second, a Mr. Maverick and they live at San Antonio, Texas.

7. Benjamin Brown Coleman (8), seventh child of William Erastus Coleman and Jane Carr Brown, born 1855, died in Chattanooga, Tenn., July 31, 1891. Unmarried.

| | |
|---|---|
| Living descendants named | 143 |
| Dead descendants named | 70 |
| Total | 213 |

X. Alfred Lewis Brown (7), born August 29, 1819, died ——. Married Elizabeth Failes. They lived in Cheyenne, Wyoming. No descendants known.

END SARAH E. W. AND BENJAMIN BROWN.

## SOME DESCENDANTS OF ANN OR "NANCY" LEWIS,

SECOND CHILD OF COLONEL CHARLES LEWIS OF "NORTH GARDEN" AND WIFE (COUSIN), MARY LEWIS.

Ann or Nancy Lewis (6), married Matthew Brown (no kin to Benjamin Brown, who married her sister Sarah Elizabeth Willis Lewis.

Do not know exact date of marriage, about 1795.

Children:

1. Howell Lewis Brown (7), born 1797, died 1860, married first a Miss Franklin. Have no further data as to issue of Ann Lewis and Matthew Brown, and no data of issue of first marriage of their son Howell Lewis Brown to Miss Franklin.

Howell Lewis Brown married, second, Jane Thompson, 1842.

Only one son by second marriage, John Thompson Brown (8), born 1844. He married, 1869, Elizabeth Waller Caldwell.

Their children:

A. John Thompson Brown (9), born 1870, married Belle C. Bolton. Children:
   a. Channing Bolton Brown (10), born 1897.
   b. Elizabeth C. Brown (10), born 1900.
   c. John Thompson Brown (10), born 1904.
   d. Belle C. Brown (10), born 1906.

B. Fannie Waller Brown (9), born 1872, married Dr. Edward C. Ambler. Children:
   a. Elizabeth C. Ambler (10), born 1900.
   b. Edward Cary Ambler (10), born 1907.
   c. John Thompson Ambler (10), born 1909.

C. David Caldwell Brown (9), born 1873, died 1873.

D. Rebekah Davies Brown (9), born 1874, married Aubrey E. Strode. Children:
   a. William Lewis Strode (10), died 1904.
   b. Mildred Ellis Strode (10), born 1906.
   c. Aubrey Ellis Strode (10), born 1908.
   d. John Thompson Strode (10), born 1910.
   e. Rebekah Elizabeth Strode (10), born 1913.

E. William Govan Brown (9), born 1876, married Mabel Simpson. Children:
   a. Germaine F. Brown (10), born 1901.
   b. John Thompson Brown (10), born 1902.
   c. David Waller Brown (10), born 1903.
   d. William G. Brown (10), born 1905.

F. Elizabeth Caldwell Brown (9), married Dr. Joseph F. Faros. No issue.

G. Howell Lewis Brown (9), born 1879, married Julie Griffith. No children.

H. David Waller Brown (9), born 1881, married Elsie Sedden. Children:
   a. Fannie Waller Brown (10).
   b. Bruce Cabell Brown (10).
   c. Sedden Brown (10).
   d. Elizabeth Caldwell Brown (10).
   e. Alexander D. Brown (10).
   f. David Waller Brown (10).

I. Ellen McBryde Brown (9), born 1883, unmarried.

J. Jane Thompson Brown (9), born 1884, married J. Baldwin Ranson. No issue.

K. W. Duval Brown (9), born 1886, unmarried.

L. R. Meredith Brown (9), died in infancy.

END NANCY AND MATTHEW BROWN.

---

## HOWELL LEWIS, HIS FAMILY REGISTER

Howell Lewis (6), son of Charles Lewis and Mary Lewis, was born July 16, 1766, died 11th day of July 1845, half past seven o'clock A. M. He married April 10, 1787, Mary Ann Carr, daughter of Thomas Carr and Mary Clarkson or Lucy Barksdale. Their children as follows:

1. Lucy Carr Lewis (7), born Thursday February 21, 1788, died Tuesday, June 13, 1807, in the nineteenth year of her age.

2. Susan Randolph Lewis (7), born July 23, 1789, died Tuesday, December 31, 1805, in the sixteenth year of her age.
3. Jane Elizabeth Lewis (7), born Thursday, June 26, 1791, died Tuesday May 28, 1811, in the twentieth year of her age.
4. Charles Warner Lewis (7), born Monday, June 10, 1792, died Saturday, October 21, 1812, in the twentieth year of his age.
5. Ann Caroline Lewis (7), born Thursday, February 19, 1795, married on February 24, 1812, Fletcher N. Taliaferro, died in the State of Tennessee, January 21, 1833, aged thirty-eight years.
6. Mary Howell Lewis (7), born Monday, August 15, 1796, married Clifton Harris, January 10, 1816, and left issue.
7. Thomas Fielding Lewis (7), born Friday, January 12, 1798, died June 13, 1862, at "Rose Hill", Albemarle County. Married February 4, 1819, Ann Anderson, born October 20, 1800, died 1844, buried at "Locust Hill", and left issue. Married second, Mrs. Mary Charlton of Suffolk. No issue by second wife. He is buried beside his first wife at "Locust Hill."
8. Sarah Meriwether Lewis (7), born Monday, March 24, 1800, married Ira Harris, March 25, 1817, died March 16, 1841. Would have been forty-one years old on the twenty-fourth following.
9. Matilda Brown Lewis (7), born Saturday, March 6, 1802, died on Sunday, October 24, 1819, in the eighteenth year of her age.
10. James Howell Lewis (7), born Saturday, November 3, 1804, married December 12, 1826, Sarah Stanford.

Children of Thomas Fielding Lewis and Ann Anderson:

1. Charles William Lewis (8), son of Thomas Fielding Lewis and Ann Anderson, born August 1819, married Martha Alexander 1859, died in Georgetown, Texas on June 7, 1869, in the fiftieth year of his age. No issue.
2. Matilda Ann Lewis (8), daughter of Fielding and Ann Lewis, born September 3, 1822, married David Henry

Wood, January 4, 1842 (died Feb. 1, 1876). David Wood, her husband died March 1876. For issue see Wood note.

3. John Marks Lewis, married Margaret Tapp.
4. Henry Grattan (8) (youngest child), died young.

## "CLAY HILL", IVY DEPOT, VA.

Children of John Marks Lewis and Margaret Tapp Lewis of "Clay Hill", Albemarle County.

1. Walter Tapp Lewis (9), born July 1, 1853, died October 4, 1860.
2. Thomas Fielding Lewis (9), born October 24, 1855, married Josephine Robinson. No issue. Adopted a son, Robert Lewis, and died on a train between Colorado Springs and Dallas, November 20, 1920. 1873—At the age of seventeen, he migrated from his father's home at "Clay Hill" to Texas; was a planter and stock breeder for some years, with tours over Western Texas on horseback. He was in the reprisal expeditions against the Indians and was severely wounded in one of these battles. He ultimately took up law and became a prominent member of the bar at Dallas to which he moved in 1879. Robert Lewis, his adopted son, was his heir. Mrs. Josephine Lewis died a few years later.
3. Mary Jouette Lewis (9), was born February 25, 1857. Died November 28, 1860.
4. Walter Jouette Lewis (9), born February 6, 1862, married Nellie ——. No issue. Adopted his niece, Sarah Meriwether Lewis.
5. John Marks Lewis (9), born May 27, 1864, married Sally Lewis, daughter of his cousin, Henry Lewis, son of James Howell Lewis.
6. William Wood Lewis, born September 2, 1867, married Annie Strayer. Issue:
   A. William Lewis (10), married, and has issue.
   B. Meriwether Lewis (10), married Mary Jaeger, March 10, 1925, of Florence, S. C.

C. Bessie Lewis (10), married. No issue. Died 1918.

7. Matilda Warner Lewis (9), born November 5, 1870, married Winston Garth. No issue.

8. Howell Carr Lewis (9), born October 17, 1873, married March 9, 1898, Bessie Smith, born November 12, 1873, daughter of Robert Worthington Smith and Lucretia Nash Johnson (English family). Issue:

A. Mathilde Warner Lewis (10), born September 12, 1899, married Robert Warner Wood, June 28, 1922. Issue:

1. Mathilde Warner Wood (11), born April 1, 1923.

B. Howell Carr Lewis (10), born October 13, 1902.

C. Mary Elizabeth Lewis (10), born June 20, 1908.

D. Catherine Lucretia Lewis (10), born June 1, 1912.

E. Lucretia Worthington Lewis (10), born May 18, 1914, died October 12, 1918.

Issue of John M. Lewis and Sally Lewis:

1. Douglas Tapp Lewis (10), born January 1886, married twice and left issue: Margaret (11), Robert (11), Carlisle (11).

2. Fielding Lewis (10), married and has Fielding.

3. Margaret Lewis (10), married Mr. Michael Owen and has issue in Dallas, Texas.

4. Robert Lewis (10), born December 9, 1899, married May 13, 1916, Emma Kathry Jaskins of Florence, Texas. Issue:

A. Robert Walker Lewis (11), born Nov. 28, 1917.

B. William Douglas Lewis (11), born Nov. 19, 1919.

C. Ruth Kathry Lewis (11), born Dec. 1, 1922.

Residence: 4410 Leroy Drive, Dallas, Texas.

5. Susie Lewis (10), married Rev. Mr. Forman. One child.

6. Sarah Meriwether Lewis (10), musical genius, adopted by her father's brother, Walter and his wife, Nellie Lewis.

7. Hunter Lewis (10), raised by his mother's brother, Fielding Lewis and his wife, Bessie Maxwell.
8. H. H. Lewis (10), Route 1, Box 59, Station A, Dallas, Texas.

## GLEN CASTLE

James Howell Lewis (7), son of Howell Lewis and Mary Carr, was born November 3, 1804, and was married December 12, 1826, to Sarah Stanford, and had issue, eleven children:

1. Susan S. Lewis (8), married Mr. Bacon, and had issue:
   - A. Susan Bacon (9), married Ernle Money, and had issue: Amile (10), Isabel (10), and Florence (10). (Isabel Money married Downing Kelley, and had issue: Isabel (11), and others.)
2. William S. Lewis (8), married Fannie Campbell. Issue:
   - A. Lelia Lewis (9), married Mr. Shackleford. Issue:
     1. Jane Shackleford (10), and others.
   - B. Fannie Lewis (9), married Mr. Mays, and has four children:
     1. Lelia Kemper Mays (10).
     2. Frank Temple Mays (10), and others.
   - C. Flora Temple Lewis (9), married Frederick William Page, and has issue:
     1. William Douglas Page (10), of Millwood, Cobham, married April 11, 1924, Margaret Caldwell Brady, daughter of Mr. and Mrs. John Archibald Brady, of Statesville, N. C.

     Frederick W. Page and Flora Lewis Page have other sons and daughters. No record supplied.
   - D. Mary Lewis (9), married Mr. E. P. Kellam of Atlanta, Georgia.
   - E. Arthur Stanford Lewis (9), of Lexington, Ky., married Jane Waldrop Lewis, and has issue: Jane Lewis and others.
3. Henry Howell Lewis (8), married Miss Sally Cleggs, and had issue:

A. Rev. Hunter Lewis (9), married.

B. Mrs. Susan (Lewis) Taylor (9), who had Lewis, died 1924. Also had a daughter who is married and lives in Arizona. Mrs. Taylor died March 1925.

C. Mrs. Brothers (9), has issue.

D. Fielding Meriwether Lewis (9), married Bessie Maxwell. No issue. (Adopted Hunter Lewis, his nephew.)

E. Sally Lewis (9), married John Lewis, son of John Marks and Margaret Tapp Lewis. Issue given under John M. Lewis and Margaret Tapp.

4. Mary Carr Lewis (8), married John J. Fry, and had issue:

    1. John Walker Fry (9), married first, Miss Ivy, and had issue:

        1. Mary Fry (10), married Mr. Pierce Rucker.
        2. Annie Fry (10), married ——.

    2. Howell Lewis Fry (9), married ——.
    3. Gordon Fry (9).
    4. Sadie Fry (9), married Aylette Everett, and has issue:

        Aylette E. Everett, Jr. (10), married, and has issue.

5. James Terrell Lewis (8), married first, Alice L. Lewis, of Castalia, daughter of Robert Walker and Sarah Craven. His second wife was Ann J. M. Wood, daughter of David H. Wood and Matilda Lewis, daughter of Fielding Lewis and Ann Anderson of Ivy.

    Issue by first marriage:

    1. George Lewis (9), who died in childhood.
    2. James Warner Lewis (9), married Lizzie Rodes. Issue:

        Warner Lewis (10), married.
        Rodes Lewis (10), married.
        Alice Lewis (10), married Berger, has five children.
        Julia Lewis (10), married.
        Mildred Lewis (10).

    3. Alice F. Lewis (9), married Harry Bruffey. Issue:

        Mildred Bruffey (10).
        Florine Bruffey (10).

Kathleen Bruffey (10), married Mr. Williams, has two children.

Bettie Bruffey (10).

Walter Bruffey (10).

4. Douglas Lewis (9), married first, Carrie Dunn. One living child: Carrie (10), married Mr. Rogers. Has several children. Married second, Miss Bruffey, had Douglas who died young. Married third, Helen Blaine, and has Sarah Lewis (10).
5. Stanford B. Lewis (9), married Mildred Jones, had Stanford Houston (10) (died), Mildred (10) who married Mr. Kelly, has Joseph (11) and Stanford (11).
6. Frederick Page Lewis (9), married Ola Wood. Had:
    1. Ola Sinclair Lewis (10), (died).
    2. Sydney Stanford Lewis (10).
    3. May Lewis (10).
    4. Carl Lewis (10).
7. Jennie V. Lewis (9), married Walter Smith, and has:
    1. Virginia Smith (10).
    2. Meriwether Smith (10), married Zona Mildred Deardorff, June 15, 1927.
    3. Alice Smith (10).
    4. Heath Smith (10).

Children by second marriage:

8. John Heath Lewis (9), married Ida Woltz. Issue: Ida (10), James (10), Annie (10), Irvin W. (10).
9. Albert Greaves (9) (named for clergyman), died in childhood.
10. Rev. David Henry Wood Lewis (9), married Louise Owen, and has David (10), Martha (10), and William Owen (10).
11. Frank Tapp Lewis (9), married Anna McIntire. Has issue: David (10), Anna (10), and Mary Jane (10).
12. Sarah Stanford Lewis, married.
13. Esther B. Lewis (9).
14. James Terrell Lewis, Jr. (9), married Helen Trim. Has issue: Ann Jane (10) and Jane Meriwether (10).

15. Matilda Wood Lewis (9).

6. Margaret D. Lewis (8), daughter of James Howell Lewis and Sarah Stanford, died young.
7. Nannie M. Lewis (8), died unmarried.
8. Julia B. Lewis (8), married Mr. A. K. Shay, and lives in Seattle, has issue, seven sons and one daughter.
9. Charles Warner Lewis (8), married Miss Carr, and went to Texas.
10. Rev. Nicholas Hunter Lewis (8), died unmarried a short time after his ordination.
11. Fielding Meriwether Lewis (8), died unmarried.

Mary Randolph Lewis (6), daughter of Charles Lewis of "North Garden", was first wife of Edward Carter of Fredericksburg and Blenheim, Albemarle County, son of Edward Carter and Sarah Champe, his wife. Among other children was Dr. Charles Carter (7) of Charlottesville. Dr. Carter married Mary Cocke. Issue:

1. Mary Lewis Carter (8), married John C. Singleton, of South Carolina, and had:
   a. Mary C. Singleton (9), married Rev. Robert Barnwell.
   b. Richard Singleton (9), married Annie Brown.
   c. Rebecca Singleton (9), married Col. Haskell. Issue: Rebecca Haskel (10).
   d. Charles Carter Singleton (9), married Miss McCullich.
   e. John C. Singleton (9), married Hattie Brown. Issue: John B. Singleton (10).
   f. Lucy Singleton (9).
2. Lucy Carter (8), married Peter Carr Minor:
   a. Hugh Frank Minor (9).
   b. Charles Carter Minor (9).
3. Charles Everett Carter (8), died unmarried.
4. Martha Champe Carter (8), married Major Green Peyton.
   a. Bernard Peyton (9), died young.
   b. Champe Peyton (9), died young.
   c. Mary Peyton (9), married Mr. Chamberlayne, and has two sons.

d. Julia Peyton (9).
e. Imogen Peyton (9), married Charles Wertenbaker. Has issue.
f. Charles Peyton (9). Has issue.

5. Charles Willis Carter (8), married Miss Franklin.
6. Edward Champe Carter (8).

Jane Lewis (6), daughter of Col. Chas. and Mary (Lewis) Lewis of "North Garden", married John Carr first, Clerk of Albemarle County, and had:

1. Dr. Charles Lewis Carr (7), (Physician at "North Garden"), married Ann, widow of Richard Watson and daughter of Richard Anderson, and his first wife, Ann Meriwether.
2. John H. Carr (7), married Malinda Clarkson.
3. Nathanial Willis Carr (Physician at Ivy, Albemarle), married Mary Ann Gaines.
4. Jane Carr (7). Most of this family went to Kentucky.

*Note.*—John Carr and this distinguished Dabney Carr, were of the family of John Carr of Bear Castle, Louisa County, who died in 1769.

Dabney Carr married Martha, sister of Thomas Jefferson, and had:

a. Peter Carr (8).
b. Samuel Carr (8).
c. Dabney Carr II (8).
d. Martha Carr (8), married Richard Terrell.
e. James Carr (8), married Miles Cary.
f. Ellen Carr (8), married Dr. Newsom of Mississippi.

* * *

## RANDOLPH

Col. William Randolph—1651, of Turkey Island (Warwickshire)

*Arms—Gules on a cross argent five mullets pierced sable.*

*Crest*—An antelope's head couped holding in its mouth a stick or.

*Motto—Fare quae sentiat.*

END CHARLES OF "NORTH GARDEN".

## WILLIAM LEWIS OF "LOCUST HILL"

Child of Robert and Jane Meriwether Lewis, was born 1733, died November 17, 1781, married 1768-9, Lucy Meriwether, born February 4, 1752, died September 8, 1837, aged 85. She was a daughter of Thomas and Elizabeth (Thornton) Meriwether.

William Lewis served as Lieutenant in the Continental Line in the American Revolution without pay—bearing his own expenses. Bounty Lands granted his heirs many years after his death were for services of seven and one half years and one month.

Reference: Land Office, Richmond, Va., Book No. 3, Page 499.

These bounty lands granted his heirs were lost through a dishonest agent who absconded with the monies for which he had sold them.

Wood's *History of Albemarle,* states:

July 11, 1775, William Lewis with twenty-seven others marched under Lieutenant George Gilmer to Williamsburg to resist Lord Dunmore, who had stolen the State's supply of powder.

September 1775, William Lewis, appointed First Lieutenant of First Company of Albemarle Minute Men, under Capt. Nicholas Lewis.

Also gives: "William Lewis" as third signature to the Albemarle County Declaration of Independence.

An old letter from William Lewis to his wife from Pages, Va., date July 21, 1776, tells his and six other companies under Col. Merideth are in pursuit of Lord Dunmore who had taken refuge on Gwyn's Island.

A confliction between the authority of the Committee of Safety and that of the Military officers, caused these troops to be changed to the Continental Line.

William Lewis (5) died, and was buried at "Cloverfields", the old Meriwether home in Albemarle, where he was taken ill when returning to the army from a visit to his family at "Locust Hill." He had taken part in the seige of Yorktown shortly before. This statement and date of his death given under oath by his wife and comrades.

The conflicting date of the inventory of his estate doubtless arose through the carelessness of clerks some years later when restoring the lost records of Albemarle County.

William Lewis's widow, married second, Captain John Marks (Revolutionary officer), and had:

1. Dr. John Marks, died unmarried.
2. Mary Garland Marks, married William Moore, and had twelve children. (Given in Meriwether family.)

William Lewis (5) and his wife had:

1. Jane Meriwether Lewis (6), born March 31, 1770, died March 15, 1845. Married 1785, Edmund Anderson, born April 1, 1763, (Good Friday), died April 19, 1810. They had nine children.
2. Meriwether Lewis (6), born at "Locust Hill", August 18, 1774, died in Lewis County, Tenn., October 17, 1809. Governor of Louisiana, Private Secretary to Thos. Jefferson and Commander of the Lewis and Clark Expedition.
3. Reuben Lewis (6), born February 14, 1777, at "Locust Hill", died February 17, 1844, at his home "Valley Point", near Ivy. Married his first cousin, Mildred Dabney, no issue. He was Indian Agent to the Mandans and Cherokees.

Jane M. Lewis and Edmund Anderson had nine children:

1. Elizabeth Thornton Anderson (7), born May 14, 1786, died in childhood.
2. Jane Lewis Anderson (7), born June 15, 1789, married Ben Wood. Issue given in the Wood genealogy.
3. William Lewis Anderson (7), born in Albemarle, December 4, 1719, died in Upshur County, West Va., November 1, 1875. Married Mary A. Webb, in Montgomery County, Tenn. She died at Buchanan, West Va., March 1858. Issue, nine children:
   A. Reuben Manderville Lewis Anderson (8), born in Montgomery County, Tenn., November 26, 1820. Died in Richmond, Va., January 1, 1838 unmarried.
   B. Mary Jane Anderson (8), born in Montgomery County, September 7, 1826, married in Albemarle County, July 29, 1845. Robert Moseby, who survived her, and died in the U. S. A. Army, Cumberland County, December

1862; had Overton A. Moseby (9). Living in Upshur County.

C. Captain Robert Meriwether Anderson (8), of the second Richmond Howitzers, C. S. A., born in Montgomery County, Tenn., October 19, 1822. Died in Essex County, from inhaling flames while rescuing his effects when his home was burned, November 9, 1880. He married Hannah or Harriet Shore Lewis, December 24, 1864. She was the daughter of Warner Lewis and Maria Isabella Shore, Essex County. They had issue:

1. Philip Lewis Anderson (9).
2. Warner Meriwether Anderson (9).
3. Henry Temple Anderson (9).
4. Robert Mandeville Anderson (9).
5. Henry Webb Anderson (9). They and their mother located in Richmond.

D. Tempte Ann Anderson (8), born in Albemarle County, Va., January 30, 1829, married in Buchanan, West Va., October 30, 1849, Kosciusco Hopkins, who died at Jackson Run, Alleghany County, Va., January 16, 1869, issue, one surviving child.

Molly Hopkins (9), married.

E. Lucy Marks Anderson (8), born in Albemarle County, March 4, 1830, died at Jackson, Tenn., May 4, 1874, married W. F. Green, Buchanan, West Va., March 16, 1856. No issue.

F. Sarah Harper Anderson (8), born in Albemarle County, December 7, 1831, died April 16, 1852, at West Milford, West Va., married Mr. Hedges. No issue.

G. Laura Lewis Anderson (8), born June 12, 1834, in Albemarle County, married December 3, 1856, William Loudin of Buchanan, West Va. No issue.

H. Richard Webb Anderson (8), Surgeon C. S. A., born in Albemarle County, Va., November 3, 1836, died at Jackson, Miss., October 22, 1867.

I. Henry Fisher Anderson (8), born in Albemarle, February 19, 1840, died in Newton County, Texas, October 18, 1869, married Laura McCoy. No issue.

4. Lucy Meriwether Anderson (7), fourth child of Jane Lewis and Edmund Anderson, was born in Albemarle County, July 30, 1795, married May 1813, Ballard Buckner, who died June 1828 in Oldham County, Kentucky, and she died in Louisville years later. And had issue:

A. Mary Jane Buckner (8), born February 17, 1814, in Clark County, Ky., died October 10, 1883, in Jefferson County, Ky., married William McCrocklan, September 18, 1854. They had no issue. Her daughter by a former marriage died unmarried.

B. Edmund Anderson Buckner (8), born December 27, 1815, in Clark County, Ky., died April 7, 1865, in Jefferson County, Ky., married twice—no surviving issue by first marriage, though had three children who died in youth. By his last wife, Mary Graff, had:

a. Edmund A. Buckner (9).

b. Meriwether L. Buckner (9), married Fanny, and has issue.

C. Maria Buckner (8), born February 14, 1820, married Mr. Davidson and had:

1. Mary Davidson (9), married Nat Ragland, and had issue:

a. Jennie Ragland (10), married Mr. Fullenwider, had Agnes, Mrs. Nash, Leah.

b. Alice Ragland (10).

c. Edward Ragland (10).

2. Ned Davidson (9), married, and has:

a. Maria Davidson (10).

b. Frank Davidson (10).

c. Harry Davidson (10).

d. Edmund Davidson, married, and has: Edward (11) and Sarah Ann (11).

D. Alice A. Buckner (8), born February 14, 1820, in Kentucky, married December 6, 1849 in Suffolk, Va., to Joseph T. Thornton, and had issue:
   1. Lula Thornton (9), married Hardin Magruder of Shelby County, and had:
      a. Bessie Magruder (10), who died unmarried.
      b. Willie Magruder (10), married.
      c. Thornton Magruder (10), married.

E. Eliza H. Buckner (8), born March 1822, died in infancy.

F. Robert M. Buckner (8), born July 13th, 1824 in Oldham County, Ky., died October 12, 1864, married Willy Abott, December 1852. And had issue:
   1. Willy L. Buckner (9), born June 21, 1855, married Mr. James Osbourne. Issue:
      a. Robert Osbourne (10), died in youth.
      b. Alfred Osbourne (10), died in infancy.

G. Caroline Buckner (8), born October 1, 1827, in Kentucky, married her cousin, Archie Anderson, September 4, 1844. He died January 18, 1865. She died years later. And had issue:
   1. Judge William Anderson (9), married, and has issue:
      a. Archie Anderson (10), m, and has issue.
   2. Robert Anderson (9), married, and has issue.
   3. Meriwether Anderson (9), married, and has two daughters. (One married in Maryland.)
   4. Alice Anderson (9), married Mr. Graves and her children are Eddie and Boyd.
   5. Lula Anderson (9), married second, Mr. McKee, and is a childless widow in Shelbyville.

5. Ann Eliza Anderson (7), born October 20, 1800, married Thomas Fielding Lewis, son of Howell Lewis and Mary Carr, of "North Garden". (Issue given in full in "Col. Chas. Lewis of 'North Garden' " line.)
6. David Anderson (7), born February 13, 1803, son of Edmund Anderson and Jane Lewis, died in Vicksburg, Miss., 1832. No issue.

7. Dr. Meriwether Anderson (7), of "Locust Hill", born June 23, 1805, died March 5, 1862. Married June 16, 1831, Lucy Sydnor Harper, born December 8, 1811 at "Spring Hill", died December 4, 1885, in Galveston, Texas. Both buried at "Locust Hill", Ivy Depot, Va.

   He studied medicine at the University of Virginia, and Philadelphia, graduating from the latter college. When first married he settled under pioneer conditions in Mississippi. He was licensed by the State in the police force for ridding the country of undesirable settlers. He lost his means through the repudiation of its bonds by Mississippi, and returned to Virginia where he practiced his profession for years in Albemarle County. He served in the Confederate hospitals in Charlottesville, and was a Member of the Virginia Legislature.

Had issue, five children:

1. Jane Lewis Anderson (8), born December 28, 1839, died November 26, 1842.
2. Lucy Anderson (8), born April 26, 1842, died August 7, 1842.
3. Meriwether Lewis Anderson (8), born August 24, 1845, killed near Fisher's Hill (Early's Campaign), October 8, 1864. (Co. K, 2nd Va. Cavalry, Fitz Lee's command).
4. Charles Harper Anderson (8), born June 28, 1848, died February 13, 1920. (Buried at "Locust Hill"). Married February 15, 1872, Sarah Travers Scott. Issue:

   A. Dr. Meriwether Lewis Anderson (9), born November 13, 1872, graduate of Virginia Medical College. He served in command of 311 Field Hospital with the 78th Division in France in 1918-19 (78th was "Lightening Division"). Married September 23, 1903, Annie Tatum of Richmond, daughter of William and Mary (Pearman) Tatum. Issue:

      a. Ann Meriwether Anderson (10), born Jan. 13, 1905.
      b. Louise Maury Anderson (10), born Dec. 21, 1906.
      c. Sarah Travers Anderson (10), born Jan. 30, 1908.
      d. Meriwether Lewis Anderson (10), b. Mar. 7, 1910.

e. Dorothea Claiborne Anderson (10), born Aug. 22, 1914.

B. Sarah Travers Scott Anderson (9), born February 1, 1874, married June 12, 1913, Geo. L. Gordon. Issue:

a. Harper Anderson Gordon (10), born March 24, 1916. Geo. Loyall Gordon, born November 25, 1918. (Loyall not a family name).

C. Charles Harper Anderson II (9), born December 3, 1875. Married April 23, 1902, Caroline Gwyn, daughter of Dr. Chas. Gwyn and Margaret Taliaferro. Issue:

a. Mary Gwyn Anderson (10), born July 1903, married June 2, 1927, James A. Crocker, U. S. N.

b. Charles Harper Anderson III (10), born February 20, 1905.

c. Caroline Anderson (10), born January 23, 1913, 8 P. M.

d. Edmund Taliaferro Anderson (10), born May 20, 1919.

D. Rev. Alfred Scott Anderson (9), born February 14, 1878, married May 1903, Katherine Morris. Issue:

a. Alfred Scott Anderson, Jr. (10), born July 24, 1904.

b. Lewis Meriwether Anderson (10), born November 18, 1905.

c. Katherine Morris Anderson (10), born July 1909, died August 2, 1914.

d. Wm. Morris Anderson (10).

e. Chas. Harper Anderson (10), born March 2, 1920.

E. Lucy Butler Anderson (9), born August 15, 1885, married June 10, 1913, Ballard Ernest Ward, son of B. E. Ward and Sophia Nuckols of Grayson County. Issue:

a. Sarah Travers Ward (10), born May 29, 1914.

b. Ballard Ernest Ward (10) } Twins—b. Jun. 27, 1916.
c. Lucien Butler Ward (10) }

d. Charles Harper Ward (10), born June 26, 1918.

e. Mary Josephine Ward (10), born May 8, 1922.

F. Rev. Alden Scott Anderson (9), born February 24, 1888, married December 13, 1916, Isabel Sterrett. Issue:

a. Alden S. Anderson (10), born October 11, 1917, died October 17, 1917.

b. Isabel Sterrett Anderson (10), born September 30, 1918.

c. Annie-Laurie Anderson (10), born January 8, 1920.

d. Alden S. Anderson (10), born December 1, 1926.

*Note.*—Isabel Sterrett, daughter of McM. Sterrett and Annie-Laurie Smith, daughter of James Bell Smith and Cornelia Wallace, son of Ballard Smith and Polly Price.

*Note.*—McM. Sterrett, son of James Reid Sterrett and Rebecca Alexander Wilson, Rockbridge County, Virginia.

G. Jane Lewis Anderson (9), born February 12, 1881, died December 10, 1882.

H. William Scott Anderson (9), born and died February 18, 1883. Both buried at "Locust Hill."

5. Mary Miller Anderson (8), born September 5, 1851, married September 27, 1877, Bradford Ripley Alden Scott, born June 28, 1851, died February 11, 1925. Issue:

A. Lucy Harper Scott (9), born August 5, 1878, married June 1904, Elmer Carpenter Griffith. Issue:

1. Lewis Scott Griffith (10), born June 1905, married Rosine Chase, has Lewis Scott Griffith, Jr.

B. Mary Anderson Scott (9), born August 27, 1880, married Chas. E. Boston. (Lives in Mexico City.)

C. John Thompson Scott (9), born February 8, 1884. Served in the Rainbow Division (42nd) in the World War; badly wounded in the Meuse-Argonne movement.

D. Sarah Lewis Scott (9), born October 2, 1886, married David Skene McKeller. Issue:

1. David Harkness McKeller (10).
2. Mary Anderson McKeller (10).
3. Alden Scott McKeller (10).

E. Dr. Bradford Ripley Alden Scott, Jr. (9), born 1888, died of influenza while a surgeon at Kelly Field, San Antonio, Texas, married Norma ——. No issue.

F. Dr. Harper Anderson Scott (9), of Austin, Texas, born January 16, 1891, married Minai Nicholson, January 29, 1923.

8. Sarah Thornton Anderson (7), born June 22, 1807, daughter of Edmund and Jane Anderson, married Gabriel Smither Harper. (Issue given in Harper genealogy).

9. Mary H. Anderson (7), born October 4, 1809, died in 1820.

## ROBERT LEWIS (5)

Youngest son of Col. Robert Lewis and Jane Meriwether, born supposedly 1738-9 since he was under age when his father's will was made 1757.

His grandmother, Mrs. Elizabeth Meriwether left him her home place of 2,000 acres in Louisa County, March 2, 1753—(Will Book 1, Louisa Records). (Marriage bond, Goochland Record). Married his first cousin, Mary Frances Lewis, daughter of Charles and Mary Howell Lewis.

He setled in Granville County, N. C. His services in State records were prominent. He was Member of the Constitutional Convention just before the Revolution. He died comparatively young. Had issue:

1. James Lewis (6).
2. Howell Lewis (6).
3. Jane Lewis (6).
4. Nicholas Lewis (6).
5. Charles Lewis (6).
6. Frances Lewis (6), married Dr. John Payne.
7. Dr. John Lewis (6), married Mrs. Latimer Posey of Maryland, settled in Warren County, Georgia.
   Ancestors of Mrs. Frank Graham of Augusta and Judge Hal Lewis of Supreme Court and others.
8. Richard Lewis (6), married Sarah Wood. Their son, William Wood Lewis (7), married Lucinda Roark of Georgia.

Their daughter, Ada Lewis (8), married Algander Bevers. Lucie Bevers (9), married Wm. Edward Schenk. Issue:

a. Lewis Bevers Schenk (10).
b. John Richardson Schenk (10).
c. Sally W. Schenk (10).
d. Fairchild Algander Schenk (10).

All of Greensboro, N. C.

*Note.*—Mrs. Gen. Gordon, also Judge Harolson of the Supreme Court of Alabama and also the first wife of Chief Justice Beckley of the Supreme Court of Georgia, descend from this line.

James Lewis (6), born August 28, 1755, married June 30, 1774, Susannah Anderson, daughter of Thomas Anderson (Revolutionary soldier). James Lewis was one of the executors of his father's will. Issue:

1. Sarah Lewis (7), born December 12, 1775, married Wortham.
2. Susannah Lewis (7), married Cottrell.
3. Elizabeth Lewis (7), born March 20, 1777, married July 26, 1792, Zadoc Daniel.
4. Witham Lewis (7), born December 16, 1780.
5. James Lewis (7), born May 25, 1784, married June 16, 1816, Mary Alston.

Elizabeth Lewis and Zadoc Daniel had issue:

1. Susanna Daniel (8), born September 10, 1793, married Dr. Thomas.
2. John Daniel (8), born December 24, 1794, married Miss Gresham.
3. Polly Daniel (8), born February 5, 1798, married Ben. Cotrell.
4. James Lewis Daniel (8), born January 6, 1800, married Matilda Gaunt.
5. Wm. B. Daniel (8), born July 26, 1802, married Miss Thomas.
6. Dudley Daniel (8), born July 1, 1804, married Miss Curtis.

7. Sarah Lewis Daniel (8), born April 23, 1806, died young.
8. Lewis Daniel (8), born February 6, 1808.
9. Zadoc Daniel (8), born September 25, 1810, married Miss West.
10. Elizabeth Daniel (8), born October 12, 1812, married Gresham.
11. Francis Anderson Daniel (8), born January 7, 1815, married Everett.
12. Charles Daniel (8), born April 24, 1817, served in Indian War and died soon after.

James Lewis Daniel (8), married October 12, 1830, Matilda or Martha Gaunt. Issue:

1. John Wilhoydt Lewis Daniel (9), born August 1, 1831, married Miss Green.
2. and 3. Twins { Mary Ann Daniel (9), Elizabeth Daniel (9), } born August 3, 1834—noted for beauty and exact likeness, married by the same ceremony, April 28, 1852—
   Wm. Thomas Simpson to Mary Ann,
   Chauncey Rodes to Elizabeth.
4. Emma Josephine Daniel (9), born May 7, 1843, married Roper.
5. Susanna Daniel (9), born June 10, 1845, married Captain Wallace.
6. Chas Daniel (9), born October 15, 1848, married Miss Turner.
7. Edwin Daniel (9), born September 1853, died in infancy.
8. Dudley Daniel (9), born January 18, 1855, died in infancy.
9. James Lewis Daniel (9), died in infancy.

Mary Ann Daniel (9) and William Thomas Simpson. Issue:

1. Caroline S. Simpson (10), born May 2, 1853, married August 23, 1870, Capt. Leonard Yancy Dean, of Edgefield, S. C., born July 18, 1843, died aged 90.
2. Eva Gertrude Simpson (10), born January 22, 1856, married John Wm. Keesee of Clarksville, Tenn.

3. Loula Leonard Simpson (10), born July 27, 1859, married October 1877, Ed. Fitzgerald, died two weeks later, October 25, 1877.
4. Lee Roy Johnston (10), born October 7, 1861, married November 5, 1883, Alice Fitzgerald.
5. Elizabeth M. Simpson (10), born October 27, 1864, married Edwin Keolin Cargill of Columbus, Ga.
6. Wm. Thomas Simpson, Jr. (10), born January 3, 1867, married Miss Malone.

Caroline S. Simpson and Captain Leonard Yancey Dean (Confederate veteran). Issue:

1. Mary Melanie Dean (11), born June 23, 1871, married October 30, 1896, Frank Percival Bakewell.
2. Willie Pearce Dean (11), born January 15, 1873, died July 26, 1876.
3. Leonard Yancey Dean (11), born March 19, 1875, married December 19, 1900, Miss Maydie Ione Thweet.
4. Loula Fitzgerald Dean (11), born June 4, 1876.
5. Ethel Bland Dean (11), born September 21, 1878, married December 14, 1893, Thomas Lipscomb Moore of Greenwood, S. C. Issue, Lewis Mathews Moore (12).
6. Elizabeth Simpson Dean (11), born January 1, 1887.
7. Caroline Simpson Dean (11), born August 16, 1889, died in infancy.

Mary Melanie Dean and Frank Percival Bakewell. Issue:

1. Yancey Dean (12).

Ethel Bland Dean and Thomas Lipscomb Moore. Issue:

1. Lewis Mathews Moore (12), born November 14, 1899.

## JANE LEWIS (5)

IV. Oldest daughter of Robert Lewis of "Belvoir" and Jane Meriwether, married first, Thos. Meriwether. Issue, eight children (See Meriwether family). Married second, John Lewis of the "Byrd", and had three sons and three daughters. Issue given under (Charles Lewis of the "Byrd").

## MARY LEWIS (5)

V. Daughter of Robert Lewis of "Belvoir" and Jane Meriwether, died 1813, married first in 1750, Samuel Cobbs, will dated September 1757, probated November 20, 1758. Married second, Waddy Thompson of Louisa and Albemarle Counties. He died 1801. His will on record in clerk's office in Charlottesville, Va. Also the marriage settlement between him and Mary Lewis Cobbs, who was his second wife, since property complications with three sets of children needed much clearness. Settlement dated December 1766, Trustee, Wm. Lewis.

Issue by first marriage:

1. Robert Cobbs (6), married Ann Poindexter, issue nine children. (Ancestor of John Meriwether McAllister, genealogist and author with Mrs. Tandy, of *Lewises and Kindred Families.*
2. Judith Cobbs (6), who died young.
3. Jane Cobbs (6), married John Waddy, had one son, Samuel, whose descendants live at Waddy, Kentucky. John J. Waddy was grandson of Anthony Waddy.

Issue of second marriage, five daughters:

1. Ann Thompson (6), married first, John Slaughter. Issue:
    a. Mary Lewis Slaughter (7).
    b. Thomson Slaughter (7).
    c. Warner Slaughter (7).

    Married second, Philip Grafton. Issue:
    a. Wm. Grafton (7).
    b. Ann Grafton (7).
    c. Mildred Grafton (7).
    d. Caroline Grafton (7).
2. Mary Thomson (6), married 1794, James Poindexter. Issue, ten children: (See Thomson family)
    a. Joseph Poindexter (7).
    b. Edwin Poindexter (7).
    c. Albert Poindexter (7).
    d. Nicholas Poindexter (7).
    e. Mary Poindexter (7), who married Gamerwell.

3. Judith Thomson (6), married 1798, Wm. Poindexter. Issue, seven children:
    1. Waddy Thomson Poindexter (7), married Miss Plunket. Issue:
        a. Wm. A. Poindexter (8).
        b. Samuel Poindexter (8).
        c. James Poindexter (8).
        d. Nicholas Poindexter (8).
    2. Mary Lewis Poindexter (7). No record.
    3. Jane Meriwether Lewis Poindexter (7), married Abraham Mills. Issue:
        Susan (Mills) Minnis and others.
    4. Wm. James Poindexter (7), married Eliza Stephens. Issue:
        a. Wm. S. Poindexter (8).
        b. James A. Poindexter (8).
        c. John T. Poindexter (8).
        d. Samuel Thornhill Poindexter (8).
        e. Ann Eliza Poindexter (8), married Gallager.
        f. Mary Frances Poindexter (8), m. Berryman.
    5. Elizabeth Poindexter (7), died at the age of fourteen.
    6. Sarah Poindexter (7), married E. Warren Lewis, lived near St. Joseph, Mo. Left descendants.
    7. Susan Mildred Poindexter (7), married Dudley Martin.
4. Susannah Thomson (6), died 1847, in Georgia. Married Jesse Davenport. Issue:
    1. James Davenport (7).
    2. Wm. Davenport (7).
    3. Charles Warner Davenport (7).
    4. John L. Davenport (7).
    5. Mary Frances Davenport (7).
5. Mildred Thomson (6), born September 22, 1775, died October 9, 1824—age 49 years. Married December 9, 1807, Dr. James Scott, born February 17, 1760, died April 14, 1822—age 62 years. Issue:

1. Mary Ann Lewis Scott (7), born October 23, 1808, married Lewis A. Boggs, February 15, 1827, died August 27, 1840. Issue: Eliza Hart Boggs (8).
2. John Thomson Scott (7), born February 26, 1810, married Huldah Lewis, January 5, 1832, and died the same year (October 9, 1832). No issue.
3. James McClure Scott, born August 17, 1811, married Sarah Travers Lewis, December 13, 1832, died July 7, 1893. Issue given in Scott family.

## MILDRED LEWIS (5)

Sixth child and fourth daughter of Robert Lewis of "Belvoir" and Jane Meriwether. Married 1755, Major John Lewis of Goochland County, born 1735, who is thus described in her father's will. Major Lewis's will on record in Goochland County dated 1796, mentions four married daughters and three sons.

Issue:

1. Mrs. Ann Mosely (6).
2. Mrs. Elizabeth Halsey (6).
3. Mrs. Mary Atkisson (6).
4. Mrs. Sarah Mann (6).
5. John Lewis (6).
6. Joseph Lewis (6).
7. William (6).

*Note.*—John Lewis Robards of St. Joseph, Mo. and Judge Joseph Lewis of Kentucky, descend from this Major John Lewis and Mildred Lewis. He was great-grandson of John Lewis of Henrico, who came to Virginia, 1660, from Wales.

John Lewis of Henrico, emigrant—1660.

William b. 1660<br>d. Dec. 24, 1706 — Sarah (No record)

| John | William | Joseph, of Goochland County |
|---|---|---|
| M.—Woodson | of Henrico | Had 3 sons and 4 daughters: |
| Jacob | | 1. John Lewis, born 1735, married |
| Jacob | | Mildred Lewis. |

2. William Lewis. No record.
3. Joseph Lewis. No record.
4. Elizabeth Robards.
5. Sarah Bedford. No record.
6. Ann Mosely. No record.
7. Fourth daughter married a Cocke.

Joseph's will speaks of grandchildren:

1. Susan Cocke.
2. Joseph Cocke.

## ANN LEWIS (5)

Seventh child of Robert Lewis of "Belvoir" and Jane Meriwether, married John Lewis (The Honest Lawyer), son of Zachary Lewis II and Mary Waller, born October 18, 1729, died September 12, 1780. His will on record, names his three sons, John Zachary Lewis, Robert Lewis and Nicholas Lewis. Another record adds Charles Lewis. Issue:

1. John Zachary Lewis (6).
2. Chas. Lewis (6).
3. Nicholas Lewis (6).
4. Robert Lewis (6).
5. Mary Lewis (6), married David Wood Meriwether and went to Kentucky.
6. Jane Lewis (6), married her first cousin, Zachary Meriwether, son of Mary Lewis and Francis Meriwether.

John Zachary Lewis, married first, Miss Woolfolk.

Issue: three children—Augustine, Ann and Bettie Lewis.

He married second, Elizabeth Brock, and had—John Zachary Lewis, Jr.

Nicholas Lewis went West, all trace of him lost.

Robert Lewis also went West, and all trace of him lost.

Mary Lewis, married 1784, David Wood Meriwether, son of Wm. and Martha Wood Meriwether.

Chas. Lewis. No record.

Jane Lewis and Zachary Meriwether. Record uncertain.

Full record of Ann's descendants in Zachary Lewis line and the Meriwether family.

## ELIZABETH LEWIS (5)

Elizabeth Lewis (5), fifth daughter of Robert Lewis of "Belvoir" and Jane Lewis, died before 1757. She married Rev. Robert Barrett, of Richmond, Rector of St. Martin's Parish. We have record of one child only. Issue:

Captain William Barrett (6), born January 2, 1756, married 1784, Dorothea Winston, they moved to Kentucky, and called their home "Rock Castle". Issue:

1. Ann Barrett (7), born in Louisa County, Va., married June 1802, Gen. James Allen, of Hopkins Division in the War of 1812. His wife died, and he moved to Illinois and died there in 1867. Issue:
    1. Rev. Richard H. Allen (8), of Philadelphia.
    2. John P. Allen (8), married Elizabeth R. Buckner. Issue:

        Betty Allen (9), married Judge B. M. Great. Issue:
        1. Buckner Allen Great (10).
        2. John Allen Great (10).
2. James Winston Barrett (7), born in Virginia 1788, died 1872, married 1812, Maria Allen—emigrated to Illinois 1835. Issue:
    1. Eliza Barrett (8), married first, Johnston, married second, Pascal Enoc.
    2. Mary Barrett. No record.
    3. Jane Barrett (8), married Chas. Ridgeley. Issue:
        1. Wm. Barrett Ridgeley (9). Issue, two daughters.
3. Mary Lee Barrett (7), married Wm. Barrett of Cumberland County, Kentucky. They lived on a sugar and cotton plantation in Louisiana, also in Texas; died at St. Louis.
4. William Perricoat Barrett (7), born in Virginia 1790, married Elizabeth Allen, sister to his brother James's wife—had six children. Issue:
    1. Robert T. Barrett (8), born 1826, died 1861 in Texas.
    2. John R. Barrett (8), born 1825, married 1846, Eliza Simpson.
    3. Mary Barrett (8).
    4. Dedie Nichols Barrett (8).

5. Overton Winston Barrett (8), born 1834. Major First Missouri Battery Artillery C. S. A.
6. Laura Barrett (8).

5. Dr. and Prof. Richard Farrill Barrett (7), born 1804 in Green County, Kentucky, died April 16, 1860, married Maria Lewis Buckner, daughter of Judge Richard Aylett and Elizabeth Buckner, November 5, 1832 at her home, Clifford, Greene County, Kentucky. Issue:
    1. Richard Aylett Barrett (8), born in Kentucky, June 21, 1833, married February 21, 1862, Mary Finny, daughter of Wm. and Jane Finny.
    2. Arthur Buckner Barrett (8), born in Illinois, August 21, 1835, died April 16, 1875, married June 5, 1859, Anna Farrer Sweringen, and had:
        1. James Barrett (9), married Miss Melton.
        2. Matty Barrett (9), married John M. Frost.
        3. Arthur Buckner Barrett (9).
    3. Dr. Wm. Lee Barrett (8), born March 5, 1837, married Nannie Lemoine. Issue:
        1. Mary Barrett (9).
        2. Maria Barrett (9).
        3. Arthur Buckner Barrett (9).
        4. Dr. Wm. Barrett (9).
    4. Julia Allen Barrett (8), born November 5, 1839, married January 1865, Dr. Chas. Alexander.
    5. Winston L. Barrett (8).
    6. John A. Barrett (8), born March 5, 1843, married ——. Issue:
        1. Richard Barrett (9).
        Daughter.
        Daughter.

## SARAH LEWIS (5)

Tenth child of Robert Lewis and Jane Meriwether of "Belvoir", married Waller Lewis, son of Zachary Lewis, and Mary Waller, of Spotsylvania County. Issue, seven children:

1. Waller Lewis, Jr. (6), married Sally Wise. Moved to the

vicinity of Russellville, Kentucky, where he died May 8, 1818. His son William writes of his father's death and mentions "Ann" (presumably his own wife), who already knew his Virginia relations.

2. Charles Lewis (6), died February 2, 1822. "Lewis's Store", Spotsylvania County, named for him. Married Susan B. Waller, probably a daughter of Wm. Waller, for whom "Waller's Tavern" was named. His widow administered on his estate. Her business letters make no mention of children, and the inference is that there were none.

3. Ann Lewis (6), married Samuel Hill (brother of John Hill, who was the husband of Mary Lewis, daughter of Zachary Lewis III.) They moved to Kentucky. A letter of Samuel Hill dated "Vale Heath", June 24, 1818 (postmark Russellville, Ky.) tells of the death of Waller Lewis, Jr., his brother-in-law. Record of two children:
    1. Robert Hill (7).
    2. Dorothea Lewis Hill (7), became second wife of Henry Wood Meriwether, son of David Wood Meriwether and Mary Lewis who was daughter of Ann Lewis and John Lewis, (The Honest Lawyer). Issue:
        1. Edward Baylor Meriwether (8), b. Dec. 1830.
        2. George Lucian Baylor Meriwether (8), born February 1832.
        3. Frederick Oscar Meriwether (8), born Oct. 1833.
        4. Lucy Ann Meriwether (8), born Jan. 28, 1835.
        5. Elizabeth Meriwether (8), born November 1837.
        6. Samuel Arthur Meriwether (8), born February 5, 1843, married Sally Baker, died August 1922. Had Lucy Meriwether and others.
        7. Sarah Harriet Meriwether (8), born 1839.
        8. Chas. Robert Meriwether, born December 1844.
        9. Frank Meriwether (8), b. Sept. 1846, d. 1887.

4. Elizabeth Lewis (6), born 1772, married in Spottsylvania, Va., John Woolfolk, born September 9, 1760, son of Joseph Woolfolk and Elizabeth Wigglesworth, who was daughter of John and Mary Wigglesworth. They moved in 1811 to

Christian County, Ky., where Elizabeth (Lewis) Woolfolk died. Her husband died in Boone County, Mo. and was buried on the farm of his son, Waller Lewis Woolfolk. This farm is now owned by this Waller's son, Robert Woolfolk. Issue:

1. Ann Waller Woolfolk (7), married Judge Benjamin Young, of Calloway County, Mo.
2. Waller Lewis Woolfolk (7), born March 19, 1794 in Spotsylvania County, Va. Moved to Christian County 1811. Married Susannah Woolfolk, daughter of Elijah and Phoebe Woolfolk, and moved to Boone County, Mo. She died 1857. He died 1874.
3. Elizabeth Woolfolk (7), born December 1797 in Virginia, died September 30. Married Thomas Beasley, October 16, 1823.
4. Sarah Woolfolk (7), moved to Kentucky with her parents. Married Joseph Holladay, born in Fayettville County, Ky. Son of Stephen and Ann (Hickman Holladay). She was daughter of James Hickman and Hannah Lewis of Culpeper County, Va.
5. Dr. John Woolfolk (7), born in Virginia. Moved to Kentucky then to St. Louis. Died unmarried, 1834.
6. Mary Woolfolk (7), born in Virginia, married in Kentucky to Washington Mansfield.
7. Chas. Woolfolk, born 1804. Moved to Kentucky then to Missouri. Married Polly Ann Payne (who lived over 90 years).
8. Alice Woolfolk (7), born in Virginia, August 15, 1805. Married December 7, 1826, Wm. Henry Tandy, at Pembroke, Kentucky. He was son of Mills and Amelia (Graves) Tandy, son of Roger and Sarah Quarles Tandy of Orange County, Virginia.

Their son Adrian (8), married his cousin, Mary Catherine Beasley, and had among others:

1. Robert Thomas Tandy, of Columbia, Mo. Married Lula May Boulton, and had eight children.

Mrs. Lula (Boulton) Tandy is widely known as a genealogist

and is co-author with John Meriwether McAllister of "The Lewises and Kindred Families".

5. Lucy Lewis (6), fifth child of Waller and Sarah Lewis, married John Wigglesworth of Spottsylvania County. Issue:
   1. Sarah Lewis Wigglesworth (7), married Henry Duerson. Had issue:
      1. Sarah Ann Duerson (8), married November 11, 1869, second wife of the Rev. Edward Glanville Baptist, son of the Rev. Edward Baptist of Powhatan County, Va. and Alabama and his wife Elizabeth Judith Cary Eggleston, daughter of Mathew J. and Ann Cary Eggleston.

   Issue of Sarah A. Duerson and the Rev. E. G. Baptist:
      1. Maude Glanville Baptist (9), born at Oakland, Marengo, County, Ala., died at Alberene, Albemarle County, Va., October 2, 1902. Age 34 years, 10 months and 7 days. Born November 25, 1870. Married Dr. Ben Dillard. Issue:
         a. Martha Dillard (10), married Major Lyndsay Pitts, died without issue.
         b. Sarah Dillard (10), married Richard Haynes, and has issue.
         c. Maude Dillard (10), married Daughety.
         d. Edward Granville Dillard (10).
         e. Benjamin Lewis (10).
         f. Alfred Magruder Dillard (10).
      2. Dr. Harry Lewis Baptist (9), born January 9, 1874, in Spottsylvania County, Va., married April 1902, Margaret Esther Boyle, daughter of the Rev. John Boyle and his wife Agnes Morton. Issue:
         a. Edward Baptist (10), died in infancy.
         b. Agnes Morton Baptist (10), born October 1904. Married.
         c. Harry Lewis Baptist, Jr. (10).
         d. Maud Baptist (10). Married.
         e. Woodson Boyle Baptist (10).
         f. Margaret Baptist (10).

g. Sarah Eggleston (10), youngest.

3. Noel W. Baptist (9), third child of Rev. E. G. Baptist and Sarah, his wife, born at Elamville, July 20, 1877. Died in childhood.

4. Maurice Jacqueline Baptist (9), fourth child of Rev. E. G. Baptist and Sarah, his wife, married Ethel Hansborough, has Garland Hansborough (10).

2. Lucy Wigglesworth (7), second daughter of John Wigglesworth and Lucy Lewis, married Warren Wigglesworth. Had issue:

1. John Wigglesworth, Jr. (8), killed in Confederate War. Unmarried.

2. Annie Wigglesworth (8), unmarried.

3. Emma Hasiltine Wigglesworth, married Wm. G. Miller, of Richmond, Va. Had issue:

1. Gay Warren Miller (9), married Frank G. Schell, and has:

Wm. Franklin Schell (10).

2. William J. Miller, Jr. (9), married Elizabeth McCalla. No issue.

3. Alton Sydney Miller (9), married Virginia Bennett. No issue.

4. Ashley Macon Miller (9), married Jessie N. Reeve. No issue.

5. Dr. Clifton Meredith Miller (9), married Mary Ashley Bell. Issue:

a. Clifton M. Miller, Jr. (10).
b. Mary Bell Miller (10).
c. Ashley Lewis Miller (10).
d. Emma Ellett Miller (10).

6. Carroll Miller (9), married Emma Guffey. Issue:

a. William Cordona Miller (10).
b. John Guffey Miller (10).
c. Carroll J. Miller (10) } Twins.
d. Joseph F. G. Miller (10) }

3. Dorothea Wigglesworth (7), married Peter Dudley, had issue. Went to Texas.

4. Elizabeth Wigglesworth (7), married John H. White, of Caroline County. Left issue:
   (Dorothea and Elizabeth Wigglesworth, daughters of John and Lucy Lewis Wigglesworth).
6. Dorothea Lewis (6), sixth child of Waller and Sarah Lewis, married Dr. Hawes Coleman, a widower of Nelson County.
7. Sally Lewis (6), seventh child of Waller and Sarah Lewis. No record.

*Baptist Note:*

Edward Baptist, Clerk of York County, Va., married first, Miss Throckmorton, and had a daughter who married Mr. Shields. Married second, Miss Russell, and had a daughter who married Burwell Coleman, and had—Burwell Coleman. Married third, Miss Glanville, and had—Wm. Glanville Baptist, married Miss Langston.

*Eggleston Note:*

Matthew J. Eggleston, married Ann Cary, and had:

1. Charles Eggleston.
2. Miles Eggleston, Judge of Supreme Court of Indiana.
3. George Eggleston, left one son and two daughters.
4. Meade Eggleston, left two sons and one daughter.
5. Samuel Overton Eggleston, left four sons and one daughter.
6. Elizabeth Eggleston.
7. John Eggleston.
8. Hugh Eggleston, married Mary Eggleston, was Judge of Circuit Court of New Orleans. Had one son—Eugene.
9. Dr. Chas. Eggleston, of Nachetoches, La. Left three children.

Richard Eggleston, brother of Matthew, both sons of Wm. Eggleston and Judith Cary Jones, married first, Miss Hill, relative of General A. P. Hill. Had:

1. Ann Eggleston, married Richard Canliff.
2. James Eggleston, married Miss Ball of Powhatan County, Va.

END OF DESCENDANTS OF ROBERT LEWIS OF "BELVOIR".

"CLOVER FIELDS"—A MERIWETHER HOME NEAR KESWICK, VA.

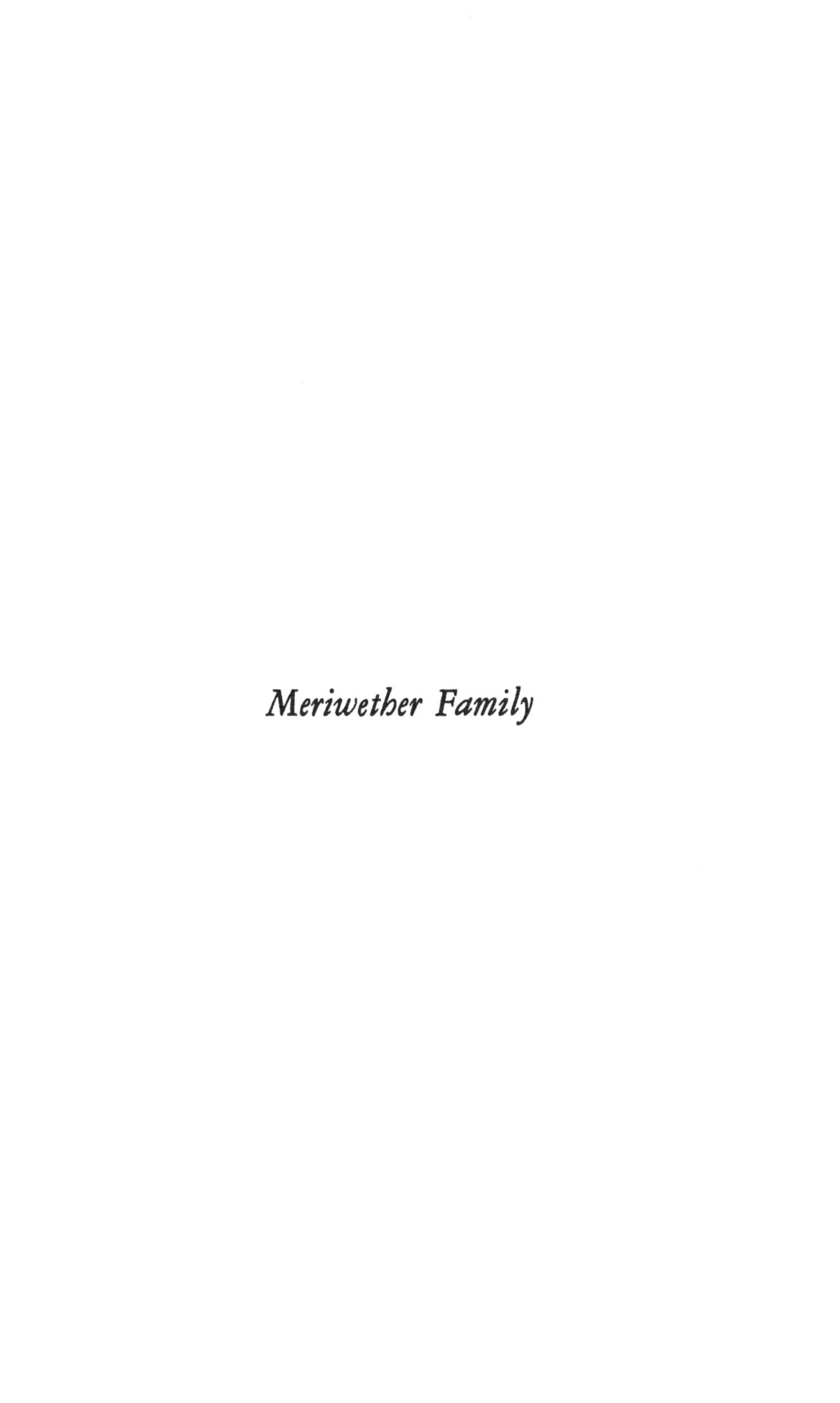

*Meriwether Family*

# MERIWETHER

## Arms

Or—three martlets (sable) on a chief azure—a sun in splendor.
*Crest*—An arm in armour embowed in the hand a sword (argent) hilt and pommel (or) entwined with a serpent (vert.).

NOTE.—The name Meriwether easily accounted for; it is found in England in the time of the Conqueror among "The Hunched Rolls". For instance, John Meryweder—varying to Mulweder and Merywedyr.

THE PREFIX.—Was much used at that period as Meryman—Merymouth, etc., a sunshiny, happy set which is depicted in the Meriwethers of today.

---

Destruction of James City records and loss of old colonial papers prevent proof of the exact time of the arrival in Virginia of the first Meriwether.

The first emigrant, Nicholas and wife, Elizabeth—and his brother, Francis and Joan, who was either the wife of Francis, or sister, of the two brothers. Destruction of James City records during the War 1860-1865 prevents proof as to Joan's status, except that she was here in Virginia, and died September 3, 1677.

So far as court records go there is some confusion between Nicholas I and Nicholas II, of New Kent. It appears that this Francis, if married, left no issue. He died March 28, 1676.

The Hanover Record, 1728—pages 22, 23, 26—gives the earliest date of Nicholas Meriwether, the Welshman, born 1631—the earliest time at which we have record of him is April 22, 1655, when he was 24 years old—the clerk of Surry County, at which time he located "Southwarke." He is supposed to have been the first clerk of Surry—that county having been formed from Isle of Wight as early as 1657. He was a large seller of land patents in different counties—and administrator of the estate of Thos. Woodhouse, 1665, as the following note shows:

"A record in Va. land registry office between 1652 and 1669 of patents to the extent of 5,250 acres in Westmoreland Co. done by Nicholas Meriwether."

He made oath May 7, 1663 that he was then 37 years old (if we consider that May is the fifth month of the year, this shows that he was born during 1631.)

He is supposed to have married Elizabeth Woodhouse. He died December 17, 1678. His wife outlived him.

The Meriwethers brought quite a large amount of wealth to the Colonies, were rich in lands, in plate and in slaves. They were men of strongly marked individuality; were noted for their integrity, determination and ingenuity.

## BACON GENEALOGY

John Bacon, married Cecilly Howe, and had:

John Bacon, married Helen Gedding, and had:

John Bacon, married first, Helena, daughter of Sir Geo. Tillot of Baugham; married second, Julia, daughter of Bradwell. He had:

John Bacon, married Margaret Thorpe, daughter of John Thorpe (who was son of William Thorpe), also granddaughter of Sir Wm. Thorpe by the daughter and heiress of Sir Roger Bacon, a very celebrated leader in the wars. "Temps" Edward II and Edward III.

Edmond Bacon, Baron of Dunkstone, and had:

Edward, married, and had:

John Bacon, married Agnes Cokefield, and had:

Robert Bacon, married Isabella, daughter of John Cage of Perkenham, Suffolkshire. He had:

Sir Nicholas Bacon, "Lord Keeper", by his second wife, Ann, daughter of Sir Anthony Cooke (1573). He had:

Ann Bacon, married Henry Woodhouse, and had:

Henry Woodhouse, Governor of Bermuda, married Frances, daughter of Sir Robert Gerunyne Penbrookeshire. He had:

Capt. Henry Woodhouse, married *Mary* or *Maria* or *Judith*. He had:

Elizabeth Woodhouse, married Nicholas Meriwether.

## WOODHOUSE

"*Charleston News*", Sept. 22, 1907—Va. Carolina, Page 112:

Captain Henry Woodhouse, Governor of Bermuda, was son of Sir Henry Woodhouse of Waxham, England, and his wife Ann, (daughter of Sir Nicholas Bacon), who was son of John Woodhouse and his wife, Alice Croft.

Captain Henry Woodhouse was in the Expedition of Isle of Ré and Rochelle; he was recommended to be Captain of Pilbury Fort and he was of the Muster of Suffolk County, England. From 1623 to 1626 he was Governor of Bermuda and was present at a council table there March 1, 1626. A few years later he petitioned King Charles to give him the Governorship of Virginia, a position which the King had promised but did not give to him.

His son, Henry II, was born in Bermuda, emigrated to Lower Norfolk, Virginia, when 30 years old and was Member of House of Burgesses from Norfolk in 1647-1652, and Commissioner of that county. He was member of the Vestry of the old church at Lynnhaven. He died 1655 leaving a wife, Mary or Judith, four sons, and several daughters—their names are:

Henry, Horatio, John, William.
Elizabeth Woodhouse, married Nicholas Meriwether
Sarah, Mary and Rachel.

Will probated 1655

He is said also to have had a daughter Lucy, married Sir Wm. Dutton Colt and a daughter Alice Woodhouse, died unmarried, and in her will, named her mother, Judith Woodhouse and her brother-in-law Jost Hane.

One authority says the father of Sir Henry Woodhouse was Sir Wm. Woodhouse of Waxam and not John Woodhouse.

NOTE.—In July, 1926 Mrs. E. C. Griffith writes of an evening spent at St. Ann's Rectory, "Port Royal", the home of Rev. E. A. Paget, Southampton, Bermuda.

"Dr. Bell keeps at his home the old church records and the communion service said to be the oldest in America and that used in the time of Gov. Woodhouse. Mr. Paget had him bring them over for us to see. I copied the following from the colonial records by Governor J. H. Lefroy, Vol. I, page 405:

" 'Capt. Henry Woodhouse in 1634 took a lease for 99 years from Sir William Killigrew dated Oct. 29, 1634 of 6 shares of land (a share is 25 acres) in Hamilton tribe (parish) with an apparent intention of returning to Bermuda, upon the nominal rental of 100 oranges, 100 lemons, 100 potatoes to be paid at the Feast of the Annunciation of the Blessed Virgin Mary.

" 'After that the rent was not paid. Woodhouse did decline to pay rent and farm the land, for we hear no more of him in Bermuda—and he describes himself as *Henry Woodhouse* of *Virginia, planter,* in a deed of sale dated April 15, 1640'."

Page 524. " 'Capt Henry Woodhouse, the second Governor of Bermuda, 1623-26'."

Issue of Nicholas Meriwether I, and Elizabeth Woodhouse:

1. Nicholas Meriwether, born October 26, 1667, died December 12, 1744; married Elizabeth Crawford, who died 1753.
2. Jane Meriwether, married William Brown.
3. Elizabeth Meriwether, married Francis Clemens of Surry County.
4. Francis Meriwether, married Mary Bathurst, daughter of Lancelot Bathurst of Gloucester, England, and his second wife, Susan Rich. He was second son of Sir Edward Bathurst who was knighted in 1643 by Charles I.

   They had four daughters:

   a. Mary Meriwether, married first, Wm. Colston; married second, Thos. Wright Bellfield, and had:
      1. John Bellfield.

   b. Lucy Meriwether, married Francis Smith, and had:
      1. Meriwether Smith, born 1730, Bathurst, Essex County.

         He was Virginia Burgess from Essex County, 1770; signed the protest against the Stamp Act; of the Westmoreland Association, February 27, 1776; Member of the Virginia Committee of 1775 and 1776. Member of Continental Congress 1778-1782. Member of Virginia Assembly, 1786-1788; Member of Virginia Committee to ratify the Federal Constitution January 26, 1790. He died January 25, 1790.

         He married Alice, daughter of Philip Lee (third in descent from the emigrant, Richard Lee), and widow of Thomas Clarke. He married second, Elizabeth Dangerfield, daughter of Col. Wm. Dangerfield of Essex. She died January 24, 1794.

He had by his first marriage:

1. Richard Lee Smith.
2. Governor George Wm. Smith, who was burned to death in the Richmond Theatre December 26, 1812. He married Sarah Adams. Issue:
   a. Richard Lee Smith.
   b. George W. Smith, born 1795, married Anna Stewart Campbell.
3. John Adams Smith, born 1801, married Lucy Williams, and had:
   a. Bathurst Smith.
   b. Thomas Smith.

c. Frances Meriwether (daughter of Francis and Mary B. Meriwether), married Theodoric Bland of Prince George County.

d. Jane Meriwether, married James Skelton, M. D. of Goochland County. Their daughter:

Sally Skelton, married Major Thos. Jones who was descended from Capt. Roger Jones (emigrant).

From her descend:

Meriwether Jones of Richmond, Va., political writer.
Gen. Walter Jones, distinguished lawyer of Washington.
Gen. Roger Jones of the regular Army.
Commodore Catesby Jones of the Navy.

5. Thomas Meriwether, son of Nicholas Meriwether I and Elizabeth Woodhouse, married Susannah Skelton, and had:

a. Susannah Meriwether, married John Armistead, of Gloucester, and had:
   1. John Armistead, Jr.
   2. Susan Armistead, married Moore Fauntleroy.
   3. William Armistead.

Thomas Meriwether lived and died near Tappahannock, Essex County, Va. His will probated January, 1703.

John Armistead's will probated April, 9, 1734.

6. David Meriwether, married, and had one child.

"Bathurst" in Essex County, the old colonial home built by Francis Meriwether (the county clerk), remained in his family for generations till sold 1810 by his descendant, Thomas Ap Thomas Jones for $20,000 when he moved to Clark County, Ky.

A picture of "Bathurst" shows a quaint roof with dormer windows of colonial pattern. One can fancy the house as the social center it must have been and deplore its passing to strangers after the so long association with the Meriwethers.

## CRAWFORD FAMILY

These Crawfords are said to be descended from Sir Roland Crawford, the grandfather of Sir William Wallace.

John Crawford, born 1600, came from Scotland to Virginia and died December 13, 1689.

David, his only son, born 1625, died 1704, came to Virginia with his father between 1643 and 1667, lived in St. Peter's, afterwards St. Paul's Parish in New Kent, now Hanover County. He was vestryman of St. Peter's 1685 to 1698. He died 1704. He came to America between 1643 and 1667, this last being date of grant of land from Sir Wm. Berkeley of 86 acres. Locating also 1,000 acres and two grants, 1672, of 1,000 acres on head-right. Other grants in St. Peter's, New Kent County, 1,350 acres, 375 acres. In 1676, 1,300; 277; 196 acres, all in New Kent County. All deeded to Captain David Crawford who may have been his son. Issue:

1. Elizabeth, died 1753, married Nicholas Meriwether.
2. ——(daughter), married Mr. Lewis and went South.
3. Angelina, married Mcguire and moved South.
4. Capt. David Crawford, born 1662, died 1761, married Ann Anderson, daughter of John Anderson and his wife, Sarah Waddy, daughter of Anthony and Sarah Waddy.
5. John Crawford, married, and had one child. (See Thomson record).

## NICHOLAS MERIWETHER II

Born in Surry County, October 26, 1667. Died in Albemarle County, December, 1744.

NOTE.—Authorities differ as to his birth date. 1647 would place his father as only 17 years his senior and I use a later date as more probable.

Like his father, he acquired large land grants. The dates of these grants which he took out in what is now Albemarle, then Goochland County, have caused him to be called by some authorities "The Father of Albemarle."

1727. Goochland County was formed—just ten years after Governor Spottswood's Expedition across the Blue Ridge at Swift Run Gap. Albemarle was formed in 1744.

June 26, 1727. Nicholas Meriwether first obtained a grant of 13,762 acres from George II. For it he was to pay yearly 21 pounds sterling—at the feast of St. Michael, the archangel, 1 shilling for every 50 acres of land—3 acres of which must be cultivated.

1730. He added a second grant of 4,090 acres to this land. "Castle Hill", "Peacholorum", "Turkey Hill", "Kinloch", "Belvoir", "Music Hall", "Cloverfields", "Cismont", are all parts of these grants.

1735. He took out a third grant of 1,020 acres which included "The Farm", his home, which was inherited by his grandson, Nicholas Lewis. (The town of Charlottesville is spreading over it now.)

His will is probated in Goochland County, as Albemarle was not cut from that county until the year after his death. He is said to be buried on the east side of the Rivanna River, but the site is not fully known. He outlived all of his children.

His colonial service followed his various changes of residence. He was Vestryman for St. Peter's Parish, New Kent County; Vestryman for St. Paul's Parish, New Kent County; Major of New Kent Troops, from 1703; Col. of New Kent Troops, from 1707 to 1733; Sheriff of New Kent, 1702; Burgess for Hanover. Hanover was cut from New Kent.

(REFERENCE.—St. Peter's Register and St. Paul's Vestry Book.)

He married Elizabeth Crawford, daughter of David Crawford of Assaquin, New Kent, which seat was inherited by their son, David.

Mrs. Elizabeth Meriwether in her will dated March 2, 1753, leaves her home place in Louisa County, of 2,000 acres to her grandson, Robert Lewis, Jr., and remaining property divided between her son-in-law, Robert Lewis, her daughter, Ann Cosby and grandson Richard, son of William Meriwether. (Will Book 1, Louisa Records.)

Issue of Nicholas Meriwether II and Elizabeth Crawford:

I. Jane Meriwether, married Col. Robert Lewis of "Belvoir" (issue given in Bel-voir Lewises.)

II. Nicholas Meriwether, born July 11, baptized August 6, 1699, married Mildred Thornton. Issue:

A. Mildred T. Meriwether, married John Syme.

III. William Meriwether, married ——, and had children: John (who 1799, married Mary Bowles) Thomas, Richard, Jane, Sarah, Mary, Nicholas.

IV. Thomas Meriwether, married ——, had a son Nicholas.

V. Col. David Meriwether, born 1690, died December 25, 1744, married Ann Holmes, daughter of Geo. Holmes, of King and Queen County. She died March 11, 1735-6.

VI. Elizabeth Meriwether, born June 20, 1703, baptized July 3, 1703, died January 1, 17—. Married Thomas Bray, and had:

A. Elizabeth Bray, married Philip Johnson, 1743, and had:

1. Thomas Bray Johnson.
2. Elizabeth Johnson.
3. Rebecca Johnson.
4. Thomas Johnson.
5. Ann Johnson.
6. Martha Johnson.

VII. Ann Meriwether, married first, Thomas Johnson; second, Mr. Cosby. She was baptized 15th of July, 1690.

VIII. Sarah Meriwether, married Wm. Littlepage of King and Queen County. She died July 2, 1733 leaving a daughter:

A. Judith Littlepage.

IX. Mary Meriwether, married first, Mr. Aylett; married second, Samuel Cobb, of Georgia.

## COL. DAVID MERIWETHER

Born 1690, died December 25, 1744. He is buried by his father on the east side of Rivanna River. (His plantation afterwards owned by Elizabeth Meriwether, wife of Thos. Walker Lewis.) His will probated in Louisa County, January 22, 1745.

He married Ann Holmes, who died March 11, 1736. Issue:

A. Thomas Meriwether, born 1714-15, married Elizabeth Thornton. He died 1756.

B. Francis Meriwether, married Mary Lewis, daughter of Zachary Lewis and Mary Waller of Spotsylvania County. They moved from Virginia to South Carolina. Issue:

   1. Zachary Meriwether, married first cousin, Jane Lewis, daughter of John Lewis, the "Honest Lawyer", and Ann, his wife.
   2. Nicholas Meriwether.
   3. Mary Meriwether.

C. Nicholas Meriwether, married Frances Morton, or Mary Pryor. He was born December 11, 1719, died May 3, 1758.

D. Ann Meriwether, born November 11, 1721, married Thomas Ballard Smith. No issue.

E. Sarah Meriwether, died in infancy.

F. David Meriwether, born October 5, 1726, married Mary Weaver, of England. They returned to England. He was in the merchant service.

G. James Meriwether, born June 1, 1729, married first, Hardenia Burnley; married second, Elizabeth Pollard. He was grandfather of Governor David Meriwether, who died 1893, near Louisville, Kentucky.

H. William Meriwether, son of Col. David Meriwether and Ann Holmes, his wife, born December 25, 1730, died December 24, 1790. He married in Louisa County, Va., Martha C. Wood, died October 17, 1801. She was daughter of Henry and Martha Cox Wood.

## THOMAS MERIWETHER

Son of Col. David Meriwether and Ann Holmes. Married Elizabeth Thornton, and had issue:

1. Col. Nicholas Meriwether, born September 7, 1736, died 1772, married December 31, 1760, Margaret Douglas, daughter of the Rev. Wm. Douglas and his wife, Nicholas Hunter of Scotland and Virginia.
2. Francis Meriwether, born October 31, 1737, married Martha Jamison, moved to Georgia 1784. He was the great-grandfather of Val and Jim Meriwether and Mrs. Tom White of Hernando, Miss.
3. David Meriwether, born September 2, 1739, married Mary Harvie.
4. Mary Meriwether, born April 4, 1742, married Peachy Ridgeway Gilmer.
5. Elizabeth Meriwether, born March 3, 1744, married Thomas Johnson ("Sheriff Tom").
6. Sarah Meriwether, born November 26, 1746, married Michael Anderson.
7. Ann Meriwether, born May 1, 1750, died August 5, 1782. She was first wife of Richard Anderson who was born June 15, 1747, died February 14, 1793. (See Anderson Record.)
8. Lucy Meriwether, born February 4, 1752, died September 8, 1837, married first, 1759, Wm. Lewis, of Locust Hill; married second, Capt. John Marks. Issue of both marriages given in Lewis and Meriwether families.
9. Mildred Thornton Meriwether, born July 25, 1753, married March 22, 1771, John Gilmer. (Her son, Nicholas Gilmer, lived on the Kentucky State line, four miles west of Cabin Row.)
10. Thomas Meriwether, born Nov. 5, 1755, died in infancy.
11. Jane Meriwether, born April 8, 1757, a short time after her father's death. She married Samuel Dabney, of Louisa County. (Ancestors of Rev. Robert Dabney of Virginia and Texas and Mrs. Vance of Memphis, Tenn.).

## PARSON WILLIAM DOUGLAS

Born in Wigtonnshire, Scotland, 1708, married 1735, Miss Nicholas Hunter, niece of Dr. John Hunter of Edinborough.

He came to Virginia 1748-50. Taught in the family of Col. Monroe, father of President Monroe. He taught also the future presidents—Thomas Jefferson and James Madison. He returned to Scotland for his wife and child, October 1751.

He was ordained to the ministry; came back with his family and settled in Goochland, serving the parish in Goochland, Louisa and Albemarle. He married 1,388 couples and performed 4,069 baptisms and had a wide clerical record.

He preached his wife's funeral on the 88th Psalm, at Beaver Dam in the year 1782. One year later he married his housekeeper, Elizabeth Burruss, 47 years his junior.

He said of her that she was a good young woman. He resigned his pastorate and retired to his farm, "Ducking Hole", in Louisa where he died—nearly 90 years old, and is buried beside his first wife near the old homestead in Louisa.

Ten years before his death he conveyed all his property except support for himself and wife to his daughter and her children.

Issue of Parson Douglas and Nicholas Hunter:

1. Margaret Douglas, born 1737, married first, in 1760, Nicholas Meriwether who died 1772 at his home "Clover Fields", Albemarle County, and left six children.

   She married second, Chiles Terrel of "Music Hall", and had:

   a. James Hunter Terrel, married Susan Vibert. No issue. Besides "Music Hall", Capt. James H. Terrel owned "Ducking Hole", Louisa County, which Parson Douglas bought from Peter Syme, 1770.

      Dr. James Hunter Minor, son of Samuel Overton Minor and Lydia Laurie Lewis, heired "Music Hall."

August 1902 a letter from Mr. W. D. Robertson Douglas, of Scotland (Ockardton Douglas Castle), was passed to me for possible answer to its inquiry regarding an old history of the Douglases which had some notes on the family by Parson Douglas.

The same claimed descent from the Dukes of Douglas. (*S. T. L. A.*).

## HUNTER OF HUNTERTON CASTLE, SCOTLAND

Hunter of Ayrhill, Fairfax County, Va.

John Hunter, son of Francis Hunter, son of Patrick Hunter who was 19th Laird of Hunterton, Scotland. He married Agnes Paul. Issue:

1. Dr. William Hunter, born at Easter Kilbridge in Lanarkshire. Died in London, November 30, 1783, and bequeathed his valuable museum to the University of Glasgow.
2. Dorothea Hunter, married Dr. Balis of the University of Glasgow (their son, Dr. Balis, physician to the King).
3. Dr. John Hunter, born February 13, 1728, married Anna Home. He went to London at the age of twenty, where his brother William was living and where he was gaining a high reputation. This stimulated John to put forth his undeveloped energies that he should in future become a power among men. He spent the summer 1740 in Chelsea Hospital 1757 he was pupil at St. Bartholmew where he received. instruction from the renowned Percival Potts, distinguished surgeon. Dr. William Douglas, his brother, wished him to be a physician and not a surgeon and so he was persuaded to be a student at St. Mary's Hall, Oxford, 1753—but only for a short time as he determined he would not spend time learning Greek and Latin—and he again returned to surgical studies.

   1754 we find him at St. George's Hospital. He added new laurels to those he had already gained and increased in reputation and ability until he was recognized as the greatest surgeon of his day. He will ever hold a prominent place in the history of science as surgeon, anatomist and philosopher.

(REFERENCE.—Burke's Landed Gentry.)

Parson Douglas' first wife, Nicholas Hunter, was a niece of Dr. John Hunter—therefore of this line of Hunters who had before this time repeatedly intermarried with the Douglases.

Her brother, John Hunter settled in Louisa 1759.

## NICHOLAS MERIWETHER

Inherited "Cloverfields", a part of the first old Meriwether land grant. This place has remained in the ownership of his descendants, one of whom, Mrs. Charlotte Randolph, now owns it.

He married Margaret Douglas, and had issue:

a. William Douglas Meriwether, born November 2, 1761, died January 21, 1845. Married 1788, Elizabeth Lewis.
b. Thomas Meriwether, born August 24, 1763, married Ann Minor, July 27, 1791. She was daughter of Garrett Minor, of "Sunning Hill."
c. Nicholas Hunter Meriwether, born January 9, 1765, married Rebecca Terrell, dau. of Richmond Terrell and Ann Overton.
d. Dr. Charles Meriwether, born August 12, 1766, married first, Lydia Laurie, a Scotch cousin. Married second, Nancy Minor, of "Woodlawn", Orange, Va. She was daughter of Dabney Minor and Ann Anderson. He married third, Mrs. Mary Walton Daniel, of Halifax County, Va.
e. Francis Meriwether, born 1768 or 9, married Catherine Davies.
f. Elizabeth Meriwether, born February 24, 1771, died March 27, 1851, married Thomas Walker Lewis, 1788.

William Douglas Meriwether and Elizabeth Lewis, had issue:

1. John Meriwether, died unmarried.
2. Nicholas Meriwether, died unmarried.
3. William Hunter Meriwether, born 1793, married first, Frances Poindexter (no living issue); married second, Kate W. Meriwether, of Bedford County. No issue. He emigrated to New Braunfels, Texas, where he built large mills.
4. Chas. James Meriwether, born 1797, married Miss Louisa Miller, no issue. They visited their Scotch relatives, and traveled in many foreign countries. Both died at "Farmington."
5. Mary Walker Meriwether, born 1800, died 1832, married Peter N. Meriwether. No living issue.
6. Margaret Douglas Meriwether, died 1880, married first, Dr. Frank Thornton Meriwether; second, Francis Kinlaw Nelson. (No issue by second marriage).
   Issue:
   a. Henry Landon Meriwether.

b. Chas. James Meriwether, married Ellen Douglas Meriwether. Issue:
   1. Bettie Meriwether, married.
   2. Addison Meriwether, m. Margaret D. Meriwether.
   3. Wm. Douglas Meriwether.
   4. Chas. W. Meriwether.

c. Mary Walker Meriwether, born April 29, 1833, died October 4, 1863, married Major Thos. J. Randolph, C. S. A. Issue:
   1. Frank M. Randolph, married Charlotte Macon. Issue:
      a. Margaret D. Randolph.
      b. Carrie R. Randolph, married E. H. Joslin.
      c. Mildred Randolph, died in infancy.
      d. Charlotte N. Randolph, married G. Rafferty, Jr. Has:
         Caroline Rafferty.
         Ann Rafferty.
         Frances D. Rafferty.
   2. Thos. J. Randolph.
   3. Margaret Douglas Randolph.
   4. Jane Randolph, died young.
   5. Frank Nelson Randolph, died young.
   6. Geo. G. Randolph, born 1863.

7. Dr. Thomas Walker Meriwether, son of Elizabeth Lewis and Wm. Douglas Meriwether, born 1803, died 1863, married Ann Carter Nelson. Issue:

a. Dr. Wm. Douglas Meriwether, married first, Phebe Gardner. Issue:
   1. Mary Gardner, married Mr. Wallace.
   2. William H. Meriwether.
   3. Bella Meriwether.
   4. Warner Meriwether.
   5. James J. Meriwether.
   6. Susie S. Meriwether.

   Dr. Meriwether, married second, Nannie Page, and had:
   7. Evelyn Page Meriwether.

b. Mildred Nelson Meriwether, married Geo. W. Macon. Issue:
   1. Thomas S. Macon.
   2. Charlotte Macon, married Frank Randolph.
   3. Betty Macon.
   4. Geo. Macon, married ——, had Harriet Macon.

c. Annie K. Meriwether, married Frederick W. Page. Issue:
   1. Jane Walker Page, married Thos. W. Lewis.
   2. Annie K. Page.
   3. Eliza Page.
   4. Geo. Page.
   5. Frederick W. Page, married Flora Lewis.
   6. Mann Page.
   7. Minnie Page.
   8. Evelyn Page.

d. Eliza Lewis Meriwether, married N. H. Massie. No issue.

e. Charlotte Nelson Meriwether, born 1834, married Major Thos. J. Randolph. Issue:
   1. Mary Walker Randolph.
   2. Charlotte N. Randolph.

Thomas Meriwether, born August 24, 1763 (second child of Nicholas Meriwether and Margaret Douglas), married Anne Minor, July 27, 1791. She was daughter of Garrett Minor and Mary O. Terrell. Anne died September 21, 1820 in Louisa. (She married second, Mr. Brockman.)

Issue:

1. Richard Terrell Meriwether, born May 11, 1792, married Elizabeth Rivers. He died December 7, 1840 in Madrid Bend, Tennessee.
2. Peter N. Meriwether, born February 7, 1796, married first, Mary W. Meriwether. Married second, Mrs. Frances W. Tapp. He died August, 1851. No issue by either marriage. He is buried beside his last wife at Cismont. He adopted George Geiger, killed at Gettysburg.
3. Mary Minor Meriwether, born July 2, 1798, married John Barker; she died March 3, 1831. She is buried at "Cloverlands", their home in Montgomery County, Tenn. Her half

sister, Virginia Brockman, Mrs. Fowlkes, is buried beside her.

4. Thos. L. Meriwether, born September 27, 1799, died July 4, 1838, unmarried.
5. Francis T. Meriwether, born 1801, died 1804.
6. Garrett Minor Meriwether, born 1794, died 1851, married Mary Anne Minor, daughter of Dabney and Lucy Herndon Minor.

Issue of Ann Minor Meriwether by second marriage:

7. Virginia Brockman, married Joseph Fowlkes.
8. Francis Brockman, married Margaret McDougal.
9. Emmet Brockman.
10. Hugh Brockman.
11. Charles James Brockman, M. D., married Margaret Terrell Cobb at "Music Hall", Va. She was daughter of Samuel Cobb and Mary Noel and was raised at "Music Hall" by James Hunter Terrell. Dr. Chas. Brockman associated in practice with Dr. Gerrard at whose home in Kentucky he died. Issue:
    a. James Hunter Brockman.
    b. Garrett Meriwether Brockman.

Issue of Richard T. Meriwether and Elizabeth Rivers:

a. Elizabeth Meriwether, married Mr. Donaldson, and had:
    1. Rivers Donaldson.
    2. Normand Donaldson.
    3. Lauchland Donaldson.
    4. Meriwether Donaldson.
b. Jane Meriwether, married Mr. Westbrook.
c. Martha Meriwether, married Mr. Thompson, had:
    1. Pauline Thompson.
    2. Georgie Thompson.
d. Margaret Meriwether, married Mr. Isler, and had:
    1. Lucy Isler.
    2. Jessie Isler.
    3. Henry Isler.
e. John Thomas Meriwether.

f. Bob Meriwether (girl), married Mr. Isler, and had:
   1. Richard Isler.

Issue of Mary Minor Meriwether, daughter of Thomas Meriwether and Anne Minor, his wife; and John Walton Barker.

1. Barbary A. Barker, married Judge A. M. Clayton, and had:
   a. Clara Clayton, married Mr. Fant.
2. Thos. L. Barker.
3. Nannie M. Barker, married Mr. Fergerson; has seven children.
4. Chiles T. Barker, married Mary L. Hutchinson of Louisa County, had:
   Eleven children who have large families, and live in Christian County, Kentucky.

Issue of Garrett M. Meriwether, born in Louisa April 25, 1794, died September 26, 1851, married September 28, 1819 at Woodlawn, Orange County, Va., and Mary Ann Minor:

1. Lucy Anne Meriwether, died young.
2. Dabney Minor Meriwether, died in infancy.
3. Louisa Meriwether, died in infancy.
4. Lucy Anne Meriwether, born May 22, 1822, died April 14, 1844, married John Hull, of Mississippi.
5. Minor Meriwether, born January 15, 1828, married January 5, 1852, Elizabeth Avery.
6. Niles Meriwether, born January 26, 1831, married Lida P. Smith.
7. Robert D. Owen Meriwether, born January 8, 1843.

Issue of Minor Meriwether of St. Louis, a talented lawyer and author, and Elizabeth Avery:

a. Avery Meriwether, born July 15, 1857, died July 22, 1883.
b. Rivers Blythe Meriwether, born July 26, 1859, married January 27, 1886, Lulie Norval, and had:
   1. Susie Lee Meriwether.
   2. Elizabeth Meriwether.
c. Lee Meriwether, born December 26, 1862. He was author of "A Tramp Trip Abroad" and other works dealing with labor conditions in various foreign lands. He married first, Millicent Nye, of California; married second, in New York, a St. Louis

girl, Jessie Gaer, December 4, 1895. Issue by first marriage:

1. Elsie Meriwether.

Nicholas Hunter Meriwether, third child of Nicholas Meriwether and Margaret Douglas, was born January 9, 1765, married Rebecca Terrell, daughter of Richmond Terrell and Anne Overton.

Issue, six children:

1. Douglas Meriwether, married Judith Bernard, and had: (six children)
   a. John N. Meriwether, married Helen Staten, and left issue.
   b. Mary Meriwether, married Mr. Wilde, and left issue.
   c. Thomas Payne Meriwether, married Georgiana Simmons, and had:
      1. Florida Meriwether who was murdered when traveling between Tennessee and Mississippi.
   d. Dr. Chas. James Fox Meriwether, married Octavia Simmons, and had three children.
   e. Robert Emmett Meriwether, married Susan Terrell, and left issue.
   f. Anne Meriwether, died in girlhood on a visit to Virginia.

   *Note.*—This family moved at an early date to Mississippi.

2. Dr. Charles Hunter Meriwether, married first, Anne E. Anderson (no issue); married second, Frances E. Thomas, and had:
   a. Margaret L. Meriwether, born May 3, 1828, died October 10, 1861, married John D. Morris, and had:
      1. Fannie Morris, married G. W. Macrae, and had: a. Margaret Macrae, married Mr. White.
      2. Mary Love Morris, married Tom Barker.
      3. Richard D. Morris, married Miss Galloway.
   b. Mary Walker Meriwether, born December 23, 1830, died 1872, married Darwin Bell, and had:
      1. Gilmer M. Bell.
      2. Francis Bell.
      3. Margaret Bell, married Dr. Williams.

c. Louisa M. Meriwether, married first, Richard Barker; married second, Gen. Wm. Quarles, C. S. A. (no issue by second marriage). Issue by first marriage:
   1. Morris Barker, married Emiline McLean.
   2. Margaret Barker, married James McClure Meriwether, of "Woodstock", 1879.
   3. Marion Walton Barker, married Wm. Douglas Meriwether, of Meriville, Kentucky, 1883.

3. Nancy T. Meriwether, married Nicholas Hunter Lewis, of the "Farm." (See issue in Lewis descent.)
4. Walker Gilmer Meriwether, fourth child of Nicholas Hunter Meriwether and his wife, Rebecca Terrell, born February 9, 1794, died July 10, 1841, married Betsy Meriwether, and had issue:

a. Francis T. Meriwether, born 1819, died 1840.

Walker Meriwether, married second Jane Warner Lewis, November 28, 1822, and had issue: (six children)

b. Betty M. D. Meriwether, married Geo. Wilson, no issue.

c. Geo. D. Meriwether, married first, Annie Wells (no issue); married second, Betty Meriwether, and had:
   1. Walker Gilmer Meriwether, married Annie McCravey, had:
      Alice C., Geo., Fontaine Gilmer Meriwether.

   Geo. D. Meriwether, married third, Elizabeth M. Anderson; married fourth, Elizabeth Miller. No issue by last two marriages.

d. Thomas Montgomery Meriwether, born 1839, died same year.

e. Franklin M. Meriwether, born March 14, 1831, married Mary C. Meriwether. No issue.

f. Alice V. Meriwether, died age 3 years.

g. Alice V. Meriwether, born June 18, 1838, married September 20, 1853, Henry V. T. Block. Issue: (10 children)
   1. Geo. M. Block, born December 10, 1856, married October 10, 1883, Helen L. Sylvester, and had:
      a. Helen Block.
   2. Robert C. Block, born July 20, 1859.

3. Jane W. Block, born May 9, 1861, died 1862.
4. Henry L. Block, born March 15, 1863.
5. Annie E. Block, born December 13, 1864.
6. Walker Meriwether Block, born July 15, 1866.
7. Sally C. Block, born June 26, 1870.
8. Alice B. Block, born September 24, 1872.
9. Mary M. Block, born May 7, 1876.
10. Helen Louise Block, born July 11, 1882.

5. Dr. Fountaine Meriwether, fifth child of Nicholas H. Meriwether and Rebecca Terrell, married November 5, 1822, Winfred Adeline Miller. This family moved to Pike and Lincoln Counties, Mo. Issue: (11 children)

a. Nicholas Hunter Meriwether, married Miss Sydnor, and had:

1. John Fountaine Meriwether.

b. Betty G. Meriwether, married Geo. D. Meriwether. (For issue, see his record.)

c. Nannie Lewis Meriwether, married Wm. Lewis, and had three children.

d. Chas. James Meriwether, born February 1829, married Lydia Laurie Wells, and had eleven children.

e. Mary Christian Meriwether, born April 18, 1831, married Franklin Montgomery Meriwether. No remaining issue.

f. Fountaine Meriwether.

g. Peter Guerrent Meriwether.

h. Walker Douglas Meriwether. Left no descendants.

i. Ellen A. H. Meriwether. Left no descendants.

j. Heath Jones Meriwether, born February, 1836, married Lydia Laurie Eastin, and had ten children.

k. Louise Rebecca Meriwether, born August 23, 1840, married Geo. G. Winn, and had two children.

6. Margaret D. Meriwether, sixth child of Nicholas H. Meriwether and his wife, Rebecca Terrell, married Thomas Terrell. This family settled in Kentucky and Tennessee where many still remain. Issue: (9 children)

a. Margaret N. Terrell.

b. Dr. Chas. N. Terrell, married Miss West.

c. Anna L. Terrell.
d. Lucian B. Terrell.
e. Sam D. Terrell.
f. Rebecca Terrell, married Mr. Upham.
g. Thomas Terrell.
h. James D. Terrell, M. D., married Miss Wilde.
i. Susan Terrell, married Robert E. Meriwether.

(See Douglas and Judith Meriwether record.)

Dr. Chas. Meriwether, fourth son of Nicholas Meriwether and Margaret Douglas, was born at "Cloverfields", August 12, 1766, moved to Kentucky 1809, died October 7, 1843 at Meriville, Todd County, Kentucky. He was educated at Edinborough, Scotland, where he took his medical degree. While there he married his cousin, Lydia Laurie. She and her infant died before he returned to Virginia. He married second, Nancy Minor, daughter of Dabney Minor, of "Woodlawn", Orange County, and his wife, Anne Anderson. Dr. Meriwether moved to Halifax County.

Dr. Chas. Meriwether and his second wife, Nancy Minor, had issue:

I. Chas. Nicholas Minor Meriwether, married Caroline Huntly Barker.

Dr. Meriwether and his third wife, Mrs. Daniel, of Charlotte County (whose maiden name was Mary Walton), had issue:

II. William Douglas Meriwether, b. 1809—never married.

III. Dr. James Hunter Meriwether, born March, 1814.

Charles Nicholas Minor Meriwether, born in Virginia August 19, 1801, died September 27, 1877, in Kentucky, married Caroline Huntley Barker. They lived at "Woodstock" Plantation in Kentucky. Issue: (5 children)

A. Chas. Edward Meriwether, born December 20, 1824. Killed in battle at Sacramento, C. S. A., December 26, 1861. He married Elizabeth Golden Sharpe, and had issue: (5 children)
   1. Maxwell Sharpe Meriwether, born September 14, 1850, married first, Nannie Warfield; married second Lillian Keene. Issue:
      a. Geo. Warfield Meriwether, born October 8, 1878.
      b. Louise Meriwether, born January 23, 1889.
      c. Catherine Golden Meriwether, born Feb. 4, 1890.

2. Chas. Nicholas Meriwether, born 1852.
3. James McClure Meriwether, born 1854.
4. Chas. Edward Meriwether, born 1857.
5. Catherine Maxwell Meriwether, born March 10, 1859, married Henry S. Barker.

B. Nancy Minor Meriwether, born March 10, 1827, married John Ferguson. Issue:
   1. Caroline Ferguson, married Douglas Meriwether, and had:
      a. Robert E. Meriwether.
      b. Lulie Meriwether.
      c. Nancy Minor Meriwether.
      d. Margaret Meriwether.
   2. James H. Ferguson, married Parthenia Kimbrough, and had:
      a. Mildred P. Ferguson.
      b. Kitty Ferguson.
      c. J. D. Ferguson.
      d. Jimmy Hunter Ferguson (girl).

C. Mary Walton Meriwether, daughter of Chas. N. M. Meriwether and Caroline Barker, born March 12, 1830, died age 94, married Robert West Humphreys, and had issue: (9 ch.)
   1. Nancy Minor Humphreys, born July 4, 1852.
   2. Betty Humphreys, born August 10, 1854.
   3. Caroline Humphreys, born August 2, 1856.
   4. Robert Humphreys, born November 1, 1860, died 1888.
   5. Edward Humphreys, born May 12, 1863.
   6. West Humphreys, born May 13, 1865.
   7. John Humphreys, born January 26, 1867.

   Nancy Minor Humphreys, married Robert Lewis Armistead. Issue:
   a. Chas. M. Armistead.
   b. Ellen Barker Armistead.
   c. Nancy Minor Armistead.
   d. West Humphreys Armistead.
   e. Wm. Christian Armistead.

Betty Humphreys, married Cary Nelson Weissiger, and had:

a. Cary Nelson Weissiger, Jr., born January 22, 1882.
b. Mary Weissiger, born October 4, 1886.
c. Elizabeth Weissiger.
d. Lucy Page Weissiger.

D. Caroline Douglas Meriwether, daughter of Chas. N. M. Meriwether and Caroline Barker, was born November 4, 1833, married M. C. Goodlett, and had:

1. Caroline Goodlett, born October 3, 1871, married, and has two sons.

E. Dr. William Douglas Meriwether, born January 1, 1837, was living with his daughter in New Orleans January 1, 1924. He married first, Mariah Kimbrough Winston; married second, Mrs. Mattie Gilmer Chase. Issue by first marriage:

1. Elizabeth Meriwether, born November 18, 1861, married Geo. O. Gilmer. No issue. (Under the name, "Dorothy Dix", she is a well known writer.)
2. Mary Meriwether, born February 1, 1863, married Geo. M. Patch.
3. Chas. Edward Meriwether, born April 7, 1869.

James Hunter Meriwether, son of Dr. Chas. and Mary (Walton) Daniel Meriwether, was born March 1814, died August 11, 1890, married Lucinda Elizabeth McClure, 1840. She was only child of Mr. McClure and his wife, Mary Overton who was sister of Judge William Overton and of Elizabeth Overton who married Lewis Taylor. Issue: (8 children)

A. Mary Overton Meriwether, born 1841, married 1866, Mr. Rowley.

B. Elizabeth Lewis Meriwether, born 1844, married 1876, Mr. Barker.

C. James McClure Meriwether, born 1846, married 1879, Margaret Douglas Barker.

D. Chas. Nicholas Meriwether, born 1849, married 1872, Miss Tutwiler.

E. John Walton Meriwether, born 1851, married 1877, Jennie Ballard.

F. Wm. Douglas Meriwether, born 1854, married 1883, Marion Walton Barker who was twin sister of Margaret D. Barker, James's wife.

G. Hunter McCann Meriwether, born 1861, married Lucy Underwood Western. Issue:

1. Wm. Western Meriwether.

H. Gilmer Meriwether, born 1864, never married.

Issue of Mary O. Meriwether and Robert Rowley:

1. Meriwether Rowley, born 1868.
2. Robina Rowley, born 1870.
3. Kelse Rowley, born 1873.
4. Lucy Rowley, born 1875.
5. Robert Rowley, born 1879.

Issue of Elizabeth Lewis Meriwether and Alex. M. Barker:

1. Lucy Barker, born August 17, 1874.
2. James M. Barker, born May 15, 1878.

Issue of James McClure Meriwether and Margaret D. Barker:

1. Richard Barker Meriwether, born 1879.
2. Mary Meriwether, born 1884.
3. Louisa Meriwether, born 1888.

Issue of Wm. D. Meriwether and Marion Walton Barker:

1. Margaret Meriwether, born 1889.

Issue of Chas. N. Meriwether and Miss Tutwiler:

1. Lucy McC. Meriwether, born August 1873.
2. Robert T. Meriwether, born January, 1875.
3. Henry Meriwether, born January, 1879.
4. Lenny Meriwether, born February, 1881.
5. Nicholas H. Meriwether, born 1886.
6. Paoli A. Meriwether, born 1888.

Issue of John Walton Meriwether and Jennie Ballard:

1. Walton Meriwether, born 1886.

Francis Thornton Meriwether, of Bedford, fifth child of Nicholas Meriwether and Margaret Douglas, born November 5, 1768 or 9, died June 1814, married June 2, 1793, Catherine Eliza Davies, born November 19, 1772. Issue: (10 children)

A. Elizabeth M. Meriwether, born October 14, 1798, died May 15, 1821, married Nov. 27, 1817 as first wife to Walker D.

Meriwether. Issue:

1. Frank T. Meriwether, died in youth.

B. George Douglas Meriwether, born May 26, 1797, died 1828, married Alice T. Lewis. No remaining issue.

C. Harriet Anne Meriwether, born February 22, 1801, married Arthur Davies. No issue.

D. Mary Catherine Whiting Meriwether, born 1803, died 1804.

E. Francis Meriwether, M. D., born August 26, 1805, died April 21, 1834, married June 8, 1826, Margaret D. Meriwether, and had:

1. Charles J. Meriwether, born March 27, 1831, married Ellen D. Meriwether, and had:
   a. James Addison Meriwether, married Emily Harris.
   b. Betty Meriwether.
   c. Margaret D. Meriwether.
   d. William D. Meriwether.
   e. Charles Meriwether.
   f. Bernice Meriwether.
   g. Francis Meriwether.
2. Mary Walker Meriwether, born April 29, 1833, died 1864. Married Thomas J. Randolph, Jr., and had:
   a. Frank Meriwether Randolph, died Sept., 1922, m. Charlotte N. Macon, lived at "Cloverfields."
   b. Thomas Jefferson Randolph.
   c. Margaret D. Randolph.
   d. Jane N. Randolph.
   e. Francis Nelson Randolph.
   f. Geo. Geiger Randolph.

   *Note.*—Thomas Randolph married second, Charlotte Nelson Meriwether, daughter of Dr. T. W. Meriwether and Nanny Page. Issue:

   g. Mary Walker Randolph.
   h. Charlotte N. Randolph.

F. James Addison Meriwether, son of Francis T. Meriwether and Catherine Davies, was born May 12, 1812, married November 28, 1832, Elizabeth Whiting Davis. Issue:

1. Mary C. Meriwether, married Mr. Clay.

2. Ellen Douglas Meriwether, married Charles I. Meriwether. Issue:
   a. James Addison Meriwether, married Emily Harris.
   b. Betty Addison Meriwether, married Mr. Scruggs.
   c. Wm. Douglas Meriwether, married Lula Oglesby.
   d. Margaret Douglas Meriwether, married Edon D. Dawson. Issue:
      1. Katherine Dawson.
   e. Charles Meriwether.
   f. Mary W. Meriwether.
   g. Bernice Meriwether, married 1898, Wm. Rucker.
   h. Francis Meriwether, married Emily Pettyjohn.
3. Kate Douglas Meriwether, second wife of Wm. H. Meriwether of Virginia and Texas. No issue.
4. Marbury Meriwether, unmarried.
5. Fanny E. Meriwether, married Henry Sommerville, had:
   a. Charles J. Sommerville.
6. Margaret D. Meriwether.
7. Nannie Meriwether.
8. Frank Meriwether.

Issue of James Addison Meriwether and Emily Harris:

1. Louise D. Meriwether.
2. Emily H. Meriwether.
3. Margaret D. Meriwether, married Henry Coon, of California, and had:
   a. Judith Coon.
4. James A. Meriwether, m. Madeline O'Hara, and had:
   a. James Meriwether.
   b. John Robert Meriwether.
5. Mary Walker Meriwether, married J. Perrow Williams, and had:
   a. James Perrow Williams.
   b. Charles Addison Williams.
6. Charles Meriwether.

Issue of William Douglas Meriwether and Lula Oglesby:

1. Charles J. Meriwether.
2. Randolph Meriwether.

3. Robert Meriwether.
4. Francis Meriwether.
5. Douglas Meriwether.
6. Lodewick Meriwether.
7. Otey Meriwether, married 1925, age 21.

Issue of Elizabeth Meriwether and Mr. Scruggs:

1. Ellen Scruggs.
2. John Scruggs.
3. Edward Scruggs.
4. Mary Scruggs.
5. Addison Scruggs.

Issue of Bernice Meriwether, married 1898, William Rucker:

1. Addison Rucker.
2. Lile Rucker.
3. Ellen Rucker.
4. Emily Rucker.
5. Charlotte Rucker.

Issue of Francis Meriwether, married Emma Pettyjohn:

1. Mary W. Meriwether.
2. Alice Meriwether.
3. Ruth Meriwether.
4. Helen Meriwether.
5. William Meriwether.

Issue of Mary Colle Meriwether, daughter of James Addison Meriwether and Elizabeth Whiting Davis, and her husband, Mr. Cyrus Clay.

1. Boyles Davis Clay.
2. Calhoun Clay.

And others.

G. Henry Landon Meriwether, born March 19, 1794, son of Francis and Catherine Eliza Meriwether. Died infant.

H. Margaret D. Meriwether, born December 1795, died infant.

I. Samuel Boyle Meriwether, born 1809, died infant.

J. William Nicholas Meriwether, fifth son of Francis Meriwether and Catherine E. Davies, born November 12, 1810, died November 8, 1887, married March 28, 1833, Martha Louisa

Manson. They lived at "Pebbleton", Bedford County, Va. Issue: (8 children)

1. Nat Manson Meriwether, born 1836, died 1880, unmarried.
2. Francis Thornton Meriwether, born March 16, 1838, died December 28, 1919, married May 2, 1872, Elizabeth J. Dawson, had:
   a. James Dawson Meriwether, born 1874, died 1880.
   b. Chas. Louis Meriwether, born 1877, married Marie Naxera.
3. William Nicholas Meriwether, Jr., born May 12, 1840, married Nov. 4, 1867, first, Mary E. Davis, and had:
   a. Wm. Nicholas Meriwether, born June 1, 1871.
   b. Mary Alice Meriwether, born September 29, 1872.
   c. John Davis Meriwether, born January 7, 1874, married Louise ——.
   d. Francis Edward Meriwether.
   e. Sally Walker Meriwether.
   f. Geo. Douglas Meriwether.
   g. Mary Bell Meriwether.
   h. James L. Meriwether.

   Wm. N. Meriwether, married second, 1889, Kate Pollard, had:
   i. William Pollard Meriwether..
   j. Garrett Meriwether.
4. George Douglas Meriwether, born September 22, 1842, married Martha Sale, had:
   a. Louisa Meriwether, born 1888, died 1910.
5. John Lee Meriwether, born July 22, 1845, unmarried.
6. Emmet Manson Meriwether, born June 4, 1848, married May 1871, Lizzy Douglas Clark, daughter of Chas. J. Clark and —— Roberts, his wife. (See Margaret D. Lewis and James Clark record.)
   Issue:
   a. Mary Christian Meriwether, born Sept. 22, 1872.
   b. Martha Louise Meriwether, born Sept. 14, 1874.
   c. Bessie Meriwether, died in infancy.

7. Sally Manson Meriwether, born June 20, 1850, unmarried.
8. James Addison Meriwether, born October 1, 1852, married 1891, Ann Clay. No issue.

Descendants of William Nicholas Meriwether and his wife, Martha Louise Manson are still living in Bedford County, Va. and also at Louisiana, Missouri, to which State some of them emigrated.

---

*Note.*—Francis Thornton Meriwether, son of Wm. N. Meriwether and M. L. Manson was born at "Pebbleton", Bedford County, Va. In this home of Christian influences and culture he developed into a ripe scholar, a teacher of rare ability and a Christian whose precepts and example became a wide influence.

1860 he graduated from the University of Virginia—his instructers; Professors Mcguffy, Shele de Vere, Gesner Harrison and Gildersleeve.

The high testimonials written for him by Prof. McGuffy and Prof. Schele de Vere he kept with his diploma. While a student at the University of Virginia the first Y. M. C. A. was formed there. He joined it and taught in a Sunday School in the near Ragged Mountains. He was a member of the Kappa Alpha fraternity there. When past 70 years of age he was a special guest of the Chicago Kappa Alpha annual banquet—his expenses borne by them—in their wish to show special honor to one of the survivors of the oldest University of Virginia fraternity.

In the War Between the States he served in Company G, Second Virginia Cavalry, Army of Northern Virginia.

After the War he came to Missouri. He was superintendent of schools, as well as accomplished teacher. Also a writer of ability of historic descriptive articles which met flattering approval. July 1st, 1900 his "Battle of Manassas" was published in the *Confederate Veteran* the summer of the reunion at Gettysburg, 1913.

His Christian belief shown in every act of his life, was fully asserted in his article—"The Resurrection of the Body." In 1872 he was one of the organizers of the Episcopal Church at Clarkesville.

Descended from Parson William Douglas of Virginia, he was confirmed in his youth, was steadfast in his service to his Maker and his Church, constant in attendance to its services, taught in its Sunday School and was vestryman and treasurer up to the time of his death. His life was filled with service in positions of trust.

He married Miss Elizabeth James Dawson, daughter of James L. and Susan (Harvie) Dawson, of "Top Lofty", Lincoln County, Missouri. He had two children, the oldest died in childhood. The other, Dr. Chas. Louis Meriwether was named in honor of his grandmother, Louisa Manson, and his Aunt Charlotte, regardless of sex.

He was buried at Old St. John's Church in whose cemetery sleep many Meriwethers. In spite of the bitter cold the crowded church bore testimony to the veneration in which he was held by all.

> "How true he was—how gracious—how sincere,
> How wept—how honored—by the friends he loved,
> Ennobled himself—by all approved—
> Peace to his manly soul—and sweetest rest—
> With that glad throng whom love of God has blest."

His little grandson Chas. Louis Meriwether, Jr., son of Dr. Chas. Louis Meriwether, at 5 years old, was a regular harvest hand at 75 cents per day—riding on Dolly hauling hay to the hay stacks. His grandfather in Europe, and the farm in charge of his 17-year-old uncle, a missing hand caused the choice to fall on Charles to meet the emergency. He rose early, rubbed his eyes, and on Dolly's back began the hot day's job of hauling hay. He said, "Some days seemed as long as from here to Europe." His mother going to see how it was with him was proud to see how he stuck to his job. Of German descent on his mother's side—on his father's he came from Col. Nicholas Meriwether (Colonial) and from Col. Wall of the Revolution. His heredity entitles him to membership in "The Sons of Colonial Wars"—and and "The Sons of the Revolution" but no titles are greater honor than that of "The Youngest Harvest Hand," in Pike County, Missouri.

Mrs. Lizzy (Dawson) Meriwether survived her husband, Francis Meriwether and is yet living (1925). She is well known for her own abilities—in literary requirement, as a writer, and her activities in patriotic and benevolant societies.

Continued record of Thomas Meriwether and his wife, Elizabeth Thornton, who was daughter of Col. Francis Thornton, of "Snow Creek", and Mary Taliaferro.

Francis Meriwether, second son of Thomas and Elizabeth Meriwether, was born October 31, 1737, married Martha Jamieson, sister of Col. Jamieson of the Revolutionary War. Francis Meriwether was spoken of by all who knew him as "The best man in the world." He had studied medicine but used his knowledge for the relief of the sickness around him without charge. He laid out a portion of his crops every year in medicines. He was without pride or vanity and of scrupulous honesty. When reminded by his son that a horse he sold was not worth the price paid, he returned the surplus to the buyer. He emigrated to Georgia 1784, and from that State descendants are widely scattered.

Issue:

A. Thomas Meriwether, married Rebecca Mathews.
B. Valentine Meriwether, married Barbara Cosby.
C. Mary Meriwether, married Wm. Barnett.
D. Elizabeth Meriwether, married Wm. Matthews.
E. Mildred Meriwether, married Joel Barnett.
F. Margaret Meriwether, married John Bradley.
G. D. Nancy Meriwether, married Wm. Glenn.
H. Lucy Meriwether, married Groves Howard.
I. Sarah Meriwether, married James Olive.
J. Nicholas Meriwether, married Mary De Yampert, and lived in Montgomery County, Alabama.

Issue of Thomas Meriwether and Rebecca Matthews: (5 ch.)

1. Frank Meriwether, married Miss Butler. No issue.
2. Dr. Geo. Meriwether, married Miss Watkins, and had:
    a. Georgie Ann Meriwether.
3. David Meriwether, married four times; first, Miss Marks, and had Emily.

    Married second, Ann Reese. No issue.

    Married third, Miss Broadus, and had Geo. Meriwether, Rebecca and Mary Meriwether.

    Married fourth, Miss Young, and had: Sally Meriwether, Louisa Meriwether, Thomas Meriwether and David Meriwether, who married Mattie Mastin of Tennessee, and had:

Mary Meriwether, married Harry Anderson.
Wheeler Meriwether, married Miss Klock.

4. Ann Meriwether, daughter of Thomas and Rebecca (Matthews) Meriwether, married Fleming Jordan, and had: two sons and two daughters.
5. Mary Gaines Meriwether, married Dr. David Addison Reese, and had:
    a. Frank M. Reese.
    b. George Reese.
    c. Ann S. Reese.
    d. Rebecca M. Reese.

Issue of Valentine Meriwether, son of Francis and Martha Jamieson Meriwether, and Barbara Minor Cosby:

1. Mrs. Dansby, of Alabama.
2. Mrs. Dansby, of Alabama.
3. Rebecca Meriwether, married Wm. White.
4. Mildred Meriwether, married Chas. Taliaferro.
5. Lucy Meriwether, married Judge Madison McGhee.
6. Chas. Meriwether, moved to Mississippi, died in Hernando.
7. Frank Meriwether, married and died in Georgia.

Issue of Mary Meriwether and William Barnett:

1. Martha Jamieson Barnett, married Francis Meriwether Gilmer. (See Mildred T. and Dr. John Gilmer record.)
2. Thos. Meriwether Barnett, married Margaret Micon.
3. Nathaniel Barnett, married Miss Hudson.
4. Mary Barnett, married David Taliaferro.
5. Lucy Barnett, married Geo. E. Matthews.
6. Frances Barnett, married Isaac Ross.

Issue of Elizabeth Meriwether and William Matthews:

1. Anne Matthews, married Nicholas Marks.
2. George Elbert Matthews, married Lucy Barnett.
3. Frank Matthews, married Sarah Burgin.

4. Charles Matthews, died unmarried.
5. Samuel Matthews, died unmarried.

Issue of Mildred Meriwether, and Joel Barnett:

1. Chas. Barnett.
2. Frank Barnett, married Miss Sarah.
3. A daughter, married Lewis Gilmer.
4. Jane Barnett, married John Gilmer.

Issue of Nicholas Meriwether and Mary De Yampert, of Montgomery, Ala.:

1. James B. Meriwether, married Sophia Taliaferro.
2. Thomas Meriwether, married Matilda Baldwin.
3. Geo. Meriwether, married Sarah Fitzpatrick.
4. Chas. Lewis Meriwether, married Fanny Baldwin.
5. Nicholas Meriwether, married Mrs. Susan Hazzard.
6. Wm. Meriwether, married Clara Baldwin.

*Note:*

MERIWETHER—TAYLOR—TALIAFERRO AND DE YAMPERT

Zachariah Taliaferro, born in Amherst County, Va., 1759. At 18 years of age was a private soldier in the Revolution and served to the end of the war as testified by the permit for him to practice law in South Carolina.

After the Revolutionary War he studied law and first practiced in the Virginia courts. Then removed to South Carolina near Pickensville, where he practiced until the courts of that place were abolished 1800.

In 1802 he returned to Virginia, and married Margaret Chew Carter, daughter of John Carter and Hannah Chew, of Caroline County. He settled three miles east of Pendleton, and continued to practice law until 1826, died 1831. He and his wife are buried in the graveyard at this home.

Issue:

1. Sarah A. Taliaferro, married Dr. O. R. Broyles.
2. Lucy Hannah Taliaferro, married Col. David S. Taylor.
3. Mary Margaret Taliaferro, married Major Richard P. Simpson.
4. Caroline Virginia Taliaferro, married Dr. H. C. Miller.

Issue of Zachary Taliaferro Taylor and Mary Meriwether:

1. Mary Rosa Taylor, married Lou De Yampert.
2. Zachariah T. Taylor, married Alma Rogers.
3. Joseph P. Taylor, married.
4. David S. Taylor, married Rebecca De Yampert.
5. James M. Taylor, married Sally Taylor Tupper.
6. William S. Taylor, unmarried.
7. Samuel G. Taylor, married Sally Tucker.
8. Gertrude Taylor, married Price Benson.

No further record.

History of Old Pendleton District with Genealogies of the Leading Families of the District S. C., by Richard Wright Simpson.

David Meriwether, third son of Thomas and Elizabeth Thornton Meriwether, married Mary Harvey. Issue:

A. Lewis B. Meriwether, married Elizabeth Johnson.
B. Martha Meriwether, married Benjamin Taliaferro.

Mary Meriwether, fourth child of Thomas Meriwether and Elizabeth T. Meriwether, married Peachy Ridgeway Gilmer, son of the emigrant, Dr. Geo. Gilmer of Williamsburg. Issue:

A. Thomas Gilmer, married Elizabeth Lewis, and lived in Georgia. Issue:
    1. Peachy R. Gilmer, married Mary Harvie.
    2. Thos. L. Gilmer, married Nancy Harvie.
    3. Mary M. Gilmer, married Mr. Taliaferro.
    4. Geo. Rockingham Gilmer (Governor of Georgia), married Eliza Frances Grattan.
    5. John Gilmer, married Lucy Johnson.
    6. Wm. Blackburn Gilmer, married Miss Marke.
    7. Chas. Lewis Gilmer, married Miss Marks.
    8. Mary Ann Gilmer, married B. L. Bibb.
B. Geo. Gilmer, lived in Rockingham, Va. where he married.
C. Elizabeth Thornton Gilmer, married Maj. Robt. Grattan, of Rockingham County. The old Grattan home is in that county. Issue:
    1. Eliza Frances Grattan, married Governor Geo. Rockingham Gilmer of Georgia.

2. Robert Grattan, married Pattie Minor of Ridgeway, Albemarle County. They lived at the old Grattan home, Rockingham. Issue:
   a. Lucy Grattan, married Maj. Geo. Chrisman.
   b. Chas. Grattan, married Elizabeth C. Finley.
   c. Geo. Grattan, married E. Heneberger.
   d. Peter Grattan, killed at Yellow Tavern.
   e. Robert Grattan, died in C. S. A.
   f. Louisa Grattan, married Thomas Doyle.
   g. John Grattan, died.
   h. Mary Grattan, married J. F. Robertson.
3. Judge Peachy R. Grattan, son of Elizabeth Gilmer and Maj. Grattan, married Miss Ferguson, and had a son and two daughters.
4. Lucy Grattan, married Dr. Geo. Harris. No issue.
5. Dr. John Grattan, of Montgomery, Alabama.

D. Lucy Gilmer, daughter of Mary Meriwether and Peachy R. Gilmer. Never married.

E. Frances Gilmer, married Richard Taliaferro.

F. Mary Peachy Gilmer. Never married.

Issue of Charles Grattan and Elizabeth Crawford Finley:

1. Mattie Grattan (Mrs. Baxter Stover), had:
   a. Elizabeth Stover.
   b. Chas. Stover.
   c. Mary Stover, m. Newton Gary Hardie, of Alabama.
2. Mrs. Warner L. Olivier, has:
   a. Warner Olivier, Jr.
3. Mary Grattan, married J. T. Stephenson.
4. Minnie Grattan, married Gilmer Weston.
5. Virginia Grattan.
6. Sarah Grattan, died.
7. Louisa Grattan, died.

Elizabeth Meriwether, married Thomas Johnson of Louisa. She was daughter of Thomas and Elizabeth Thornton Meriwether.

## JOHNSON FAMILY

Col. Richard Johnson of Lincolnshire, England came to Virginia early in the 17th Century, settled in King and Queen County, was member of Council 1696, died 1698. Married first in England, and had:

A. Judith Johnson who married Sir Hardiff Westneys.

Col. Johnson, married second, (probably in Virginia) Mary ——. Her tombstone is in King and Queen County. A son, Thomas.

Thomas Johnson, (died 1734) married Ann Meriwether. He was in the House of Burgesses from King and Queen County, 1798-1720-1722.

A. Nicholas Johnson, married Elizabeth Hudson.

B. Richard Johnson, married Dorothy Powers, Nov. 14, 1769.

C. Jane Johnson, married Richard Chapman.

D. William Johnson, married Elizabeth Hutcherson.

E. Ann Johnson, married Thomas Coke.

F. Thomas Johnson, married Ursula Rowe.

Nicholas Johnson and Elizabeth Hudson, had:

1. Thomas Johnson, Jr., married Elizabeth Meriwether.
2. Richard Johnson, married Susanna Garrett.
3. Henry Artislaw Johnson, married Annie Michie.
4. Mary Johnson, married Richard Anderson.

Thomas Johnson, Jr. served in House of Burgesses for Louisa County, 1758-1759-60-61-62-63-64-65-69-70-74-75-76, was Member of Colonial Congress, Member of Committee of Safety, Member of Convention 1774, 1776, High Sheriff of Louisa County.

He married Elizabeth Meriwether, and had:

a. Nicholas Johnson, married first, Mary Marks; married second, Miss Gilmer of Alabama.
b. Francis Johnson, married Miss Mitchell.
c. David Johnson, m. Mary Tinsley of Hanover County.
d. Thomas Johnson, married first, Harriet Washington; married second, Martha Winston.

e. Mary M. Johnson, married John Winston.
f. Elizabeth Johnson, married Rev. John Poindexter.
g. Rebecca Johnson, married Joe Winston.
h. Lucy Johnson, married William Quarles.
i. Sarah Johnson, married Richard Overton.
j. Nancy Johnson, married Charles Barrett, (parents of Dr. Layton Barrett, of Louisa Courthouse).

David Johnson, born April 7, 1778, died in Orange County, January 12, 1833. He is buried at "Bloombury", the home of his sister, Lucy Quarles. He married September 12, 1805, Mary Tinsley, daughter of Thomas and Susanna (Thomas) Tinsley. She died September 22, 1819, age 33, and is buried at the Tinsley home, "Totopotamoi" (a royal grant).

Issue:

1. Thomas Johnson, married Elizabeth Norval.
2. Lucy Ann Rebecca Johnson, married Wm. Tinsley.
3. Peter Tinsley Johnson, married first, Nannie Clack; married second, Georgianna Cave.
4. Wm. Galt Johnson, born February 11, 1813, married first, Evelina Davenport; married second Mrs. Mary Coghton.
5. Harriet Susan Johnson, died in infancy.
6. Elizabeth Johnson, died in infancy.
7. Mary Tinsley Johnson, married Samuel Crofton Greenhow, descendant of Benjamin Lewis and Martha Bickerton. Mary T. Johnson was born September 24, 1839, died August 19, 1877.

Mary Tinsley Johnson and Samuel Crofton Greenhow, had:

a. Maria Flemming Greenhow, married first, Samuel Boyle; married second, Rev. F. Baker.
b. Elizabeth L. Greenhow, married Robert H. Maury.
c. Mary Tinsley Greenhow, unmarried, and invalid. She was the originator of Home for Incurables, Richmond, Va.
d. Geo. Greenhow, married first, Ella Roberts; married second Octavia Claus, of Florida.
e. Samuel Greenhow, twin, died infant.
f. James Greenhow, twin to Samuel, died infant.
g. Fanny Nelson Greenhow.

h. Sally Williams Greenhow, died August, 1923.
i. Lucy Johnson Greenhow, m. Andrew Langstaff Johnson.
j. Harriet Greenhow, m. John Overton Smith. No issue.
k. Samuel Crofton Greenhow.

*Note:* MERIWETHER, JOHNSON AND CHAPMAN.

Ann Meriwether, seventh child of Nicholas Meriwether and Elizabeth Crawford, married Thomas Johnson, and had six children. Their daughter, Jane Johnson, married Richard Chapman, and their descendant, Jane Chapman, married Dr. Thomas Slaughter, son of Dr. Philip Slaughter.

Richard Chapman bought of his mother-in-law, Ann (Meriwether) Johnson, "Chericoke", King William County, Va.

He and Jane Johnson had:

A. Richard Chapman, Jr., married Elizabeth Reynolds, and had:
   1. Reynolds Chapman, married Rebecca Madison, and built "Berry Hill", near Orange, Va.
   2. Jane Chapman, married Dr. Thomas Slaughter, and had seven sons in Confederate service.
      a. Dr. Alfred Slaughter, surgeon, 13th Virginia Stonewall Brigade.
      b. R. Chapman Slaughter, Capt. in Engineer Corps, C. S. A., settled in Vicksburg after the war, and died there.
      c. Philip Peyton Slaughter, commanded a regiment at Cold Harbor, was terribly wounded, but lived years afterwards.
      d. James Slaughter, private in Stonewall Brigade, 13th Virginia, died years later at Meridian, Miss., of yellow fever. He never missed a battle, was never wounded and never had a furlough.
      e. Richard Slaughter, a midshipman, C. S. N., was of Jefferson Davis's escort after the surrender, died long after the war of typhoid fever.
      f. Mercer Slaughter, lieutenant in Fry's battery, was never wounded, and never missed a battle in which his battery participated.
      g. (Name not given) was a private in the Stonewall brigade.

Their grandfather, Captain Philip Slaughter, was one of seven brothers who served gallantly in the Revolution.

John Madison Chapman, son of Reynolds Chapman and Rebecca Madison, married Susan D. Coles, and had eleven children.

a. Mary Ella Chapman, married Dr. Nat. Chapman.
b. Susan Ashton Chapman, married Calvin Perkins.
c. Sally Foote Alexander Chapman.
d. Jane Slaughter Chapman, died aged 12.
e. Cora Chapman, died aged 16.
f. John Chapman, died in infancy.
g. Belle Chapman, married Wm. Moncure.
h. Ashton Alexander Chapman, m. Nanny Easton Gregory.
i. Emma Chapman, married first Capt. Robt. V. Boykin; married second Samuel Culver.
j. Constance Chapman, twin to Emma, died in infancy.

Belle Moncure and her husband, William Moncure, of Orange County, Va. and Raleigh, N. C., had issue:

1. Son.
2. Daughter.
3. Vivienne Moncure, married William Allen Butler, of New York, grandson of William Allen Butler, author of the celebrated poem, "Miss Flora McFlimsey."

William Moncure is son of Chas. Moncure and Ann Daniel, daughter of United States Supreme Court Judge Peter V. Daniel and Lucy Randolph, daughter of Edmond Randolph.

Sarah Meriwether, sixth child of Thomas Meriwether and his wife, Elizabeth (Thornton) Meriwether, born November 26, 1746, married Michael Anderson, of Louisa County, son of Pauncy Anderson and his wife Elizabeth. In his will Michael Anderson portioned to each son 500 acres of land in Kentucky.

Issue: (8 children)

1. Thomas Meriwether Anderson.
2. Ann Anderson, married Edward Thompson.
3. Pauncy Anderson.
4. Reuben Anderson.
5. William Anderson.
6. Edmond Anderson.

7. Richard Anderson.
8. Elizabeth Anderson.

(No further record known of this line.)

Lucy Meriwether, eighth child of Thos. Meriwether and Elizabeth Thornton, born February 4, 1752, died September 8, 1837, married first, 1769, Lieutenant William Lewis of "Locust Hill" (her father's first cousin). He died a short time after the siege of Yorktown in which he participated. His young widow remarried, shortly, Capt. John Marks, Revolutionary officer.

Issue by first marriage:

A. Jane M. Lewis, married Edmund Anderson—left issue. (See Anderson family.)
B. Meriwether Lewis, Private Secretary to President Jefferson and by him appointed to command the Lewis and Clark Exploration of the Missouri and Columbia Rivers. Also was Governor of Louisiana. Died unmarried.
C. Reuben Lewis, married his first cousin, Mildred Dabney. No issue.

Issue by second marriage:

D. Dr. John Marks, died unmarried. He was three years older than his sister.
E. Mary Garland Marks, born May 8, 1788, married Wm. Moore, of Broad River Settlement, Ga. They left a large family, now scattered through Alabama and Texas.

Captain Marks emigrated to Georgia and died there in Oglethorpe County. Mrs. Marks returned to "Locust Hill", Va. which was owned by Meriwether Lewis who inherited it under the primogeniture law.

Mrs. Lucy Marks, as she is best known, was a remarkable woman, possessing great firmness of character, unlimited courage and readiness of resource under all circumstances—which qualities she transmitted to her son, Meriwether Lewis, "The Explorer". Her memory is still revered by all ranks in the neighborhood where she lived, as well as by all branches of her family who are scattered through the whole United States.

Her position as head of a large family connection combined with the Spartan ideas in those stirring times of discipline developed in her, it is said, a good deal of the autocrat. Yet she is said by those who knew her well to have had much sweetness of character, to have been a devoted Christian, and full of sympathy for all sickness and trouble. As it was often impossible to obtain a physician in those days she became an authority in medical remedies and the "Locust Hill" garden yielded a crop of medicinal herbs which she dispensed under her own sound judgment.

Her activity in old age was remarkable. A grandnephew of Wm. Lewis' in passing to his home in Spotsylvania County after a tour through Kentucky and Missouri, stopped at "Locust Hill" to pay his respects to "Aunt Marks." She was not home; though between seventy and eighty years of age she had gone on horseback eight miles to minister to some one who was ill.

Many anecdotes are told of her, each illustrative of some point of character. On one occasion her first husband, Wm. Lewis, had a hunting party staying with him at "Locust Hill." The gentlemen under Wm. Lewis's guidance started out full of hope, the dogs having already gotten on the track of a deer. Later in the day the Negroes came running to their mistress to tell her a deer was passing; she ran out and made the servants with their dogs bay it in a chimney corner, then shot it herself. And the Negroes being still afraid of it, she cut its throat and had it properly prepared for the huntsmen's supper. After many hours the hunting party returned, worn out and unsuccessful, having lost the deer a short time after they left the house. Their surprise, when they went to supper and saw the saddle of venison on the table, was only surpassed when they heard of their hostess's exploit.

When she and her second husband, Captain Marks, were moving to Georgia he bade her and the wagons to start on, saying he would follow in a few hours, but meeting some friends he was detained, and did not follow for some days. Meanwhile, Mrs. Marks finding the overseer drunk and incapable of conducting the procession of vehicles and Negroes, took charge herself—riding the saddle horse of one of the wagons and driving till they reached their destined stop where Captain Marks found them later.

When the Burgoyne command of captured English was in barracks near Charlottesville, the officers under parole were allowed to visit the families in the vicinity; on one occasion some young officers calling on her blew out the light for a lark. She ordered them out, calling in the servants to insure obedience and, accounts say, emphasized it with a gun.

Raised in the Established Church she became a Methodist and gave the land on which Shiloh Church is built from the "Locust Hill" place. She died aged nearly 86 years and is buried in the old "Locust Hill" graveyard.

Mary Garland Marks and William Moore, of Georgia, had issue:

A. Lucy Jane Moore, named for her Grandmother Marks and her Aunt Jane Anderson. Lucy J. Moore married Dr. Flemming Jordan, and had:

 1. Mary Lewis Jordan.
 2. ——.
 3. Chas. Edwin Jordan.
 4. ——, married, and had issue: Lucy, Holman, Bessie, Mary, Chas., Flemming, Clara, married Mr. Alexander.
 5. Martha Jordan, married ——, issue: Flemming.
 6. Sarah J. Jordan.
 7. Lucy Gaines Jordan.
 8. Reuben Jordan.
 9. William Jordan.
 10. Turner Jordan.
 11. Maggie Jordan.
 12. Ella Jordan.

B. John Moore, civil and mining engineer, married first, Anna King; married second, Mariette Conklin.

 Issue by first marriage:

 1. Wm. Edwin Moore, married Mary Collins.
 2. Mary Moore, married first, Mr. Jones; married second, Mr. Senkler. Issue:
    a. Hattie Jones.
    b. Annie Jones.
    c. Maggie Senkler.
 3. Margaret Moore, married Mr. Meaclin, and had issue:
    a. Cornelia Meaclin.
    b. Bessie Meaclin.
    c. Hattie Meaclin.
    d. Wm. Harvey Meaclin.

Issue by second marriage:

4. Hannah Conklin Moore.
5. John Henry Moore.
6. Chapman Moore.
7. Sally Moore.
8. Cornelia Moore, married Mr. Evans, and had issue:
    a. Druce Evans.
    b. Hattie Evans.
    c. Edith Evans.
    d. John Evans.

C. Dr. Wm. H. Moore, son of Wm. and Mary Marks Moore, married Elizabeth Dixon, and had issue:

1. Matthew Moore, married first, Miss Grayham; married second, Miss Crawford.
2. Samuela Moore.
3. Lucy Barnett Moore.
4. Wm. Hastings Moore.
5. Reuben Moore.
6. Effie Moore, married Mr. Calhoun, had:
    a. Elizabeth Thornton Calhoun, married R. H. Norton.
    b. Lucy Meriwether Calhoun, m. Georges Noel Nicot.
7. Edwin Moore.
8. Elizabeth Moore.
9. Mary Moore.
10. George Moore, married Miss Merrit, had:
    a. Geo. Moore.
    b. Wm. Moore.

D. Nicholas Moore, married first, Miss Taliaferro, lived in Texas. Issue:

1. Mary Moore.
2. Margaret Moore, married Mr. Posey.

Nicholas Moore, married second, Eliza Stivins, and had:

3. Lucy Corker Moore.
4. Susan Moore, married Mr. Nelson, and had:
    a. Albert Nelson.
    b. Molly Nelson.
    c. Maggie Nelson.
5. Oscar Moore.

6. Wm. Harvey Moore.
7. Fred Moore.
8. Laura Moore.

E. Reuben Moore, died young.

F. Edmond Moore, died young.

G. Frederick Moore, merchant and manufacturer, unmarried.

H. Augustine Moore, chemist, unmarried.

I. Dr. Meriwether Moore, son of Mary Marks and William Moore, married Georgie Spratlin, and had issue:

1. Mary Moore, married Mr. Williams, and had:
    a. John D. Williams.
2. Ida Moore.
3. John Wm. Moore.
4. Annie Moore.
5. Flemming Moore.
6. Frederick Moore.

J. Judge Geo. Moore (Texas Supreme Court), married Susan Spyker. Issue:

1. Baldwin Moore.
2. Lizzie Moore, married first, Mr. Glascock; married second, Mr. Lloyd. Issue:
    a. Frank Glascock.
    b. Annie Lloyd.
3. John Moore, married Essie Grace, and had:
    a. Fleming Moore.
    b. George Moore.
    c. Mary Moore.
    d. John Moore.
4. Walker Moore.
5. Fanny Moore, married Dr. Shelton, of Nelson County, Virginia and Waco, Texas. Issue:
    a. George Shelton.
    b. Joe Shelton.
    c. Lucy Shelton.
    d. Leslie Shelton.
    e. Mary Shelton.
    f. Francis Eugene Shelton, born December, 1896.

6. Mary Moore, married Mr. Evans, and had:
   a. George Evans.
   b. Howard Evans.
   c. Aubrey Evans.
7. Susan Moore.

K. Mary Moore, youngest daughter of Wm. and Mary Marks Moore, married Mr. Yuille, a Frenchman. Issue:
1. Gavin Yuille, Jr.
2. William Yuille.

OBITUARY OF MARY (MOORE) YUILLE, NOV. 8TH MOBILE, ALA.

"Mrs. Mary (Moore) Yuille, 84 years of age, who was half niece of Meriwether Lewis, explorer of the Northwest, 1803-1806, died tonight at "Fair Hope", Barwin County, after an illness of 50 years, being an invalid nearly the entire time."

Her mother was Mary Garland Marks, half sister of Meriwether Lewis, and was a great pet with him.

EXTRACT FROM A LETTER WRITTEN BY EFFIE MOORE CALHOUN, JUNE, 1934.

"My grandmother was married at "Locust Hill" and went directly to her plantation in Georgia, which she inherited from her father, and began housekeeping in the house in which she was born. When her father died she was five years old and her father and his friend Mr. John Moore, the father of William Moore, betrothed the two little children, boy and girl—Mary Garland Marks and William Moore—in the old English fashion because their plantations adjoined. My grandmother said she never thought of marrying any one else, and when my grandfather was twenty-one he came to Virginia to see her and they were married the next spring. They lived happily together for sixty years. They had twelve children, raised seven sons and two daughters; and I can say with pardonable pride that in whatever community they lived these seven sons were loved and respected by all, both rich and poor."

Mildred Meriwether, ninth child of Thomas Meriwether and Elizabeth Thornton, was born July 25, 1763, married March 22, 1771, John Gilmer, born April 26, 1748. Issue: (nine children)

A. Dr. John Thornton Gilmer, born in Amherst County, Va., February 20, 1774. Married October 4th, 1803, Martha Gaines Harvie, and left nine children, many of whom emigrated to Georgia and Missouri.

B. Nicholas Meriwether Gilmer, born May 25, 1776, married Amelia Gatewood Clark. They lived in Kentucky and Tennessee on the State line.
C. George O. Gilmer, married Miss Johnson—issue four children.
D. Francis Gilmer, married Martha Jamison Barnett—issue seven children.
E. David Gilmer, married Virginia Clark—issue six children.
F. Harrison Blair Gilmer, the eldest daughter, married Gabriel Christian, a Methodist minister—issue six children.
G. Elizabeth V. Gilmer, married Wm. McGehee.
H. Sally Gilmer, married Mr. Taliaferro.
I. Jane Mildred Gilmer, daughter of John and Mildred Gilmer, was born June 4, 1792, married first, Thos. Johnson; married second, Abner McGehee. Issue:
   1. Elizabeth McGehee, married James Gilchrist.
   2. Sarah McGehee, married Mr. Graves.

These families live in Alabama and Georgia.

Jane Meriwether, born April 3, 1757, youngest child of Thomas and Elizabeth T. Meriwether, married 1776, Samuel Dabney, of Louisa County. Issue:

A. Wm. Dabney.
B. Samuel Dabney.
C. Thomas Dabney.
D. Elizabeth Dabney.
E. George Dabney.
F. Charles Dabney, married Miss Price, of Hanover. Issue:
   1. Wm. Dabney.
   2. Rev. Robert Lewis Dabney, Historian and Theologian, Stonewall Jackson's Chief of Staff; Professor at Union Theological Seminary of Virginia., and of Divinity, University of Texas. He married Lavinia Morrison. Issue:
      a. Charles Wm. Dabney, born June, 1855. He has filled many positions of note, among them was President of University of Cincinnati 1904-1920. He married Mary Brent, of Paris, Ky., August 24, 1881.
      b. Samuel Dabney, well known lawyer of Houston, Texas, married and has several children.
      c. Lewis Dabney.

3. Frank Dabney.
4. Ann Dabney, married Mr. Payne. No issue.
5. Betty Dabney, married Mr. Johnson, and had two sons and a daughter, Harriet.
6. George Dabney, married Louisa Dabney, has:
    a. Frank Dabney.
    b. Robert Dabney.

G. Frank Dabney, son of Jane Meriwether and Samuel Dabney, Captain U. S. A. 1812, died unmarried 1847.

H. Richard Dabney, poet, burned to death in the Richmond Theatre.

I. Mildred Dabney, married Reuben Lewis, brother of Meriwether Lewis. No issue. Buried at "Locust Hill."

K. Edmund Dabney, married Ann Blount.

L. John Dabney, married Eliza Blount.

M. Samuel Dabney, married first, Miss Hopkinson, and had issue:
1. Samuel Dabney, married Cordelia Minor, of "Woodlawn", Orange County, Va., and had issue: 5 children.
2. Wm. Dabney, married Fredonia Marable. No issue.
3. John Lewis Dabney. Never married.
4. Jane Dabney, married Dr. Thos. Rivers, and had issue:
    a. Dr. Thomas Rivers, Jr., of Paducah, Kentucky.
5. Mildred Dabney, married Jack Rivers.
6. Martha Dabney, married Mr. Caldwell.

Samuel Dabney, married second, Elizabeth Jane Harrison, of Caswell County, N. C. Issue:

7. Frank Dabney.
8. Edmund R. Dabney, married Ellen V. Manson. Left large issue.
9. Almira Dabney, married John F. Hughes.
10. Margaret L. Dabney, married O. F. Vance, of Memphis, Tenn., and had three children.
11. Elizabeth Dabney, married David Wall.
12. Louisa Dabney, married Geo. F. Dabney, of Bay St. Louis, La.
13. Lucy Dabney, married Col. C. H. Smith.

THIS ENDS THE RECORD OF DESCENDANTS OF THOMAS AND ELIZABETH THORNTON MERIWETHER.

## NICHOLAS MERIWETHER

Nicholas Meriwether, the third son of David Meriwether and Ann Holmes, married Mary Pryor (or Frances Morton). Issue:

1. Nicholas Meriwether, born 1741, died 1741.
2. John Meriwether, born and died 1743.
3. Reuben Meriwether, born December 15, 1743, married Miss Dorsey, died 1800. He was a member of Congress.
4. George Meriwether, born 1745, died 1782.
5. Ann Meriwether, died in infancy.
6. Nicholas Meriwether, born June 4, 1749, died 1828.
7. Mary Meriwether, born March 1, 1752, married Dr. Shadrach Vaughan. (Descendants, Keans and Vaughans of Goochland County, Va.)
8. Francis Meriwether, born 1754, died 1757.

Issue of Reuben Meriwether and Miss Dorsey, of Howard County, Maryland:

a. Thomas Beal Dorsey Meriwether, born September 29, 1786, died July 24, 1836 in Howard County, Md. He married Maria Handy February 15, 1810. She was born October 21, 1795, died July 27, 1848. Issue:
    1. Eleanor Jane Meriwether, died unmarried.
    2. Sarah Ann Meriwether, married Dr. R. R. Riggs.
    3. Reuben H. Meriwether.
    4. Thomas B. Meriwether.
    5. Margaret Elizabeth.
    6. Camilla Meriwether.

b. Nicholas Meriwether, married Elizabeth Hood. He lived at Elk Ridge, Howard County, Md. He was born June 14, 1778, died 1872 at West Liberty, Ohio. Issue:
    1. Reuben Meriwether, born 1803, died 1885.
    2. John Hood Meriwether, died 1863, left seven children.
    3. Rachel Meriwether, born March 5, 1805, died February 4, 1842, married Romulus Riggs Griffith, of Baltimore.
    4. James H. Meriwether, died December 21, 1846 at Cincinnati, Ohio, married Miss Jupalitz. No issue.
    5. Thomas H. Meriwether, died 1850 at Springfield, Ohio. Unmarried.

6. Elizabeth H. Meriwether, died unmarried, 1850.
7. Sarah Meriwether, married Reuben Dorsey of Howard County, Md., and had:
   a. Sally Dorsey, married Dr. Rogers, and had two sons.
8. Nicholas Meriwether, died 1850 at Cincinnati, married Miss Gateman, and had five or six children.
9. William Meriwether, born 1815, died 1869 in Covington, Ky., married Rachel Ann Hood, and had a son and daughter.

c. Mrs. Charles Hammonds lives in Maryland.
d. Mrs. Daniel Warfield lives in Maryland.

Issue of George Meriwether, son of Nicholas and Mary Pryor Meriwether, and his wife, Martha:

a. Reuben Meriwether, died at 20 years of age.
b. Frances Meriwether, married first, Basil Prather, and had five children; married second, James R. Williams. Three of her children left issue.

   Mary Prather, married Elias Newman. Thomas Prather, married Miss Cox. Martha Prather, married Warwick Miller. All of Louisville, Kentucky.

Issue of Nicholas Meriwether, son of Mary Pryor and Nicholas Meriwether, and his wife, Elizabeth Thornton:

a. Frances Meriwether, married Martin Daniel.
b. Morton Meriwether, born 1773, died 1784.
c. Nicholas Meriwether, born 1775, died 1784.
d. Richard Meriwether, born October 10, 1777, married first, Elizabeth Thornton; married second, Susannah Thornton, daughter of Dr. Henry F. Thornton (Anthony—Anthony—Francis—William), and his wife, Ann Rose Fitzhugh, of Bel-Air, Stafford, Va.
e. William Meriwether, born 1782, died 1784.

Issue of Richard Meriwether and first wife, Elizabeth Thornton:

1. Richard Meriwether, died unmarried.

Issue by second wife, Susannah Thornton:

2. Thornton Meriwether, born 1824, died March 1868, married July 12, 1864, Elizabeth Davis Allen.
3. Anthony Meriwether.

4. Elizabeth Meriwether, born 1831, died 1854.
5. George W. Meriwether.

Issue of Thornton Meriwether and his wife, Elizabeth D. Allen:

a. Sue Thornton Meriwether, born August 14, 18—, married James Williamson Henning, September 6, 1887, and had:
    1. Sue Meriwether Henning, born July 29, 1888.

## DAVID MERIWETHER

David Meriwether, son of Col. David and Ann Holmes Meriwether, was called "English David" or "Sailor David" as he sailed a merchantman vessel between England and America. He was born October 5, 1726, married Mary Weaver, of England. Issue:

1. Thomas Meriwether, unmarried.
2. General James Meriwether (D. S.), married Susan Hatcher, 1817, in Georgia.
3. David Meriwether, married Miss Smith and lived in Coweta County, Georgia.
4. Elizabeth Meriwether, married first, Mr. Patterson; married second, Mr. Carson.

Issue by first marriage:

a. Mrs. Early.
b. Mrs. Sturges.

Issue by second marriage:

c. Elizabeth Carson, married Mr. Abercrombie, of Georgia.

Issue of Gen. James Meriwether (D. S.) and Susan Hatcher:

a. Alexander Meriwether, ordinary of Dooley County, Ga.
b. James A. Meriwether, member of Congress from Georgia 1841-1843, was one of the Supreme Court judges of Georgia, member of State Legislature and speaker of the House of Representatives at the time of his death, 17th of April, 1843.
c. Mrs. Thomas M. Berrian.
d. Mrs. Dr. Robins.

Issue of David Meriwether and his wife, Miss Smith:

a. George Meriwether.
b. Stephen Meriwether, married Miss Stone.
c. Charles Meriwether, married Miss Dupree.

d. James Meriwether, married Frances Bradshaw.

Issue of James Meriwether and Frances Bradshaw:

1. Peyton S. Meriwether, born 1820, died 1891, married Charlotte Wood.
2. Mrs. Sarah Lazenby.
3. Lizzie Meriwether, married first, Mr. Lee; married second, Mr. Herring.
4. William D. Meriwether, of Newnan, Ga., married Martha D. Simmons.
5. James B. Meriwether.
6. Martha Meriwether, married Mr. Harris.
7. Cornelia Meriwether, married Mr. Stone.
8. Joseph B. Meriwether.

Issue of Peyton S. Meriwether and his wife, Charlotte Wood:

a. Fannie Meriwether, married Mr. Key, and had one daughter.
b. Preston Meriwether.
c. Irene Meriwether, married Mr. Thurmond.
d. Callie Meriwether, married Mr. Thurmond.
e. Edgar J. W. Meriwether.

Issue of William D. Meriwether and Martha D. Simmons:

a. Robert S. Meriwether, of Vicksburg, Miss.
b. Leonce Meriwether, of Brunswick, Ga.
c. James B. Meriwether, of Vicksburg, Miss.
d. Annie T. Meriwether.
e. Mattie Meriwether.
f. Fannie S. Meriwether.
g. Willie R. Meriwether.
h. Benjamin Meriwether.
i. Clara Meriwether.
j. Thomas P. Meriwether.

This family lived mostly in Newnan and Coweta County, Georgia.

## JAMES MERIWETHER

James Meriwether, seventh child of David Meriwether and Ann Holmes, was born June 1, 1729, married first, Judith Hardenia Burnley; married second, Elizabeth Pollard.

Issue by first marriage:

1. Gen. David Meriwether, born 1754 or '55, married Frances Wingfield. He died October 13, 1822.
2. Gen. James Meriwether (Dabney's Legion), born 1756, died October 24, 1801 or 1817. He married Sarah Meriwether.
3. William Meriwether, born 1760, died February 10, 1842, married Elizabeth Winslow.

Issue by second marriage:

4. John Meriwether, married Miss Bell.
5. Thomas Meriwether, married 1796, Miss Mary Anderson. (Marriage Bond in Louisa County, Va.).
6. Robert Meriwether, died unmarried.
7. Ann Meriwether, married Horatio Gates Winston.

Gen. David Meriwether, born 1754, died 1822, married 1782, Miss Frances Wingfield, of Wilkes County, Ga., and had issue:

a. John Meriwether, of Alabama.
b. Major James Meriwether, married several times—had a daughter, Fannie Meriwether who married Thomas Cobb, of Georgia.
c. Dr. Wm. Meriwether.
d. Francis Meriwether.
e. George Meriwether, married Martha M. Williams.
f. David Meriwether, married first, Miss Collier, of Alabama; married second, Miss Eliza J. Deberry, and had Mattie D. Meriwether.
g. Thomas Meriwether.
h. Judith Meriwether, married Rev. Mr. Henning. (Descendants living in Memphis, Tenn.).

George Meriwether, son of Gen. David and Frances Wingfield Meriwether, married Martha M. Williams, of Clark County, Ga. He died 1847 or '48. Issue:

1. Fannie Meriwether, married Thomas Berry, of Pearsal, Texas. Issue: one son.
2. Mary Jane Meriwether, married B. W. Humphreys, M. D. Issue:
   a. Henrietta Humphreys.

b. Fannie M. Humphreys, married J. M. Abbott, and had three boys and one girl.
c. Thomas M. Humphreys.
d. Mary M. Humphreys.
e. Mattie M. Humphreys, married Mr. J. R. Christian, of Texas, and had two sons and a daughter.
f. Maude M. Humphreys.

3. Frank Meriwether, Jackson County, Texas, married, and has children.
4. John Meriwether, died 1889, left three children.
5. George Meriwether, killed at Goliad, left five daughters. He was a lawyer and member of the Texas Legislature.
6. Thomas Meriwether, member of Texas Legislature. Issue: one son.
7. James Meriwether, of Pearsal, Texas, married, and has several sons.
8. Mattie Meriwether, married first, Mr. Huff; married second, Mr. Ramsay. Issue: two sons and three daughters.

Dr. William Meriwether, third son of Gen. David Meriwether and Frances Wingfield, married Sarah Thomas Molloy. Issue:

1. Sarah Frances Meriwether, died unmarried, age 19 years.
2. Thomas Molloy Meriwether, married four times. Married first, Henrietta L. Andrew, daughter of Bishop J. O. Andrew of the Methodist Church. She had six children, three died infants. T. M. Meriwether, married second, Mary Ann Price (no issue). He married third, Henrietta Caroline Smith (her mother was Cynthia Lewis, of Georgia, of a noted family of that State). He married fourth, Mrs. Cornelia Elizabeth Florance, née Cooper who survived him twenty-five years. No issue.

Issue of Thomas Molloy Meriwether and first wife:

a. Henry Meriwether, Confederate soldier and courier for Gen. Edward L. Thomas and was at the siege of Petersburg, died there a few weeks before the army moved to Appomattox Courthouse.

b. Ann Amelie Meriwether, died age thirty, unmarried.

c. Henrietta Elizabeth Meriwether, married James Gay Lester, had:

1. Paul W. Lester.
2. Eugene Lester.
3. Annie May Lester, married Paul Walker.

Issue by third marriage:

d. Carietta Howard Meriwether.
e. Octavia Meriwether, died age 6 years.
f. Clara Lewis Meriwether, married A. C. McMekin.
g. Fanny Fletcher Meriwether, died age 11 years.
h. Thomas Molloy Meriwether, Jr., married Neta Kendricks, and has:

1. Carolyn Meriwether.

i. Myra Osborne Meriwether, married E. C. Bullock.

Carietta Howard Meriwether is a well known writer of historical articles, author of *Grandmother's Tales of the Land of Used To Be,* a compilation of most interesting historical matter. She married Watkins Price Lovett, and has issue:

1. Isabella Lovett, died in infancy.
2. Frances Lovett.
3. Caroline Lewis Lovett (named for grandmother).
4. Heyward Meriwether Lovett, student at the University of Georgia (1925).

Gen. James (D. L.) Meriwether, son of James and Judith Meriwether, married Sarah Meriwether, daughter of William and Martha C. Meriwether. Issue, seven children:

a. William W. Meriwether, M. D., married Amanda Smith.
b. Richard Meriwether.
c. Mildred Meriwether.
d. Elizabeth Meriwether.
e. Judith Meriwether.
f. Sarah Meriwether.
g. Jane Meriwether.

Thomas Meriwether, son of James Meriwether and his second wife, Elizabeth Pollard; grandson of Col. David Meriwether and

Anne Holmes, was raised in Louisa County, Va. and married there, Miss Mary Anderson, 1796. They emigrated to Kentucky in 1806, and had issue:

A. Albert Gallatin Meriwether, died in Washington, D. C., 1848, while in service in United States Government.

B. Sarah Meriwether, married Benjamin Edwards, died 1840.

C. James Meriwether, born in Virginia 1805, died in North Missouri, 1889 (issue).

D. Elizabeth Meriwether, married Wm. Edwards, died 1855.

E. David Meriwether, died 1887 in Kentucky.

F. Martha Meriwether, married Leonard Yates, died 1888.

G. Thomas Meriwether, living in Kentucky.

Issue of James Meriwether, born 1805, who married 1828, Elizabeth McMurry:

1. Dr. Lindsay Meriwether, born in Kentucky 1829, lived in Paragould, Ark., married in 1850, Miss M. E. Chaney. Issue:
   a. Daniel W. Meriwether, married Miss Lou T.
   b. Mollie E. Meriwether, born 1853, married A. P. Mack.
   c. James Albert Meriwether, born 1858, married Ella Simmons.
   d. Lindsay C. Meriwether, born 1861, married Miss Theo. Wells.
   e. Nannie I. Meriwether, born 1866, m. John Blackshine.
   f. Jessie R. Meriwether, born 1870, married George Counts.
2. Sarah (or Mary) E. Meriwether, born 1837, married 1850, Wm. D. Keach. He died 1855. Issue:
   a. John H. Keach, died 1877.
   b. Alice M. Keach, born 1853, m. 1872, John E. Seaman.
3. David W. Meriwether, born 1838, married first, Eliza Shacklett. She died 1867. He married second, Sarah A. Brener, 1869.

   Issue by first marriage:

   a. Edgar Meriwether, born 1864, died 1871.

   Issue by second marriage:

   b. Georgiana Meriwether, born 1873.
   c. Lou Ella Meriwether, born 1875.

d. Maude Meriwether, born 1882.

This family lived in Knox County, Mo.

4. Albert G. Meriwether, born 1842, murdered in North Missouri, July, 1866 by the Union League, on account of his Southern sympathies.
5. Annie Meriwether, born 1846, married Mr. Reese, and died 1872.
6. Maggie Meriwether, born 1848, married W. M. Weber in 1871. Issue:
   a. Albert E. Weber, born 1872.
   b. Ceril H. Weber, born 1875.
   c. Ernest David Weber, born 1878.
   d. Eugene M. Weber, born 1881.

   This family live in Louis County, Mo.
7. John Thomas Meriwether, born 1851, died 1873.

Issue of William Meriwether, son of James and his first wife, Judith H. Burnley Meriwether and his wife, Elizabeth Winslow. Issue, six children:

a. James Beverly Meriwether, married Anna Smith, Shelby County, Kentucky.
b. David Meriwether, ex-Governor of New Mexico, Senator, Congressman, etc., married Sarah Leonard of Massachusetts. Issue, seven children:
c. William Meriwether.
d. Albert G. Meriwether, married first, Edna Miller; married second, Anna C. Dabney.
e. Catherine Meriwether, married Dr. Wm. Davis.
f. Thomas Meriwether, married Dorothy Dabney, daughter of General Isaac Dabney, of Kentucky.

Issue of James Beverly Meriwether, son of Wm. and Elizabeth Winslow Meriwether, married Anna Smith of Shelby County, Ky.:

1. Mildred Meriwether.
2. Emily Meriwether, married William H. Meriwether.

Issue of David Meriwether, ex-Governor of New Mexico, son of Wm. and Elizabeth Winslow Meriwether and his wife, Sarah Leonard of Massachusetts:

1. Catherine H. B. Meriwether, married Edmund Graves, of Kentucky, and had:
   a. William Graves.
   b. Edmund Graves.
   c. Charles Porter Graves.
   d. John Graves.
2. William Augustus Meriwether, married first, Lily Morselle, and had:
   a. Travilla Meriwether.

   W. A. Meriwether, married second, Mrs. Julia Morselle Tryon, and had four children.
3. James Beverly Meriwether, married first, Martha Reed; married second, Rebecca Reeder. Issue:
   a. Frank Meriwether.
   b. James Meriwether.
4. Elizabeth Winslow Meriwether, married John Williams, and had:
   a. Belle Williams.
   b. Lizzie Williams.
   c. Mary Thomas Williams.
5. Orlando R. Meriwether, married Martha Rebecca Owen.
6. Mary Leonard Meriwether, married John Bartlett, and had:
   a. Eliza Booker Bartlett, and others.
7. David Albert Meriwether, m. Alice Armistead, and had:
   a. Dixie Meriwether.

Issue of Albert Gallatin Meriwether, born 1802, died 1852, son of Wm. Meriwether and Elizabeth Winslow; and grandson of James Meriwether and Judith H. Burnley, and his wife, Edna Miller:

1. Edna C. Meriwether, married Robinson Smith, and had:
   a. Albert G. Smith.
   b. John W. Smith.
   c. Cassie Smith.

Issue by second marriage, to Mariah Catharine Dabney:

2. Wm. Winston Meriwether, married Sarah E. Trippitt. He was Captain in Confederate States service and aide to Gen.

Stephen D. Lee. William Winston Meriwether issue:
a. Ida May Meriwether.
b. Robert W. Meriwether, married Kathleen Hays.
This family lived in Paragould, Ark.

3. Robert Miller Meriwether, married Juliette O. Dabney, of Hopkinsville, Ky. Issue, three children:
   a. Winston Meriwether.
   b. Dixie Meriwether.
   c. Nettie Meriwether.
4. Hannah Anne Meriwether, married James Quigly, and had:
   a. Mattie Quigly.
5. Mariah Catharine Meriwether, married Thomas Jerdon (no issue).
6. James David Meriwether, killed in Confederate War, unmarried.
7. Sarah Chew Meriwether, married Lilburn Lewis, and had:
   a. Lilburn Lewis.
   b. Winston Lewis.
8. Harriet Winslow Meriwether, married James T. Tipton, had:
   a. Hattie Tipton.

## WILLIAM MERIWETHER

William Meriwether, born December 25, 1730, died December 24, 1790, son of David and Ann Holmes Meriwether, married Martha Cox Wood, died October 17, 1801, daughter of Henry and Martha Cox Wood, of Louisa County. William and his wife were raised in Louisa County, and emigrated to Kentucky. Issue:

1. Elizabeth Meriwether, died November 27, 1784, married Nicholas Meriwether. (Issue under Nicholas and Mary F. Pryor Meriwether).
2. Martha Meriwether, died August 1786, married George Meriwether. (Issue given under Nicholas and Mary F. Pryor Meriwether).
3. David Wood Meriwether, born 1756, died 1797, married Mary Lewis who died 1801. She was daughter of John

Lewis the "Honest Lawyer", of Spotsylvania County. [Zachary; Zachary] and his wife, Ann Lewis, daughter of Robert Lewis and Jane Meriwether.

4. William Meriwether, born 1757 or '58, died 1814, married May 24, 1788, Sarah Oldham, born 1772, died 1830, was daughter of Samuel and Jane Cunningham Oldham, of Louisa, Kentucky.
5. Mildred Meriwether, married Thomas Mitchell, died 1782.
6. Sarah Meriwether, married Gen. James Meriwether, (Dabney's Legion).
7. Valentine Meriwether, married Priscilla Pollard.
8. Ann Meriwether, born October 12, 1767, died 1820, married Major John W. Hughes.

Issue of David Wood Meriwether and his wife, Mary Lewis:

1. Anne Meriwether, born July 6, 1783, married John Burruss, and had:
   a. John Henry Burruss, born 1808, died 1882.
   b. Mary Ann Lewis Burruss, died age 8.
   c. David Nelson Burruss, born 1813, died 1853, married Frances Burruss Henly.
   d. Barbary Terrell Burruss, died unmarried.
   e. George Lewis Burruss, born February 15, 1820, married Maria J. Wood, had seven children.
   f. Barbary Terrell Burruss (2), died 1854, married Mr. Winston.
2. Martha Meriwether, married Robert Pollard. No issue.
3. Jane Meriwether, married John P. Tunstall. Several of her children intermarried with the family of Henry Wood Meriwether.
4. Henry Wood Meriwether, married 1811 his first cousin, Jane Meriwether, daughter of William Meriwether and Sarah Oldham; married second, Dorothea Lewis Hill, granddaughter of Waller Lewis and Sarah Lewis.
5. Mary Meriwether, married Dr. Samuel Meriwether, son of William and Sarah Oldham Meriwether.
6. Sarah Lewis Meriwether, born September 9, 1794, married

first, David Fernsley, January 2, 1814; married second Ebenezer Williams, September 3, 1832. She died in 1854.

Issue of Henry Wood Meriwether and first wife, Jane Meriwether: (eleven children)

1. Mariah Meriwether, born November 8, 1811, died infant.
2. Mary Meriwether, born September 25, 1814, died infant.
3. Letitia Meriwether, born October 14, 1815, married first, John Hopkins Cobb. Issue:
    a. Jane Cobb, married Wm. Goggin, and had:
        1. Fannie Goggin.
        2. Emma Goggin.
        3. Letitia Goggin.
        4. Georgia Goggin.
        5. Pleasant Goggin.

    Letitia Meriwether, m. second, Henry Johnson, and had:
    b. Fannie Johnson.
    c. Henry Johnson.
4. Mildred Meriwether, born April 5, 1817, married first, Nicholas Tunstall; married second, John Floyd. Issue:
    a. Maria Tunstall, married Frank Stewart, and had:
        1. Frank Stewart.
        2. Carrie Stewart.
    b. John Tunstall.
    c. Malcolm Tunstall.
    d. Walter B. Floyd.
    e. Alice Floyd.
5. Nicholas Henry Meriwether, born December 16, 1818, died July 20, 1885, married Mary J. Tunstall, January 22, 1839. Issue:
    a. Algernon Meriwether, born 1840, died infant.
    b. Anna Tunstall Meriwether, born 1844, died 1866.
    c. Jane Tillots Meriwether, born July 17, 1845, died January 22, 1923, married Albert H. Armstrong, of Springfield, Ill. Six of her eight children survive her.
        1. Anna E. Armstrong.
        2. Grace Armstrong.

3. Harry Armstrong.
4. Roy D. Armstrong, of Portland, Ore.
5. John D. Armstrong, Springfield, Ill.
6. Mrs. F. E. Paule, of Akron, Ohio.

d. Mary Quarles Meriwether, born 1848, died 1878, married John S. Cummings.
e. Maria Pierce Meriwether, born 1851, died 1865.
f. Henry Pierce Meriwether, born 1860.

6. Wm. Alexander Meriwether, born April 14, 1820, married Mary Gasser; married second Laura Kennaday.

Issue of first marriage:

a. Wm. A. Meriwether, Jr., married Alice Short, and had:
1. Alvira Meriwether.
2. Jennie Meriwether.

Issue of second marriage:

b. Henry W. Meriwether, married Lou Andrews.
c. Fannie Meriwether.
d. Marion G. Meriwether.

7. Marion Meriwether, born December 25, 1821, died August 29, 1873, married James W. Gilson of Jeffersonville, Ind., December 24, 1840. Issue:

a. Elizabeth Gilson, born December 9, 1841, died 1867.
b. Mary Frances Gilson, born November 1845, married October 22, 1867, M. S. Bromme, and had:
1. Loula M. Bromme.
2. S. Gilson Bromme.
3. Ada F. Bromme.

c. Sarah Gilson, born 1847, died infant.
d. Martha Gilson, born May 24, 1849, married December 14, 1871, Hugh H. Herdman, and had: (six children)
1. Hugh H. Herdman, Jr., born November 10, 1875, married and lives in Portland, Oregon.
2. Albert W. Herdman, born September 15, 1883, married and lives in Buffalo, New York.
3. Jessie W. Herdman, born 1881, died infant.

4. Marian Gilson Herdman, born June 2, 1873, died unmarried.
5. Ellis Herdman, born 1886, died infant.

e. Edward P. Gilson, born 1851, died unmarried.

f. Geo. Herbert Gilson, born September 15, 1853, married Mary Preston.

g. Henry Gilson, born 1854, died 1857.

8. Jane Meriwether, daughter of Henry Wood Meriwether and his first wife, Jane Meriwether, born 1823, died infant.
9. John Lewis Meriwether, born 1825, died 1846.
10. Martha Wood Meriwether, born October 4, 1826, married Fenelon Trabue, April 9, 1844.
11. David Samuel Meriwether, born 1828.

Issue of Martha W. Meriwether and Fenelon Trabue:

a. Olympia Trabue, born 1846.

b. Letitia Trabue, born 1850, died 1875.

c. Luther Trabue, born March 31, 1853, married Sarah Harlan, and had three children.

d. Marion Trabue, born 1855, married Robert McCause, and had:

1. Fenelon McCause.
2. Robert G. McCause.
3. Frank M. McCause.

e. Eliza Trabue, born 1857, died 1860.

f. Haskins Trabue, born 1860.

g. Aaron Trabue, born March 10, 1865.

This family now lives in Kensley, Kansas.

Issue of Henry Wood and his second wife, Dorothea Lewis Hill, married 1829, died 1860. [His first wife died August 18, 1828, he died 1856].

12. Edward Baylor Meriwether, born December 31, 1830, married September 27, 1865, Lucy A. Green, and had:

a. Edward D. Meriwether, born 1862.

13. George Lucian Meriwether, born February 20, 1832, married November 11, 1858, Elizabeth J. White, at Shipman, Illinois. Issue:

a. Eugene Meriwether, married Miss Sweet, and had:
   1. Rhoda L. Meriwether.
   2. Maude Meriwether.
   3. George Meriwether.
b. Henry W. Meriwether, born 1862, died 1868.
c. Eva Meriwether, born 1870.
d. Cora Meriwether.

14. Frederick Oscar Meriwether, born October 1, 1833, married February 22, 1855, Lititia Reynolds, and had:
a. Stella Meriwether, died infant.
b. Gertrude V. L. Meriwether, born 1858, died 1886, married July 2, 1884, John C. Davies.
c. Alfred P. Meriwether, born 1862.
d. Guy Meriwether, born 1871, married Jessie L. Brown, 1889.
e. Frank L. Meriwether.

15. Lucy Anne Meriwether, born January 28, 1835, married C. Merritt, had:
a. Ella Merritt, married George C. Kenney, and had:
   1. Ray G. Kenney.
   2. Norma Kenney.
   3. Lucy Kenney.
b. Leon E. Merritt, married Kate Stark, and had:
   1. Ella Merritt.
   2. Leon Merritt } twins.
   3. Loving Merritt }
c. Arthur H. Merritt, married Rose S. ——, and had:
   1. Bessie Merritt.
   2. Arthur Merritt.

Lucy A. Meriwether, married second, Dave Rorick, had:
d. Dave Rorick.

16. Elizabeth Meriwether, died unmarried.
17. Laura Harriet Meriwether, born April 28, 1839.
18. Samuel Arthur Meriwether, born February 5, 1843, married Sarah Baker, July 20, 1870.
19. Charles Robert Meriwether, born December 26, 1844.

20. Frank Meriwether, born September 29, 1846, died April 12, 1887.

Samuel Arthur Meriwether, married Sarah Margaret Baker, who was born December 12, 1846, near Burkeville, Kentucky, died August 15, 1922, at her home in Raymond, Illinois. She was daughter of Daniel and Lucy H. Baker. She was one of eight children, two of whom married. Madison Baker, her brother, still lives near Burkeville, Kentucky. Samuel A. Meriwether and his wife, Sarah Baker, lived first at Auburn, Ky. In 1873 they moved to Shipman, Ill., then to Raymond, Ill. Both are buried in Asbury Cemetery. He died December 22, 1912.

Issue of Samuel A. Meriwether and Sarah M. Baker:

a. Arthur B. Meriwether, who lives in the old home near Raymond, Ill.
b. Dorothea Meriwether lives in Raymond.
c. Lucy L. Meriwether lives in Raymond.
d. Elizabeth Meriwether lives in Raymond.
e. Owen W. Meriwether, of Hillsboro, Ill.
   Grandchildren: George G. Meriwether, Lyman A. Meriwether, Robert L. Meriwether, James C. Meriwether.

Sarah Lewis Meriwether, sixth child of David W. Meriwether and Mary Lewis, born September 9, 1794, married first, David Fernsley, January 2, 1814; married second, Ebenezer Williams, September 3, 1833.

Issue by first marriage:

1. Mary Rebecca Fernsley.
2. James Martin Fernsley.
3. David Henry Fernsley, M. D.
4. Wm. Joshua Fernsley.
5. Martha Elizabeth Fernsley.
6. David Albert Fernsley.

Issue by second marriage:

7. Leah Ann Williams, married Charles R. Atmore.
8. Sarah Ebenezer Williams, married Samuel Taylor Suit.

Issue of Leah Anne Williams and her husband, Charles Rawson Atmore:

a. William Ebenezer Atmore.
b. Charles Rawson Atmore.
c. Mary Lloyd Atmore.
d. Annie Atmore, married Paul Caine, December 1880, had:
    1. Sydney A. Caine.
    2. Idelle Meriwether Caine.

Issue of William Meriwether and his wife, Sarah Oldham. (He was son of William Meriwether and Martha Cox Wood.)

1. George Wood Meriwether, born October 10, 1789, married Anne E. Weir, widow of George W. Weir and daughter of John W. and Martha Blackburn Price. George Meriwether held high offices of trust under various presidents. His home, Louisville, Ky. He was also a distinguished genealogist and historian of the Meriwether family.
2. Samuel C. Meriwether, M. D., born August 10, 1791, married Mary Meriwether, daughter of David Wood Meriwether and Mary Lewis.
3. Jane Meriwether, born July 10, 1893, married David Wood Meriwether, son of David and Mary Lewis Meriwether.
4. David Holmes Meriwether, born May 6, 1795, married 1819, Lydia Clark Williams; he died December 12, 1860.
5. Valentine Meriwether, born 1797, married Lucy Carter, died 1833. No issue.
6. William J. Meriwether, M. D., born June 15, 1799, married Miss Hathaway, issue: three children. He died 1841.
7. Lewis Meriwether, born 1801, died 1859, unmarried.
8. Lucy Anne Meriwether, born April 14, 1803, married Alexander Barker.
9. Louisa Matilda Meriwether, born September 14, 1805, married Aaron M. Moffett, died February 11, 1850. No issue.
10. Caroline Meriwether, born 1806, died 1841, married William Reay.
11. Charles Scott Meriwether, born 1809, d. 1829, unmarried.

12. Mary Meriwether, born 1813, died infant.

Issue of George Wood Meriwether and his wife, Mrs. Anne (Price) Weir:

a. George Meriwether, born June 6, 18—, died unmarried, September 9, 1870.
b. Martha Price Meriwether, born February 27, 18—, died November 4, 1851.
c. Emeline Price Meriwether, born February 2, 18—, married February 9, 1876, Udolpho Snead, son of Chas. Scott Snead and Martha Raphael Snead; great-great-grandson of Gen. Chas. Scott, one of Gen. Washington's staff officers and fifth Governor of Kentucky.
d. William Meriwether, born April 8, 18—.
e. Charles Meriwether, born Aug. 30, 18—, married October 13, 1874, Patti Stewart Barbour, daughter of John and Annie Coleman Barbour, and had issue:
    1. Coleman Meriwether, born July 14, 1875.

Issue of Dr. Samuel Meriwether, son of William and Sarah Oldham Meriwether and his wife, Mary Meriwether, daughter of David Wood and Mary L. Meriwether.

a. Mary Lewis Meriwether, born October 20, 1814, died March 10, 1837, married Mr. Connor.
b. Samuel Oldham Meriwether, born 1819, died 1819.
c. Letitia Meriwether, born September 23, 1821, married James Harvie McCampbell.
d. Walter Lewis Meriwether, born April 23, 1824.
e. Samuel Ann Meriwether, born December 13, 1827, married Mr. Walker, died November 14, 1864. No issue.
f. Virginia Wood Meriwether, born May 10, 1831, died February 13, 1837.
g. Martha Louisa Meriwether, born May 26, 1834, died November 17, 1845.
h. Martha Jane Meriwether, died 1829, at age of 12 years.

Issue of Letitia Meriwether and her husband, J. H. McCampbell:

1. George Meriwether McCampbell, born September 9, 1841,

married first, Mary Jane Hall, June 27, 1866; married second, Caroline Moore, October 8, 1888.

2. Mary Jane McCampbell, born November 17, 1845, married December 18, 1866, J. K. Demarest.
3. Louisa A. McCampbell, born July 17, 1848, died August 27, 1873.
4. Margaret Allen McCampbell, born November 1, 1852, married October 21, 1883, Henry Cole Smith.
5. Annie Walker McCampbell, born May 16, 1857, married August 21, 1883, Rev. J. M. Hutchinson. Issue:

a. James Harvie McCampbell Hutchinson, born May 6, 1888, Louisville, Kentucky.

Issue of Geo. M. McCampbell and his first wife, Mary J. Hall:

a. Letitia Hall McCampbell, born November 10, 1868.
b. George Meriwether McCampbell, born October 18, 1870.
c. William Hall McCampbell, born January 28, 1872.
d. Elizabeth Anderson McCampbell, born April 10, 1874.
e. David Tilford McCampbell, born August 3, 1875.

Issue of second marriage to Catherine Moore:

f. Sarah Meriwether McCampbell, born August 27, 1887.
g. James Harvie Reid McCampbell, born October 19, 1888.

Issue of Mary Jane McCampbell and her husband, Rev. J. K. Demarest:

a. Bertha Demarest, born January 13, 1869.
b. Letitia Meriwether Demarest, born August 3, 1878.
c. Cornelius Agnew Demarest, born May 3, 1883.

Caroline Meriwether, daughter of William and Sarah Oldham Meriwether, granddaughter of William and Martha Wood Meriwether, married William Reay. Issue:

1. Sarah Jane Reay, born 1826, died 1841.
2. Charles Scott Reay, born 1826, died 1872.
3. Anne Reay, born 18—, married first, Robert D. Miller; married second, July 11, 1861, Orpheus A. Knapp. Issue:
    a. Herman M. Knapp.
    b. Charles Reay Knapp.

4. John Otto Reay, married Martha Neville in 1860, and had:
    a. John Otto Reay, born November 18, 1872.
    b. Neville Reay, born March 20, 1875.

David Holmes Meriwether, son of William and Sarah Oldham Meriwether, and grandson of William and Martha Cox Meriwether, and great-grandson of David and Anne Holmes Meriwether, great-great-grandson of Nicholas and Elizabeth Crawford Meriwether, great-great-great-grandson of Nicholas Meriwether, the Emigrant, and wife, Elizabeth Woodhouse, married Lydia C. Williams. Issue:

1. Evans W. Meriwether, married Elizabeth Armstrong.
2. Mary Jane Meriwether, m. Martin D. McHenry, and had:
    a. David M. McHenry.
3. Henry Clay Meriwether, born December 1829, was a gallant Confederate officer, died unmarried.
4. Charles Lewis Meriwether, born February 1831, unmarried.
5. Lydia Meriwether, born November 1835, married Capt. Frank Carter. No issue.
6. Emily Meriwether, born August 18, ——, married Eben Milton, 1863. Issue:
    a. David Meriwether Milton, married Ellen Fink, daughter of Albert Fink and granddaughter of A. V. Hunt, banker of Louisville, Kentucky.

Issue of David M. Milton and Ellen Fink:

1. David Meriwether Milton, Jr., married May 14, 1925, Abbie Rockfeller.
2. Albert Milton.
3. Ellen Milton.

Valentine Meriwether, son of William and Martha Cox Wood Meriwether, married Priscilla Pollard. Issue:

1. Thomas Meriwether, married Miss Woolfolk, and lived in Kentucky.
2. Priscilla Meriwether.
3. Mildred Meriwether.
4. Martha Wood Meriwether.

5. David Meriwether, moved to Indiana, name of descendants unknown; some live near Vermillion, Indiana.
6. George Meriwether, (Presbyterian minister), born December 8, 1800, married November 8, 1827, Eliza Dodds. He was born in Virginia, died in Indiana, December 12, 1847. Issue: (five children).
   a. Dr. Samuel D. Meriwether lived and died in South West, Missouri, married first, Miss Jane Bowles who had a son. Married second, Miss ——.

      Issue by first marriage:
      a. Judge Robert Meriwether, of Phelps County, Mo. married Alice Bondurant, of Louis County, Mo.

      Issue by second marriage:
      b. Charles Meriwether.
      c. Josephine Meriwether.
      d. Antoinette Meriwether.
      e. Bonaparte Meriwether.
      f., g., h. Triplets—Ada, Eda, Ida Meriwether.
   b. Valentine Meriwether, died.
   c. Thomas H. Meriwether, married Henrietta Tompson, and had:
      a. Wm. H. Meriwether, born March 15, 1863, married.
      b. Henry B. Meriwether, b. March 26, 1865, unmarried.
   d. Joseph Meriwether, married Laura M. Turner, and had issue:
      a. Joseph Derling Meriwether.
      b. Clara E. Meriwether.
      c. Frank M. Meriwether.
      d. Ella Bessie Meriwether.
      e. Thomas Dewitt Meriwether, married Stella Lieche.
      This family is of Pike County, Louisiana, Mo.
   e. George R. Meriwether, married Jane Gregory, lived in La Belle County, Mo. Issue: (nine children).
      a. Mary Jane Meriwether, born 1855.
      b. Thomas H. D. Meriwether, born 1857, married.
      c. Annie E. Meriwether, born 1859.
      d. Elizabeth L. Meriwether, born 1863.

e. Richard H. Meriwether, born 1866.

f. Walter G. Meriwether, born 1869.

g. Hattie A. Meriwether, born 1871.

h. Wm. H. Meriwether, born 1876.

i. Georgie Meriwether, born 1880.

Anne Meriwether, eighth child of William and Martha Cox Wood Meriwether, married Major John Neville Hughes. He was born in Powhatan County, Va., August 11, 1763, at the age of 15 he left Hampden-Sydney College and enlisted in the Revolutionary army, and served until the close of the war. At the age of twenty he married Anne Meriwether, and they were the parents of twenty-six children, fourteen of whom arrived at maturity. He went West in 1786. Served again in the second war with England in 1812, died at his farm on the Ohio River six miles below Louisville, December 11, 1842. He survived all of his children but five. His wife died in 1820.

"His granddaughter, Miss Martha Hughes of Jefferson County, Ky. now (1890) over 70 years of age, is of bright intellect and full of genealogical lore."

(Extract from *The Meriwethers* by Louisa H. A. Minor, of Virginia and Eolia, Pike County, Mo.).

Issue of Anne Meriwether and John N. Hughes: (twenty children given).

1. John Hughes, born October 18, 1784, died November 4, 1847, married Esther Cox, and had issue:
   a. Judith A. Hughes, born 1810, married Robert Sadler, of England.
   b. Richard T. Hughes, born December 1815, married Sarah J. Hughes.
   c. Martha Hughes, born 1818, unmarried—living in 1890 on the old home place settled by her grandfather, Major John N. Hughes, near Louisville, Ky.
   d. John Woodson Hughes, born 1822, married Lucy Hughes (cousin).
   e. Emily Neville Hughes, born 1828, married John Russell Smith (dead).

2. Jane B. Hughes, born May 5, 1786, died September 17, 1800.
3. Martha Hughes, born February 10, 1788, died September 30, 1797.
4. William M. Hughes, born October 15, 1789, died September 1, 1819.
5. Judith Hughes, born December 23, 1790, died November 6, 1800.
6. Tarlton Hughes, born September 27, 1792, died October 6, 1794.
7. Sallie Hughes, born November 26, 1793, died 1817.
8. Lucy Hughes, born August 22, 1794, died 1842.
9. Mary M. Hughes, born September 22, 1795, died March 6, 1835.
10. Stephen Hughes, born February 11, 1798, died 1852.
11. Elizabeth Hughes, born November 13, 1799.
12. Martha J. Hughes, born March 25, 1801, died 1811.
13. Benjamin J. Hughes, born January 17, 1803, died October 15, 1815.
14. James Neville Hughes, born December 20, 1804, died May 3, 1874.
15. Henry W. Hughes, born December 19, 1805.
16. Washington Hughes }
17. Madison Hughes } Triplets, born January 19, 1807, died 1807.
18. Jefferson Hughes }
19. Esther Hughes }
20. Edward Hughes } Twins, born May 1810, died 1810.

END RECORD DAVID AND ANN HOLMES MERIWETHER

## THOMAS MERIWETHER

Thomas Meriwether, born 1708, died 1756 (probably son of William, son of Nicholas and Elizabeth Crawford Meriwether), married Jane Lewis, oldest daughter of Robert Lewis, of "Belvoir", and Jane Meriwether. The record of Jane Lewis's second marriage is given under Charles Lewis of "The Byrd". Issue:

1. William Meriwether, born 1751.
2. Robert Meriwether, born 1752.

3. Thomas Meriwether, born 1754.
4. Jane Meriwether.
5. Elizabeth Meriwether.
6. Nicholas Meriwether.
7. Mary Meriwether, married Richard P. White.
8. Richard Meriwether.

William Meriwether, son of Thomas and Jane Lewis Meriwether, married, and had issue:

a. Thomas Meriwether, born 1781.
b. Jane Meriwether, born 1783.
c. Frances Meriwether, born 1785.
d. Matilda Meriwether, born 1790.
e. William Meriwether, born 1792.
f. Robert Meriwether, born 1795.
g. Lucinda Meriwether, born 1800.

Issue of William Meriwether, Jr. [William; Thomas].

1. Robert Meriwether, born 1828.
2. Mary Ann Meriwether, born 1830.
3. Eveline Meriwether, born 1832.
4. William A. Meriwether, born 1834.
5. Susan Meriwether, born 1837.
6. Moody B. Meriwether, born 1839.
7. Thomas Meriwether, born 1843.
8. C. V. Meriwether (Mrs. Furlow), born 1846.

C. V. Meriwether and Chas. C. Furlow, married 1864, had issue:

a. Floyd Furlow, married Miss Johnston.
b. Felda Meriwether Furlow.
c. Chas. F. Furlow, Jr.
d. Eugenia Furlow.
e. Hal Furlow.

Mary Meriwether, born 1763, daughter of Thomas Meriwether and Jane Lewis, died in Harris County, Ga., 1840; married 1782, Richard P. White. Issue: (five children).

a. Thomas M. White.
b. William White.

c. Nicholas White.

d. Clement B. White.

e. Malinda Lewis White, born April 18, 1789, married Pleasant Moon Benning, and had issue:

(Six oldest children died in infancy).

Seventh child, Sarah Amanda Benning, died at 17 years.

8. Gen. Henry Lewis Benning, born April 2, 1814. Was a lawyer, served a term of six years on the Supreme bench of Georgia. Brigadier General in the C. S. A., in command of Toombs Brigade of the 2nd, 13th, 17th, 20th Georgia Regiments which was part of Hood's command. 1839, married Mary Jones, daughter of Col. Seaborn Jones, of Columbus, Ga. where General Benning lived.

Issue of Gen. Henry Lewis Benning and Mary Jones:

a. Richard Edwin Benning, born 1818, married Frances Simpson.

b. Carolina Matilda Benning, born 1824, died 1856, married Benjamin Yancy.

c. Augusta P. Benning, born August 18, 1827, married in 1852, Madison Lewis Patterson, a son of Col. Edward Patterson and his wife, Mildred Lewis of Spartanburg, S. C., descendant of John Lewis, of Hanover. Issue:

1. Pleasant Benning Patterson, born 1856.
2. Edward Morris Patterson, born 1861.
3. Mildred Lewis Patterson, born 1863.
4. Jerome Augustine Patterson, born 1869.
5. Madison Lewis Patterson, born 1870.

END OF MERIWETHER PAPER

## *MAJOR LAWRENCE SMITH OF GLOUCESTER COUNTY

VOL. 21 OR 22, *Virginia Historical Magazine*

Major Lawrence Smith, died 1700, came to Virginia early in the seventeenth century. In order to stop Indian depredations the Governor, in March 1673, ordered forts to be built on the Rappahannock and Potomac, placing Major Smith in charge of them all. In 1679 the Assembly granted him lands five and a half miles long by four miles wide if he would seat there fifty armed men and two hundred others. He was included in this force with legal jurisdiction.

In 1651 he laid off Yorktown. Temple Farm on which later took place the surrender of Cornwallis, was sold to Major Smith in 1686.

He was recommended by the Governor to sit in King's Council, but died before taking his seat.

He bore Arms of Smiths of Totten, Devonshire, England. He married before 1685, Mary ——. His will which was proved in 1700 gives these names of his children:

I. Elizabeth, married Capt. John Battaile.

*II. Sarah, married Col. John Taliaferro.

III. Charles Smith of Essex, surveyor 1706. (*Virginia Historical Magazine,* Vol. II, p. 5.)

IV. John Smith, married Elizabeth, daughter, John Cox and Arabella Strachy. He was Lieutenant, Gloucester 1706; King and Queen 1707; died 1719-20. Issue: 1. William, 2. Hon. John, 3. Lawrence, 4. Burgess.

V. William Smith, died 1759, married Miss Ballard (?).

VI. Lawrence Smith, died 1739, was sheriff of York, member of House of Burgesses, married first, Mildred Cheeseman; married second, Mildred Reade, widow of Col. Goodwin, and sister of Margaret Reade who married Scotch Tom Nelson.

Augustine Smith, a descendant of Major Lawrence Smith, married Alice Grymes Page, and had: John Smith, the Councillor; Lawrence Smith; William Smith; Augustine Smith; Charles

Smith; and Elizabeth Smith, who is said to have married Captain John Battaile of Essex, a man of prominence.

An Augustine Smith (mentioned in Howe's *History of Virginia*) lived in Essex, St. Mary's Parish. In 1722 he qualified as one of the first justices of Spottsylvania. His children were: Thomas Smith of Prince William County, Va. and Mary Smith, who married Robert Slaughter.

The Nelsons of Albemarle were also descendants of Col. Lawrence Smith. Robert Nelson Smith, raised in Albemarle moved to Fayette County, Ky. and had there a classical school. He married Mary Margaret Fry, daughter of Reuben and Ann Coleman Slaughter Fry. They had ten children:

1. Eliza Nelson Smith; 2. Reuben Augustine Smith; 3. Robert Burwell Smith; 4. Hugh Nelson Smith; 5. Joseph Fry Smith; 6. Henry Smith, died infant; 7. Alice Page Smith; 8. Phillip Fry Smith; 9. Lucius Calthorpe Smith; 10. Frances Coleman Smith. (*Virginia Historical Magazine,* page 90, Vol. 23.)

## TALIAFERRO

*Taken from "Some Prominent Virginia Families" by Mrs. Louis Pecquet Bellet—Vol. II, page 230.*

"Of all the old legends and traditions which have come down to us as the origin of our Colonial ancestry in America there is no story more interesting and certainly none more ancient than that of the origin of the Taliaferro family for it carries us back to Julius Cæsar and his camp in Gaul in the year 58 B. C.

"It is said that Cæsar while inspecting his camp at twilight was surrounded by Gallic barbarians who would have killed him had it not been for the intervention of one of their number who admired Cæsar's courage and bravery in defending himself, and who refused to let him be murdered. In return for this kindly assistance Cæsar made this man one of his personal attendants and allowed him to carry arms. Taliaferro, it is said, comes from the Latin words, *tutum ferro* which expressed this man's pride in the privilege accorded him, a most unusual one for a stranger in the camp.

"A branch of this family wandered to Normandy coming from there to England with William the Conqueror. Baron Taliaferro, called the Hero of Hastings, for his bravery, received large grants of land in Kent, handing it down to his descendants who became the

Earls of Pinnington. In Bulwer's novel *Harold* we have the story of a troubadour named Taliaferro who was the personal friend of William the Conqueror and who died a gallant death at Hastings.

"In 804 a Taliaferro was created Duke of Angouleme by Charles the Bold of France. And in Hume's *History of England* we find Isabella Taliaferro, daughter of the Count of Angouleme, married King John of England. From them descend a long line of kings and queens, also linked through the Dukes of Plantagenet with the Norman kings and with the older line of English rulers—Edward the Confessor and others."

"*Arms*—shield—a chevron gu. *Crest*—trunk of an oak tree shooting out young branches ppr. three on one side, two on the other. Motto—Viresco."

## ESSEX RECORD

Tuscan family of Italian origin. Virginia emigrants Protestants, probably came away from religious persecution. Extracts and records always write name Taliaferro except when misspelled by clerks.

First in Virginia—Robert Taliaferro, gentleman, married daughter of Rev. Charles Grimes. First grant to him in Gloucester County 1655. Name written "Tolliver." Large grants later in Rappahannock County, one of these 6,300 acres patented conjointly with Col. Lawrence Smith of Gloucester County. Issue: 1. FRANCIS lived in Gloucester 1682, justice in Essex 1695, married Elizabeth Catlett. 2. JOHN died 1720, was lieutenant commanding company of rangers against Indians 1692, justice of Essex 1692-5, sheriff 1699, married before 1683, Sarah, daughter of Col. Lawrence Smith. 3. RICHARD in Richmond County 1711. 4. CHARLES in Essex 1724. 5. ROBERT of Essex died 1726, married Sarah Catlett, had grant of land 1672-3 in Rappahannock adjoining Mr. Corbin and Mr. Grimes. 6. CATHERINE married Col. John Battaile who married second Elizabeth Smith.

John and Sarah Smith Taliaferro, had: 1. LAWRENCE, sheriff of Essex 1721. 2. COL. JOHN TALIAFERRO of Snow Creek, Spotsylvania County, born 1687, died May 3, 1744 (tombstone at Hickory Neck Church near Williamsburg). He settled Snow

Creek 1707, justice of Spotsylvania 1720, Vestryman of St. George Parish 1725, married Mary, daughter of Capt. John Catlett and Elizabeth Gaines. Issue: *a.* Lawrence who married Susan Power, and had one daughter. *b.* William. *c.* Martha. *d.* Mary. *e.* Lucy married Col Charles Lewis of "Cedar Creek." 3. MARY married Col. Francis Thornton. 4. ELIZABETH married John Catlett. 5. ZACHARIAH died unmarried 1745. 6. CHARLES married Ann Kemp. 7. SARAH. 8. ROBERT married Elizabeth Mathews. 9. CATHERINE. 10. RICHARD married Elizabeth Eggleston. 11. WILLIAM married Miss Hay, and their son Col. William married Eliza Holden.

Philip of Hockley, King and Queen County was son of Col. William and Eliza Holden Taliaferro. He was Captain in the second Virginia Regiment, Troop of King and Queen, member of House of Delegates 1708, sheriff 1791, justice 1784, married Lucy, daughter of Col. Thomas Baytop. A son of this union was James Taliaferro of "Roaring Springs" who married first, Kate Booth and second, Elizabeth, widow of Francis Thornton.

Thomas, son of James and Kate Booth Taliaferro, married Mary Sinclair and their daughter, Margaret (born October 28, 1850, died January 1901), married April 25, 1868, Dr. Charles Gwyn, and had Caroline, who married in Galveston, April 23, 1902, Charles Harper Anderson, Jr. (See Anderson).

Robert Taliaferro, the emigrant from Cornwall England settled in Totopotomy Swamp, Gloucester 1655 with Col. Lawrence Smith patented 6,300 acres of land on the Rappahannock giving, doubtless, their respective sons, John Taliaferro and Augustine Smith, an interest in the future Fredericksburg. Col. John Taliaferro getting a larger portion of that land through his wife, Sarah Smith.

Dr. William, son of Philip and Lucy Baytop Taliaferro, married first, Mary and, second, Harriet Throckmorton, daughters of Col. Philip Throckmorton of Church Hill, Gloucester County. One of these ladies was mother of WARNER THROCKMORTON TALIAFERRO who married first, Fanny Booth; second Leah Selden; also COL. ALEXANDER TALIAFERRO of Gloucester and Culpeper Counties.

The other wife was mother of DR. WILLIAM TALIAFERRO of

Gloucester, one of the most elegant gentlemen of his day; he was noted as having several affairs of the heart, the most serious with Ann Carmichael of Fredericksburg. She was a celebrated beauty and wit and had great personal charm. She married William Kinsey of New York and died a year or so later. Her stepson, Edward Kinsey, the sculptor, when a Union soldier sought knowledge of her home and her people and in a letter to a friend told of her coming into his home when he was six years old, of his admiration and devotion to her, also that his character and life would have been better under her influence.

Warner T. Taliaferro owned historic "Belleville" which he inherited through his wife, Fanny Booth, whose ancestors had it as a royal grant. Their only child, William Booth Taliaferro, general C. S. A., married Sally, daughter of Hon. James Lyons, and their children still own and live upon a part of this place.

Warner T. Taliaferro by his second wife, Leah Selden of Fredericksburg had: 1. Dr. Philip Alexander Taliaferro, died childless; 2. Susan, married Judge B. R. Welford; 3. Edwin Taliaferro; 4. Warner T. Taliaferro, Jr.

## THORNTONS OF EAST NEWTON, YORKSHIRE, ENGLAND

The name *Thornton* appears in old works as an evolution from *Thorton,* Oxfordshire.

*Ancient Arms*—a chevron between three hawthorn sprays. These appear in a sculpture of the fifteenth century in Stonegar Church. In the seventeenth century the sprays were changed into trees.

*Crest*—on a wreath argent and sable, a lion's head crossed purpure gorged with a crown of the first.

*Motto*—*Nisi Christus Nemo.*

William Thornton m. Isabella, daughter and co-heiress of
Lord of East Newton (1313-1333) — William de Newton (——d. 1336)

| Thomas | Isabel | Agnes | Elizabeth |
|---|---|---|---|
| died 1345, m. Jean, dau. of Peter Nellison (living in 1364) | m. John de Acoster of Herlmsley | m. Clement de Shaklethorp; m. 2nd, Wm. Crawton, 1349 | m. Peter de Carleton |

| William, | Robert, | Thomas | Joan |
|---|---|---|---|
| Lord of East Newton in 1350 m. Alice de Eston | heir to his brother Wm., 1374, died circa 1401-2, m. Marjory | m. —— had daughter Elizabeth | m. Wm. Kirkly of Ampleford 1390 |

| Robert (died 1418) | Elizabeth | Beatrice |
|---|---|---|
| m. Isobel de Gray | 1401 | |

| Robert | John | William | Alice |
|---|---|---|---|
| Lord of East Newton 1418, m. 1st, Agnes; 2nd, Isobel (remarried in 1465 John McKylfield) | friar 1416 | (living 1438) | 2nd wife of Wm. Brown 1410 |

William (son of Robert) living at Tirkleby 1456, settled East Newton on his son, Robt. 1485. Will dated 1487, probated at York. Married Annis, daughter of Richard Oldborough.

Robert (born 1454) m. Jane, dau. of Wm. Laton of Sproxton. Issue, eleven children, namely:

| | | |
|---|---|---|
| 1. Wm. m. Marjory Leigh<br>\|<br>whence Alice Thornton born 1653, died 1702, married 1668, Thomas Comber, D.D., Dean of Durham. This branch stayed in England | 2. Thomas 1545<br>3. Francis, died April 12, 1566 m. 1st Delosier 2nd Joan<br>4. Robert<br>5. Martin, a clerk<br>6. Robert<br>7. Richard | 8. Gregory<br>9. Thomas, a clerk<br>10. Anne E., married Leonard Wildon<br>11. John, a monk. |

Francis (d. April 12, 1566), had

| William | Thomas | Marjory m. Wilson |
|---|---|---|
| will dated May 5, 1600, m. Barbara | 1566 1600 | |
| William (1600) | John | |

## THE YORKSHIRE THORNTONS OF AMERICA

William Thornton, gentleman, settled in York County (now Gloucester County) Petsworth Parish before 1646, built a home four miles north of Gloucester Point and called it "The Hills" after his Yorkshire home in England. Late in life he lived in Stafford County. He had three sons:

1. William born March 27, 1649, died February 15, 1727, married three times—first, August 24, 1671; second, November 11, 1688; third, October 20, 1720, and had nineteen children.

2. Rowland, died about 1701, was a planter in Rappahannock and Richmond counties, married Elizabeth, daughter of Alexander Fleming. No issue.

3. Francis, born November 5, 1651; settled in Stafford County before 1700, married first, Alice Savage; second, Mrs. Jane Harvey. No issue.

I have no certain record of ancestry of Alice Savage; a partial record of Capt. Anthony Savage, justice of Gloucester 1773. Will on record in Richmond County, or Henrico, date 1795, supposed to be son of John and Alice Stafford Savage.

Issue of Francis and Alice Savage Thornton:

1. Francis, born January 4, 1682, of Snow Creek in 1703; Burgess from Spotsylvania in 1723 to 1726, also justice in Caroline County. Married Mary Taliaferro.
2. Elizabeth, born January 3, 1674.
3, 4. Twins { William, died 1742-3.
Sarah, b. Dec. 17, 1680, m. Lawrence Taliaferro.
5. Margaret, born April 2, 1678, married William Strother, sheriff of King George County 1726.

6. Anne, born March 22, 1689.
7. Rowland.
8. Anthony.

Col. Francis Thornton of "Snow Creek" and Mary Taliaferro, his wife, had issue:

1. William, who established Montpelier.
2. Alice, married James Taylor (granduncle of President Zachary Taylor.
3. Daughter, married Slaughter.
4. Mildred, born 1721, married first, Nicholas Meriwether; second, in 1741, Dr. Walker. (See Walker record.)
   By first marriage had only one child—
   Mildred T. Meriwether, died before 1764. She married John Syme (son of Col. Syme), and had: Sarah, born November 5, 1760, died May 15, 1814; John Syme, and others.
*5. *Elizabeth, married Thomas Meriwether.*
6. Daughter, married Woodford.
7. Reuben (died 1768), married Elizabeth Gregory. No issue. She married four times.
8. Col. John served in French and Indian War. Was justice in 1742, sheriff 1751, Burgess 1753, colonel of Colonial militia in Spotsylvania 1756, married Mildred Gregory, had four daughters.
9. Col. Francis, married November 3, 1736, Frances Gregory, commissioned by Governor Gooch as colonel in colonial troops of George II 1742; was member House of Burgesses 1745; lived in Spotsylvania, died a little over thirty years of age, left four sons.

Children of Col. John and Mildred G. Thornton:

1. Mildred, born 1739, died 1764, married Samuel, brother of General Washington.
2. Mary, married General Woodford of the Revolution.
3. Elizabeth, married John Taliaferro.
4. Lucy, married John Lewis (only son of Col. Fielding Lewis

and Catherine Washington), and left one child:
Mildred Lewis, married Col. William Minor.

Col. Francis Thornton and Frances Gregory, his wife had:

1. Francis, married Ann (widow of Butler Brayne), daughter of Rev. John Thompson and Lady Spotswood.
2. George, married Mary, daughter of John Alexander.
3. William, married Mary or Martha Stuart.
   Progenitors of the Rappahannock or Mountain Thorntons. Homes were "Montpelier" and "Hawthorn", this last name derived from a marriage between Frances *Thorn*ton and Dr. Ayler *Haw*es.
4. John, married Jane Washington, niece of General Washington, lived at "Thornton Hill" near "Montpelier." (*William and Mary Quarterly,* Vol. —, page 197.)
5. Mildred, married Charles, youngest brother of General Washington.
6. Mary, married first, William Champe; second, Churchill Jones.

## DR. THOMAS WALKER

Born 1715 in King and Queen County, died 1794. Student at William and Mary. At 26 years of age married Mildred Thornton (widow of Nicholas Meriwether), through whom he obtained "Castle Hill". Explored in Kentucky and Southwest Virginia. Named Cumberland Mountains and River, Walker Mountain, etc. Commissary of Virginia troops under Braddock, and was at Braddock's defeat. Appointed to treat with Indians of New York and of Pennsylvania. On commission to fix boundary between Virginia and North Carolina 1778. Burgess successively for Hanover, Louisa, Albemarle. Trustee for Albemarle 1763 to sell lots of Charlottesville, the new county-seat.

Children: (12)

1. Mary, born 1742, married Nicholas Lewis of "The Farm" 1760.
2. John, inherited "Belvoir", married Elizabeth Moore, granddaughter of Governor Spotswood.
3. Susan, born 1746, married Henry Fry 1764.

4. Thomas (1748-1798), married Margaret Hoops 1773, lived at "Indian Fields".
5. Lucy, born 1751, married Dr. George Gilmer of "Pen Park" 1771.
6. Elizabeth, born 1753, married Rev. Matthew Maury 1773, of old Walker's church.
7. Mildred, born 1755, married 1770, Joseph Hornsby, of Williamsburg and removed to Shelby County, Kentucky.
8. Sarah, born 1758, married Col. Reuben Lyndsay, of Albemarle 1778.
9. Martha, born 1760, m. George Divers 1780. No issue.
10. Reuben (1762-5).
11. Francis (1764-1806), married Jane Byrd Nelson 1798, daughter of Governor Nelson, of Yorktown, Virginia.
12. Peachy, born 1767, married 1787, Joshua Fry.

John Walker, died 1809. Aide to Washington in Revolution. Member of House of Burgesses. U. S. Senator to fill vacancy occasioned by death of Wm. Grayson. For years commonwealth's attorney for Albemarle. Married Elizabeth Moore, their only child Mildred, married Francis Kinloch of South Carolina; and their daughter, Eliza Kinloch married Hugh Nelson (son of Governor Thomas Nelson.) Hugh Nelson came to Albemarle 1802, lived at "Belvoir", was speaker in House of Delegates. Member of Congress 1811-23, then was minister to Spain, died 1836.

Children:

1. Francis K. Nelson.
2. Mildred, married Thomas Nelson of Clark.
3. Ann, married Dr. Thomas Meriwether.
4. Dr. Thomas Nelson of Elk Hill.
5. Rev. Cleland K. Nelson.
6. Keating Nelson.
7. Dr. Robert W. Nelson.

Thomas Walker, Captain in 9th Virginia Regiment of Revolutionary Army, married Margaret Hoops, and had:

1. M. L. Walker.

2. Elizabeth, married Robert Michie.
3. Maria, married Richard Duke of Louisa County.
4. Jane, married William Rice of Halifax.
5. Mildred, married Tarleton Goolsby.
6. John.
7. Thomas
8. Martha.

Francis Walker, married Jane Byrd Nelson and succeeded to "Castle Hill", was a magistrate, member of House of Delegates, representative in Congress, colonel of 88th Regiment, died 1806. Issue:

1. Jane Frances, married 1815, Dr. Mann Page, son of Major Carter Page of Cumberland County, lived at "Turkey Hill." He was magistrate of the county 1824, died 1850. 11 children: Maria, Ella, Jane, Charlotte, William, Francis W., Carter H., Mann, Thomas, Dr. R. Channing Page of New York and Frederick W. Page, married Anne K. Meriwether.

2. Judith, married Hon. Wm. C. Rives (died 1868). He served in the Legislature, U. S. Senate and as minister to France, was one of the most finished orators of his day. Their descendants now own "Castle Hill."

Maria Walker, married 1806, Richard Duke (died at "Morea" 1849.) He was magistrate 1819, sheriff 1847. Issue:

1. William J. Duke, married Emily Anderson.
2. Lucy Duke, married first, David Wood son of Drewry Wood and Malinda Carr; married second, John H. Betts, of Tennessee.
3. Mary J. Duke, married William T. Smith.
4. Mildred Duke, married Christopher Gilmer.
5. Martha Duke.
6. Margaret Duke, married Robert Rodes.
7. Charles Duke.
8. Col. Richard T. W. Duke, died 1898, married Elizabeth Eskridge of Staunton. Col. R. T. W. Duke, 48th Virginia Regiment, C. S. A. Served as commonwealth's attorney. Delegate to Legislature. Member of Congress, father of

Judge R. T. W. Duke and William Duke of Charlottesville, Virginia.

NOTE.—James Duke (brother of Richard), died 1838, married Miss Biggers of Louisa. Issue:

1. Richard, moved to Nelson County. His daughter married John Cole.
2. Horace Duke, of Mississippi.
3. Charlotte, married Dr. William Carr.
4. Lucy, married Thomas Ballard.

Alexander Duke of Hanover, 1835, married Elizabeth (daughter of Alexander Garrett), and was father of Mrs. Horace Jones.

*(Walker and Fry Note)*

Col. Joshua Fry, born in England, educated at Oxford, professor of Mathematics at William and Mary College, Va., was present when Albemarle was organized. Was made one of its first magistrates, its county lieutenant and its surveyor. Was appointed Colonel of a regiment raised in Virginia at outbreak of French and Indian wars, 1754. George Washington was the lieutenant-colonel and succeeded him in command when Mr. Fry died at the rendezvous, Fort Willis, Cumberland, Maryland. He married Mrs. Mary Micou Hill, who was daughter of Philip Micou, physician and surgeon, a Huguenot refugee.
Issue:

1. John Fry, married Sarah Adams 1764, sister of Thomas Adams of "Blair Park".
2. Henry Fry, died in Madison County 1823 in 85th year, deputy clerk of Albemarle. Married Susan Walker.
3. Martha Fry, married John Nicholas, clerk of Albemarle.
4. William Fry, died unmarried.
5. Margaret, married John Scott.

John Fry and Sarah Adams Fry, sister of Thomas Adams, at one time owner of "Blair Park", Albemarle County, had Joshua, William and Tabitha.

Joshua Fry, married Peachy Walker, daughter of Dr. Thomas Walker and Mildred Meriwether Thornton. Joshua Fry was a noted teacher, magistrate and member of legislature for Albemarle.

In later years moved to Kentucky and taught a classical academy. He had numerous descendants—Frys, Greens, Bullitts and Speeds. He and his wife are buried at Danville, Kentucky.

Thomas Walker Fry, son of John and Peachy Fry of "Spring House", Kentucky, married Eliza Smith, sister of Hon. Speed Smith of Kentucky. Their widowed daughter, Mrs. Mary Fry Lawrence, became second wife of Rev. Dr. Lewis Warner Green, D. D. Issue:

1. Julia Green, married Mathew Thompson Scott of Bloomington, Illinois.
2. Letitia Green, married Hon. Adlai Stevenson.

Henry Fry and Susan Walker, had issue, nine children, of whom were:

1. Reuben Fry, father of Joseph L. Fry for twenty years Judge of Wheeling Circuit.
2. Henry Fry, married December 27, 1796, Mildred Maury (died September 14, 1861), daughter of Rev. Matthew Maury and Elizabeth Walker. Issue:
   Frank Fry, long Commissioner of Revenue for Albemarle.
3. Wesley Fry, who was the father of Capt. W. C. Fry.

## MAURY

Rev. James Maury, born April 8, 1717, died June 9, 1769. Son of the emigrant, Matthew Maury, and Mary Ann Fontaine, was rector of Frederickville Parish; was noted as a teacher, having among other pupils Thomas Jefferson, noted also as the suitor in the celebrated Two-Penny Act or Parson's Cause which was defeated through Patrick Henry's eloquence. He did not live at the Glebe, but on his own farm on the edge of Albemarle and Louisa.

November 11, 1743, he married Mary Walker, born November 22, 1724, died March 20, 1798, daughter of Capt. James Walker and Ann Hill, widow of Leonard Hill, who lived near Bowler's on the Rappahannock River. James Walker was a physician of King and Queen County. Issue:

1. Rev. Matthew, married Elizabeth Walker, daughter of Dr. Walker and Mildred Thornton Meriwether.
2. James, married. Appointed U. S. Consul to Liverpool, England 1789-1837.

3. Richard, married Diana Minor, daughter of John Minor, parents of Commodore Matthew Maury, and grand-parents of General Dabney Maury, C. S. A.
4. Ann.
5. Mary.
6. Walker, married Mary Dawson, daughter of Rev. Musgrove Dawson. Issue, ten children. Was noted teacher of many distinguished men, among them John Randolph of Roanoke. He moved to Norfolk. His descendants prominent in letters and literature.
7. Catherine, married James Barrett.
8. Elizabeth, married James Lewis of Spotsylvania.
9. Abraham Maury.
10. Fontaine Maury.
11. Benjamin Maury.

Rev. Matthew Maury (2), married Elizabeth Walker. He succeeded his father as rector of Frederickville parish. Lived at the same place, also taught a classical school and among other pupils who afterwards became distinguished was Meriwether Lewis. Issue:

1. Matthew Maury, married Fry.
2. Thomas Walker Maury, died 1842, married Elizabeth Clarkson, daughter of Julius Clarkson and granddaughter of Jesse Lewis. He was a member of the Albemarle bar. Magistrate in 1816. He also taught school.
3. Reuben Maury, died 1869, married Elizabeth Lewis, daughter of Jesse Lewis, and had one child:
   Jesse Lewis Maury, married Lucy Price. He inherited his father's home "Piedmont". (Issue, see Price note.)
4. Francis Fontaine, married Matilda Fry.
5. Mary Ann, married William Michie.
6. Mildred, married Fry. Issue: Frank Fry.
7. Elizabeth.
8. Catherine, married Francis Lightfoot.
9. John Maury, married Winston.
10. James Bickerton Maury.

James Frank Fry, son of Mildred Maury and Henry Fry, died 1880. Married Mary Jane Barksdale, daughter of Nelson Barksdale and Jane Lewis, daughter of Jesse Lewis and Nancy Clarkson. He was sheriff of Albemarle for years, Assessor and Commissioner of the Revenue. Issue:

1. Thomas Wesley Fry, married Sarah Jane McLaurin. Issue:
   Edward James, born 1846.
   Clara Thomas, born 1849, married Frank Starr.
2. Matthew Henry Fry, born 1824, married Sarah Taliaferro Heiskell. No issue.
3. Mildred Jane Fry, born 1825, married James S. Barksdale, son of Rice G. Barksdale. Issue:
   Mary Elizabeth, 1852.
   Frank Nelson, 1855.
   Sarah Lewis, born 1858.
   Mildred Fry, 1860.
   James Rice, 1864.
4. John Nelson Fry, born 1828, married Elizabeth Goodman.
5. Jesse Lewis Fry, born 1829, married Frances Dunkum. Issue:
   William Dunkum, born 1857.
   Frank Barksdale, born 1859.
   Jesse Lewis, born 1861.
   John Thomas, born 1863.
6. Elizabeth Fry, married James D. Goodman, and had Mary Mildred, born 1858, married 1887, James W. Garnett of Culpeper County.
7. Mary Catherine Fry, born 1837, married John L. Jarman, had:
   Frank Dabney Jarman, born 1861.
   John Thomas Jarman, born 1864.

## COL. HENRY WILLIS

"Topman", according to Colonel Byrd, of the seven "feoffers" who held the charter of Fredericksburg. His name is second on the list, Augustine Smith and John Taliaferro are next.

Francis Willis, the first of this family, settled in York County, later in Gloucester from which county he and Walter Gwin were first delegates to the House of Burgesses, 1652. He returned to England leaving his estate on Ware River to his nephew, Francis Willis of Gloucester, who left two sons: COL. FRANCIS WILLIS the third, and COL. HENRY WILLIS. This Col. Francis Willis lived at "White Hall" where Col. Byrd visited him. For the last three generations this place has been owned by the Byrds. Col. Francis married Lady Ann Rich, who is buried in the chancel of old Ware Church. Their descendants are to be found in the *Willis Family* by Byrd Charles Willis of Fairfax County. Among them are the children of Claudia Marshall Willis who married W. W. Scott; Edward Jones Willis of Pembroke, near Richmond; the Madisons of Orange; etc.

Col. Henry Willis was a rich and a good man as well as a marrying man. He courted three maids and married all three of them as widows. His first wife was Ann Alexander, widow of John Smith of Purton. The second wife was Mildred Howell, the widow Brown. The third wife was Mildred Washington, widow of Roger Gregory. Some accounts give this as her third marriage, claiming that her first husband was a Lewis. She had three Gregory daughters, who married Thorntons.

Issue by first marriage:

1. John Willis, whose daughter, Mary married Col. Wm. Dangerfield.
2. Henry Willis.
3. Mary Willis, married Hancock Lee, hence General George Chittenden, C. S. A.
4. Francis Willis.
5. David Willis.
6. Robert Willis.

Issue of Col. Henry Willis by his second and third marriages, were:

1. Elizabeth Willis, married Howell Lewis and went to Granville County, N. C.
2. Ann Willis, married Duff Green and went to Kentucky.
3. John Willis.

Col. Henry Willis and his third wife had a son, Col. Lewis

Willis, an officer in the Revolution, who married first, Mary Champe who was sister of Jane, the wife of Samuel Washington. By a second marriage he had a son, Col. Byrd Willis who lived at "Willis Hall", Fredericksburg, and later moved to Florida, and whose daughter married Achille Murat. His several times granddaughter, Consuela Vanderbilt married the Duke of Marlborough.

Children of Col. Lewis Willis and Mary Champe:

a. Mildred Willis, married Landon Carter, and had:

  1. Mrs. Robert Mercer.
  2. Lucy L. Carter, married General John Minor of Fredericksburg.

b. John Willis, had three daughters.

c. Henry Willis, whose daughter married Gen. McComas, of Mississippi.

d. Mary Willis, married Mr. Battaile.

e. William Champe Willis, married, and left issue.

Lucy Carter and General John Minor, had:

a. Lt. John Minor, a lawyer and well known in Fredericksburg. He died a bachelor.

b. Lucius Minor, married Miss Berkley of Hanover, and had: Fannie, Landon, Tamaria, Charles, who was a noted teacher, Berkley, and Robert Minor.

c. Dr. Lewis Minor, U. S. N.

d. Mrs. Mary Blackford, of Lynchburg.

Ann Willis and Duff Green, had:

a. Willis Green, 1772, emigrated to Kentucky; 1783, married Sarah Reid, was clerk of Lincoln County, Kentucky. His youngest son was Rev. Lewis Warner Green, who was born January 28, 1806, at Waveland Plantation, near Danville, Kentucky, and married first, Eliza Montgomery, no issue; married second, Mrs. Mary Fry Lawrence, issue:

  a. Mrs. Matthew Scott.
  b. Mrs. Adlai Stevenson.

b. William Green, soldier at Valley Forge when fifteen years of age, later moved to Kentucky, married daughter of Markham Marshall, was father of Gen. Duff Green, who was editor of *Washington Telegraph* in the time of Andrew Jackson.

## LAWRENCE WASHINGTON

Son of John Washington of Warton, Lancashire.

Lawrence Washington of Northampton and Gray's Inn, Grantee of Sulgrave Manor, Mayor of Northampton 1533-1546. He died February 19, 1584. His wife was Ann, daughter of Robert Pargiter of Gretworth. She died October 6, 1564. Both are buried in Sulgrave Church.

Robert Washington, son of Lawrence, died 1619, buried in Sulgrave Church. He married first, Elizabeth, daughter of Robert Light of Radway, Warwickshire; second, Anne Fisher of Han-Slop, Bucks. He had two sons: Lawrence and Robert, who died 1622 and with his wife is buried in Brington Church.

Lawrence Washington of Sulgrave and Brington, died December 13, 1616, buried in Brington Church. He married Margaret, daughter of William Butler of Tees, Sussex. She died about 1650. Their son:

Rev. Lawrence Washington, M. A. Fellow of Brasenose College, Oxford; Rector of Purleigh, Essex, 1632 to 1643; died about 1650. He married Amphilliss Roades, who died January 16, 1665, buried at Tring, Hertfordshire. Their two sons, John and Lawrence, both emigrated to Virginia, 1657.

John Washington, son of the Rev. Lawrence, was born at Tring, 1634. His second wife was Ann, daughter of Nathaniel Pope, and their children were John, Lawrence and Ann.

Lawrence, son of John and Ann Pope Washington, died 1697. He married Mildred Warner, and had issue:

A. John Washington, married Catharine Whiting and had Catharine, who was the first wife of Col. Fielding Lewis of Gloucester.

B. Augustine Washington, died April 12, 1743, married first, 1715, Jane Butler, daughter of Caleb Butler. He married second, 1730, Mary Ball.

C. Mildred Washington, married Roger Gregory, and after his death she married Col. Henry Willis.

Children of Augustine Washington and Jane Butler, who died 1728:

1. Butler Washington.
2. Lawrence Washington, died 1752, married 1743, Ann Fairfax. He lived at Mt. Vernon.
3. Augustine Washington, married Ann Aylett, lived in Westmoreland.
4. Jane Washington.

Children of Augustine Washington and his second wife, Mary Ball:

5. George Washington, married 1759, Mrs. Martha Custis.
6. Betty Washington was the second wife of Col. Fielding Lewis.
7. Samuel Washington, married first, Jane Champe; second, Mildred Thornton; third, Lucy Chapman.
8. John Augustine Washington, married Hannah Bushrod.
9. Charles Washington, married Mildred, daughter of Francis Thornton.
10. Mildred Washington, died infant.

NOTE: John Augustine Washington, born at Berkley, 1821, the last to own Mt. Vernon, served on the staff of General R. E. Lee, and was killed when on a reconnoitering party near Richmond, 1861.

William H. Washington, born in North Carolina, 1814, was of the Virginia family, was a prominent statesman, in United States Congress 1841-3, and also served many terms in the North Carolina Legislature.

## COBBS FAMILY

Originally spelt their name with the final S, later we find families who have dropped this final letter while claiming these original Cobbs ancestors.

Note the family of Cobb of Robeson County, North Carolina, which claims Joseph Cobbs, 1613, as its ancestor. (Excursus in Harper family.)

Again the Cobb family of Georgia has done the same.

Joseph Cobbs came to Virginia, 1613.

1624 his wife and sons, Joseph and Benjamin followed him.

1635 Joseph Cobbs appears as taking out land grants.

Date of emigration of Ambrose Cobbs not known.

1635 he also took up land grants in Virginia.

Robert Cobbs, born 1620, is presumably from Ambrose Cobbs. He is on the records of York County. Was church warden of York County, 1651; Justice of the Peace for York County, 1667; High Sheriff, 16—; County Commissioner, 1681. He left four sons:

1. Edmund Cobbs (Administrator of his father's will, dated 1682, probated 1692-3.) Edmund in his will gives his entire estate to his three brothers, Robert, Ambrose and Otho, whose names seem to confirm this statement of a Holland ancestress, as stated in the Robeson Co., N. C. record.

There appears in the records of Henrico and Goochland Counties from 1736 to 1750—these sons of Robert Cobbs II:

Thomas Cobbs, 1706.
John Cobbs, 1708.
Robert Cobbs, 1710.

Samuel Cobbs' and his brothers Edmund and John of Albemarle, lived in Louisa, sons of John Cobbs and Susannah. In 1750, Samuel Cobbs, married Mary Lewis, daughter of Robert Lewis and Jane Meriwether.

Samuel Cobbs' will written in 1758, shows his wife Mary survived him, also they had three children: Robert, Jane, and Judith. After providing fully for his wife and children, he wills 1,000 acres of land to be divided between his two brothers, Edmund and John.

His youngest child, Judith, died in childhood. His other daughter, Jane, married John J. Waddy, of Louisa County, whose will is dated 1775—and tells of his beloved wife, Jane, daughter of late father-in-law, Samuel Cobbs, and gives her his land in Bedford County, and wills his son Samuel Waddy, his patrimonial estate; one of executors to be his dear friend Waddy Thompson, attorney-at-law, Louisa County. Judith Cobbs, witness.

Codicil read, if his son Samuel die without issue, his part of the estate to go to John J. Waddy's brothers and sisters: Samuel, Ann, Francis, Elizabeth and their heirs.

Samuel Waddy, son of John J. and Jane Cobbs Waddy, was raised by his grandmother (Mary Lewis Cobbs); he later went to Kentucky with his Thompson relations. He married first, his cousin, Mary Thompson, daughter of Anthony and Ann Bibb Thompson; she did not live long, and died childless. He married second, Sally Dupuy, who also died childless.

He married third, Elizabeth Hobbs, mother of all his children who reached maturity. They left descendants, the only one of whom I know is Mrs. Louise Waddy Baily, wife of Landon Baily, Esqr. of Shelby County, Ky. She states a tradition that Samuel Waddy was visited on one occasion by his cousin, Meriwether Lewis.

Robert Cobbs, born 1754 in Louisa County. Was only son of Samuel Cobbs and his wife, Mary Lewis.

He entered the Revolutionary service from Louisa County, in the regiment commanded by his uncle, Col. Chas. Lewis.

He married after the war, Ann G. Poindexter, daughter of John Poindexter, of Louisa and Bedford Counties. He moved to the latter county in 1788, where he had inherited a large landed property from his father, Samuel Cobbs. In 1795 his widow moved to Campbell County where he also owned valuable lands. His Bedford property was inherited by his son, Chas. Lewis Cobbs. He had named his Campbell home "Plain Dealings". This name was indicative of his own character and straightforward methods of business.

He died 1829. His widow survived him twelve years, dying 1842. She lived with her daughter Sarah, wife of Capt. Wm. C. McAllister. She drew a pension in her latter years, as widow of Robert Cobbs, who rose to be Captain in the Revolutionary War.

Although a person of reticent nature, Robert Cobbs' strong dependence on the intervention of God in an emergency is shown by the following incident:

On one occasion when he returned home from a journey, he found his manager ill, and given up to die by the doctor. Robert Cobbs declared he would not give up Bosher, and hastening to the home of the sick man, called them all to prayers. He was not in the habit of public prayers, but on this occasion astonished all with his fervent commendation of Bosher's fitness to live, and their need of him in the community as example of a husband, parent and citizen. Going further, he enumerated by naming a long list of others who would not be missed if taken away, and presented them a sacrifice for the restored Bosher. This astonishing prayer was answered in Bosher's recovery, and has afforded amusement for neighbors and Robert Cobbs' descendants. He left issue, nine children:

1. John Poindexter Cobbs, born May 27, 1785, graduate of Hampden-Sydney College, 1808, of Philadelphia College, 1810. Married Jane Garland, daughter of the Hon. David Garland of Amherst, who was in the U. S. Congress for years, and his wife, Miss Meredith. They had a daughter, Jane Cobbs, who married a Mr. Thwing. Issue:
   a. Jane Henry Thwing, married Horace Smith.
   b. Sarah Florence Thwing.
   c. Franklin Thwing, married Elizabeth Smith. Issue:
      1. Franklin. 2. Harriet. 3. Ellen.
   d. Virginia Thwing, married S. J. Peterson-Halstrom, and had:
      1. James. 2. Charles. 3. Mary.
2. Mary Lewis Cobbs, born July 11, 1787, married first, William Armistead. They had a son, Dr. John O. Armistead. She married second, William McLean, and had two sons.
3. Robert Lewis Cobbs, born December 25, 1789, graduate of Hampden-Sydney. Never married.
4. Samuel Cobbs, died single, age 21 years, served in the War of 1812.
5. William Cobbs, born in Campbell County, March 2, 1792, died 1850. He bought "Poplar Grove" which is still owned by the family. He married Marion Scott of Bedford County, and had:
   Emily Cobbs, married Edward Sextus Hutter.
6. Charles Lewis Cobbs, born in Campbell County, March 12,

1800, married Ann Scott of Bedford County. Removed to Indiana. Had issue:

a. Wm. Scott Cobbs.
b. Maria Louisa Cobbs.
c. Nanny Cobbs.
d. Harriet Cobbs.
e. Mary Emma Cobbs.

7. Sarah White Cobbs, born February 12, 1797, at "Plain Dealings", married Capt. Wm. C. McAllister, born 1789, died 1841, age 52. Will probated at Campbell Courthouse 1841. Issue, two sons:

a. Robert Cobbs McAllister, M. D., was graduate of Virginia Medical College, Richmond. He married Miss Moore of Appomattox. No issue.

b. John Meriwether McAllister, born October 3, 1833, in Campbell County, Va., married August 18, 1857, Miss Frances Ann Dibrell. He graduated 1856 from the law school of Washington College, Lexington, Va., died March 9, 1906. He was joint editor with Mrs. Tandy of *Lewis and Kindred Families.* He practiced his profession in Campbell and Appomattox counties; in 1878 removed to Morgan County, Tenn., where he practiced for many years. Later he was employed in railroad business in Atlanta, Ga. Issue:

1. Frances Elizabeth McAllister, who died May 18, 1901. She was of unusual intellect, graduate of the best Georgia schools. She specialized in literature, and was widely and favorably known as a writer of character, and dialect sketches, and other short stories. She married December 8, 1897, Dr. Wm. Herring Leyden whom she survived some years. They had:

   a. Estelle Dibrell Leyden.
   b. John M. Leyden, who later took also the given name of his father.

2. Robert Lewis D. McAllister, born in Atlanta, Ga., December 2, 1872. Graduated at Auburn College,

Alabama, and the University of Virginia. His profession is law. He married Sarah Elizabeth Smith of St. Louis, Mo. and has:

a. Lesene M. McAllister.
b. Dorothy Lee McAllister.
c. Robert McAllister.
d. Cornelia McAllister.

8. Ann Elizabeth Cobbs, born in Campbell County, Va. 1802, died in Amelia County 1886—age 82 years. She married Joel Mottley of Nottoway County. They had five children.

1. Robert Cobbs Mottley, born 1824. Graduate of Hampden-Sydney, 1845, also Medical College, Philadelphia, 1847. Married Indiana Vaughan, of Amelia County, and had six children:

1. Elizabeth, never married.
2. Robert Milton, never married.
3. John Egbert, married Miss Lee of Buckingham County.
4. Jefferson Davis, married Miss Bayly of Amelia County.
5. Wirt, never married.
6. William Henry.

2. John Lewis Mottley, born 1826, in Nottoway County, married Anna Gill. Had issue: (nine children)

a. Mary Elizabeth, m. William Vaughan, 1891.
b. Emma Lewis, m. C. Butler, 1882.
c. Sarah Roberta, m. James Wooton, 1889.
d. Alice Armistead, m. Henry W. Hubbard, 1880.
e. Anna Adkisson, m. Samuel Hubbard, 1887.
f. John Meriwether, died April 29, 1890.
g. Charles Adolphus, never married.
h. Joel Wm., never married.
i. Robert Miller, never married.

3. Meriwether Cobbs Mottley, born 1828, unmarried. C. S. A.
4. Joel William Mottley, unmarried. C. S. A.
5. Charles Adolphus Mottley, unmarried, C. S. A.

9. Meriwether Lewis Cobbs, born March 4, 1805. (Youngest son of Capt. Robert Cobbs and Ann G. Poindexter.) Graduate of Hampden-Sydney, 1825, and of Medical College, Philadelphia, 1827. Practiced in Surry County, died 1828, buried at Surry Courthouse. Never married.

## THOMSON FAMILY OF VIRGINIA

The ruthless destruction of Virginia County records—some in the Revolutionary period, later more largely by the Union Army—causes many gaps in the early records of many of the families of this State. Old church registers and family papers scattered through many lines of such families partially cover some of these gaps. The records of this Thomson family suffered greatly. Some years ago in conjunction with Mr. George C. Downing, a genealogist of Frankfort, Kentucky (who descends from Anthony Thomson, and Ann Bibb) with some addresses furnished me by J. M. McAllister, whose genealogical records cover many lines, I gathered many points concerning the Thomsons. Later there came to me other tracings furnished by descendants of Waddy Thomson, Sr., of Hanover, Louisa and Albemarle counties.

This description of the Thomson arms furnished by Mr. R. H. Earle of Marietta, Georgia, has been preserved by the South Carolina Waddy Thompsons, and is the same as given in the Visitation of Hertfordshire in early times to the Thompsons of Walton-at-Stone.

Or on a fesse lancette azure three estoiles of the field (or)—

On a canton of the second (azure)—the sun in glory (or).

Crest—an arm erect vested gules; cuffed, argent, holding in the hand proper, five ears of wheat.

Visitation of Hertfordshire gives this descent:

Robert Thom(p)son came out of the North.

Maurice Thom(p)son, married Katherine Harvey.

Robert Thomson, married Elizabeth Harsnett, of Wooten, Hertfordshire, who was living in 1634.

| Maurice | Col. George | Paul | Robert | Mary | Elizabeth. |
|---|---|---|---|---|---|
| Thompson | b. 1603 | b. 1610 | | m. Wm. | Married |
| came to | came to | came to | | Tucker | Stokes |
| Va. 1620. | Va. 1623 | Va. 1628 | | came to Va. | |

The first five of these all came to Virginia as is borne out by record.

Robert Thomson, married Judith.
Died 1702. Died 1709.

| David Thomson | Robert Thomson | Susanna | Hannah | Martha |
|---|---|---|---|---|
| b. 1686 | b. about 1687 | | | |

David Thomson b. 1686 m. probably Elizabeth Waddy and had among others:

Waddy Thomson
d. 1801 (Hanover record); m. first, Elizabeth Anderson; 1766, m. second, Mary Lewis (Mrs. Cobbs), d. 1813.

Mildred Thomson
(by second marriage), b. Sept. 21, 1775; m. Dr. James Scott.

James McClue Scott
m. Sarah Travers Lewis.

Anthony Thomson possibly nephew, but more probably son of Robert, married 1758, Ann Bibb, daughter of Henry Bibb. She was born in Louisa County, Va., 1735, died in Kentucky, 1798. Emigrated 1785 to Woodford County, Ky., that being date of land grants.

All of their children except Robert went to Kentucky with them.

Issue of Anthony Thomson, died 1794, and Ann Bibb:

1. Eleanor (1759-1827), married her cousin, Rev. David Thomson, who was born the same year, 1759, and died the same year, 1827. Their tombstones are yet visible in the old family burying-ground near Versailles, Kentucky. Issue:

Anderson, Judith, Elizabeth, Ann, Mary, Sarah, William, David and Louisa.

2. Judith, married Thomas Bell. Issue:
   Robert, Thomson, Samuel, Thomas, Jefferson.
3. Robert (said to have remained in Virginia.)
4. Susanna, married Edmund Vaughan, had Mary and James.
5. Anthony.
6. Elizabeth, died unmarried, 1799.
7. Sarah, died unmarried, 1800.
8. Mary, first wife of Samuel Waddy, grandson of Samuel Cobbs and Mary (Lewis) Cobbs. No issue.
9. Henry, died unmarried—1810.
10. Nathaniel (1764-1833), married 1795, Frances Major, daughter of John and Elizabeth Redd Major, had issue:
    Zoraida (1807-1859), married Thomas Crutcher (1810-1887).

    Ann Crutcher, married 1870, Jerry Downing.

    George C. Downing, married 1914, Clare Churchill, daughter of Wm. Churchill and Miss Cocke; has a son, Churchill Downing.

*Note.*—Benjamin Bibb of King William County, Va., died 1768, in Louisa County. Married Mary ——, had:

Henry Bibb, of Frederickville Parish, died before 1763, when estate was settled, he married. Issue: (ten children)

1. David, died unmarried.
2. John, died unmarried.
3. Henry, died unmarried.
4. Benjamin, was his father's executor.
5. Thomas, lieutenant in French and Indian War.
6. Charles.
7. Robert Flemming, died 1812, married Justiana ——.
8. Elizabeth, married Nathaniel Garland.
9. ——, married Joseph Woolfolk.
10. Ann, married Anthony Thomson.

## DAVID THOMSON

Born September 4th, 1690.

Tradition says—Married Elizabeth Waddy, daughter of Anthony Waddy and his wife, Sarah. This Thomson-Waddy marriage is the only one on record of this period, and the conclusion is that David and Elizabeth had several sons, who through their descendants perpetuated the name of "Waddy Thomson." The South Carolina Waddy Thomsons will be cited later.

## WADDY THOMSON

Son of David and Elizabeth, who lived at various times in Hanover, Louisa and Albemarle, left many well known descendants.

He was widely known as a lawyer of valued legal knowledge, as well as a reliable citizen. His name therefore figures on many legal documents. Old Mr. Jesse Maury of Albemarle told me that (though born some years after the death of Waddy Thomson) he had heard often of him as talented in business affairs and his advice much sought.

On the Louisa records he figures often in public service, and in church affairs.

*Early Settlers* by Saunders on page 492—refers to Waddy Thomson and his son, Waddy, of Louisa County.

1775—Waddy Thomson on a committee for care of the county poor—Associates: George Meriwether, Charles Yancey, Wm. Peters, etc.

1778—Waddy Thomson took deposition as Commissioner. (Virginia *Gazette.*)

1747—He appeared on records of Frederickville Parish Book.

1768—As Justice of Peace for Louisa.

1774—The court of His Majesty's Justice of Peace for Louisa, are: Waddy Thomson, Robert Anderson, Thomas Johnson, Nathaniel Anderson, gentlemen.

*Virginia Historical Magazine* cites Waddy Thomson as one of the commissioners of Louisa County, and—(Vol. V) date May, 1775,

Waddy Thomson, member of Louisa County Committee of Safety.

Waddy Thomson, married first, Elizabeth Anderson, daughter of Nelson Anderson, Sr., who died 1786, of Hanover County, and had six children.

Children of Waddy Thomson and Elizabeth Anderson:

1. Nelson Thomson, died 1798, married Sarah Kerr, daughter of James Kerr and Sarah Rice. He was a Revolutionary soldier. (See *History of Albemarle,* and Colonial list of Revolutionary Soldiers.)
2. Sarah Thomson, married John Lewis, son of "Planter" John Lewis and Sarah Shelton, of Scottsville, Va.
3. Waddy Thomson, married first, Elizabeth Anderson; married second, Miss Onesbey.
4. Anderson Thomson, married first cousin, Ann Thomson, daughter of Col. Nelson Thomson, Jr. and Miss Ball.
5. David Thomson, married Eleanor Thomson, daughter of Anthony Thomson and Ann Bibb. David Thomson was a Baptist minister. 1770 was pastor of Gold Mine Church, Louisa County, Va. 1778 he emigrated to Kentucky and served Boone Creek Church and Tate Creek Church. (Semple's *Virginia Baptist Ministers.*)
6. Elizabeth Thomson, apparently died unmarried. Her father's will stated he had already portioned her, thus left her no more property.

## NELSON THOMSON

Born 1725, died February 13, 1798, married Sarah Kerr, April 2, 1776, she was born June 10, 1760, died July 22, 1799. She was the daughter of James Kerr and Sarah Rice. (See note.)

Nelson Thomson was one of those from Albemarle who in July 11, 1775, marched under Lieutenant George Gilmer to Williamsburg to demand satisfaction of Lord Dunmore for the removal of the State's supply of powder. (Reference: *History of Albemarle.*)

This same history gives date of his death, 1798. His name also appears in the list of Revolutionary soldiers of Virginia, indicating fuller service. He had issue:

1. Elizabeth Thomson, born January 30, 1777, died November 13, 1840, married September 8, 1802, Nathaniel Morton. Issue:
   1. Mary W. Morton, married Nicholas Hocker.
   2. James Morton.
   3. Elizabeth Morton, married James Duncan.
   4. Lucy Jane Morton, married Abraham Cummings, U. S. Congressman.
2. Sarah Thomson, born July 22, 1788, died June 18, 1828, unmarried.
3. Nelson A. Thomson, born December 24, 1781, died June 7, 1839, in Kentucky. Married Hannah Blain.
4. Mary Waddy Thomson, born February 7, 1780, died September 17, 1812. Married Thomas Gay.
5. Ann Thomson, born December 2, 1783, died July 6, 1827.
6. James W. Thomson, born August 26, 1785, died September 2, 1827. Married the daughter of a Presbyterian minister in one of the Carolinas.
7. Maria Thomson, born April 30, 1788, married Alexander Reid. Issue:

   Nelson Reid, Samuel Reid, Sally Reid and Maria Reid.
8. Susanna Thomson, born May 31, 1790, married April 21, 1807, Edmund Shackleford.
9. Lucy Ann Thomson, born April 26, 1792, died 1842. Married George Lee.
10. Sophia Thomson, born June 19, 1794, married first, Francis Lightfoot Lee; married second, Geo. Carpenter.
11. Amelia Rice Thomson, born November 11, 1796, married John Montgomery.

Nelson Anderson Thomson, born September 24, 1781, died 1839; September 30, 1805, married Hannah Blain, who died October 3, 1827. Issue:

1. Sarah Nelson Thomson, born August 29, 1806, died January 18, 1828, married —— Lee.
2. Elizabeth Morton, born April 3, 1808, died November 15, 1840, married Walter Nichols.
3. James Waddy Thomson, born June 10, 1810, died September 3, 1827.

4. Lucy Ann Thomson, born April 3, 1812, died December 7, 1828.
5. Nelson Anderson Thomson, born June 11, 1814, died April 25, 1886, married on December 23, 1841, Margaret Bledsoe.
6. George M. Thomson, born January 12, 1816, died June 6, 1862, married Susan Pemberton.
7. John Rice Thomson, born November 20, 1817, married Martha Caldwell.
8. Mary Waddy Thomson, born December 11, 1819, died June 7, 1844, married Will Nichols.
9. Frances Jane Thomson, born December 10, 1821, died January 24, 1844, married Robert Blain.
10. David Drury Thomson, born January 6, 1824, died April 22, 1904, married Ella Enders in Texas.
11. Andrew Carr Thomson, born May 23, 1825, died July 27, 1851, married Milly Morland.
12. Hannah Ann Thomson, born September 3, 1827, died August 3, 1843.

Lucy Ann Thomson, ninth child of Nelson A. Thomson and Sarah Kerr, born April 26, 1792, died 1842; married George Lee in 1812, in Kentucky, Lincoln County, born 1792, in Amherst County, and moved to Kentucky. Issue:

1. Elizabeth Shelton Lee, married Rev. Wm. Dickon at age of 14.
2. Nelson Thomson Lee, married Lucy Weisiger.
3. Geo. Frank Lee, married Susan Jane Miller, had:
   - Eugene Wallace Lee, married Clara Louise Warren, and had:
     - Virginia Lee, married April 18, 1917, Louis Bryant. Their address: Roberta, Scott County, Tenn.
4. Pamelia Lee, died age 15 years.
5. Josiah Ellis Lee, married first, Elizabeth Miller; married second, Fanny Bell.
6. Lucy Ann Lee, married Wm. Chrisman.
7. Ambrose Lee, died unmarried.
8. Richard Lee, married Sarah, and had one son.

9. James Lewis Lee, died age 18 years.
10. Mary Lee.
11. Sarah Lee.

Lucy Ann Lee, sixth child of George Lee and Lucy Ann Thomson, born July 12, 1828, died February 16, 1889, married May 16, 1848, William Chrisman, born November 23, 1822, died January 27, 1897. Issue:

a. Geo. Lee Chrisman, born August 8, 1851, married Charlotte Duke, 1872, and had Luke Duke; married second, Miss Gales.
b. James Lee Chrisman, born 1853, died 1872.
c. Margaret Chrisman, born June 12, 1855, married May 10, 1877, Logan O. Swope, born February 27, 1847, died February 23, 1900. Had issue:
    1. Wm. Chrisman Swope, born March 29, 1878—named for grandfather. Died September 6, 1909.
    2. Frances Hunton Swope (father's mother's full name), born December 9, 1879, married, has two children.
    3. Thomas Hunton Swope, born August 23, 1882, married Maude Moseley.
    4. Logan O. Swope, born January 11, 1884, died infant.
    5. Lucy Lee Swope, born July 1, 1886, married —— Byrn.
    6. Margaret Chrisman Swope, born May 21, 1888, married Thomas T. Miller.
    7. Lo, born October 19, 1890, died August 1891.
    8. Stella Swope, born October 12, 1893, married James G. Eurengy.
    9. Sarah B. Swope, born February 12, 1896, died July 3, 1916.

Thomas Hunton Swope and Maude Mosely, had issue:

1. Maude Louise Swope, born September 14, 1907.
2. Julia J. Swope, born May 28, 1909.
3. Thomas Hunton Swope, born December 17, 1911.
4. Margaret Swope, born July 27, 1912.
5. Lucy Lee Swope, born October 31, 1914.

Issue of Margaret Swope and Thomas T. Miller, married December 21, 1912:

1. Margaret Nancy Miller, born October 31, 1913.
2. Stella Miller, born January 1, 1915.
3. Thomas T. Miller, Jr., born December 8, 1917.
4. Ruth Miller, born July 11, 1919.

Alexander Kerr, born in Scotland 1867 or 1869.

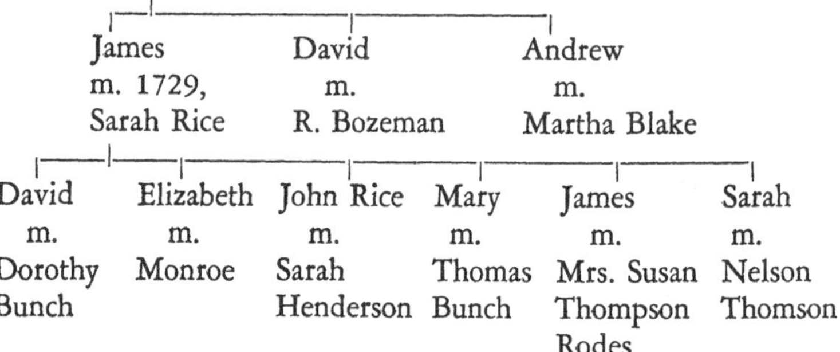


*Note.*—John Rice had: David Rice, married Blair; Sarah Rice, married James Kerr.

*Note.*—Kerr family noted for its many Presbyterian ministers.

## ANDERSON THOMSON

Lieutenant Third Regiment Revolutionary War, married Ann Anderson, who is supposed to have been his first cousin, she was the daugher of Col. Nelson Anderson, Jr., born in Hanover, died 1826 in Bedford County. He married *Ann Ball,* and their issue:

1. Ann Anderson (above).
2. Jesse Anderson, married Elizabeth West Jones, lived in Bedford County Issue:
   1. Mary Lightfoot Anderson, married Samuel Garland.
   2. Elizabeth Anderson, married Dr. Nathaniel W. Floyd.
   3. Charles Dandridge Anderson, married Mary Harrison.

Issue:

1. Dr. Nat. Waddy Thomson, who was for a year in the Legislature from Bedford County, Va.
2. Nelson Thomson.
3. Jesse Thomson.
4. Ann Thomson.
5. Frances Thomson.

I know little of these descendants. 1908 a letter to Mr. Nat. Waddy Thomson, grandson of Anderson Thomson of Peakville, Bedford County, states that he, and his children and his brother, Dr. Alexander Spottswood Thomson, were the only members of this family remaining in Bedford County.

1829, Jane Meriwether Poindexter (daughter of Anderson Thomson's half sister, Judith Thomson), visited the homes of her uncles, Anderson and Waddy Thomson and says of them: "These uncles had large families, good homes and many slaves." Some years before when at the age of fifteen, she had lived at her uncle Anderson's. Her letter gives the above list of her children.

Further descendants:

Spottswood E. Thomson, deceased. Born in Bedford County, June 30, 1864. Son of Dr. A. S. and Mrs. M. R. Thomson, who died some years ago. He married Miss Jessie Frances Penn, and had:

Harry P., Marion, Lillian, Edith, Louise, Pauline, Virginia, Mrs. M. L. Slaughter, Louis E. Thomson, of Collins, Tex., James R. Thomson, of Houston, Tex., Wm. A. Thomson, of Hattiesburg, Miss.

He leaves also, his brother Henry Thomson, of Goodes, Va., and sisters, M. L. and C. A. Thomson, of Chicago.

Mrs. Boyle, 515 South Kenmore Ave., Los Angeles, California, descends from Waddy Thomson, Sr.'s first marriage, but her line not fully known.

## WADDY THOMSON, JR.

Married Elizabeth Anderson, daughter of Richard Anderson and Ann Meriwether. She was born April 5, 1769, married August 8, 1787.

*Brock's Anderson* gives a list of their children:

1. Ann Meriwether Thomson, born March 15, 1789.
2. Elizabeth, born July 17, 1791.
3. Mary Louise, born March 15, 1793, died April 1862, married Nicholas W. Owen. Issue given.
4. Richard Anderson Thomson and
5. Jasper Thomson were twins, born November 1, 1795.
6. Nelson A. Thomson, born March 2, 1797.

7. Nicholas Thomson, born December 26, 1799.
8. Louise Thomson, born November 20, 1801, married 1824, Yancey Harris. Issue given later.
9. David W. Thomson, born September 6, 1803.
10. Frances Thomson, born May 6, 1805.
11. Cecilia A. Thomson, born January 15, 1808, married Jordan W. Rucker and had: Jas. W. Rucker and Ann E. Rucker.
12. Sarah E. Thomson, born January 7, 1811.

Waddy Thomson, married second, Susanna Overby, "a fine woman and good wife", Mrs. Mills' old letter testifies.

Waddy Thomson was also a Revolutionary soldier, must have been quite young and, I have heard from his nephew (my father), was of a reckless courage and spirits.

My father told me of an incident when his uncle Waddy was in the Revolutionary Army and closely pursued by the British, he stopped at a house for a toddy. While he was "tasting", the enemy surrounded him as they thought. Turning, he drank to them and putting spurs to his horse cleared a very high fence which the enemy were depending upon to pen him—and was soon beyond pursuit.

Mary Louise Thomson, born March 15, 1793, died April 11, 1862, married Nicholas W. Owen, born January 17, 1792, died July 20, 1869. Had issue:

1. Bernard L. Owen.
2. Judith Ann Elizabeth, married Joseph Rucker.
3. Maria L., married Henry Gibbs.
4. James Francis Meriwether Owen, born January 24, 1824, died November 26, 1895, married Harriet Agnes Watson, born 1828, died 1866, and had issue:
    a. Wm. Henry Owen, born January 6, 1846, married October 5, 1871, Nanny Caroline Spencer. Issue: Jenny Owen, married F. E. Moss, Louisiana, Missouri.
5. Cecilia A. Owen, married Thomas Key. Issue:
    a. David Key.
    b. Mary Key, married Bernard Gibbs.
    c. Henry Key.
    d. Robert Key.

6. Mary V. Owen, married William Mitchell, issue: Thomas B. Mitchell.
7. Nicholas W. Owen, Jr., born 1833.
8. Martha M. Owen, born 1836.
9. Jane T. Owen, born 1840.

*Owen Note*

William Owen, born September 3, 1748, died December 22, 1821. Married Agnes Wilkerson. Died May 6, 1820.

*Son,* Bernard Owen, born July 26, 1768, died February 3, 1847. Married Judith Palmer. Died November 20, 1855.

*Son,* Nicholas W. Owen, married Mary Louise Thomson.

Henry and Maria L. Owen Gibbs. Issue:

1. Ann, married Edwards.
2. Sarah, married George Gett.
3. William N.
4. Alice V., married Powell Gibbs.
5. Addison B.

Yancey Harris and Louise Thomson, had:

1. Mary E.
2. Maria L., married Wm. Elliott.
3. John N.
4. Martha A.
5. Mary P.
6. William Y.
7. Francis.

Mrs. Jane Martin of Columbus, Georgia, descended from Eleanor, daughter of Anthony Thomson and Ann Bibb, and the Rev. David Thomson, son of Waddy Thomson, Sr. and Elizabeth Anderson. States that: "The wife of David Thomson, first *was* Elizabeth Waddy", daughter of Anthony Waddy and Sarah. And also states that the Rev. David Thomson's family claimed kin with Spottswoods, Dandridges and Crawfords.

David Crawford III, married Ann Anderson, daughter of John and Sarah Waddy Anderson, sister of Elizabeth Waddy.

We find another Waddy Thomson line: Samuel Thomson, possibly nephew of Waddy Thomson, Sr., of Louisa, Amelia and Pittsylvania counties, married Ann Jennings. A son, Waddy

Thomson, went to Kentucky. His daughter, Mary Thomson, married. They had: Captain Ed. Porter Thomson, who married his first cousin on his father's side, Marcella Pitts Thomson. Their daughter, Elizabeth Thomson, married John Orr. Issue: Frances Orr, of Frankfort, Kentucky.

## SARAH THOMSON

Daughter of Waddy Thomson, Sr. and Elizabeth Anderson, married John Lewis, born 1749, died 1804, son of "Planter" John Lewis of Albemarle, and his wife, Sarah Shelton.

John Lewis's will dated July 16, 1780.

Will:

> I bequeathe to Sally Ming all property which came by first wife, her mother—To John Waddy Lewis all property except ½ to beloved wife Sarah Lewis for her lifetime—to John Waddy and Elizabeth Anderson Lewis all property that came by present wife, of which she has one third.
>
> Brother Owen Lewis and Zachary Lewis, Executors.
>
> Probated Feb. 6, 1804.

### SECOND MARRIAGE OF WADDY THOMSON, SR.

Waddy Thomson, of Hanover, Louisa and Albemarle counties, married second, Mrs. Mary (Lewis) Cobbs, widow of Samuel Cobbs, of Louisa County. The marriage settlement between them is dated December 12, 1766, with William Lewis of "Locust Hill" as trustee. Each already had children by former marriages, so property complications between three sets of children needed much cleverness of statement. They lived on land inherited through Robert Lewis's will situated four miles from Ivy, Albemarle County. Here they raised five daughters. A cedar tree on a hilltop which overlooked the old home marks their burial ground.

I. Ann Thomson, married twice.

Married first, John Slaughter, died 1797, surveyor of the county, had:

1. Mary Lewis Slaughter, born 1790, died November 10, 1849. Who inherited a Negro girl, Lucy by her grandfather's will.

2. Waddy Thomson Slaughter, married Frances Ballard.
3. Warner Slaughter.

Married second, Philip Grafton, had:

1. "Sally Scott" Grafton.
2. William Grafton.
3. Ann.
4. Mildred.
5. Caroline Grafton.

Record: Furnished by Miss Alta G. St. Clair, 510 N. Martin Street, Kahoka, Clark County, Mo.

Mary Lewis Slaughter, born 1790, died November 10, 1849. Married approximately 1808 or 1809 to William L. Slaughter, born January 20, 1783, died November 8, 1854. Son of Reuben and Ann (Poindexter) Slaughter, of Culpeper and Bedford counties, Virginia.

Mary and William Slaughter moved to Clark County, Mo. in 1837. Both are buried at Chambersburg Cemetery, Clark County, Missouri. Children:

A. William Lewis Lightfoot, born September 18, 1811, died August 3, 1889, born at Culpeper, Va., married January 7, 1845 to Miss Rebecca McKinney Cooper, born April 8, 1823, died May 23, 1876. Daughter of Jacob Manson Cooper II and Hannah McDaniel of Ohio County, Ky., and granddaughter of Jacob Cooper I, Captain in Revolution, from Camden District, S. C. and Rebecca McKinney.

Wm. Lewis Lightfoot Slaughter and his wife resided many years in Clark County, Mo. and are buried at Peaksville Cemetery, Clark County, Mo. Seven children:

1. Harriet L. Slaughter, born October 20, 1845, married Sewell Arthur St. Clair, who was born May 8, 1845, married April 9, 1872. Has one child: Alta G., born May 31, 1883.

S. Arthur St. Clair is a son of James and Polly Emerson Sherman St. Clair, who came to Clark County, Mo. from Washington County, Ohio.

James St. Clair's father and mother, William and Alice

Smith St. Clair were early residents of Belmont County, Ohio, near St. Clairsville.

2. Sarah L Slaughter, born September 13, 1847, married March 2, 1871, Virgil A. Jones. Two sons:
   a. William Otis, born April 24, 1872.
   b. Claude A., born October 11, 1874, Waverly, Neb.
3. William Cooper Slaughter, born September 8, 1849, died December 23, 1921, married November 23, 1879, Alice Pierson, of Kahoka, Mo. One child:
   a. Alberta C., born August 26, 1880, married August 26, 1912 to James M. Shackleford, of Kahoka, Mo.
4. Jacob Manson Slaughter, born March 13, 1851, married December 22, 1883 to Emma Gray, daughter of Robert and Julia Graham Gray of Athens, Clark County, Mo. Two children:
   a. Julia M., born January 29, 1884, married J. W. Woodford. Children: James, Gilbert and Margaret. Residence: Tulsa, Oklahoma.
   b. Bertie E., married B. B. Hickman.
5. Charles T. Slaughter, born January 2, 1853, died November 21, 1913, married December 29, 1886, to Miss Mina Woodford, born February 9, 1864, died July 9, 1906, daughter of Wm. and Emily Woodford of Watertown, Ohio. Seven children:
   a. Mabel, born November 6, 1887, married April 23, 1913 to Jeff Sinnett, a widower with three children. Issue:
      1. Dora, born July 2, 1914.
      2. Nora, born September 8, 1916, and
      3. Flora, born September 9, 1916, died September 9, 1916, were twins.
   b. Maude, born October 21, 1889, died September 11, 1906.
   c. Lucy, born March 21, 1892.
   d. Charles, born January 30, 1895, married December 17, 1915, Mary Balentine Green. Issue:
      1. Chas. Aaron, born September 27, 1916.

2. Roy Edward, born January 13, 1918.
3. Cecil Boyd, born July 23, 1919.

e. Chester, born November 19, 1897, married August 27, 1918, Winnie Mae Haddock. Issue:
1. Elizabeth Lucile, born August 5, 1919.
2. Ralph Lawrence, born July 11, 1921.

f. Jessie, born May 5, 1900.

g. Julia, born June 27, 1903.

6. Mary Hannah Slaughter, born January 29, 1855, died May 1, 1904, married November 24, 1878 to Addison F. Clarke of Kahoka, Mo. Issue.
a. Ray E., born October 2, 1879.
b. Myrta.

7. Susan Amanda Slaughter, born August 18, 1859, died February 13, 1894, married March 12, 1884 to William E. Leach, of Clarke County, Mo. Three sons: George, Earl and Roy.

B. Henry Holloway Slaughter, son of William and Mary Slaughter, died October 24, 1870, married Mary J. Denny. Issue:
1. Chalmer, died young.
2. Emma, married William Nixon, has a son, perhaps others.
3. Adelia, married Chas. Becker, of Alexandria, Mo. Issue:
Gladys and Nellie, died unmarried.
Sadie Marion, unmarried.
4. Ella, married Wilbur Dwight, has one son, Benjamin, who married, and has one daughter, Louella.
5. Eva, married Booco, and has:
Florence Booco, married Alfin Johnson. Residence: Honolulu, Hawaiian Islands. Two small children.
6. Rosa, married Coombs. Several children. Residence: Boston, Mass.
7. Laura, married Henry Becker, brother of Chas. Becker:
a. Jessie, married ——, of Rockford, Ill.
b. Marion, married ——, of Keokuk, Iowa.

C. Charles Meriwether Slaughter, married Fannie Kemmer, moved to Utah. Many descendants. Has staff given to his father in Clark County, Mo., by Lewis and Clark on exploring expedition.

D. Reuben Pendleton Slaughter, married first, Mary Gray, of Athens, Mo.; married second, Miss Mary Mason.

Peter, son by first marriage has descendants in Nebraska.

E. Mary, A. E. (Aunt Polly), born February 8, 1826, married Samuel Allison, born June 1, 1820. Issue:

a. Wm., deceased.

b. Eddie Allison.

c. Anna, unmarried.

END OF MISS ALTA ST. CLAIR'S RECORDS

II. Mary Thomson, daughter of Waddy Thomson and Mrs. Cobbs, married 1794, James Poindexter, son of Joseph Poindexter and Elizabeth, of Louisa and Bedford counties. Issue:

1. Lewis, born August 30, 1795.
2. Joseph.
3. Edwin Waddy.
4. Warner, born June 14, 1801, died February 3, 1871, married first, Margaret Caldwell.
5. Albert.
6. Nicholas.
7. Hartland.
8. James Monroe.
9. Mary, married —— Gamewell, of St. Louis, Mo. (See Poindexter Record.)

These moved to Kanawha, West Virginia.

III. Judith Thomson, married, 1798, Wm. Poindexter, died 1834, son of Joseph and Elizabeth G. Poindexter, born near Ivy Depot, Va., 1779, died October 24, 1844 in Montgomery County, Missouri. Issue:

1. Waddy Thomson Poindexter, married Miss Plunkett, from near Lynchburg, Va. Moved to Caloway County, Mo.
   a. William Auborn.
   b. Samuel.
   c. James.
   d. Nicholas.
2. Mary Lewis Poindexter.
3. Jane Meriwether Lewis Poindexter, born 1803, lived to be

over ninety. Named for maternal grandmother and the explorer. Married Abraham P. Mills. Issue:

a. Susan Ann Mills, married first, Joel Trotter, who was killed in war. Issue, six children. Married second, Sam Bristow, had one child. Married third, Chas. Minnis.

b. Sarah Judith Mills, married first, Samuel Castile, had six children. Married second, Ransome Wait, had: Marcus T. Wait.

c. Robert Waddy Mills, died September 25, 1844, age 15 years.

4. William James Poindexter, born 1806, married Eliza Stephens. Issue:

a. William Stephens Poindexter, lives in Colorado.

b. James Archie Poindexter, lives in Nevada.

c. John Thomson Poindexter, lives in Montgomery County.

d. Samuel Thornhill Poindexter, lives in Collins County, Texas.

e. Ann Eliza, married Gallager, lives in Collins County, Texas.

f. Mary Frances Poindexter, married Berryman, lives in Collins County, Texas.

5. Elizabeth Poindexter, died age 14.

6. Susan Mildred, married Dudley Martin, died in Montgomery County, Mo., left issue.

7. Sarah Poindexter, died near St. Joseph, Mo. Married Edward Warren Lewis, son of Fielding Lewis, of North Carolina, left descendants.

IV. Susanna Thomson, daughter of Waddy Thomson and Mrs. Cobbs, died 1847, married Jesse Davenport, died 1822. Issue:

1. James Thomson Davenport, went to Georgia.

2. William, went to Georgia. (William and his mother visited their Virginia relations several times.)

3. John L., died in Richmond or Charlottesville.

4. Charles Warner.

5. Mary Frances.
6. Susan Mildred.

V. Mildred Thomson, born September 22, 1775, died October 9, 1829, age 49; became second wife of Dr. James Scott of Pennsylvania and Virginia, born February 17, 1760, died April 14, 1822. Issue:

1. Mary Ann Lewis Scott, born October 23, 1808, died August 27, 1840, married Lewis A. Boggs, February 15, 1827, one child—Elizabeth Hart Boggs, m. Valentine Johnson.
2. John Thomson Scott, born February 26, 1810, died October 19, 1832, married January 5, 1832, Huldah Lewis, born March 18, 1812, died October 5, 1836. No issue.
3. James McClure Scott, born August 17, 1811, four miles from Ivy at the home of Waddy Thomson, died July 7, 1893, married December 13, 1832, Sarah Travers Lewis, born November 7, 1813, died December 19, 1891. (For issue see Scott record.)

## THE WADDY THOMSONS OF SOUTH CAROLINA

(Record of Mr. Richard H. Earle, of Marietta, Ga.)

Waddy Thomson, born in Cumberland County, Va., son of Josiah Thomson and Mary Swann, his wife, while yet a young man—in 1769—emigrated to Willis County, Ga., married in Washington, Ga., Eliza Williams, daughter of James Williams, a distinguished Revolutionary officer of Virginia.

Later, Waddy Thomson moved to South Carolina, and became prominent in the politics of that State.

Through the generations of these Waddy Thomsons of South Carolina, this name persists and has passed to other States through them. Evidently descended from Waddy Thomsons of Virginia, Georgia and South Carolina—was

"Waddy Thomson, b. at Pickinsville, S. C., Sept. 8, 1798. d. in Tallahassee, Fla., Nov. 23, 1868. An American Polititian, he was Whig member of Congress from South Carolina, 1835-41 and U. S. Minister to Mexico 1842-44. He wrote *Recollections of Mexico* in 1846."

(Quoted from *Century Dictionary of Proper Names.*)

## EX-GOV. HUGH THOMSON

New York *Tribune,* 1904.

("Gov. Thomson Dead.) Hugh Smith Thomson, twice governor of South Carolina, born in South Carolina, January 24, 1836. . . was grandson of Waddy Thomson, Senior, who for 26 years was Chancellor of South Carolina. His uncle, Gen. Waddy Thomson, Junior, was Congressman from South Carolina and Minister to Mexico. This ex-Governor Hugh Thomson, was son of Henry Tazewell Thomson and Agnes Smith, married April 6, 1858, Elizabeth Clarkson, who survived him. Had issue, five sons and two daughters.

"Graduated from South Carolina Military Academy, 1856; Prof. of French and Belles Lettres at Arsenal Academy, 1857; Capt. of battalion of State Cadets in Civil War and Principal of Columbia Academy after war till 1876; State Superintendent of schools till 1882, instituting many reforms; elected Governor of South Carolina, 1882; reëlected, 1884; resigned June 30, 1886 to become Assistant-Secretary United States Treasury; served under Secretary Manning, later under Senator Fairchild; named Democratic member Civil Service Commission, February 18, 1889 by Cleveland. Senate did not ratify nomination but he was appointed by President Harrison the following May, and served under Roosevelt till spring of 1892. Then became Controller of New York Life Insurance Co., and moved to New York City. Member of Century and Reform Clubs; Confederate Veteran Association; New York Alumni, Alpha Tau Omega Fraternity, and for many years President of Southern Society."

Children of Gov. Hugh S. Thomson:

1. Lt.-Col. Henry T. Thomson, Columbia, S. C. Second, S. C. Regiment in Spanish War.
2. Thomas C. Thomson, Chattanooga, Tenn. Prominent insurance man.
3. John M. Thomson, 115 Broadway, New York City. Real estate broker.
4. Waddy Thomson, Atlanta, Georgia. Author of *History of United States* in general use in the South.
5. Hugh S. Thomson, Jr., 44 Wall Street, New York. Real estate broker.
6. Daughter, married James G. Zachary, 44 Wall Street, New York. Real estate broker.
7. Caroline Thomson.

*Note.*—James M. Scott, son of Mildred Thomson and Dr. James

Scott, with his wife and daughter, Mildred, being at the Rawleigh Springs, Va., 1891 were addressed at the supper table by a Mr. Tom Thomson, who had been impressed by Mr. Scott's exact resemblance to his own father, the Hon. Hugh Thompson, Representative in Congress from South Carolina, also by the resemblance of his daughter, Mildred Thurman, to his own aunt, "Mildred Thompson". Mr. Thompson said he was of the Thompsons of South Carolina. He married the adopted daughter of Mr. Berry, of Baltimore, a wholesale merchant.

FINIS

## THE SCOTT-McCLURE FAMILY OF CHAMBERSBURG, PENNSYLVANIA AND VIRGINIA

NOTE.—The children of Dr. James Scott of Pennsylvania and Virginia, were very young at the time of his death and retained only a few points of tradition of his family.

These were:

1. His parents—Scott, whose wife was a Miss McClure, were both of immediate emigrant families from the north of Ireland, who had settled at Carlisle, Pa. All sons of this family, except Dr. Scott, had died early without issue. The two daughters married, and with their families moved West.

2. And in 1812 Dr. Scott and his wife with their three children had visited the old Scott home in Pennsylvania, then owned by his brother John.

Many years ago my brother, J. Z. H. Scott through legal friends made an unsuccessful attempt to find record of this Scott McClure family at Carlisle, Pa.

January, 1904, I also made an attempt at Carlisle, assisted by C. H. Humrich, a lawyer, who most kindly sent me much interesting record. But none of it bore positively on my search.

Knowing of the lifelong friendship of Dr. Scott and Mr. Henry Thomson (not a relative) of Chambersburg, Pa. and later of "Pine Grove", Stafford County, Va., I returned to my original inference that Dr. Scott had come from the vicinity of Chambersburg, also. This surmise proved correct. My father being very young when his parents died and not especially interested on this point had been mistaken.

A letter addressed to the "Office of Registers and Wills" at Chambersburg brought me the address of a reliable and distinguished genealogist, G. O. Seilhammer, who at once located in that office the land patents and will of my great-grandfather, John Scott, with full list of his children, and later record of them in the settlement of their father's estate. (Evidence so clear upon which B. R. Alden Scott said a suit could have been won.)

Mr. Seilhammer was then editor of an historical magazine regarding the families of original settlers of Cumberland County, Pa. which originally stretched to the Ohio. I supplied for this magazine the record of Dr. Scott's descendants in Virginia.

October 12, 1912, Mr. Seilhammer wrote me he had obtained McClure record also. Consultation with "our clan" brought a resolve to secure this paper so interesting to our family; and this was accomplished financially by Dr. Zachary T. Scott of Austin, Texas, B. R. Alden Scott, Alfred L. Scott, both of San Antonio, Texas, and Richmond L. Scott, Sr. of Clifton, Texas. Thus this record was fully recovered after being lost to us for one hundred years.

The children of James McClure Scott are the only descendants of John Scott and Mary McClure who bear the Scott name.

## THE SCOTT McCLURE FAMILY

William McClure, a pioneer of what is now Montgomery Township, Franklin County, Pennsylvania, in the Cumberland Valley, was apparently a brother of David McClure of Donegal in Lancaster County, and of John McClure of Letort's Springs at Carlisle. Genealogically speaking he was the first of the McClure family to come to the Valley. On the west branch of Conococheague he built a mill, probably before 1746. He died in 1747. His will divided his lands between his wife and his son, Patrick. He also mentioned his daughter Mary. His mill was probably abandoned during the French and Indian War and fell into decay. The name of William McClure's wife as given in his will was Margaret.

Issue:

1. John McClure.
2. Thomas McClure.
3. Andrew McClure.
4. Samuel McClure.

5. Patrick McClure.

*6. Mary McClure, married John Scott, who died in 1790. She died presumedly in 1794.

John Scott was an early settler on one of the tributaries of the Little Antietam in what is now Washington Township, Franklin County, Pa. He was taxable in Antrim Township, which then included Washington. In 1751 he obtained a Maryland Patent for 187 acres of land on the Greencastle and Waynesboro turnpike November 8, 1762, also a Pennsylvania Patent for 109 acres and 21 perches September 25, 1770.

His plantation was partly in Antrim and partly in Washington Townships; he lived there till his death. His will dated March 1st, 1782, was proved May 11, 1790.

It is believed that Mr. Scott was a son of David Scott, an early settler in the Great Cove, Fulton County, Pennsylvania.

It is recorded in the votes of Assembly that in 1763 David Scott gave his bond to pay and maintain twenty men of a scouting party for three months for the purpose of driving back Indians who invaded the Cove. This enabled farmers of the Cove to reap crops. David Scott was appointed guardian for Patrick McClure, son of William McClure in 1755.

Children of Mary McClure and John Scott:

1. William Scott, died early.
2. David Scott, died in 1800, was in bad health when he visited his brother, Dr. James Scott in Virginia. Dr. Scott went back home with him and nursed him till his death.

*3. James Scott, M. D.

4. Mary Scott, married William Lowrey.
5. Martha Scott, married John Gaff.
6. John Scott, married Elizabeth Gaff. No issue.
7. McClure Scott, died young.

John Scott, Jr., died 1812. He obtained the Scott homestead patented by his father which he sold to Henry Funk, July 7, 1812, for $11,065.94. At his time it consisted of two tracts containing, respectively, 166 acres, seven perches, and 54 acres, 141 perches. The homestead is now owned by Benjamin Funk, grandson of Henry. Mr. Scott's will dated July 11, 1812, and proved August

10, 1812. During his last illness he was nursed by his brother, Dr. James Scott, who brought his family from Virginia that he might remain at his brother's bedside till his death. With Mildred, his wife, Dr. Scott executed a release for his interest in the old Scott homestead June 30, 1812. Mr. Scott was married, but left no issue. (His wife married second, Col. John Fletcher, as his second wife, and left children: John Calvin Fletcher, William Scott Fletcher, James, Robert and Elizabeth Fletcher.)

(John Scott's wife was a sister of Hugh Gaff.)

Mary Scott, daughter of John and Mary (McClure) Scott, married William Lowrey. Had issue: Margaret Lowrey.

They went West before the close of 18th century. When the Scott family accepted the award of the arbitration for settlement of the Scott estate, William Scott, the oldest of the brothers signed for his sister, Mary Lowrey.

Martha Scott, daughter of John and Mary (McClure) Scott, married John Gaff, son of Hugh Gaff of Antrim Township, Cumberland, now Franklin County, Pennsylvania. They seem also to have gone West. Their history has been lost.

Issue:

1. David McClure Gaff.
2. Mary Maria Gaff.
3. Elizabeth Gaff.

## DR. JAMES SCOTT

Son of John and Mary McClure Scott, was born February 17, 1760, near Chambersburg, Pa., and died April 14, 1822, in Orange County, Va. He was a physician of talent and distinction, highly educated, and far ahead of his day in diagnosis and treatment of diseases. (Possibly educated at Dickerson College, Va.) Before 1794 he came from his Pennsylvania home and established himself in Virginia, settling first in Spotsylvania County, where he lived at the time of his first marriage.

After his second marriage he lived at Hydraulic Mill which he established in Albemarle County, Va. He subsequently returned to Spotsylvania County, living for a time in Fredericksburg, and finally removed to his farm on Mine Run where he and his second wife died, and are buried in the garden there, their graves being reserved in the deed of sale of the place by his children. Dr. Scott had a passion for mills and owned many mill sites on various rivers. The hydraulic mill which he had built in Albemarle County at the junction of Ivy Creek and the Rivanna River, was a place which later became an active business center in the time of flat-boat transportation down the Rivanna River into the James River to the Richmond market. Warehouses and shops gathered around it, but the coming of railroads with quicker facilities of transportation destroyed its trade. The old mill finally washed away in a big flood about 1870.

At Mine Run also he had a thrifty mill under the charge of an expert miller. Dr. Scott was an active practitioner all his life. During the latter part of his life he did much of his practice on foot, being a fine walker—and taking advantage of paths through plantations to shorten distances.

While very popular and most successful in his practice, he was dissatisfied with the immaturity of medical knowledge, and in his latter years would not charge for his services. His patients did not share his doubts, but eagerly trusted to his methods which were often original and were practiced later, generally, by scientific physicians.

A few of his letters have been preserved and are filled with discussions speculative of the progress of medical science and its future development. These addressed to his brother-in-law, Dr. Richmond Lewis while the latter was a "Student of Physick" at Philadelphia, are full of inquiries for later methods of practice taught there, and commissions for late works on these subjects.

He was a man of warm sympathies and exceeding generosity, who never cared to accumulate much property, although he left his children a competency. On one occasion he met a former schoolmate walking from some point in the South to his home in the North, who had lost his horse and used up his money through his delayed journey. With characteristic liberality Dr. Scott forced him to accept his horse and purse as a gift, when this friend had declined to accept an urgent invitation to stop and pay the Doctor a prolonged visit.

The ford across Mine Run, at Dr. Scott's mill was on a thoroughfare to Fredericksburg, and between deep banks. When draft horses were checked to drink in the stream, the start up a steep bank with a heavy load was hard for them. Dr. Scott put in a public water trough piped from his spring beside his boundary fence, that those teams might drink and have a level road on which to start again.

Note: Years later Dr. Scott's grandson, B. R. A. Scott, of San Antonio, Texas, put up a similar watering place on a desert road in Texas—in commemoration of Dr. Scott.

A letter dated October 10th, 1800, tells of his oldest brother, David, coming to him in Virginia, and of his plans for some sort of sanatorium which were interrupted by his going back to Pennsylvania with him to give him care on the journey.

In 1812, he again went to his old home taking his wife and children, to visit his brother John Scott.

He married July 28th, 1795, Ann Overton Lewis, daughter of Zachary Lewis III and Ann Overton Terrell of Bel-air, Spotsylvania County. She was dying with consumption and lived only until September 11, 1795. Her wish was that Dr. Scott should become closely identified with her family, and that he should be with her constantly in her illness. He was devoted to her and everyone related to her; he called her parents father and mother and was a loving son to them.

Her brothers and sisters also showed him the same love as if he were their very brother. Col. Lewis wished him to accept Ann's portion. This Dr. Scott refused, but eventually did accept a small legacy after Zachary Lewis's death.

He changed his place of residence several times—but as an old slave said of him: "Master would never live out of reach of Bel-air" (this Zachary Lewis' home).

He married second, December 9, 1807, Mildred Thomson, daughter of Waddy Thomson and Mary (Lewis) Cobbs, daughter of Col. Robert Lewis of Bel-voir and his wife Jane Meriwether.

Mildred Thomson was born September 22, 1775, died October 9, 1829. She shared Dr. Scott's affection for his first wife's family. He and she died before their three children were grown, and the two brothers of Dr. Scott's first wife and his sister-in-law,

Mrs. Huldah (Lewis) Holladay raised his children. All three of them married into the family of his first wife, Ann Lewis.

Issue:

1. Mary Ann Lewis Scott, married Lewis Alexander Boggs, and left one child, Eliza Hart Boggs. (Her descendants given later.)
2. John Thomson Scott, married Huldah Lewis, daughter of Dr. Richmond Terrell Lewis and his wife, Elizabeth Travers Daniel. No issue.

*3. James McClure Scott, born August 17, 1811, married December 13, 1832, Sarah Travers Lewis, daughter of Dr. Richmond T. Lewis and his wife, Elizabeth T. Daniel.

## MARY ANN LEWIS SCOTT

Daughter of Dr. James and Mildred Thomson Scott, born in Albemarle County, Va., October 23, 1808, died August 27, 1840, married February 15, 1837 to Lewis Alexander Boggs, of Livingston, Spotsylvania County, Virginia. Issue, one daughter:

A. Eliza Hart Boggs, married Valentine Johnson. Issue, nine children:

1. Mary A. Johnson, married David Meade. Issue:
   a. David Pratt Meade.
   b. Eliza Hart Meade.
   c. Jane Lewis, married April 3, 1913 to Mr. Snell, has issue.
   d. Catherine Meade.
   e. Dorothy Wythe Meade.
2. Louise, died young.
3. Alfred R. Johnson, married first, Miss Yost. Issue:
   a. Henry Mason Johnson.
   b. Caroll Hart Johnson.

   Alfred R. Johnson, married second, Louise Rawlings. Issue:

   c. Clara Johnson.
   d. James R. Johnson.
   e. John, died infant, and
   f. Eliza, died young—twins.

4. Lewis Johnson, married and has, Marjory Adair Johnson.
5. Dunbar Hanson Johnson, married and has two children.
6. Valentine Mason Johnson, married and has issue.
7. Rev. John Scott Johnson, married Louise ——, graduate of University in Washington, D. C. and of Union Theological Seminary, Richmond, Va.
8. Henry Branch Johnson, married.
9. Livingstone Spottswood Johnson, married, has two children.

## JOHN THOMSON SCOTT

Son of Dr. James Scott and Mildred (Thomson) Scott, was born February 6, 1810, died October 19, 1832. He attended and was educated at Hampden-Sydney College. Married January 5, 1832 to Huldah Lewis, daughter of Dr. Richmond and Elizabeth T. Daniel Lewis, born March 18, 1812, died October 5, 1836. No issue. He died in Savannah, Ga., where he had gone in search of health. His body brought back to "Brecknock", Spotsylvania County, Va. for burial. His wife died at the Fauquier White Sulphur Springs some years later, and is buried beside her husband at the "Sunset Tree" which was the meeting place of a literary club of their circle of young associates, with many romantic remembrances.

## "BEL-AIR" SCOTTS

### JAMES McCLURE SCOTT

Son of Dr. James and Mildred (Thomson) Scott, was born in Albemarle County, Va., at the home of his grandmother, Mrs. Mary (Lewis) Thomson, August 17, 1811, and died July 1893, at Bel-air. He was educated at Hampden-Sydney College and was married to Sarah Travers Lewis, born November 7, 1813, died December 18, 1891, at "Prospect Hill", the home of Waller and Huldah (Lewis) Holladay in Spotsylvania County on December 13, 1832.

They lived at "Bel-air", the old Lewis home, which Mrs. Scott inherited from her father, Dr. Richmond Lewis, in the comfort of people of means of that day. "Bel-air" and "Prospect Hill", as the homes of representatives of these Lewises, were famed for their hospitality and were centers to which widely scattered Lewises who had spread out to other States came back for long visits to their kin.

Mr. and Mrs. Scott had fifteen children, twelve of whom were born at "Bel-air" and the older ones grew to manhood and womanhood there, being educated by private teachers under the supervision of Mrs. Scott whose education was of high order. One of her sons said of her she gave him more preparation for his college course than he got from professional teachers.

In 1852 Mr. Scott bought a farm in Stafford two miles from Fredericksburg, where he built a handsome home and where he lived for many years, his two youngest daughters being born there. Mrs. Scott called the place "Little Whim."

Selling this place some years before the Confederate War, he for a time rented and lived at "Kenmore" the former home of his kinsman, Fielding Lewis and Betty Washington, his wife. He finally bought "Pine Grove", the former home of Dr. Scott's friend, Mr. Henry Thompson of Chambersburg, Pa. and Stafford, Va. He planned to build a permanent home here but the breaking out of the Confederate War and advancing armies caused him to return to "Bel-air" where he lived the remainder of his life.

Here on neutral ground between the armies he was subjected to many inconveniences and two raids—Stoneman's Raid from Fredericksburg to Frederick's Hall on the C. & O. Railroad, and Sheridan's troops the day before the Battle of Trevilians.

As Mr. Scott with his wife and daughters sat and silently looked on the looting of their home by Northern soldiers, their chief thought was, "Does General Lee know what this move of Yankee troops means?" The answer came with Hampton's scouts who rode up from one direction as the Yankees had just left.

Before the war Mr. Scott had been advised to transfer his money and his family abroad that the latter might avoid being in the thick of a military struggle. He replied, "I have no more right to do so than others and will abide by the fortunes of my State." His loyalty caused him to invest his means in Confederate bonds, he lost all except his lands, which in their depreciated value served only to pay some loans he had incurred. He paid the last dollar that he owed and was moneyless. He and his family led a life of privation at "Bel-air" for the rest of his life.

His five oldest sons served in the Confederate Army; providentially none were killed, though serving creditably in the hottest parts of battlefields. Like their comrades, after Appomattox, they turned their energies to the care of their parents, younger brothers and sisters, each later finding a profession and independency.

At "Bel-air" in 1882, was celebrated Mr. and Mrs. Scott's golden wedding—all ten living children gathering from widely scattered homes to be together for once; the oldest children having left home before the four youngest were born. In parting they knelt around their parents to receive their blessing.

Mr. Scott was long an elder in the Presbyterian church in Fredericksburg and afterwards at the "Kirk O' the Cliff", near "Bel-air".

He and his wife lie side by side in the old Lewis burial-ground at "Bel-air". Their descendants are widely scattered but their life's work is accomplished in the example they have given of Christian rectitude and scholastic ideals.

They stood for the right rather than for expediency.

Children:

1. John Thomson Scott, born January 7, 1834, died January 16, 1869, in Galveston, Texas, where his remains are buried. He received an excellent education and was for a time at West Point Military Academy, but at the outbreak of the war entered the Confederate service, rising to the rank of major.

   He married in Houston, Texas, May 18, 1865, Gracie McMorris, later the wife of Judge Geo. Mann. She died January, 1925. Issue:

   a. James M. Scott, died age 13.

   b. John Scott, died age 22, unmarried.

2. Elizabeth Lewis Scott, born December 21, 1835, died July, 1917, married September 4, 1851, to Dr. John Minor, son of James and Catharine Thompkins Minor.

3. Alfred Lewis Scott, born February 12, 1838, died 1915, married Fanny Taylor, July, 1862.
4. Mary Ann Lewis Scott, born October 6, 1839, died October 18, 1861, in Richmond, Va. Buried at "Bel-air".
5. James McClure Scott, born July 13, 1841, died December 13, 1913.
6. John Zachary Holladay Scott, born March 14, 1843, died January 4, 1904.
7. Richmond Lewis Scott, born September 21, 1845, died March 30, 1847.

*8. Sarah Travers Lewis Scott, born March 31, 1847, died February 6, 1926.

9. Lewis M. Scott, changed to Richmond Lewis Scott.
10. Lucian Minor Scott, born December 11, 1849, died March 2, 1854.
11. Bradford Ripley Alden Scott, born June 28, 1851, died January 13, 1925. (B. R. A. not a family name.)
12. Anne Elizabeth Scott, born December 25, 1852, died August, 1914.
13. Mildred Scott, born April 1, 1855, at "Little Whim", died January 10, 1935.
14. Frances Greenhow Scott, born July 18, 1857, at "Little Whim".
15. William Wyndham Scott, born October 19, 1861, died October 1, 1862. (Wyndham not a family name.)

## ELIZABETH LEWIS SCOTT

and Dr. John Minor. Issue:

a. Lucian Minor, born August 12, 1852, died a man of high attainments, having received his education at the best classical schools. Superintendent of Southern Express; lived at Nashville. Married Lizzie Webb of Bowling Green, Kentucky.

Issue: (six children)

1. Webb Minor, married Jean Holladay, had:
    a. Lucian.
    b. John.
    c. Elizabeth.

2. Dr. Harry Fisher Minor.
3. Lucian Minor, died young.
4. Dr. Dabney Minor, married Mary Harrison, had Mary Dabney Minor.
5. Frank Minor.
6. Joseph Minor.

b. Dr. James Minor of Memphis, ear, eye and throat specialist, married Margaret Rogers. No issue.

He graduated in medicine at the University of Virginia, then went to New York, where he became assistant to Dr. Noys. Dr. Minor has a national reputation. He reported the first use of cocaine in eye surgery. He had for years been a professor in the Memphis Medical School, and has to his credit many wonderful operations and treatments. He has use of both hands in operations. In answer to my query Dr. Minor states that he was "one of the first to use cocaine as a local anæsthetic and the first to operate for the removal of cataract under the effects of that drug." Associated with him is his nephew, Dr. Harry F. Minor.

c. Katherine Minor, married Edward Jenkins. No issue.

d. Mary Love Minor, married Lewis Littlepage Holladay. Issue:

1. Lewis L. Holladay, married.
2. Elizabeth, died young.
3. Frances Greenhow, married Robert Somerville, November 8, 1922, and has issue:
   Robert Somerville, Jr., born 1924; Lewis L. Somerville; Mary Love Somerville.
4. James Scott Holladay, married Martha Trigg, October 18, 1922, and had issue:
   Barbara Scott Holladay and Frances Holladay.
5. Margaret Holladay.

e. Lucy Landon Minor, died infant.

f. John Bailey Minor, born April 25, 1869, died September 11, 1883.

g. Elizabeth V. Minor, born May 12, 1874.

## ALFRED LEWIS SCOTT

Born in Spotsylvania County, Virginia, February 12, 1838, married Fanny Herbert Taylor, born in Butler County, Alabama, March 1, 1845. They were married in Greenville, Ala., July 22, 1862.

He had a classical education at the University of Virginia. Was a planter in Alabama at the beginning of the Confederate War, entered the service as a private, declining the grade of an officer, preferring to go to the front as one of the rank and file. He was a member of the 9th Alabama Regiment, Co. G, Wilcox Brigade, Anderson's Division; but later he served as aide on the Staff of General E. A. Perry.

He was in the principal battles in Virginia, and was in the charges in the re-taking of the lines at Bloody Angle, and The Crater. (His wife, daughter of Dunklin Bonar Taylor and Katherine Herbert, of Greenville, Ala.)

(Record given by A. L. Scott, Sr.)

Children:

a. Alfred Lewis Scott, born November 19, 1863, baptized July 10, 1864, married Mary Macey. No issue.

b. Augusta Daniel Scott, born April 28, 1865, baptized November 10, 1867, died October, 1924. Married Dr. Houston Chaney, May 31, 1888, had:

    1. Marie Chaney, married Harry Fisher. No issue.
    2. Ellis Chaney, married ——, has three sons: Price Chaney, Ellis Chaney and Reeder Chaney.

c. Edward Perry Scott, born January 5, 1867, baptized November 10, 1867, married Annie Hadden. No issue.

d. Catherine Taylor Scott, born September 18, 1868, baptized May 7, 1871, died December 24, 1896. Unmarried.

e. Frances Greenhow Scott, born February 7, 1871, baptized May, 1871.

f. James McClure Scott, born March 15, 1873, baptized December 13, 1873.

g. Dunklin Bonar Taylor Scott, born January 31, 1875, baptized May 21, 1876.

h. Sarah Travers Scott, born July 4, 1877, baptized November 25, 1877, married Frank Dullnig, and has:
   1. Francis Scott Dullnig, married.
   2. Marie Dullnig, married Mr. Gilliland, has a daughter, Sarah L.
   3. Catherine Dullnig.
i. Nathan Virginia Scott, born July 15, 1879, died infant.
j. Richmond Lewis Scott, born February 12, 1884, baptized March 28, 1885, married April 1916, Susan Fletcher, and has:
   1. Richmond Lewis Scott, Jr.
   2. Alfred Herbert Scott.
k. Hillary Herbert Scott, born April 21, 1888, has two daughters by his second marriage. He was a captain of artillery with the 42nd Rainbow Division in France. His guns bore on Sedan while waiting for the Armistice, and the advance of the French troops.

## DR. JAMES McCLURE SCOTT

Was born July 13, 1841, died December 13, 1913. Married first, Sally L. Dickerson, February 24, 1875; married second, Laura Payne, June, 1902, who has one daughter, Jean Lindsay Scott.

He was educated at a classical school, later at Washington College which is now Washington and Lee. He graduated in Medicine at the University of Virginia after the close of the War Between the States, during which conflict he was in the Confederate service from the outbreak of the war until the surrender at Appomattox.

He inherited the warm sympathies and generosities of his grandfather, Dr. Scott. This disposition was shown even to his foes; for instance his admiration of the bravery of Lieutenant Dewes, U. S. A. at the Battle of Brandy Station was not impaired when the Federal officer left a dent in James Scott's sword in the effort to cut him down in the mêlée.

He enlisted with the Fredericksburg Artillery, C. S. A., May, 1861. He re-enlisted in the Cavalry, Co. F, 10th Virginia (Albemarle) Rangers and served with it to Appomattox. At Gettysburg separated from his command by Stuart's absence, he volunteered with the 9th Alabama and fought the three days' battle with them, and was wounded there.

Wounded and captured in the second battle at Brandy Station and a prisoner at Point Lookout for sixteen months, he was sergeant and was given the oversight of 100 prisoners to nurse and care for. His inherited love of the medical profession, which he later adopted, enabled him to be a great comfort to those suffering illnesses.

a. Issue by first marriage:
   1. McClure Scott, born November 13, 1876, married Dr. Jessie Thornton. Issue:
      a. McClure Scott, died young.
      b. William T. Scott.
      c. James McClure Scott.

b. Cassie D. Scott, born June 25, 1879.

c. Nan Brooke Scott, born June 29, 1885, married J. W. McMullin, and has:
   a. Jere McMullin.
   b. Edward McMullin.
   c. James McMullin.
   d. Francis Lewis McMullin.

## JOHN ZACHARY HOLLADAY SCOTT

Born March 14, 1843, died January 18, 1904. He was a student at the University of Virginia at the opening of the War Between the States. Although but 17 years old at the time he entered the Confederate Army, with which he served until the close of hostilities, being with General Johnston when the latter finally surrendered.

He joined Wise's Brigade in the Albemarle Rangers, later Company F, 10th Virginia Cavalry. His special service was that of a scout in which capacity he acted for Stonewall Jackson and General Chambliss and for General R. E. Lee at Gettysburg. He was captured twice, at Hagerstown, and again near Petersburg. Exchanged he followed the retreat and surrendered with General Johnston in North Carolina.

He went to Texas after the war; studied law and rose high in this profession. After the great Galveston Flood, he was appointed by the governor of Texas as City Attorney of Galveston, his special duty being to rehabilitate the City Finances, and establish the Commission Government of the city.

His death which was a sudden one, was widely deplored, and his obsequies were marked by civic honors and every evidence of the warm appreciation in which he had been held by his fellow citizens.

He was married first, to Lucy Prentis Doswell, daughter of Richard Doswell and Helen Prentis, October 10, 1872.

Married second, Mary Claudia Keenan, June 20, 1903.

Issue by first marriage:

a. Helen Sarah Scott, married Frederick von Harten, no issue.
b. Lewis Raymond Scott, married Helen Smith, 1900, has issue.
c. Lucy Estelle Scott, married Chas. Waters Cannon, no issue.
d. James M. Scott, born April 2, 1879, married, and has issue.
e. Richard Doswell Scott, born February 17, 1881, married Nan, and has:
    1. Helen Scott, married 1929, Alfredo Santilli, has Helen.
    2. Richard Scott.
    3. Lucy Scott, married Mr. Frazier.
    4. John Z. Scott.
    5. Mary Scott.
    6. Catherine Scott.
    7. Richmond Lewis Scott.
f. Mary Travers Scott, married Richard Tiernan, 1904, has issue:
    1. Helen Tiernan, married.
    2. Richard Tiernan.
    3. Virginia Tiernan.
g. Caroline Prentis Scott, born August 15, 1884, died in childhood.
h. Elizabeth Scott, born September 17, 1885, died an infant.

Second marriage:

i. Margaret Keenan Scott, born June, 1904, married September 12, 1923, Thos. F. Hanrahan, of Houston, Texas. Issue: Claudia and Tom.

## SARAH TRAVERS LEWIS SCOTT

Born March 31, 1847, married February 15, 1872, Charles Harper Anderson of "Locust Hill." She died February 6, 1926, at the home of her son, Dr. M. L. Anderson, Richmond, Va.

## RICHMOND LEWIS SCOTT

(Christened Lewis Minor Scott), born September 17, 1848, died, 1933. He entered the Confederate service in Wise's Brigade, Pate's Co. at the beginning of the war, being between the age of twelve and thirteen, and served the campaign of the year 1861 in West Virginia. He had a severe attack of measles and was dismissed from the service as too young and too weakened for further service. He made a later effort to enter the service but arrived at Appomattox the morning of the surrender. He was educated partly at Hampden-Sydney and at private classical schools.

He removed to Texas in 1869, where he lived at Clifton, Bosque County. He married first, Abby Boyle, October 14, 1874, who was born July 13, 1855, and died March 27, 1895. She was from Bryan, Texas.

He married second, Annie Estill of Huntsville, Texas, no issue.

Issue by first marriage:

a. Lewis Alden Scott, born July 10, 1875, died October 5, 1889, being accidentally killed while wolf hunting. His remains are buried by those of his mother at Clifton, Texas.

b. Zachary Thomson Scott, born December 25, 1880, graduated from the Texas University School of Medicine at Galveston, Texas. At the time the great flood occurred (1900) at Galveston he was in a hospital, and rendered heroic service in carrying patients from a ward that was being wrecked to a part of the hospital which withstood the storm. Others who were assisting stopped from exhaustion and terror, but he in spite of exhaustion, did not stop till the last patient was moved. Quite a large number owed their lives to his individual efforts.

He married June 2, 1909, Sally Lee Masterson, born March 6, 1882, daughter of Robert Benjamin Masterson and his wife Ann Exum Masterson. Issue:

1. Abby Ann, born July 11, 1910, married 1931, Lawrence R. Hagy.
2. Zachary Thomson, born February 21, 1914, married Miss Anderson.
3. Mary Lewis.

c. Pauline Lewis Scott, born July 14, 1883, married October 5, 1911, William Green Poindexter, of Morgan City, Miss. Issue:
1. Wm. Green Poindexter, born September 25, 1912.
2. Richmond Lewis Scott Poindexter, and
3. Mildred Poindexter, born January 25, 1915, were twins.

d. Abby E. L. M. A. Scott, born July 14, 1885, married January 12, 1909, William Poindexter Kimbrough, of Itta Bena, Miss. Issue:
1. Wm. Poindexter Kimbrough, born September 25, 1910.
2. Lewis McCaskil Kimbrough, born July, 1913.

e. Joseph Boyle Scott, born December 4, 1889, married April, 1915, Catherine Irene Jones. Issue:
1. Stephen Franklin Scott, born January 19, 1916.
2. Joseph Boyle Scott, born 1920, died infant.
3. Joseph Boyle Scott, born September 12, 1926.

## BRADLEY RIPLEY ALDEN SCOTT

Born July 28, 1851, died January 13, 1925, in San Antonio, Texas, his home for twenty years. He was educated at classical schools and graduated from the law department of the University of Virginia, 1873. In 1873 he established himself in practice at Galveston, Texas. In the great storm that worked wide havoc in that place, he was obliged to carry his family to a haven of safety in the center of the city, his home and belongings being wiped out by the wind and water. The ruins of his home were filled with the bodies of many unfortunate refugees.

He removed to San Antonio, Texas, where he practiced his profession and ranked as a leading member of the bar.

He was married September 27, 1877, to Mary Miller Anderson, of "Locust Hill", Albemarle County, Va.

*Note.*—B. R. Alden Scott's name was in honor of Col. Bradford Ripley Alden, Superintendent of West Point, who was a friend of John Scott when a cadet at West Point. (Therefore not a family name.)

Issue of B. R. A. Scott and his wife, Mary Miller Anderson:

a. Lucy Harper Scott, born August 5, 1878, married June 29, 1904, Elmer Carpenter Griffith, of New York City, and has:
   Lewis Scott Griffith, born June 11, 1905, married October 27, 1934, Rosine Chase.

b. Mary (Polly) Anderson Scott, born August 27, 1880, married Chas. Boston, of Missouri and Mexico.

c. John Thomson Scott, born February 17, 1884. Served with the 42nd (Rainbow) Division in the Meuse-Argonne Advance, was desperately wounded, and after a year of hospital care—is a pensioned soldier. The fragment of shell in his chest is too near a vital point to risk removal. He has been a good soldier in civil as well as military life.

d. Sarah Lewis Scott, born October 2, 1886, married David Skene McKellar, who was born in New Zealand of a Scotch family. The McKellars are septs to the "Campbells of Argyle." (See McKellar note.)

   Issue:

   1. David McKellar, born December 18, 1911, San Antonio, Texas.
   2. Mary McKellar, born September 27, 1917, Palestine, Texas.
   3. Alden McKellar, born October 9, 1920, Eagle Pass, Texas.

e. Dr. Bradford Ripley Alden Scott, born December 13, 1888, died in U. S. A. service, November 12, 1918, in San Antonio, Texas. August, 1918, he married Norma ——. No issue.

   He was a talented young physician—was a graduate of the Texas Medical School at Galveston, Texas. Just beginning a life of great promise, he was worn out in serving in the great epidemic of influenza of 1918, and succumbed to the disease. At the time of his death he was Flight Surgeon for aviators at Brooks Field, near San Antonio, Texas.

f. Dr. Harper Anderson Scott, born January 16, 1891, was of the Naval Reserves in the World War, graduated in medicine

THE HALL AT "BEL-AIR"

from Texas University, at Galveston, Texas. He married January 29, 1923, Minai Nicholson, daughter of Mrs. Mabel C. Nicholson, and lives at Austin, Texas, and has a daughter, Minai C. Scott.

## MILDRED SCOTT

Born April 1, 1855, married April 11, 1882 to John R. Thurman. They had no children of their own, but were deeply interested in the circle of young people around them, particularly those of the Bel-air school in which Mildred Thurman also taught, her efficiency reaching out to many emergencies in its problems.

They lived at "Aldermarsh", near Lewiston, Spotsylvania; later settled in Fredericksburg. John Thurman died after prolonged ill health in Mississippi at the home of William G. Poindexter, March 17, 1924, and is buried beside his parents at the cemetery of South Plains Church, Keswick, Va. She died January 10, 1935 in Fredericksburg and is buried at Aquia in Stafford County.

## ANN ELIZABETH SCOTT

Born Christmas Day, 1852 at "Bel-air", died in Austin, Texas, August 5, 1914. From her childhood she was remarkable in character and mind, of deeply Christian piety, and brilliant intellect. Under many difficulties she obtained an education of high order, and chose teaching as a profession. After some years of teaching with marked success in private families, she instituted at "Bel-air" (which she had inherited) a classical school. She had students from many States who now, from their widely scattering homes, look back at this formative influence as their inspiration of all that was intellectual and noble and good. She had their devotion always, and now their lasting gratitude.

They have placed a memorial cross to mark her grave in testimony of their affection. At its unveiling, a group of her white pupils stood on one side of her grave—facing them on the other side stood a group of gray-headed Negroes who had been her pupils in a Sunday School she had organized for them in her early life. The ceremony, impressive and simple, was conducted by her former pupils whose addresses told of the inspiration she had been to them.

## FRANCES GREENHOW SCOTT

Born at "Little Whim", July 18, 1857, was associated with her sister, Ann Elizabeth Scott in the Bel-air School, and has been a teacher also of marked ability in other schools in Virginia and Mississippi.

She has been a stay and comfort always in many lives—always self-sacrificing in help to others. Her home is in Fredericksburg, and she now shares it with her sister, Mildred Thurman.

## WILLIAM WYNDHAM SCOTT

Born October 19, 1861 at Pine Grove, Stafford County, died October 1, 1862 of membranous croup at Bel-air.

These children of James M. Scott cited in the family register already given should have had a fuller record which is now added.

## LUCIAN MINOR SCOTT

Born at Bel-air, died in childhood at "Little Whim", buried at Bel-air.

## JOHN THOMSON SCOTT

Oldest son of James M. Scott, was educated at private classical schools and at West Point Military Academy. In spite of Col. B. R. Alden's protest discouragement caused him not to complete his course at West Point—to his own later regret.

He settled in Kansas until the political situation there was too strained for Southern principles. He then turned to cotton planting on the Brazos River in Texas.

At Richmond, Va., 1861, he enlisted in the Confederate service. As no Texas troops had arrived in Virginia, he was first with the 2nd S. C. Regt., then transfered to the 5th S. C. Regt. to be with his former Kansas partner, Mr. Blassingame. In this command he served that summer, and in the first Battle of Manassas received a cut on his forehead from a piece of shell.

November 1861 he returned overland to Texas, and joined a Texas command as a private soldier (at Shreveport, La.) Promotion sought him, and he served on the staffs of several generals as he was needed; first, under Gen. Richard Taylor's command, then as Major on General Hawes's staff in the defense of Galveston, 1864-5.

He was cited for special efficiency in the shortage of officers in the yellow fever epidemic among the troops there. He also had a severe attack of the same disease. He was paroled at Houston, Texas. He bravely faced reverses, and business embarrassments, dying just as he had overcome them. His two sons died in youth, unmarried.

### MARY ANN LEWIS SCOTT

Fourth child of James M. Scott (named for his only sister), died, age 22, in Richmond, Virginia, of typhoid fever at the home of her relative, Thos. Cushing Daniel, October 18, 1861, and is buried at Bel-air.

Intellectual, and lovely in person and character, she has left among all who knew her an unhealed sorrow.

*McKellar Note:*

David Harkness McKellar, born in Scotland, married Jane Katherine Skene, born in Victoria, Australia. Their son, David Skene McKellar, born September 12, 1876, in Invercargill, Otago, New Zealand, married Sarah Lewis Scott in San Antonio, Texas, on January 31, 1911.

## THE ANDERSON FAMILY OF HANOVER COUNTY, VA.

Our knowledge of the origin of this family is copied from a collection of notes from various sources. S. T. L. A. *Americans of Gentle Birth* by Mrs. H. D. Pitman, of St. Louis, Mo. states that the Virginia family of Anderson originated in Scotland and appears later in Northumberland County, England—where Sir Edmund Anderson is found, as Chief Justice.

Mrs. Hester Dorsey Richardson, genealogist of Baltimore, Md. supplied me with some old records on the Anderson families, taken from Louisa records which were most useful in genealogies and dates. She also contributed the following extract, from *Tyler's Quarterly Magazine,* Volume I, No. 3, page 127:

"The *Journal* of the Rev. Samuel Davies, of Hanover County, who was at that time in London getting subscriptions for the erection at

Princeton of the first substantial 'Nassau Hall', states: 'Thursday, Feb. 14, 1754. Daniel with Mr. Anderson of the South Sea House, a friendly, polite gentleman and a secretary of the Correspondents here with the society for Promulgating Christian Knowledge in Scotland. I find his uncle was grandfather of the Andersons in Hanover.'

"This Mr. Anderson with whom the Rev. Mr. Davies dined was Adam Anderson (1692-1755), who was for 40 years Clerk in the South Sea House. He was a native of Aberdeen, and author of the History of Commerce to 1763."

*The Anderson Family* by Edward Lowell Anderson states that on July 4, 1635, Richard Anderson, age 17, left England for the colonies, and was followed July 1st by Richard Anderson, age 53, presumably his father. Before sailing both took the oath of allegiance and supremacy. These seemed to have been the progenitors of the Anderson family of Hanover County, Va. They intermarried with Massies, Cloughs, Poindexters, Overtons, Garlands, Dabneys and Sheltons.

*I. ROBERT ANDERSON, SENIOR, died 1712, aged nearly 72 years. The land office register, April 16, 1683 (page 272, Book 7) states him as a grantee for 727 acres of land in New Kent County for importing fifteen persons. He was Vestryman for St. Peter's Parish, 1686, and for St. Paul's Parish, 1704-1712, until his death. He married Cecilia Massie, who was of a family who came to Virginia about the same time as the Anderson family. Her parents were D. Massie and Lucelia Poindexter.

Issue, nine children:

1. Richard Anderson, Magistrate of King and Queen County, 1699-1702.
2. David Anderson, whose son was an officer in New Kent Militia, 1700.
3. John Anderson, grandfather of Capt. John Anderson of 5th and 3rd Va. Regts., who married Mary Anderson, daughter of Robert Anderson the third. (See page 285.)
4. Thomas Anderson.
5. Matthew Anderson.
6. Nelson Anderson.
7. Cecilia Anderson.
8. Mary Anderson.

*9. Robert Anderson, Jr., married Mary, said to have been daughter of Wm. Overton and Mary E. Waters.

One of the younger sons married Miss Garland.

*ROBERT ANDERSON, JR., was born 1663, and died 1716, age 53 years. He married Mary Overton, who died 1734. He was Vestryman of St. Peter's Parish, New Kent, 1702; Vestryman of St. Paul's Parish, 1705; Captain for New Kent, from 1705 to 1713; and Justice for New Kent County., 1714. His widow, Mary Anderson, is cited in processing of her land in St. Paul's Vestry Book. This Robert Anderson, Jr. took up 727 acres in New Kent County which had been relinquished by his father and on the same date, October 23, 1690, received 1,200 acres for the importation of twenty-four persons, he being designated Captain Robert Anderson; his father being designated as Robert Anderson, Senior.

Issue, nine sons:

1. Richard Anderson.
2. James Anderson.
3. Garland Anderson, who held many properties in Hanover, Louisa and adjoining counties. He was an able and progressive man, and was member of House of Burgesses, and delegate to Virginia Convention, 1775. He married Marcia Burbridge of Norfolk, Va., and left descendants, who became distinguished in *Belle Lettres* and for their refinement.
4. Matthew Anderson, Burgess in place of John Symes in 1734, married Mary Dabney, daughter of George Dabney. His tombstone, his wife's, and that of their only child are in a graveyard in Gloucester County.

*5. David Anderson of Hanover and Albemarle, married Elizabeth Mills. (Full record on page 286.)

6. Robert Anderson (third), of "Gold Mine", Louisa County, married Elizabeth Clough.
7. Nathaniel Anderson.

   *Note:* Could this name be for Nathaniel Massie, born August 2, 1727, who may have been brother to Cecilia, wife of Robert Anderson the first?

8. Charles Anderson, married Janet Claiborne.

9. John Anderson, father of Cousin Jack Anderson (Captain), who married Mary Anderson, daughter of Robert Anderson (third).

Louisa, Va. *County Record,* Vol. VI, Part 3, page 258, gives a conveyance from David Anderson, of Louisa County, to his brothers and sisters—Robert, John, Ann, Susannah, Kitty and Sally Anderson—of his rights in a tract of land in Louisa on Peter's Creek, whereon in his lifetime our father, the late Robert Anderson was possessed, the said David reserving to himself one-seventh part, the residue to his six brothers and sisters. (Recorded July 8, 1782.)

The early Andersons settled in York County, Va. When York was divided in 1654, they found themselves in New Kent. Then again in 1720, they found themselves in Hanover, which had been taken from New Kent. "Gold Mine", formerly in Hanover, is now in Louisa County. and named for a creek which runs through the estate and empties into the North Anna River.

Robert Anderson of "Gold Mine", Louisa County, was born January 1, 1712, died 1792, will probated January, 1793. He was Burgess for Louisa County, 1745; Magistrate for Louisa, 1768. His will gives son Robert 410-acre plantation, son George 820 acres, son Samuel 820 acres—slaves and personalty divided among children and grandchildren. His son Matthew Anderson of Gloucester County, probably given lands in that county. Richard Clough Anderson probably given "Gold Mine."

Robert Anderson, married July 3, 1739, Elizabeth Clough (1722-1779). She was a daughter of Richard Clough, who is said to have been a native of Wales and whose wife was a daughter of (?) Massie and Lucilla (Poindexter) Massie, and granddaughter of George Poindexter, the "Emigrant." Her name is variously given as Cecilia, Anne, and Caroline by different authorities. Her marriage date 1718. (St. Peter's Parish Register.) Richard Clough, died 1751. He was the son of George Clough, Clerk of New Kent County, 1720 until his death, 1740.

*Note:* A George Clough was a grantee of 610 acres of land in King and Queen County, 1669. There is a tombstone in the Jamestown Church to the memory of Rev. John Clough, he having been minister to the church. Died January 3, 1683 or 1684.

Issue of Robert and Elizabeth C. Anderson, twelve children:

1. Richard Anderson, died young.
2. Robert Anderson, born August 26, 1740, died February 1, 1805, married Elizabeth Stratton or Shelton. Their second son, Charles Anderson, was buried in Kentucky at "Soldiers Retreat", and was father of Samuel C. Anderson, grandfather of Mrs. Samuel Anderson Bailey, of Lynchburg.
3. Matthew Anderson, born December 6, 1742, died December 24, 1805, married Elizabeth Dabney, and lived in Gloucester.
4. William Anderson, born April 15, 1744, died July 22, 1822, married ——.
5. Ann Anderson, born January 21, 1745, died between 1779 and 1782, was first wife of Col. Anthony New, Revolutionary officer and U. S. Congressman from Virginia and from Kentucky. Issue:
   a. Mary Anderson New, born October, 1779, married William S. Wyatt, of Caroline County. They were great-grandparents of Mrs. Martha B. Wyatt Williams, of Berwick, Pa., who was born at "Edgewood", Caroline County, the home of her paternal grandparents; and was raised partly at "Clifton", the home of her maternal grandparents, near Shadwell, Albemarle County.

   *Note.—Richmond Times-Dispatch,* March 3, 1823:

   > "In Hanover County by the Rev. Charles Talley on Thursday, March 3rd, Wm. W. Tate of Hanover to Miss Ann L. New, daughter of Col. Anthony New of Kentucky, who was born in Gloucester County, served in the Revolution as Colonel, and as Congressman of Virginia (1793-1805), later as Congressman from Kentucky."
6. Cecilia Anderson, born August 2, 1748, died September 8, 1802, married April 3, 1768, Wm. Anderson ("Old Field Billy"), born April 16, 1744, died July 22, 1792.
7. Richard Clough Anderson, born January 12, 1750, died October 16, 1826, married November 24, 1787, Elizabeth Clark, daughter of John Clark and Ann Rogers, and sister of George Rogers Clark and Wm. Clark (of the Lewis and Clark Expedition). She died January 5, 1795. Richard

Anderson married second, September 17, 1797, Sarah Marshall, daughter of William and Ann McLeod Marshall, of Caroline County.

8. Elizabeth Anderson, born November 24, 1752, married Reuben Austen.
9. George Anderson, of "Newington", born May 27, 1755, died April 25, 1816, married first, Miss Presberry, of Baltimore, Md.; married second, Jane Tucker. (John Howard was his grandson.)
10. Samuel Anderson of Cumberland County, born January 25, 1757, died 1826, married Ann Dabney.
11. Mary Anderson, born August 18, 1759, married Captain John (Jack) Anderson. She married second, the Rev. Elkannah Talley. (See Bishop Mead's *Old Churches and Families of Virginia.*) She had two daughters by her first marriage.
12. Charles Anderson, born May 10, 1762, died unmarried.

## RICHARD CLOUGH ANDERSON

In 1775 he was active in the Committee of Safety.

In 1775 he was Quartermaster for the Hanover Minute Men.

In 1776, March 7, was Captain of a Company of Regulars, his cousin John Anderson being his first lieutenant.

In 1779, March 20, he was promoted to Major of 1st Va. Line, and served in the Southern Campaign at Savannah, Ga. and Charleston, S. C.

On September 14, was a prisoner at Charleston until May 12, 1780.

In May, 1781, he was exchanged.

Later was Lieutenant-Colonel of LaFayette's Staff. (His personal statement to his grandson, E. L. Anderson.)

As Captain he was assigned to the 5th Va. Regiment commanded by Col. Peachy—Lieut.-Col. William Crawford.

Richard inherited "Gold Mine", but having had heavy losses through his brother George, he emigrated to Kentucky, buying 500 acres of land near Louisville on which he built his future home "Soldiers Retreat". He was appointed General Surveyor of Western Lands. He and his wife, Elizabeth Clark, whose family also emigrated to the vicinity of Louisville, had issue:

a. Richard Clough Anderson, Jr., born August 4, 1788, in Louisville, died July 28, 1826 at Tabuco. He graduated at William and Mary College, Va., studied law with Judge St. George Tucker, practiced with distinction in Louisville, was a member of the Kentucky Legislature, Member of Congress, 1817-1821, Minister to Colombia, 1823, Envoy Extraordinary to the Panama Congress, 1826, but died on his way there.

b. Larz Anderson, removed to Cincinnati, Ohio, died 1878, married Miss Longworth, daughter of Nicholas Longworth.

c. ——.

d. Anne Anderson, married Richard Logan. Issue:
   1. William Logan, married Elizabeth Hackworth, and had:
      a. Susan Elizabeth Logan, married James Cleve Ritchey, M. D., and had a daughter, Jane Gamble Ritchey, who married Gideon Gilpin Brinton, and had Gideon Gilpin Brinton, Jr.

Richard Clough Anderson, Sr., and his second wife, Sarah Marshall had several children, of whom were:

e. Robert Anderson, born June 14, 1806, graduate of West Point, 1825, Major in command at Fort Sumter, S. C., 1861, was promoted to Brigadier-General U. S. A., died at Nice, October 26, 1871.

f. William Marshall Anderson, born 1808, died January 7, 1881, at Cedarville. He was among the first to cross the Rocky Mountains, and made a scientific journey through New Mexico at the age of sixty years.

g. John Anderson, of Chillicothe, Ohio.

h. Charles Anderson, Governor of Ohio, 1865. He made a speech before the Secession Meeting at San Antonio, Texas, 1861, in favor of sustaining the Union. He lived later at Kuttawa, Ohio.

DAVID ANDERSON, of Hanover and Albemarle counties, Va., married Elizabeth Mills of England, according to Edward Lowel Anderson in *Anderson Family*. They came from Hanover to Albemarle about the end of the Revolutionary War, and lived on a plantation in Albemarle not far from Scottsville. He died 1791; she died 1804. (Wood's *History of Albemarle.*) Issue:

A. William Anderson went to England, settled in London as a merchant. He married Mary Guest, daughter of Wm. Guest (who later administered on the Anderson estate.) Having no issue, William adopted his nephew, Francis, son of Richard Anderson, also Mary Guest, the niece of his wife. William Anderson's estate was held by the Crown. The Master of Rolls advertised for heirs, and some of the claims were settled to applying heirs, but the amounts were very small. The same was done from William's widow's dowery. *Note:* Charles Harper Anderson and his sister, Mrs. Mary M. Scott, received the portion of their father, Dr. M. L. Anderson, Sr. in this last division which amounted to $100 only.

B. Nathaniel Anderson, who died 1812, married 1767 (Marriage Bond), Sarah Elizabeth Carr, daughter of John Carr of Bear Castle, Louisa County, and sister to Dabney Carr, who married Martha Jefferson, sister to Thomas Jefferson. Nathaniel lived on the Old Glebe of St. Anne Parish, on Totier Creek, which he purchased in 1796. He also had several grants in Southwest Virginia owned later by his children, some of whom moved to that region.

Issue of Nathaniel Anderson and his wife, Elizabeth:

1. William Anderson.
2. Nathaniel Anderson, married Sarah Elizabeth, and had:
   a. Martha Anderson, married Stephen Woodson.
   b. Mary Anderson.
   c. Dabney Minor Anderson.
   d. Overton Anderson.
3. Mary Anderson, married Mr. Mosby.
4. Elizabeth Anderson, married Mr. Laurence.

C. David Anderson received from his father, 300 acres of land in Hanover County, but lived in Albemarle.

D. Richard Anderson, born June 15, 1747, died February 14, 1793, married first Anne Meriwether, who died August 5, 1782. Her funeral was preached by the Rev. Wm. Douglas.

Richard married second, Millie Thompson, February 9, 1784. She was born April 4, 1755, died August 22, 1828. She married second, Mr. Jackson. Richard Anderson left issue by both marriages. He had valuable lands in Kentucky, which were afterwards a subject of suit in Kentucky.

E. Matthew Anderson, of Louisa County, married 1772, Elizabeth Anderson, daughter of Col. Richard Anderson (son of Pauncy and Elizabeth Anderson), and his wife Mary Johnson, whose parents were Richard Johnson and Ann Meriwether. Matthew Anderson lived to be 90 years old, his wife 85.

F. Thomas Anderson, of Buckingham County, Virginia.

G. Ann Anderson, married Dabney Minor, of "Woodlawn", Orange County.

H. Sarah Anderson, born July 20, 1758, married March 19, 1783, Christopher Hudson, born March 30, 1758.

I. EDMUND ANDERSON, received the tract of land of 210 acres in Hanover County, on the north side of New Found River, below the confluence of said river, the same land on which his father formerly lived. He was born April 1, 1763, died April 19, 1810. He married Jane Meriwether Lewis, of "Locust Hill".

J. Samuel Anderson, who received lands from his father on New Found River, in Hanover County, Va.

K. A daughter, who married Mr. Barrett.

*Note:*

## PAUNCY ANDERSON

Received a grant of land August 17, 1725, as attested in the Land Office at the Capitol Registry for land grants in Hanover County, in the year 1725. He married Elizabeth, and resided in Louisa County, after that county was cut off from Hanover. His will recorded in Louisa. His children were:

1. Michael Anderson, married Sarah Meriwether, daughter of Thomas and Elizabeth Meriwether.
2. Judith Anderson, married James Dabney, of Albemarle.
3. Richard Anderson, married Mary Johnson, daughter of Nicholas and Elizabeth Hudson Johnson, married second, a

daughter or granddaughter of John Woodson and Dorothea Randolph. Richard Anderson was born 1735, died April, 1819, aged 84 years. He was Justice of the Peace 1762, Colonel of the county 1772, Member of the House of Burgesses 1769-1774. He represented the county for ten terms as associate with Patrick Henry.

Ann Anderson, daughter of David and Elizabeth Mills Anderson, married Dabney Minor, of "Woodlawn", Orange County, and had issue:

1. Sarah Elizabeth Minor, born September 6, 1775, died January 3, 1833, married William Anderson, died September 22, 1822.
2. Mary Minor, born 1777, died young.
3. Dabney Minor, born July 22, 1779, died March 8, 1822, married September 30, 1800, Lucy Herndon, born 1779, died 1833.
4. Ann Minor, born April 20, 1781, died August 19, 1801. She was the second wife of Dr. Charles Meriwether, married September 15, 1800. Dr. Meriwether married three times: first, Lydia Laurie; third, Mrs. Mary Walton Daniel.
5. Sarah Minor, born August 24, 1783, died September 27, 1864 at "Ridgway", Albemarle County, married June 28, 1808, Dr. John Gilmer, of "Edgemont", Albemarle County. He was born April 20, 1782, died February 12, 1834.

Sarah Elizabeth Minor and William Anderson, had:

a. William Anderson, born October 11, 1794, died September, 1822.
b. Ann Eliza Anderson, born March 6, 1796, married Dr. Charles Hunter Meriwether.
c. Dabney Minor Anderson, born February, 1798, unmarried.
d. Overton Carr Anderson, born March 25, 1800, married Miss Diggs.
e. Martha Ann Anderson, born June 6, 1802, married Stephen Woodson.
f. Mary Parks Anderson, born December 30, 1805, married Mr. Morrison.

Dabney Minor, son of Dabney Minor and Ann Anderson, of "Woodlawn". Married Lucy Herndon, daughter of Joseph Herndon, of Fredericksburg and his wife, Nancy Minor, daughter of John Minor and Sarah Carr. Issue:

1. Mary Ann Minor, born March 25, 1801, died May 21, 1833. Married Garrett Minor Meriwether, born 1794, died 1851.
2. Nancy Meriwether Minor, born August 11, 1803, died July 13, 1872. Married Peter Scales on June 22, 1827.
3. James Lewis Minor, born May 5, 1805, died February 28, 1826.
4. Henry Laurie Minor, born March 16, 1807, died September 5, 1832. Married Margaret Whitelaw Herndon on November 18, 1829.
5. Cornelia Lewis Minor, born May 4, 1810, died March 12, 1842 in Kentucky. Married Dr. Samuel Hobson Dabney December 8, 1829. He died August 20, 1846. He was a grandson of Jane Meriwether and Samuel Dabney.
6. Ellen Minor, born December 14, 1811, died March 2, 1826, unmarried.
7. Dabney Minor, born October 18, 1814, died August 29, 1862. Married Jane Hull on February 10, 1835.
8. John Mercer Minor, born 1816, died 1831.
9. Francis Minor, born August 15, 1820, died February 19, 1892. Married Virginia Louisa Minor on August 31, 1843.

Sarah Minor, daughter of Dabney Minor and Ann Anderson, married Dr. John Gilmer of "Edgemont", Albemarle County, son of Dr. George Gilmer, of "Penn Park", and Lucy Walker. Issue:

1. Lucy Ann Gilmer, born 1810, died 1881. Married Benjamin Franklin Minor.
2. Juliet Minor Gilmer, born July 16, 1811, died 1837.

Sarah Anderson, daughter of David and Elizabeth (Mills) Anderson, was born July 20, 1758, died April 3, 1807; married 1783, Christopher Hudson, born March 30, 1758, died May 1, 1825. Issue:

1. Christopher Anderson Hudson, born March 30.
2. Elizabeth Anderson Hudson, born July 6, 1784.
3. George Hudson.
4. Anna Hudson.
5. Anne Hudson, born July 6, 1787.

Elizabeth A. Hudson, married George Gilmer. Issue:

1. Thomas Walker Gilmer, Member of Virginia Legislature, Governor of Virginia, Member of Congress, Secretary of the Navy in Tyler's Administration. He was killed by the bursting of a cannon on the steamer "Princeton" on the Chesapeake Bay; at which time three other members of the President's Cabinet were killed—Upshur, Kennon and Gardner.
2. George Christopher Gilmer, married first, Leanna Lewis, of Scottsville; married second, Matilda Duke.
3. John H. Gilmer.
4. Sarah Gilmer, married Dr. Samuel W. Tompkins.
5. Georgia Gilmer, married Collin C. Spiller.
6. Maria Gilmer, married Samuel J. Adams.
7. Ann Gilmer, second wife of Peter McGhee, of Ivy. No issue.
8. Martha Gilmer, unmarried.
9. Lucy Gilmer, second wife of Edward Pegram. No issue.
10. John Harmer Gilmer, married his cousin, Mary Anderson, who was daughter of William and Mary Goodwin (Woodson) Anderson and granddaughter of Matthew and Elizabeth Anderson, of Louisa.

    Issue given under the Matthew Anderson line.

Richard Anderson, son of David and Elizabeth Mills Anderson, married first, Ann Meriwether, daughter of Thomas and Elizabeth Thornton Meriwether. Issue:

A. David Anderson, born February 1, 1776. Married first, 1801, Susan Moore, daughter of Reuben Moore, of Culpeper County. Issue:

1. Catherine Price Anderson, born January 13, 1802, died January 28, 1825. Married January 28, 1819, Jefferson Epps Trice, of Richmond. (Heirs in Kentucky.)
2. Reuben Moore Anderson, born August 14, 1804, died August 16, 1805.
3. Ann Meriwether Anderson, born September 10, 1806, died January 13, 1840. Married April 15, 1821, William Porter.
4. Dr. Richard Anderson, born November 10, 1809, married first, Margaret Clark, daughter of James Clark and Margaret D. Lewis. Issue:
    a. David M. Anderson, married Nannie Anderson, and had David McM. Anderson.
    b. Maggie D. Anderson, married Mr. Stonebreaker, and had one child.

    Dr. Richard Anderson, married second, Mrs. Jane W. Lewis Meriwether. No issue.
5. Meriwether Lewis Anderson, born March 20, 1812, died October 6, 1872. Married December, 1831, Eliza Leitch, daughter of his stepmother, Mary Walker Lewis Leitch Anderson.

David Anderson (A), married second, Mrs. Mary Walker Lewis Leitch. No issue. She was daughter of Thos. W. Lewis and Elizabeth Meriwether, of Charlottesville.

She and her first husband, James Leitch had three children; the youngest, Eliza M. L. Leitch, born August 23, 1815, died February, 1866. Married December, 1831, Meriwether Lewis Anderson. Eliza inherited "Pantops", her mother's home. This name meaning "all eye" was selected for it by Mr. Jefferson because of its wide and beautiful view.

## "PANTOPS" ANDERSONS

Meriwether L. and Eliza M. L. Anderson, had issue:

1. Susan Moore Anderson, born February 23, 1833, married 1860, John R. Macmurdo, and had issue:
    a. Eliza L. Macmurdo, died young.
    b. John R. Macmurdo, died young.

c. Cunningham Wardlaw Macmurdo.
d. Susan Macmurdo, married Mr. Burr. No issue.

2. David Johnson Anderson, born April 15, 1837, died 1845.
3. James Anderson, born 1839, died 1859.
4. Mary Lewis Anderson, born January 2, 1842, died 1924, married 1870, John McGehee, and had issue:
   a. Eliza L. McGehee, died unmarried.
   b. Ellen McGehee, died young.
   c. Martha McGehee, died young.
   d. Mary McGehee, is a trained nurse, Waynesboro, Va.
5. Ann Eliza Anderson, married Dr. David Anderson, and had:
   a. Dr. David Macmurdo Anderson.
6. Margaret Douglas Anderson, married, and has issue.
7. David Meriwether Anderson ("Met"), born April 16, 1850, married 1889, Miss Mary Matthew, and has issue:
   a. Meriwether L. Anderson, married, has issue and lives in Texas.
8. Ellen Overton Anderson, born July 28, 1853, married Meriwether Macmurdo, and has issue.
9. Rev. Richard Warner Lewis Anderson, born May 12, 1857. He married Mary Beatty, and has issue:
   a. Richard Warner L. Anderson.
   b. Dr. Wm. Douglas Anderson, and
   c. Dr. Troy Beatty Anderson, twins.

END "PANTOPS" RECORD

---

B. Elizabeth Anderson, born April 5, 1769, daughter of Richard and Ann Meriwether Anderson, married August 8, 1787, Waddy Thomson, Jr. (See Thomson family.)

C. Sarah Anderson, born March 28, 1771.

D. Cecily Anderson, born September 20, 1780, married Wm. Kerr. Died July 19, 1820, in Hickman County, Kentucky.

E. Nicholas M. Anderson, born December 14, 1773, died 1824. Married ——.

F. Nancy Anderson, married first, Richard Watson; married second, Lewis Carr. She was born August 2, 1782.

G. Frances Anderson, born December 14, 1779.

H. Jasper Anderson, born April 18, 1772, and married Susan Cole, daughter of William Cole, of "North Garden".

Richard Anderson and his second wife, Milly Thomson, had issue:

I. Edmund Anderson, born April 30, 1785, married December 2, 1807, Frances Moore, sister of David Anderson's wife. She died in Charlottesville on February 6, 1814. He married second, Ann Cole, daughter of Wm. Cole of "North Garden". He lived at Milton, Albemarle County, but moved to Richmond and was of the firm, Anderson & Woodson, later, Anderson, Woodson & Biggers. Issue:

a. Charles Anderson, a druggist in Richmond, later moved to Roanoke, where he died. (*History of Albemarle.*) Fuller record later.

Issue of Cecily Anderson and Wm. Kerr:

1. Sarah Ann Kerr, born January 26, 1802, died September 5, 1857.
2. Nicholas Meriwether Kerr, born July 1, 1804, died November 13, 1876. Married and had eight children—given later.
3. John Thornton Kerr, born 1807, died 1860, unmarried.
4. Elizabeth Frances Kerr, born 1809, died 1810.
5. Lucy Caroline Kerr, born 1812, died 1825.
6. Mary Harriet Kerr, born 1815, died 1819.
7. James Richard Kerr, born 1818, died 1825.
8. Wm. Richard Kerr, born July 30, 1821, married, and had seven children.
9. Maria Burch Kerr, born February 25, 1824, died 1856, married June 12, 1842, James Craig, and left five children.

Issue of Nicholas Meriwether Anderson and his wife:

1. Caroline V. Anderson, married Cary W. Lambert.
2. Mary F. Anderson, married John C. Waggener, of Hancock County, Illinois.
3. Martha Anderson, married Baldwin L. Samuels, of Fort Worth, Texas. Issue:
   a. Sarah Samuels, married Mr. Hall.
   b. Amelia Samuels, married Mr. Foster.

4. Sarah Anderson, married Wm. B. Mason, of Hopkinsville, Kentucky.
5. Ann Anderson, married S. T. Waggener. Issue:
   a. Jasper Waggener, of Cincinnati, Ohio.
   b. Olivia K. Waggener, married F. W. Waller, of Russelville, Logan County, Ky.
6. Louisa V. Anderson, married Edmund Ware. Issue:
   a. Sue B. Ware, married F. Runnion.
   b. Gertrude Ware, married John D. Dickinson.
   c. Nicholas M. Ware.
   d. Charles Ware, of Trenton, Todd County, Ky.
   e. Jasper A. Ware.

Issue of Edmund Anderson and his first wife, Frances Moore:

1. John Mortimer Anderson, born February 6, 1809.
2. Pamelia Mildred Anderson, born February 1, 1810, died March 21, 1873. Married 1833, Philip S. Fry, of Stanardsville, Va. He died August 15, 1858.
3. Sarah Frances Anderson, born April 26, 1811, married November 25, 1833, David Michie, of Richmond, Va.
4. Louisa Virginia Anderson, born July ——, died September, 1812.
5. Louisa Virginia Anderson (2), born 1813, died 1819, at the residence of John A. Marshall, Culpeper, Va.

Issue of Edmund Anderson by his second wife, Anne Cole:

6. Susan Eliza Anderson, born 1815, died 1851, in Richmond.
7. Mary Anderson (1st), born 1816, died 1817.
8. Mary Anderson (2nd), born 1818, died 1819.
9. Amanda Marshall Anderson, born July 6, 1820, died 1844. Married Benjamin F. Peter.
10. Charles Everett Anderson, born February 29, 1824, married November 27, 1856, Sally A. Epps, born 1837, daughter of John C. and Ann Epps, of New Kent County.
11. Dr. Edmund Anderson, born April 23, 1827, died December 9, 1871. Married October 26, 1853, Ellen Rowena Pemberton, daughter of R. K. Pemberton, of Powhatan County, Va. She died July 26, 1877.

Issue of Pamelia Mildred Anderson and Philip Fry:

1. Alexander M. Fry, born November 1, 1849, died 1858.
2. Philip H. Fry, born June 30, 1834, married August 6, 1873.
3. Edmund Fry, born May 6, 1835, died September 1, 1862.
4. Thomas S. Fry, born February 25, 1838, m. 1865, ——.
5. Charles W. Fry, born May, 1842, married 1869 ——.
6. Luther C. Fry, born November 20, 1844.
7. Rebecca M. Fry, born July 2, 1847, married 1872, ——.

Issue of Charles Everett Anderson, M. D. and Sally Epps:

1. Charles Edmund Anderson, born January 2, 1858.
2. Roger Anderson, born November 29, 1859.
3. Infant son died.
4. Nathaniel C. Anderson, born 1863, died 1864, and
5. Nancy C. Anderson, born 1863, died 1864, twins.
6. Florence Michie Anderson, born June 22, 1864.
7. Temple Cole Anderson, born March 17, 1868.
8. Everett Anderson, born March 16, 1873.
9. Letitia Anderson, born July 25, 1875.

Issue of William Edmund Anderson, M. D. and Ellen Rowena Pemberton:

1. Charles P. Anderson, born March 1, 1855.
2. Robert P. Anderson, born July 1, 1856.
3. William Anderson, born July 26, 1858.
4. Sally C. Anderson, born October 14, 1860.

Issue of Ann Anderson and her first husband, Richard P. Watson, died 1812. He was son of Wm. Watson, died 1784, who came, 1762, from Charles City County to the vicinity of "North Garden", Albemarle County, Va.:

1. William Watson.
2. Lucinda Watson, married Wilson Gregory, of Henrico County.
3. Ann Watson, married Francis Staples, of Henrico County.

Mrs. Ann (Anderson) Watson married second, her cousin, Dr. Charles Lewis Carr, of "North Garden".

END OF RECORD OF RICHARD ANDERSON AND FIRST AND SECOND WIFE.

Issue of daughter, ——, eleventh child of David Anderson and Elizabeth Mills. She married Mr. Barrett:

1. Anderson Barrett, of Richmond, married Miss Sutton. Issue:
    a. Anne Barrett, married Linden Waller.
    b. Jane Barrett, married Mr. Griffin.
    c. William Barrett, married his cousin, Lucy Jane Wood, daughter of Ben Wood and Jane Anderson, of Ivy, Albemarle. Had issue: Lucy Barrett (never married) and several other children who died in infancy.
    d. Ellen Barrett, married Mr. Jones of Richmond.
    e. Mary Barrett, married her cousin, Mr. Sutton, of Richmond.

Matthew Anderson, son of David Anderson and Elizabeth Mills, married Elizabeth Anderson, daughter of Col. Richard Anderson and Mary Johnson, of Louisa County. Issue:

A. Richard Anderson, married first, Maria Eggleston; married second, Mrs. Blair, of Williamsburg, daughter of Governor Page. She died a year later. Her infant son did not survive her. Her two daughters by her first marriage intermarried with her stepsons. Richard Anderson settled first, at Milton, Albemarle County, later in Richmond and was of the firm of Anderson and Blair and Anderson. He established a cotton factory and exported cotton and tobacco. He owned his own ships, one being called the "Richard Anderson." Having made a large fortune he retired, and after a visit to Europe with his daughter, Fanny, he returned and purchased a plantation in Powhatan County.

    Issue of Richard Anderson and Maria Eggleston:

    1. Richard Anderson, graduate of University of Virginia, finished his education in France. Died in Richmond, Va., unmarried.
    2. Benjamin Eggleston Anderson, died 1890, married Fanny Blair.
    3. Marion Anderson, married Edward Barker, of Clarksville, Tenn. Left issue.

4. Maria Anderson, married Charles Barker. Their only son is supposed to have been killed in the Confederate War, but not known where.
5. William Anderson, married Mary Ann Blair, left several children.
6. Archie Anderson, while in Virginia, married his cousin, Caroline Buckner, granddaughter of Edmund and Jane Lewis Anderson, Ivy, Va., and went to Louisville, Ky. Issue:
   1. Robert Anderson, married Laura Vandyke, of Mercer County, Ky., near Harrodsburg. Issue:
      a. Claude Anderson, of Bullit County, Kentucky.
      b. William Anderson, lives in Louisville, Ky., is Vice-President of Indiana Truck Co.
      c. Love Anderson, unmarried, lives with her mother at Jefferson Town, near Louisville.
   2. Meriwether L. Anderson, married ——, left two daughters—one married in Maryland.
   3. Judge William Anderson, born August 15, 1850, at Ivy, Va., died April 9, 1907, aged 56 years. He was finely educated, taught school in early life, read law and became an able lawyer. He served in the Kentucky Senate and was Chief of a Division in the General Land Office at Washington, D. C. under Hoke Smith, Secretary of Interior. Again under President Cleveland, he was Registrar of Land at Enid, Okla. Later he settled at Lawton, Okla. He was a Christian gentleman of an unostentatious and methodical character. His death occurred suddenly on a train. He married Jennie Coots, of Kentucky, and left one son:
      a. Archibald Wilson Anderson, who married Ora Avenette Westgate, daughter of Sylvester S. Westgate. They were married Wednesday, September 21, 1904, 106 North Topeka Ave., Wichita, Kansas. They have two daughters, Mary and Alice.
   4. Alice Anderson, married Mr. Graves, of Louisville. Issue:

a. Roy Graves.

b. Eddie Graves.

5. Lula Anderson, married Mr. McKee, lives in Shelbyville. No issue.

6. Archie Anderson (girl), died unmarried.

7. Frances Anne Anderson, daughter of Richard and Maria Eggleston Anderson, died 1890, age 73 years, at her home in Powhatan County, Va. She married first, Alexander Ludlow. Issue:

1. Cora Ludlow.

2. Richard Ludlow.

She married second, Jacob Michaux. Issue:

3. William Michaux.

4. Maria Michaux.

B. Dorothea Anderson, daughter of Matthew and Elizabeth Anderson, married a Mr. Thomson, who was her brother-in-law. Her sister, Mary, first wife of Mr. Thomson left three children, all of whom stood well in character and position in Louisa, where they lived and died. They were:

1. Sarah Thomson.
2. Mary Thomson.
3. Nathaniel Thomson.

C. William Anderson, married his half first cousin, Mary Goodwin Woodson, of Hanover, granddaughter of Col. Richard Anderson and his second wife. William Anderson settled in Richmond and acquired a fortune as a merchant. In later life although in delicate health he yet occupied positions of public trust. "Warsaw", his luxurious home is now owned by the "Little Sisters of the Poor." Its former beautiful grounds are now a vegetable garden. He died age 51, in 1836, his widow died 1837. Issue:

1. Matthew Anderson, died in infancy.

2. Mary Elizabeth Anderson, died age 4.

3. William Anderson, died in infancy.

4. Mary Elizabeth Anderson (2nd), born 1821, married 1840, her cousin, John Harmer Gilmer. They lived at

Ivy, Albemarle, at Charlottesville, and later at Richmond, where Mr. Gilmer practiced law. He was injured in the Capitol disaster at Richmond and died 1879. Mary E. Anderson Gilmer was a most remarkable woman, cultured and intelligent, she retained her interest in keeping up courses of study, sciences and languages, also on all topics of general information and fine literature up until the time her sight was virtually gone through cataracts in her very old age. She lived to be 90 years old, with a clear intelligent mind to the last. (The author knew her intimately. S. T. L. A.).

She had issue:

1. John Harmer Gilmer, Jr., graduate of V. M. I. Later graduate in law, was in the C. S. A. as Lieutenant of Engineers. He came out of the service in broken health and died in 1867, unmarried.
2. Junius Mercer Gilmer, died age 4.
3. Mary Elizabeth Gilmer, died age 5 years.
4. Lucy Walker Gilmer, born 1845, married Edward B. Meade of Richmond. Issue:
   a. Mary Gilmer Meade, married James Gordon, and has several children.
   b. Everard Benjamin Meade, unmarried.
   c. Jenny Hardaway Meade, unmarried.
   d. Ellen Walker Meade, married Mr. Macon.
   e. Lucy Skelton Meade.
   f. Charlotte Williams Meade.

5. William Loundes Anderson, fifth child of William and Mary Goodwin Woodson Anderson, married Martha Grey, daughter of Gabriel Jones Grey and Sarah Pendleton Barbour, sister of General James Barbour and of Judge Philip Barbour. William Anderson lived in Culpeper, was killed at Malvern Hill. Issue:
   1. Fannie Anderson, married Zack Daniel of Culpeper. Issue:
      a. Beverly David Daniel.
      b. Martha Daniel, married, and left issue.

2. John Randolph Anderson, unmarried.
3. Richard Dabney Anderson, 1859-1899, married Miss White.

These two brothers owned and for years operated "The Corner Bookstore" at the University of Virginia. Richard Dabney Anderson and his wife, Caroline White had:

a. Martha James Anderson, married Ephraim Roland Mulford, M. D., of Bridgewater, New Jersey.
b. John R. Anderson, married ——.
c. Maria Caroline Anderson.
d. Richard Dabney Anderson, M. D., married Constance Bainbridge, daughter of Mrs. Lydia Price Bainbridge and has: Constance and Richard, Jr.
e. William R. Anderson, married Eliza Scull.
f. Annie Belle Anderson, married John White Page of Batesville, Va., and has: Annie Belle, John, Betty, and Caroline Page.

Dr. and Mrs. Mulford have:

a. Caroline Westcott Mulford, married Joseph Lee Walsh, of New Haven, and has Sheila Caroline Walsh.
b. Ephraim Mulford.
c. Martha Mulford.
d. Louisa Gray Mulford, married Joseph Conway Hiden, and has: Louise Battaile Hiden, born July 9, 1934.
e. William Pinkerton Mulford, medical student at University of Virginia.
f. James M. Mulford.
g. David B. Mulford.

6. Richard Woodson Anderson, son of William and Mary Woodson Anderson, educated at the University of Virginia, married Philippa Barbour Grey, who was sister of William Loundes Anderson's wife. They lived in Albemarle County, near Gordonsville for many years, then in Cumberland County. He was in the C. S. A.; was wounded and taken prisoner, was taken to Fort McHenry, Md. His wife died not long after the Confed-

erate War. In 1880 he accepted the position as teacher at the Male Orphan Asylum in Richmond, was honored as a man of highest honor and integrity and unflinching Christian character. Issue:

1. Richard Grey Anderson, of Cumberland County, married Anna Davis, of that county. (His widow and children lived in Waynesboro, Va.)
2. Nora Anderson (lives with her brother, Rev. John G. Anderson, in Florida.)
3. Lucy Barbour Anderson, married Mr. Surber, near Clifton Forge.
4. William Anderson, lives in Monroe, Texas.
5. Nina Anderson, died 1890.
6. Elizabeth Anderson, married John B. Handy, of New York City.
7. Philip Barbour Anderson, lives in Monroe, Texas.
8. Rev. John Grey Anderson, Presbyterian minister, married Fanny Davis, sister of his brother Richard's wife. He had several children.

7. John Randolph Anderson, seventh child of William and Mary Goodwin Woodson Anderson, married Martha Heiskell, daughter of Mr. Potterfield Heiskell, of Staunton, Va. He was for years Proctor of Washington and Lee University. Issue:
   1. Maude May Anderson, died in her 18th year at Mary Baldwin Seminary, Staunton.
   2. Alexander Kerr Anderson, living in Richmond.
   3. Sarah Heiskell Anderson, married W. J. Venable, of Sherman, Texas.
   4. William Anderson, of Richmond, engineer, was educated at Washington and Lee. He was connected with direction of the new State Library.
   5. Katie Anderson, educated at Mary Baldwin Seminary, Staunton, married Professor Brown Ayres, of Tulane University, New Orleans, La.
   6. Douglas L. Anderson, educated at Tulane University, is now professor of Physics at that institution.

8. James Monroe Anderson, son of William and Mary Goodwin Woodson Anderson. Unmarried.

9. Willianne Anderson, born 1834, was educated at Patapsco Institute, Md., married Dr. Mercer Winston Quarles, son of John Todd Quarles, of Louisa County. She died 1884, leaving four sons, who live in the West.

D. Ann Anderson, fourth child of Matthew Anderson and his wife, Elizabeth, married Mann Valentine Satterwhite. She lived in Louisa County on a farm given her by her father.

E. David Anderson, son of Matthew Anderson and his wife, Elizabeth, married Sarah Ann Moseby, daughter of Samuel Moseby and —— Anderson, of Hanover County. David died 1892, age 85. He was very poor, having gained and lost several fortunes by speculation. Issue:

1. Lula Anderson, married Hon. Thomas E. McCorkle, and had one daughter:

   Mrs. Sadie Alexander (McCorkle) Boppell, a consecrated missionary to Africa. She died in that mission field at Baraka, age 30 years. She was descended on her father's side from the Alexanders and from Lieutenant McCorkle of the Cowpens battle, both of them being grandfathers in the fourth degree. On her mother's side she was descended from Col. Richard Anderson of the Revolution.

*Note from Mrs. Bellamy, of Mississippi:*

Ethel Price who married James Bellamy was daughter of Napoleon Price and Molly Milligan of Kentucky.

Napoleon Price was son of William A. Price, Jr. and Sarah Ann Duke, of Virginia.

William A. Price, Jr. was son of Wm. A. Price and Dorothy Trice, daughter of James Trice and Elizabeth Anderson (who was daughter of Matthew and Elizabeth Anderson.)

This Elizabeth Anderson was daughter of Richard and Mary Anderson, daughter of Cornelius and Elizabeth Hudson Johnson.

# ANDERSONS OF "LOCUST HILL"

## IVY, ALBEMARLE COUNTY, VA.

*Edmund Anderson, ninth child of David Anderson and Elizabeth Mills Anderson, was born April 1st (Good Friday), 1763, in Hanover County. He died at "Locust Hill", April 19, 1810, his grave being the second one placed in the old graveyard. He married Jane Meriwether Lewis, of "Locust Hill", born March 31, 1770, died March 15, 1845. She was the daughter of William Lewis, of "Locust Hill" (died November 14, 1781) and his wife, Lucy Meriwether (born February 4, 1752, died September 8, 1837).

Issue of Edmund and Jane Anderson, nine children:

1. Elizabeth T. Anderson, born May 14, 1786, died in early girlhood.
2. Jane Lewis Anderson, born June 15, 1789, married Ben Wood. Issue:
   a. Mrs. Marian Rogers.
   b. Mrs. Alice Price.
   c. Mrs. Lucy Barret.
   d. Mrs. Martha Perkins, married first, Daniel Perkins; second Captain Flynn. (See Wood family.)
3. William Lewis Anderson, born December 4, 1792, married Miss Webb. Issue: Capt. Meriwether Anderson of Richmond Howitzers, C. S. A., and others.
4. Lucy M. Anderson, born July 30, 1795, married Ballard Buckner. Their children settled near Louisville, Ky.
5. Ann E. Anderson, born October 20, 1800, married Thomas Fielding Lewis.
6. David Anderson, born February 13, 1803, died of cholera in Natchez, Miss.

*7. Dr. Meriwether L. Anderson, born June 23, 1805, died March 5, 1862, married Lucy S. Harper.

8. Sarah T. Anderson, born June 22, 1807, married Gabriel Harper.

   Descendents: Terrys, Toppings, Mrs. Martha Harper Cobb, and family of Wm. Woods, Charlotte County, Va.

9. Mary H. Anderson, born October 4, 1809, died 1810, buried beside Edmund Anderson at "Locust Hill."

*Dr. Meriwether Lewis Anderson, of "Locust Hill", born June 23, 1805, died March 5, 1862, studied medicine at the University of Virginia; graduated in medicine at Philadelphia. He married June 16, 1831, Lucy Sydnor Harper, daughter of Charles Harper and his second wife, Lucy Smither. She was born December 8, 1811, at "Spring Hill", Ivy, Va., died December 4, 1885 at Galveston, Texas, buried at "Locust Hill". Issue:

1. Jane Lewis Anderson, born December 28, 1839, died November 26, 1842.
2. Lucy Anderson, born April 26, 1842, died August 7, 1842.
3. Meriwether L. Anderson, born August 24, 1845, killed at "Brook's Run", near Fisher's Hill, October 8, 1864. He was a member of Co. "K", 2nd Va., Col. Munford's Brigade, Fitzhugh Lee's Command, age 19.

*4. CHARLES HARPER ANDERSON, born June 28, 1848, died February 13, 1920, married February 15, 1872, Sarah Travers Lewis Scott.

5. Mary Miller Anderson, born September 5, 1851, died in Austin, Texas, 1932, married September 27, 1877, Bradford Ripley Alden Scott, of Galveston, Texas. He was born in Virginia.

Dr. Anderson's certificate after much preamble in Latin concludes with these words, "We the Prefects and Vice Prefects and Professors of the University of Pennsylvania grant willingly the grade of Doctor in the Art of Medicine to Meriwether L. Anderson, an excellent man of Virginia."

Dr. Meriwether Lewis Anderson, Sr. and his wife as owners of "Locust Hill" sustained its position as a family center whose hospitality reached out widely. For years they were childless, but Mrs. Anderson's mother heart called her to be a mother to a succession of orphan children, from a motherless baby during its short life while she was a bride in her Mississippi home, to the whole families of orphan nieces and nephews after her return to live in Virginia at "Locust Hill".

DR. MERIWETHER L. ANDERSON ON JOHN HARMON

Dr. Anderson's and his wife's high standards and her gentle Christian influence flowed out into these young lives, who later held before their children the examples of "Uncle Merrie and Aunt Lucy" as the highest one could follow. The three children born later to the Doctor and his wife, were enthusiastically welcomed by their orphan cousins who received them as their younger brothers and sister.

The Doctor was a devoted Mason, and his wife had taken the degree permitted the wives of Masons. In 1865 Mrs. Anderson widowed, and further bereaved by the death of her oldest son, Meriwether (killed in battle, 1864) had with her at "Locust Hill", the wife and children of the Hon. Randolph Tucker, who were refugees from their own home. March 1865, Sheridan's cavalry passed through Albemarle on their way towards Richmond, its soldiers pillaging the county along their route. Mrs. Anderson fearing lawlessness from these Union soldiers, overrunning her house, held up the Masonic Apron, Dr. Anderson had inherited from his uncle, Meriwether Lewis, and asked of any Mason present protection for the family of a Mason. A Union soldier spoke, saying while not a Mason he would like to look at this apron, lifting one corner of it and leaving on it the stain from his muddy, wet hand. The house was at once cleared of soldiers and no others came in afterwards.

Mrs. Anderson's second son, Chas. Harper Anderson, a boy under military age, was with the reserves under General Taliaferro at Charlottesville. He was sent up the road towards Ivy to note the advance of the Federals and on encountering them, was chased by them and repeatedly fired on for some miles, escaping through the speed of his horse. He rejoined the Reserves and was one of the two last men to cross the burning bridge over the Rivanna River. With a group of officers on the field near "Pantops", he watched the advance of the Union troops. The group being fired on by the Federals, Harper dropped to the ground to avoid markmanship and was supposed killed by his first cousin, Dr. Richard Anderson, who was a prisoner and had recognized him. Fortunately this rumor did not reach his mother. The enemy crossed the river at Secretary's Ford but made no advance.

The Reserves reinforced later by a considerable Confederate force of cavalry, returned to Charlottesville to find Sheridan had taken another route towards Richmond.

C. Harper Anderson had also served with a group sent from the University to render first aid to wounded soldiers on the battlefield. In this capacity he was at the battles around Fredericksburg. This is a copy of his Certificate:

*Charlottesville, May 8/64.*

This will Certify that Mr. Harper Anderson visits the Army as a Member of the Albemarle Committee for the relief of wounded Soldiers from Albemarle County, appointed by authority of the County Court of said County.

Given under my hand this 8th day of May, 1864.

ROBT. R. PRENTIS,

*Chairman of Albemarle Military Committee.*

Mary Miller Anderson and B. R. Alden Scott, had issue:

1. Lucy Harper Scott, born August 5, 1888, married June 1, 1904, Elmer Carpenter Griffith, of Bronxville, N. Y., and has:
    a. Lewis Scott Griffith, born June 11, 1905 (Alumnus of V. M. I.), married Rosine Chase, has Lewis, Jr.
2. Mary Anderson Scott, married June 15, 1917, Charles E. Boston. He was born in Toledo, Indiana, May 9, 1871. No issue. They live in Mexico.
3. John Thomson Scott, of San Antonio, Texas. Member of the "Rainbow Division", was badly wounded in the Meuse-Argonne Drive.
4. Sarah Lewis Scott, married January 31, 1911 in San Antonio, Texas, David Skene McKellar, born, Invercargill, Otago, New Zealand, September 12, 1876. He was son of David Harkness McKellar, born in Scotland and Jane Katherine Skene, who was born in Victoria, Australia. The McKellars live in Mexico, at Mariposa Ranch, Coahuila.

    Issue of Sarah Lewis Scott and David Skene McKellar:
    a. David Harkness McKellar, born San Antonio, Texas, December 18, 1911.
    b. Mary Anderson McKellar, born Palestine, Texas, September 27, 1917.

c. Alden Scott McKellar, born Eagle Pass, Texas, October 9, 1920.

5. Dr. Bradley Ripley Alden Scott, married Norma ——, no issue. He was surgeon of the Flying Field, San Antonio, Texas. He died in service, November 12, 1918.

6. Dr. Harper Anderson Scott, also graduate of the Medical School of the University of Texas, married Minai Nicholson, and lives in Austin, Texas. They have a daughter, Minai Scott.

CHARLES HARPER ANDERSON and his wife, Sarah Travers Lewis Scott, had issue:

1. Dr. Meriwether Lewis Anderson, born November 13, 1872 at "Locust Hill", married September 23, 1903, Anne Tatum, of Richmond, Va., born May 22, 1874, daughter of Wm. Tatum and Mary Pearman. Issue: (Dr. Anderson died in Richmond, August 4, 1936, is buried in Hollywood.)
   a. Ann Meriwether Anderson, born January 13, 1905, married Wm. Goodridge Sale, and has:
      1. Ann Goodridge Sale, born June 18, 1930.
      2. Grace Wilson Sale, born December 11, 1932.
      3. Jane Lewis Sale.
   b. Louisa Maury Anderson, born December 21, 1906, married Dr. Fred M. Hodges, and has:
      1. Fred Hodges, Jr., born February 26, 1931.
      2. Louise Meriwether (Meri) Hodges, born March 27, 1933.
   c. Sarah Travers Anderson, born January 30, 1909, married September 14, 1933, Wm. Garland Tarrant, of Richmond, and has:
      1. Wm. Garland Tarrant III, born May 13, 1935.
   d. Meriwether Lewis Anderson, born March 7, 1912.
   e. Dorothea Claiborne Anderson, born August 22, 1914.
2. Sarah Travers Scott Anderson, born February 1, 1874, married George L. Gordon, June 12, 1913. Issue:
   a. Harper Anderson Gordon, born March 24, 1916.
   b. George L. Gordon, Jr., born November 25, 1918.

3. Charles Harper Anderson, born December 3, 1875, married April 23, 1902, Caroline Gwynne. Issue:
    a. Mary Gwynne Anderson, born July 10, 1903, married Lieut. James Crocker, U. S. N., and has:
        1. James Anderson Crocker, born March 21, 1928 in Galveston, Texas.
        2. Robert Warner Crocker.
    b. Charles Harper Anderson III, born February 20, 1905, married Miss Tarrant.
    c. Caroline Anderson, born January 23, 1913.
    d. Edmund Taliaferro Anderson, born May 23, 1919.
4. Rev. Alfred Scott Anderson, born February 14, 1878, married May, 1903, Katherine Morris. Issue:
    a. Alfred Scott Anderson, born July 24, 1904, married Anne Curd.
    b. Lewis Meriwether Anderson, born November 18, 1905 at Memorial Hospital, Richmond, Va., married Mary Wood. He was baptized April 23, 1907 by Dr. Strickler, Union Theological Seminary.
    c. Katherine Morris Anderson, born at Gastonia, N. C., July 27, 1909, died at Waynesville, N. C., August 3, 1914.
    d. William Morris Anderson, born July 3, 1917, Hopkinsville, Ky.
    e. Charles Harper Anderson, born March 2, 1920, Hopkinsville, Ky.
5. Jane Lewis Anderson, born at "Locust Hill", February 12, 1881, died at "West Locust Hill", December 10, 1882.
6. William Anderson, born at "West Locust Hill", and died the same day, February 18, 1883.
7. Lucy Butler Anderson, born August 15, 1885, at "West Locust Hill", married June 10, 1913, Ballard Ernest Ward. Issue:
    a. Sarah Travers Ward, born May 29, 1914.
    b. Ballard Ernest Ward, and
    c. Lucien Ward, twins, born June 27, 1916.

d. Charles Harper Ward, born June 26, 1918.
e. Mary Josephine Ward, born May 8, 1922.

8. Rev. Alden Scott Anderson, born February 24, 1888; graduate of Union Theological Seminary, Richmond, 1917, married December 18, 1916, Isabel Sterrett. Issue:
   a. Alden Scott Anderson, died infant, 1917.
   b. Isabel Anderson.
   c. Annie-Laurie Anderson, born January 8, 1920.
   d. Alden S. Anderson, born December 1, 1926.

END OF DESCENDANTS OF DR. M. L. ANDERSON, OF "LOCUST HILL".

Lucy Meriwether Anderson, daughter of Edmund and Jane Lewis Anderson, born July 30, 1795 in Albemarle County, Va. She married Ballard Buckner and went to Kentucky and settled in the vicinity of Louisville—Peewe Valley. Issue:

1. Mary Buckner, married first, ——, and had a daughter who died unmarried. Married second, Mr. Cunningham, no issue. Married third, Mr. Mc'Clockin, no issue.
2. Robert Buckner, married Miss Bullett, and had:
   a. Willa Buckner, married James Osborne, and had two sons, Robert and Alfred, who both died young.
3. Edmund Buckner, married first, ——, had three children, who died unmarried. Married second, Mary Graff, died September, 1917, aged 80. Issue:
   a. Edmund Buckner, never married.
   b. Meriwether L. Buckner, married ——, has issue.
4. Maria Buckner, married Mr. Davidson, of Kentucky. Issue:
   a. Mary Davidson, married Nat Ragland, Jefferson County, Kentucky, and had:
      1. Jennie Ragland, married Mr. Fullenwider, and left issue.
      2. Edmund Ragland, married ——, and left issue.
      3. Alice Ragland, married ——, no issue.
   b. Ned Davidson, married twice. By his first marriage he had:

1. Maria (Pet) Davidson, who was adopted by her aunt, Mrs. Mary (Davidson) Ragland.

By his second marriage he had:

2. Eddie Buckner Davidson, married ——, and had:
   a. Edward K. Davidson.
   b. Sadie Anna Davidson, and others.

5. Alice Buckner, married Mr. Thornton. Issue:
   a. Lula Thornton, married Hardin Magruder, and had:
      1. Bessie Magruder, died unmarried.
      2. Willie Magruder, married ——, in West Virginia.
      3. Thornton Magruder, married ——.

6. Caroline Buckner, married Archibald Anderson, son of Richard Anderson and Maria Eggleston. (See Matthew Anderson Line.)

## MERIWETHER, ANDERSON, AND JORDAN RECORD

From Prince George County, Va. (Supplied by C. A. Wyche, Rosemary, N. C.)

Dr. William Meriwether (brother of Lord Charles Meriwether of England, who died unmarried), married Miss Scott of New Kent County, Va. She was sister of Governor Scott of Kentucky and first cousin of General Winfield Scott. Issue:

A. Judge Joseph Meriwether, of Arkansas.

B. Sarah Scott Meriwether, born January 20, 1805, married July 14, 1819, Joseph B. Anderson, son of Henry and Elizabeth Bass Anderson, of Amelia County, Va. (Bible Record.) Joseph was born June 9, 1795. He was in the War of 1812, was a ruling Elder of the Presbyterian Church. With small assistance he built the first Presbyterian Church in Amelia County, "Mt. Zion". Issue:

   1. Mary C. Anderson, born November 11, 1829, married Josiah Jordan, of Prince George County, Va. on December 16, 1845, Rev. Theodrick Pryor officiating. He was son of Joseph M. Jordan, Sr., who was born October 24,

1789, died October 19, 1834 and Rebecca Heath, who died January 29, 1852. She married second, Mr. Roane.

2. Josiah M. Anderson, born January 12, 1824, died at his residence, "Clermont", Prince George County. He married first, Mary C. Jordan; second, Miss Hill, of Petersburg. Issue:
   a. Sarah Rebecca, born September 10, 1846.
   b. Mary, born August 4, 1849.
   c. Josiah Anderson, born March 31, 1852.
   d. Lemuel Peebles Anderson, born April 17, 1855, married Frances Lewis, daughter of Dr. Willis Lewis of Granville County, N. C. (See Warner Hall Lewises.) Issue:
      1. Lemme McKenzie Anderson, married C. A. Wyche, of Rosemary, N. C., and has issue.
   e. Watson Pendleton Anderson, born Feb. 24, 1860.
   f. Charles Berthier Anderson, born April 1, 1862.
   g. Willianne Gregory Anderson, born Dec. 4, 1864.

   Issue by second marriage (to Miss Hill):
   h. Susan Anderson.

END ANDERSON.

# HARPER

INCLUDING THE FAMILY CONNECTIONS OF WOOD, PRICE, MAURY, SLAUGHTER, MAVERICK, AND JEAN ANDERSON OF SOUTH CAROLINA, AND COBBS OF NORTH CAROLINA.

## HARPER GENEALOGY

(Compiled by S. T. Anderson from tradition given by Mrs. Lucy Anderson and Mrs. Eliza J. Wood to their children; the Locust Hill Bible; and some data sent S. T. Anderson by William Walton Harper (late of the town of Orange, Virginia.)

As far back as I have been able to trace the Harpers is the following note from William Walton Harper—E. T. Gaffery Co., 350 Broadway, New York City.

*Note:*

"I have traced the Harpers in an unbroken series to:

"1. John Harper, died 1714, who with his brother settled on an estate in Oxford township, County of Philadelphia in April, 1682. John Harper and his wife were Quakers; among other children they had a son,

"2. Joseph Harper, who had by his wife, Ann, a number of children, the eldest of whom was—

"3. Robert Harper, whose wife was Sarah ——. They too had a large family. He was a planter and died leaving landed estate and much gold. Robert and Sarah Harper's tenth child was—

"4. Capt. John Harper of Philadelphia, Pa. and Alexandria, Virginia.

"WILLIAM W. HARPER."

S. T. L. Anderson.

## HARPERS OF "SPRING HILL"

### ALBEMARLE COUNTY, VA.

(From a memorandum made by Charles Wood, June 22, 1897, from information given by his mother, Eliza [Harper] Wood which coincides with the statements of her sister, Mrs. Lucy Harper Anderson.)

These Harpers are descended from Capt. John Harper of Philadelphia, Pa. and later of Alexandria, Virginia, who was born October 3, 1728. He lost his father when a boy. He and his mother were in reduced circumstances. He overheard his uncle and a family friend urging his mother to bind him out to a trade. To this he was unwilling, so he ran away to sea.

The captain of the vessel died on the voyage and he being of sufficient education was the only one of the crew who understood navigation and he was chosen captain, though not twenty-one years old at the time. On one voyage he was shipwrecked on the coast of France and swam ashore, holding his father's watch in his mouth. Eventually he became a large ship owner and accumulated quite a fortune. He suffered losses through the French naval depredations, and his claims are still in abeyance under the French Spoilation Act.

Capt. Harper married twice; first, Sarah Wells of Philadelphia by whom he had twenty children. (A piece of her wedding dress came to Mrs. Lucy [Harper] Anderson and was later in the possession of Mrs. B. R. Alden Scott.) He married second, Mary Reynolds by whom he had nine children. Capt. Harper is said to have been much chagrined over this last nine, since Mary Reynolds had been a childless widow. Tradition says, furthermore that she induced him to cut off his first twenty children with nine shillings each and leave his large property to these nine younger children.

He was a Presbyterian of the strait-laced order and the church he attended in Alexandria was on Fairfax Street, two blocks from the river. Despite his rigid church standards there are laughable anecdotes extant of occasional lapses into "sailor a-shore" delinquencies.

The following list of John Harper's children was sent S. T. L. Anderson by W. W. Harper. Mrs. Lucy S. Anderson and Mrs. Eliza Wood stated that a good many of John Harper's children died young, some in infancy, others in early youth; thus leaving no descendants, their names may have been lost. W. W. Harper insisted that Charles Harper of "Spring Hill" was a child of the second marriage; but this does not accord with his own statement to his children that he was a younger child of the first marriage, one of the twenty children of the first marriage, nor accord with the fact that he was just fifty years old when his youngest child was born. Eliza Jane (Harper) Wood was born December 27, 1817. This would make his birth in 1767 or 68. (Mrs. Mary Reynolds was born June 4, 1756 in Londonderry, Ireland. She was only eleven years old when Charles Harper was born 1767-8. Thus she could not have been Charles Harper's mother. Q. E. D.)

Captain John Harper was born October 3, 1728, died 1803 or 4. He married first, Sarah Wells; second, Mrs. Mary Reynolds (born June 4, 1756 in Londonderry, Ireland.)

"THE TWENTY"

I. Joseph Harper, born July 27, 1751, married Sally or Eliza Pearson, of Newark, N. J.

II. John Harper, born May 29, 1753, married Margaret Pearson Territt.

III. Sarah Harper, born April 16, 1755, married Peter Lloyd, had a son, John.

IV. Robert Harper, born April 2, 1757, married Sarah Washington.

V. Rebecca Harper, born August 16, 1759, married Joseph Greenway, son of the Captain Greenway of the ship, "Welcome" upon which Penn arrived in 1682.

VI. William Harper, born March 14, 1761 (Captain in Revolution), married Mary Scull, of Philadelphia, and had issue:

A. Dr. Wm. Harper, married Mary Thomas Newton, and had:

1. Wm. Walton Harper, and others.

B. Washington Territt Harper, married Ann Elicott.

C. John Harper, married Sarah Davis.

D. Robert Harper.

E. Edward Harper.

F. Joel Zane Harper.

G. Col. Charles Harper.

H. Joseph Harper, unmarried.

VII. Edward Harper, born August 1, 1763 (a lawyer).

VIII. Samuel Harper, born January 24, 1765, married Rachel or Sarah Brooke. Issue:

A. Rachel Harper, married Dr. John Eversfield Berry.

B. Judge Samuel Harper, married first, —— Magruder; second, Julia Harper, and had:

1. Sarah Brooke Harper, married R. W. P. Garnet.

IX. Elizabeth Harper, born 1767, married Rev. Dr. Thomas Blucher, who was for fifty years pastor of the Presbyterian church in Georgetown, D. C.

*X. Charles Harper, of "Spring Hill".

XI. Fanny Harper, born 1769, married Joshua Biddle, of Alexandria, Va.

XII. Mary Harper, born February 28, 1772, married Thomas Vowell, and had:

A. Mary Vowell, married Norman Fitzhugh.

XIII. Margaret Harper, born 1775, married John C. Vowell, and had:

A. Eliza Vowell, married John Douglas, and had issue:

1. Margaret Douglas, married Mr. Fairfax Herbert Whiting, and had:

a. Margaret Whiting, and others.

## "THE NINE"

Issue of Captain John Harper and Mary Reynolds:

I. Robert Harper, born December 5, 1784, lost at sea—supposed childless.

II. John Harper, born April 4, 1786.

III. Sarah Harper, born September 8, 1787.

IV. James Harper, born December 30, 1788, married Eliza Ward, daughter of Gen. Thomas Ward in U. S. Congress from New Jersey.

V. Sarah Ann Harper, born December 12, 1790.

VI. Sophia Harper, born September 22, 1797.

VII. Joshua Harper, born April 13, 1796, married Sarah Thomas of Maine, daughter of Hushaie Thomas and Hannah Cushman Thomas, his wife.

VIII. Nancy Harper, born May 4, 1794, married first, Mr. King; second, Rev. Wells Andrews, Presbyterian minister, of Alexandria, Va.

IX. Ruth Harper, born 1798.

*Note:* At Chesterton, England A. D. 959, lived Hugo le Harper (Dugdale of London College of Heraldry), had three sons.

1. Sir Robert Harper, whose son was Sir Gilbert le Harper.
2. Laheries Harper.
3. Roger Harper.

Sir Gilbert le Harper, married Haurie, daughter of Elmedon. Their son was Sir John le Harper, who had three sons, Crusaders, knighted by Richard of England. They were Sir Robert Harper, Sir Wm. Harper (Lord Mayor of London), and Sir Henry Harper.

From Sir Robert Harper (Crusader) is descended Sir Robert Harper of Ireland, whose son or grandson, John Harper had a son or grandson, Robert Harper, who was the father of Captain John Harper of the twenty-nine children.

AUTHORITY—Wm. Walton Harper's papers.

Mrs. Lucy Harper Anderson stated: "Several of John Harper's children were named Robert—and most of them died infants." Also that Capt. Harper's sons, James and Joshua moved from Alexandria to New York, living on a farm near that city, and that her brother, William Harper, visited them there in 1831.

Notes made at St. Louis, given me by John Slaughter (son of Sarah Harper). Addresses:

John P. Slaughter, Burlinghame, Kansas.

Joshua Harper, Jenessee County, Illinois.

Lucy Snow (formerly Andrews), granddaughter of Capt. John Harper, lived at Jenessee, Illinois 1814. (See Slaughter note.)

## *CHARLES HARPER OF "SPRING HILL"
### ALBEMARLE COUNTY, VA.

He was son of Capt. John Harper and Sarah Wells, and was born 1767 or '68, died at "Locust Hill" 1848 (?), married first, Sarah Janney, issue, a son and daughter; married second, Lucy Smither; issue, nine children.

He was born in Philadelphia and with his brothers and sisters and parents came to live in Alexandria, Va., just before the Revolutionary War. Mrs. Lucy Anderson says that Charles Harper told his children how he, at the age of eight years, helped his father, Captain John Harper, hide money and other valuables in the cellar from the British. Hearing the roar of the cannon, Captain Harper said, "Charles are you afraid?" Charles Harper told his children, "I was quaking in my boots, but I answered, "Not at all, Sir."

He and his second wife lived in Culpeper County, (in that part which became Rappahannock County) and owned much land in various tracts. His home was a handsome, large place on Robertson's River. He and his wife were very happily situated there, yet concluding that the influences for fast living were too tempting for him and his sons, he disposed of his property at a disadvantage and removed to "Spring Hill", Albemarle County in 1812.

His wife always regretted the separation from her early friends though she and her husband made many more in their new location, being much beloved, and honored by all who knew them.

Mr. Harper's influence was strong and lasting over his children. His high standards influenced them throughout life. They loved their mother, but turned in reverent love to their father's strength of mind for guidance always. Even in their old age and weakened faculties they cited him as their ideal.

The student body of the early days of the University of Virginia did not appeal to him as associates for his sons, therefore he did not send them to the University but himself supervised their courses of reading.

He and old Mr. Southal originated a circulating library of standard books in Charlottesville, which in cultivating influence reached out over the county for many years.

His rigid early religious training reacted in giving him far gentler views which for him seemed to lead to the highest religious character (though these views in the light of his earlier training were not orthodox).

His first wife was a Quakeress which perhaps influenced him in his original departure from the strict tenets in which he had been raised.

He became blind in his later years, and with his wife lived with Dr. and Mrs. Anderson (son-in-law and daughter). He died at "Locust Hill" and with his wife is buried in the "Locust Hill" graveyard amid the graves of beloved friends and relatives—81 years of age says the obituary.

From this obituary the following is an extract:

"Mr. Charles Harper died at 'Locust Hill', Tuesday 9, ——, had been a resident of Albemarle County for 35 years; began as a merchant in Alexandria, a successful career opened for him in that business in which he made several voyages to the West Indies. But his preference was for a country life, and a strong desire to devote his life to agriculture overcame every other consideration. He removed to that part of Culpeper now known as Rappahannock where he lived for eighteen years, acquiring the reputation of a successful farmer, originating in his vicinity a spirit of improvement needed in Agriculture then and so prevalent at the present day.

"He removed to Albemarle where he again, as a successful farmer, stimulated improved methods.

"He had the esteem and respect of all who knew him. He possessed a vigorous mind improved by reading and reflection. His big aim in life was for the happiness, enlightenment, and elevation of our race. He was a good conversationalist, well up on the affairs of the world which pointed to a bright day for humanity. Love for his fellowman was excelled only by his gratitude and affection for his Heavenly Father in whom his trust was perfect. He was charitable to the faults of others and to their errors, liberally helping the needy or distressed, seeking out and helping particularly the widows and orphans.

"His loss of sight some years before his death was borne with patient resignation. This compelled his retirement from business. He carefully put his house in order and cheerfully made ready to depart this life when the Father should call him."

Charles Harper married first, Sarah Janney, and had issue:

A. Joseph Harper, married first, Eliza Greenway (his father's niece and ward), and had issue:

1. John Harper, and others, who removed to Missouri. Descendants given later.

Joseph married second, Mrs. Mary Ann Wood (neé Miller), an English lady, no issue. She lived later at "Farmington", near Ivy, Va. Still owned by descendants of her first marriage (1926).

B. Sarah Harper, married Wm. Slaughter of Culpeper County, and had issue:

1. William Slaughter.
2. John Slaughter, who has two sons and others probably. They live in Kansas and Missouri, (I met them at the World's Fair, St. Louis.) Slaughter record given later.

Charles Harper married second, March 28, 1797, Lucy Smither, daughter of Mark Smither and Wilmoth Sydnor Smither. Issue:

A. Mary Harper, born May 23, 1798, married Dr. Wm. Glascock, and had:

1. Judge Wm. Glascock of Oakland, Calif., married Margaret ——. Issue.

a. Hon. John Glascock, Congressman-at-Large from California, married Mary W——, and left issue.
b. Mary Glascock, married Mr. Blew, left issue.

B. William Harper, born May 1, 1800, married Miss Coleman, issue lived in Tennessee. (See letter for issue.)

C. Charles Bennet Harper, born May 13, 1802, married Anna Price, and had:

1. George Harper of Georgetown, Texas, married Margaret Sharpe, and had issue:
   a. Lucy Harper.
   b. Sally Harper.
   c. Harriet Harper, and others.
2. Charles Harper, married, and left issue in Missouri.
3. Jane Harper, married Erastus Brown, no issue.

*Note:* Margaret Sharpe's people were from Abington, Va. and scattered into North Carolina and Kentucky—Vances, Sharpes, Tulkersons. She is a cousin of Rev. John Paxton, Presbyterian missionary from Danville, Virginia.

D. Gabriel Smither Harper, born May 17, 1804, died January, 1872, married Sarah Thornton Anderson (born ——, died September 20, 1857. Issue:

1. Mary Jane Harper, born September 5, 1825, died October 19, 1845, married William A. Woods, January, 1843, and left issue:
   a. William Harper Woods, married Emily Gwathmey Smith.
2. Lucy Wilmoth Harper, born December 4, 1827, died in youth at Ivy, Va., buried at "Locust Hill". Unmarried.
3. Ann Lewis Harper, born April 24, 1830, died September 15, 1849.
4. Sally Eliza Harper, born September 5, 1832, died May 23, 1856, married November 10, 1852, Dr. N. G. Terry, and had:
   a. Nat Terry, m. Miss Elizabeth Sydnor, and had:
      1. Elizabeth Terry, married 1907, Dr. Boland, U. S. N., and has:
         a. John Boland.

2. Sarah Terry, married Mr. Coleman.
3. Mary Terry, married Heywood Merritt.
4. Delia Terry, married Robert Tait, Jr.
5. Natalie Terry, married H. W. Withers.
6. Giles Terry, M. D., practicing in Paris, France.

5. Alice Willie Harper, born June 19, 1835, died September 20, 1858, married Joel Daniel, and had:
   a. Harper Daniel, died in childhood.
   b. Sarah Anderson Daniel, married Nathan Blount Topping, had:
      1. Nat Topping, Jr., died unmarried.
      2. Harper Topping, died in France, married, no issue.
      3. Ruth Topping.
6. Robert Meriwether Harper, born October 19, ——.
7. Charles Harper, born April 20, 1847, died June ——, buried at "Locust Hill", married Alice Gates, and had:
   a. Martha Harper, married Mr. Cobb, and has:
      1. Mary Harper Cobb.
      2. John Charles Cobb.
      3. Wm. Stephen Cobb.
      4. Edward Cobb.
      5. Frederick Cobb.

      (See Cobbs Record.)

William Harper Woods, only child of Mary Jane Harper and William A. Woods, married Emily Gwathmey Smith, and had:

1. William Harper Woods, born February 1, 1872, died February, 1892.
2. Emily Gwathmey Woods, born February 8, 1873.
3. Larkin Smith Woods, died an infant.
4. Kate Storrow Woods, born September 20, 1876, married William C. Scott, of Charlotte County. (Address: 618 Denver Street, Tulsa, Oklahoma.)
5. Albert Triplett Woods, born September 5, 1880. (Address: 724 S. Flores Street, San Antonio, Texas.)

He married Estelle Grant, Coffeville, Kansas, and has:

a. Emily Grant Woods.
b. Virginia Estelle Woods.
c. Mary Catharine Woods.
d. Louise Young Woods.

Emily Gwathmey Woods, married Robert Bradley Wilson, and has:

a. Emily Gwathmey Wilson, married Robert Maxwell Jenkins, and has issue:
    1. Robert Maxwell Jenkins, Jr. (3rd.)
    2. Bradley Wilson Jenkins.
    3. Emily Gwathmey Jenkins, died age 4½ years.
    4. Margaret Eugene Jenkins.

Kate Woods and her husband, Wm. C. Scott, have:

a. William Woods Scott, born 1901.
b. Ruth Josephine Scott, born 1902.

E. Robert Burns Harper, son of Charles Harper and Lucy Smither, was born June 7, 1816, married Eliza Coleman, and has:

1. Fielding Harper.
2. Gabriel Meriwether Harper.
3. Anna Harper.
4. Maria Harper.

F. Lydia Anna Harper, born February 24, 1809, married Stephen Price, and had:

1. Charles Price, married first, Alice Wood (issue given under Price record), married second, Sally Woods, and had:
    a. Dr. Woods Price.
    b. Gertrude Price.
2. Robert Price, married Linda ——, and had:
    a. Annie Price.
    b. Bob Price.
3. Daniel Price, married Harriet Harper, and had:
    a. Margaret Price.
    b. Meriwether Price.
    c. George Price.

4. Lucy Price, married Jesse Maury.
5. Sally Price, married Mr. Pride.
6. Betty Price, married Mr. Earle.
(See Price and Maury records.)

G. *Lucy Sydnor Harper, born December 8, 1811, married Dr. Meriwether L. Anderson, and had issue:
1. Meriwether L. Anderson, killed in C. S. A., unmarried.
2. *Charles Harper Anderson, married S. T. L. Scott.
3. Mary M. Anderson, married B. R. Alden Scott.

H. Nancy Harper, born September 27, 1814, married Uriah Bennet, and had:
1. Charles Bennet.
2. Lewis Bennet.
3. Lucy Bennet, and other daughters in Missouri.

I. Eliza Jane Harper, born December 27, 1817 when her father was fifty years old, married John Wood, Jr., and had issue: (eleven children)
1. Charles Wood, born February 3, 1836, married Clara Hargraves, had:
 a. Hargraves Wood, died unmarried.
 b. Waddy B. Wood, m. Lyndsay Lomax, and had:
  1. Lyndsay Wood, married.
  2. Virginia Wood.
 c. Virginia H. Wood, artist, married Charles Franc Goddard.
 d. Nanny F. Wood.
 g. Eliza Wood, died 1923, married Dr. Sperow, no issue.
 h. Rosa Wood, married G. Glenn, and has issue:
  1. Gerard Glenn.
  2. John Glenn.
 i. Charles Meigs Wood, U. S. A., died 1930, married but no issue.
2. Elizabeth Wood, born March 28, 1839, married Clem Fishburne, had:
 a. Jack Fishburne, married Mary Lyons, and had five daughters and three sons.

b. Junius Fishburne.
c. Walter Fishburne, died unmarried.
d. Clem Fishburne, married Annie Price, and had:
    1. Clem Fishburne III.
    2. Lydia Fishburne.
e. George Fishburne, married Esther Moon. No issue.

3. Lucy Wood, born November 14, 1841, married Waddy Butler, C. S. A. No issue.
4. Lydia Wood, born April 28, 1844, died unmarried.
5. Alfred Wood, born May 25, 1846, died in childhood.
6. John Snowdon Wood, born May 13, 1848, died 1933, unmarried.
7. Walter Wood, born July 14, 1850, died unmarried.
8. Maria Wood, born June 3, 1853, died unmarried.
9. Lewis Wood, born April 5, 1855, married Jacky Baker, no issue.
10. Ben. Wood, born February 14, 1862, died in childhood.
11. Alfred Griffith Wood, died in childhood.

A letter Mrs. Lucy Anderson received from her brother, William Harper, Hickman, Kentucky, 1865, stated that—

". . . his brother, Charles, living sixteen miles from St. Louis, had gotten through the Civil War with life and better means than he expected; he and his wife, Anna, were in good health.

". . . William says of himself, that he was ruined by the war. His losses being $75,000—all he had. (Depredations of Union Army.)

"He says that his youngest son, George Kent Harper, entered the army very young and served the whole four years—"but got home safely one night and is in good health."

He tells of a visit of a troop of blacks to his farm a few weeks before, who took off his remaining slaves.

His wife and daughters were doing all their own work. He mentions six children: Sally; Eliza, with five children, living at Owensboro, Ky.; Mary, with her husband and three children, living in Paducah; Charles, living on a farm near Hickman, Ky., has four children; Bernice and George Kent, unmarried, and living with him and his wife.

Eliza J. (Harper) Simmons writes to her Aunt Lucy Anderson from Kenton, February 6, 1879—tells of hearing her cousins, Bob and Betty Price talk lovingly of her Aunt Lucy; and speaks of her own seven children. Her oldest daughter, Sally, married to Dr. Ewing, had one child, and had been living in Arkansas, but moved to Wise County, Northern Texas. Sally at home for a visit, her brother Amus Simmons would go back with her. Eliza mentions her Aunt Lucy's namesake, Lucy Simmons, just three years old. Eliza opposed to Mr. Simmons' wish to move to Texas.

## JOSEPH HARPER

(Son of Charles Harper and Sarah Janney)

He lived for many years near Ivy Depot, then moved with his first wife, Eliza Greenway (his father's niece) to Missouri as did his children, also. After his first wife's death while on a visit to Virginia, he married second, Mrs. Mary Ann Wood née Miller, daughter of Capt. Miller, an Englishman. They had no children and after some years in Missouri they returned to Virginia, where Joseph died. He is buried at "Locust Hill", Ivy Depot. He died at the home of Gabriel Harper, "Red Banks" (afterward owned by Peter McGee.) A letter of inquiry from Mrs. Lucy Stone, Harrisonville, Mo., regarding her paternal ancestor, Lieutenant Hudson Martin, of the Revolution, brought out the fact that her mother was a daughter of Joseph Harper and Eliza Greenway. She furnished the following list of Joseph Harper's descendants. His children were: (six children)

1. Lucy Ann Harper, married Norbourne Martin, brother of Hudson J. Martin. Issue.
    a. Maria Martin.
    b. Joseph Martin.
    c. David Martin.
2. John Smither Harper, married Juliet Amanda Butts, and had:
    a. Charles Harper, died young.
    b. Eliza Catharine, died.
    c. Mary Ann, living.
    d. Joseph Harper.

- e. Juliet B. Harper.
- f. Frances Ella Harper, died young.
- g. John Slaughter Harper, died young.
- h. William Edward Harper, living 1923, in Missouri.

3. William Harper, married Nanny Kirk. They died childless in California.
4. Charles Harper, married Sarah Katherine Butts, sister of Juliet A. Butts, wife of John Harper. Issue:
   - a. Mary Juliet Harper.
   - b. Wm. Thomas Harper, living in California.
   - c. Sarah Katherine Harper, dead.
   - d. Lucy Harper, living in 1923.
   - e. John Harper, died in infancy.
   - f. Ida Thomas Harper, died in 1923.
   - g. Susan Broadus Harper, dead 1923.
   - h. Eliza Anne Harper, living in California, 1923.

   (Given more fully.)
5. Mary Eliza Harper, married Hudson J. Martin, and had issue:
   - a. Joseph Martin, died young.
   - b. Lucy Ann Martin, born June 2, 1847, married August 4, 1866, David Stone, deceased, 1923. Issue:
     1. Henry Stone, born 1867, married Minnie Sygnar, died February 2, 1919. Issue:
        - a. Jean L. Stone, Harrisonville, Missouri.
        - b. Frank Stone, Long Beach, California.
        - c. David Stone.
6. Twyman Harper, married Elizabeth Hopkin, and had:
   - a. Mary Harper, dead.
   - b. Charles Harper, living in California.
   - c. John Harper, living in California.
   - d. Lulu Harper, living in California.
   - e. Joseph Harper, living in California.
   - f. Netty Harper, living in California.
   - g. George Harper, dead.
   - h. Sarah Harper.
   - i. Milton Harper.

The six children of John Smither Harper and Juliet Amanda Butts:

1. Charles Harper, died young.
2. Eliza Katherine Harper, married John Stone, and had:
    a. Charles Harper Stone.
    b. Wm. Thomas Stone.
    c. Harry Broadus Stone.
3. Joseph Harper, married Florence Watson. He died in 1918. They lived in Nevada, Mo., and had issue:
    a. John Sherman Harper, Long Beach, California.
    b. Juliet Anna Harper, lives in Oklahoma.
    c. Twyman Harper, lives in Nevada, Missouri.
    d. Joseph H. Harper, lives in St. Louis, Missouri.
4. Mary Ann Harper, married Dr. G. C. Waters (dead), lives in Marshall, Mo., and has issue:
    a. Clara Waters, dead.
    b. Horace Waters, living.
    c. Grover Waters, living.
    d. Walter Waters, died in infancy.
    e. Joseph Harper Waters.
    f. Julia Waters.
    g. George Waters.
5. John Slaughter Harper, died young.
6. Wm. Edward Harper, married Lucy Rockhold, and lives in Nevada, Mo. Issue:
    a. Nelly Harper, living.
    b. Joseph Lewis Harper, dead.
    c. Ruth Harper, living.

Charles Harper and his wife, Sarah Katherin Butts, had issue:

1. Mary Juliet Harper, married Charles Clark, and had:
    a. William T. Clark, married, and has issue.
2. William Thomas Harper, married three times; first, Nelly Jonester, and had Elizabeth Harper, who married Charles Metey, and has two sons. W. T. Harper, married second, Hatty Hooper; third, Janie Martin.

3. Sarah Katharine Harper, married Allan Price, and has:
    a. Charlie Price.
    b. George Price.
    c. Margaret Price.
    d. Belle Price.
    e. Frank Price.
4. Lucy Harper, married C. L. Orth, and had:
    a. Estelle Orth.
    b. Nancy Orth.
    c. Ann Eliza Orth.
    d. Harper Orth.
    e. Florence Orth.
5. John Harper, died young.
6. Ida Harper, married George S. Wilson, of Greenfield, Mo., and had:
    a. Ethel Augusta Wilson.
    b. Zelma Catharine Wilson.
    c. Leustry Wilson.
    d. Mabel Claire Wilson.
    e. Ancer Wilson.
    f. John Wilson.
    g. Georgia Wilson.
7. Susan Broadus Harper, married Bert Cowler, and had:
    a. Ruth Cowler.
    b. Corrine Cowler.
8. Eliza Ann Harper, living in Los Angeles, California.

END OF DESCENDANTS OF JOSEPH HARPER, OF VIRGINIA AND MISSOURI.

## THE WOOD FAMILY

Combining their Hunter descent (taken from official records compiled by Mrs. Susan Hunter Bull), to which is added later records of Woods of this family, who settled at Ivy, Albemarle County, Virginia.

HUNTER of Abbots Hill and Parks, County Ayre, Scotland.

Robert Hunter, Provost of Ayre, born 1657, married Agnes Patterson and had issue:

Barbary Hunter, married Robert Fullerton, of Creghale.

Robert Hunter, married Agnes Smith, and had one son:

James Hunter, Provost of Ayre, born 1698, married 1726, Janet, oldest daughter of James Hunter of Abbots Hill and Parks. Issue:

1. Mary.
2. Sarah.
3. Jean Isabell.
4. James Hunter.
5. Andrew Hunter.
6. Robert Hunter.
7. John Hunter, born 1746, married Jane Broadwater. 1767 settled in Virginia, and had issue:
   a. Ann, married Mr. Gunnell.
   b. James Hunter.
   c. Robert Hunter.
   d. George Washington Hunter.
   e. John Hunter.

WOOD FAMILY of Burlington, N. J. and Fairfax County, Va.

This family entered in visitation of Leicestershire, England, 1583. They descend from Sir John Wood, Lord Mayor of London, who married Catherine Clarck of Leicestershire from whom descended William Wood, native of Leicestershire who came to America in the fly boat "Martha" 1677, and landed at Burlington, N. J. He married Mary Parnell with whom he had fallen in love on the voyage.

Issue: 1. John, married Susan; 2. William, never married; 3. Martha, married Mr. Newbold; 4. Sarah, married Mr. Stevens.

John and his wife Susan, had issue:

1. William.
2. John.
3. Hester, married James Montgomery, of Edlington, Monmouth, N. J.

*Note:* Mrs. Susan Wood, married second, William Montgomery of Upper Freehold, son of William and Isabell Montgomery, of Brigned, Scotland.

John Wood (son of John and Susan Wood) and his wife, Mary, had issue, seven children:

1. Susan, married Mr. Hartshorne.
2. Joanna, married Mr. Joseph Craig, a banker of Alexandria.
3. Mary Wood, married M. Ritche Leonard.
4. Joseph Wood, moved to Ohio, and left issue there.
5. William Wood, married Miss Parsons, issue, three children:
    - a. Marion M. Wood, married and had issue.
    - b. William Wood.
    - c. James Wood, left issue:
        1. Mollie E. Wood.
        2. James P. Wood.
6. Thomas Wood, married Ann Reading, and had issue:
    - a. Harriet Bullock Wood, married her cousin, Gen. Wm. Reading Montgomery.
    - b. A son.
    - c. A son.
    - d. George Wood, born at Burlington, N. J., 1813, graduated from Princeton, 1835, made L. L. D. Hambleton College 1842, made L. L. D. Union College 1845. He practiced law in New York and became one of its eminent lawyers. It is related that Daniel Webster asked William C. Preston of South Carolina, who was his opponent in a case before the United States Supreme Court, to which Preston replied, "That sleepy looking Wood." Webster said, "If it is George Wood I advise you to look out how you wake him." George Wood died unmarried in New York, and is buried in Burlington, New Jersey.
7. John Wood, married Alice Coward. They married young and left New Jersey soon after the Revolutionary War and settled on a farm in Fairfax County, Virginia. They thought the sudden worthlessness of Federal script caused the loss of their wealth; but their son Ben visited the New Jersey home after he

was grown and found that the estate might have been recovered by the proper exertion.

Alice Coward and her first cousin, Hannah Randolph were married at the same time and with the same ceremony. Hannah married a Mr. Longstreet and moved to Georgia.

Thus these Woods were related to the Longstreets of New Jersey, some of whom came South. Two of these were General Longstreet, C. S. A., of Georgia and Judge Longstreet, of Georgia (author of "Georgia Scenes", of "Flush Times in Alabama", and many shorter articles).

John and Alice Coward Wood had four sons:

a. John Wood, married Elizabeth Myers, lived in Alexandria.
b. William Wood, married Margaret Ridgeway, and lived in Frederick County, Va.
c. Benjamin Wood, by his first marriage had a child who died. He married second, Jane Meriwether Anderson, daughter of Edmund and Jane Anderson, of "Locust Hill."
d. Thomas Wood, never married.
e. Mary Wood, married Robert Hunter, son of Col. George Washington Hunter, of Fairfax County.
f. Susan Wood, married Robert Abercrombie, issue:
    1. Martha Alice Abercombie.

Issue of John Wood and Elizabeth Meyers: John Junior; Thomas; Robert, and four daughters.

1. John Wood, Jr., born at Alexandria, July 14, 1811, died March 16, 1889 at "Spring Hill", buried in Charlottesville. Married February 12, 1835, Eliza Jane Harper, born at "Spring Hill", December 27, 1817, died at "Spring Hill", August 19, 1907, buried at St. Paul's Church, Ivy Depot. Their issue:
    a. Charles Wood, born February 3, 1836 at "Spring Hill"; married 1866, Clara Hargraves at Columbus, Ga. She died March 14, 1916 and was buried at St. Paul's. Issue given later.
    b. Elizabeth Wood, born March 28, 1839, died October, 1920, married Clement D. Fishburne, June 11, 1867. Issue given later.
    c. Lucy Wood, born November 14, 1842 or '41, died at

"Spring Hill", May 25, 1921. She married W. B. Butler, July 3, 1861. He was killed, May 3, 1863 at the battle of Chancellorsville. Was an officer in the Florida Brigade, commanded by Gen. E. A. Perry. His body lies beside his wife at St. Paul's Church, Ivy. No issue.

d. Lydia Wood, born April 28, 1844, died August 30, 1879 at "Spring Hill."

e. Alfred Griffith Wood, born May 25, 1846, died April 28, 1854 in consequence of his leg being crushed in a bark mill. He is buried at "Locust Hill."

f. John Snowden Wood, born May 13, 1848 at "Spring Hill", died there, 1933, unmarried.

g. Walter Wood, born July 14, 1850, died April 24, 1873 and was buried in Charlottesville.

h. Maria Wood, born June 3, 1853, died October 13, 1853. Buried at "Locust Hill."

i. Lewis Wood, born April 5, 1855, lives at Lampazas, Texas. Married Jackie Baker, 1887. She died without issue.

j. Benjamin Wood, born February 14, 1862, died April, 1869, and is buried in Charlottesville.

Issue of Charles Wood and Clara Hargraves:

1. John Wood, died infant.
2. Hargraves Wood, born ——, died March 8, 1921 at the Walter Read Hospital, Washington, D. C., unmarried. Buried at St. Paul's, Ivy.
3. Waddy Butler Wood, born ——, married Lindsay Lomax, issue:
   a. Lindsay Wood.
   b. Virginia Wood.
4. Virginia Hargraves Wood, born March 1872, artist. She married Mr. Charles Franc Goddard, of New York.
5. Ann Forsythe Wood, born March 19, 1874.
6. Eliza T. Wood, born ——, married October, 1903, Dr. Cliff Sperow. She died 1923 and was buried at St. Paul's. No issue.

7. Clara Wood, died in infancy, buried in Charlottesville.
8. Lydia Wood, died young, buried at St. Paul's Church.
9. Rosa Aubrey Wood, born ——, married Gerard Glenn. Issue:
   a. Gerard Glenn.
   b. John Forsythe Cobb Glenn.
10. Major Charles Meigs Wood, U. S. A., married, no issue. He died 1930, buried at St. Paul's, Ivy Depot, Va.

Issue of Elizabeth Wood and Clement Fishburne.

1. John Wood Fishburne, married Mary Lyons, issue:
   a. Mary.
   b. Elizabeth, died young.
   c. Eleanor.
   d. Catherine B., born 1905, married October 14, 1924, Addinell Hewson Michie.
   e. Lucy.
   f. Jack.
   g. Thomas, died young.
   h. Junius.
2. Junius Fishburne, died young. Married. No issue.
3. Clement D. Fishburne, Jr., married first, Annie Price; married second, Florence ——. Issue by first wife:
   a. Clement D.
   b. Lydia, married 1927, Dr. Staige Davis Blackford.
4. Walter Fishburne, died April, 1902, unmarried.
5. George Fishburne.

Thomas, second son of John and Elizabeth (Myers) Wood, married Lydia Learned, who was daughter of Gen. Learned, U. S. A. and his second wife, Lydia Gates. Issue:

a. Learned (Naval officer), born ——, died August 25, 1922. Buried at St. Paul's, unmarried.
b. Thomas Longstreet, died unmarried.
c. John Wood, born ——, married Sally ——. Has a son John.

d. Emily Wood, died February, 1937, married Henry White. Issue:
   1. Harry White.
   2. Thomas White.
   3. Lydia White, married Carstairs Douglass. Issue:
      a. Carstairs Douglass.
   4. Samuel White.
   5. Garland White, died in infancy.

Robert L. Wood, third son of John Wood and Elizabeth Myers, was killed in a railroad accident. He was a member of the firm of Ashley and Wood, Alexandria. Married Melissa Hussey, daughter of Capt. Samuel Hussey (nephew of George Bancroft, the Historian). Issue, two daughters:

a. Ida Melissa Wood, married George Roberts Hill, and had: Melissa Ann Hill of Alexandria.
b. Frances Bancroft Wood, married James Clinton Smoot.

Harriet Wood, fourth child of John Wood and Elizabeth Myers, never married.

The fifth child, Susan Wood, was the second wife of Daniel Harmon, Sr. No issue.

The sixth child, Mary Elizabeth Wood, was the first wife of Daniel Harmon, Sr., and had issue:

a. Charles Harmon, married Miss Warwick, and left issue.
b. Mamie Harmon, died unmarried.
c. Daniel Harmon, Jr., married Miss Murphy, and left issue.
d. Lizzie Harmon, married Dr. Moss, and left one son.
e. John Harmon.

The seventh child, Ann Maria Wood, married ——.

William Wood, second son of John Wood and Alice Coward, was several times elected to the Virginia Legislature from Frederick County, Va. He married Margaret Ridgeway, and had six sons:

1. Algernon Ridgeway Wood, married Louise Cogswell, of New Jersey. Issue:
   a. Annie Wood, lives in Europe.

2. David Henry Wood, died March 18, 1876, of Ivy and Washington, D. C. and last of New York City, married January 4, 1842, Matilda Lewis, daughter of Thomas Fielding Lewis and his wife Ann Anderson, born September 3, 1822, died February 1, 1876. Issue:
   a. Margaret Lewis Wood, married Francis Lobban. No issue.
   b. Henry Wood, married Miss Hudspeth, and left issue.
   c. Paulus Powell Wood, married and left a son.
   d. Ann Jane Meriwether Wood, second wife of James Terrell Lewis, had issue:
      1. John Heath Lewis, married Ida ——, and has issue.
      2. Albert Greaves Lewis, died in childhood.
      3. Rev. David H. Lewis, married Louise Owen, and has David and a daughter.
      4. Frank L. Lewis, married Anna McIntire and has David and Anna.
      5. James Terrell Lewis, married Helen ——, and has two daughters.
      6. Sarah Stanford Lewis of New York, married Arthur Milner.
      7. Ettie B. Lewis.
      8. Matilda Lewis, of Richmond.
3. Thomas Wood, son of William and Margaret R. Wood, died young.
4. Dr. John Dean Wood, married Miss Burwa, of Louisiana. He was killed at the battle of Shiloh, C. S. A.
5. William Wood, unmarried.
6. Joseph Wood, lieutenant in C. S. A., wounded and died a few years after the War Between the States.

Ben Wood, third son of John and Alice Coward Wood, married Jane Anderson. Issue:

1. Marion Wood, married Dr. William G. Rogers (relative of Geo. Rogers and Wm. Clark through their mother Ann Rogers). Issue:
   a. Jennie Rogers, died young.

b. Maggie Rogers, died young.
c. Ella, married Alfred Wood, one child.
d. Ben Rogers, died unmarried.
e. Willie Rogers.

2. Martha Wood, married first, Daniel Perkins; second Capt. Flynn, no issue. Issue by first marriage, Joseph and Jane Lewis Perkins.
3. Alice Wood, married Charles Price. (See Price record.)
4. Lucy Wood, married William Barrett, and left issue: Lucy, who died unmarried, and several others who died young.

Joseph Perkins, married Sally Maupin. Issue:

1. Cabell Perkins, married Mr. Norris.
2. Marie Mildred Perkins, married first Gillum, had one son. She married second, Mr. Morecock, and has issue.
3. Daniel Perkins, married, no issue.
4. Joseph Perkins, died unmarried.
5. Rhett Perkins.
6. Jane Perkins, married Mr. Brazee.
7. Mason Perkins.
8. John Perkins.
9. Eloise Perkins, married Campbell Littleton, and has a girl and a boy.

Jane Lewis Perkins, married Dr. Walker, of Baltimore, had issue:

1. Mary Walker, married Rev. Miller, has Rhett, Esther and Joe.
2. Joseph Walker.

END OF WOOD RECORD.

## PRICE NOTE

*Extract from a Letter dictated by Mrs. Lucy Price Maury.*

"My father was Stephen Price, son of Lucy Coleman and Daniel Price. My great-grandmother was Miss Lucy Allen. My great-grandfather was killed in the Revolution. My great-grandmother lived twenty-five miles from Danville, near Pittsylvania Courthouse on a farm now the site of Chatham; with her lived her sister, Mrs. Barksdale, who lived to be 110 years old. She cut a new set of teeth in her old age; she lay on a couch, not having walked for years and died from the effects of a fall from this couch. Her descendants—Barksdales of Halifax Courthouse, and near Scottsville, Albemarle County, I think. Great-grandmother Coleman lived 101 years. Her oldest daughter married a Ward, lived in Georgia, had a son, Rowan Ward. (His son in War C. S. A., died in Virginia, his body was sent back to Georgia.)"

Mrs. Lucy P. Maury states that both of her grandmothers and her great-grandmother Coleman were living at the time of her birth, all of them being named Lucy. She was named for the three.

Issue of Lydia Harper and Stephen Price, six children:

A. Lucy Price, married Jesse Maury. Issue:

- 1. Nanny, married 1872, Fontaine Maury. Issue:
    - a. Lucy, married Gordon Granger, and had issue:
        - 1. Gordon Granger.
        - 2. Margaret Granger.
        - 3. Agatha, died in infancy.
    - b. Bessie, first married Chas. Haynes; second, Mr. Coombs, has:
        - 1. Ann Haynes.
        - 2. Alice Haynes, married September 8, 1924, Chas. Mesmer Montgomery.
    - c. Loundes Maury, married Nanny Perkins, and had:
        - 1. Reuben Maury.
        - 2. Jessie Lewis Maury.
        - 3. Lydia Maury, and others.
- 2. Lizzie Maury, married Dr. Lemon. They had:
    - a. Nan Lemon, married John Lightfoot. No issue.
    - b. Bob Lemon, married ——, and had issue.
- 3. Reuben Maury, died January 2, 1923, married Mrs. Joey Weyman Houston. They had no children.
- 4. Stephen Price Maury, married Lizzie Stribling. Issue:
    - a. Eleanor Maury, married, no issue.
    - b. Lucy Maury, married Mr. Peyton, no issue.
    - c. Judith Maury, married Mr. Tice, had:

1. Maury Tice, and two others.

d. Lola Maury, married, and had one child.

e. Fontaine Maury, married Mr. Thraives, and had:

1. Mercy Thraives.

2. Patricia Thraives.

f. Lewis Maury, married.

5. Mat Maury, married second, Florence ——, no issue.

6. Jane Maury, married Albert Maverick, of San Antonio.

7. Ellen Maury, married James L. Slayden. No issue.

The children of Albert and Jane Maverick are:

a. Jesse Maverick, married Mr. McNeil, has issue.

b. Agatha Maverick, married Norval Welsh, has issue.

c. Ellen Maverick, married Mr. Wright, has Ellen Wright.

d. Mary Maverick, married and has issue. McGaurow.

e. Albert Maverick, married Lillian ——.

f. Phillip Maverick, married Jean ——.

g. Virginia Maverick, married Murray Crossette, and has issue.

h. Reuben Maverick, died unmarried.

i. George Maverick, married Ruth Newell, issue:

1. Ruth Maverick, born 1918.

2. Fontaine Maverick, born 1920.

j. James Maverick, married, and has issue.

k. Hon. Maury Maverick, married Miss Terrell, and has:

1. Maury Maverick, Jr.

B. Charles Price, married first, Alice Wood; second, Sallie Woods. There were five children by the first marriage and two by the second. They were:

1. Jane Lewis Price, married Mr. Villineuve, no issue.

2. Lydia Price, married first, Mr. Ford, no issue. She married second, Mr. Bainbridge, issue:

a. Constance Bainbridge, married Richard Anderson, issue:

1. Constance Anderson.

2. Richard Anderson, Jr.

b. Frederick Bainbridge, married July 7, 1924, Cornelia W. Burnley, daughter of Charles Horace and Cornelia Burnley (cousins).

3. Lucy Price, married Dr. Albert Wilson, issue:
   a. Price Wilson, died in childhood.
   b. Lydia Wilson.
   c. Albert Wilson, married and has issue.
   d. Lewis Wilson, married.
   e. Jesse Wilson, died unmarried.
   f. Alice Wilson, married.
4. Meriwether L. Price, married Hester Maloney, issue:
   a. Harper Price, married.
   b. Meriwether Price.
   c. Elizabeth Price, married.
5. Charlie Price, married Anna Euker, daughter of Charles Euker, of Marburg, Germany and Augusta Krache, of Richmond, Va., 1862. Issue:
   a. Honor, died 1926, married Chris. Green, no issue.
   b. Ben Wood Price, born 1912, married Miss Newton.
6. Dr. James Woods Price, married Sophie Hoener.
7. Gertrude Price.

C. Robert Price, married Linda ——. They had:
   1. Annie Price, married Clem Fishburne, and had:
      a. Clem Fishburne.
      b. Lydia Fishburne, married Dr. Staige Blackford.
   2. Bob Price, married Sue Johnson, and has:
      a. Richard Price.
      b. Robert Price.

D. Daniel Price, married Harriet Harper, granddaughter of Chas. Bennet Harper and Anna Price. Issue:
   1. George Price.
   2. Margaret Price.
   3. Meriwether L. Price.

E. Sally Price, married Mr. Pride.
   1. Lucy, married Mr. Gilbert, and had:
      a. Sarah Gilbert.
      b. Lucy Harper Gilbert, married.

2. Bessie Pride.
3. Jack Pride, married.
4. Meriwether Pride.

F. Betty Price, married Mr. Earle, and had:

1. Lydia Earle, married, no issue.
2. Harry Earle, married.
3. Lewis Earle.
4. William Earle.

END OF PRICE RECORD.

## SLAUGHTER

This record completed from a family Bible record given to Mr. Slaughter Ficklin by John Slaughter of Illinois (husband of Sarah Harper) when shortly before his death he was on visit to Virginia, 1857.

(Copied by his daughter, Mildred M. Russell, of Henry, Ill.)

Between 1720 and 1730 Frances and Robert Slaughter, brothers, moved from near Williamsburg to Orange County. Tradition says they were sons or grandsons of a Welshman of that name who emigrated to Virginia at an early age. Francis settled on land later held as Glebe of Rev. John Woodville and took up large land grants around it. He had four sons:

1. Francis, married Miss Coleman, had Francis and three or four other sons. Several of them served in the Revolution.
2. Cadwallader, married Miss Randall, of Fauquier County.
3. Reuben.
4. John—commanded a regiment of Militia in Virginia. First married Milly Coleman, born March 6, 1736, died May 1, 1758), daughter of Robert Coleman; had Ann, Cadwallader, and Robert, born April 16, 1758. Married second, December 22, 1758, Elizabeth, born March 11, 1742, daughter of Edgewood Suggett and Elizabeth, his wife, of Richmond County. Issue, seven sons:
   1. Cadwallader, born December 18, 1756.

2. Robert, born April 16, 1758—officer in Revolution.
3. John, born November 2, 1759—officer in Revolution.
4. William, born April 19, 1761—officer in Revolution.
5. Lucien, born March 7, 1763.
6. Francis Lightfoot, born May 22, 1765.
7. Thomas K.

Daughter Elizabeth, born June 1, 1767.

John's daughters married Col. Thomas Barber; Gen. Joshua Barber; Col. Ben Fields; Major G. Long and C. C. Robertson.

William Slaughter, married April 10, 1785, Lucy S. Brown, born February 26, 1769, daughter of Wm. and Mary Brown, and had:

1. Elizabeth, born February 2, 1786, died April 13, 1786.
2. Elizabeth, born March 25, 1787, married Paul Yates.
3. John, married Sarah Harper; moved from Albemarle County to Zanesville, Ohio, 1831. Issue:
   - a. Lucy Ann, married Uriah Parks, of Zanesville (now living in Illinois)—three children.
   - b. Mary Ann, married James Dowell, settled in Ohio. Four children.
   - c. Sarah E., married John McClure, settled in Ohio. Four children.
   - d. Mildred M., married John T. Russell, of Virginia, settled in Illinois. No issue.
   - e. William, married ——, settled in Illinois. Two children.
   - f. Hannah G., married Samuel Graves, settled in Illinois. Three children.
   - g. Rebecca, married P. H. Kipp, of Missouri. Four children.
   - h. Joseph, married ——. Two sons and two daughters.
   - i. John, died 1862, unmarried.

# FAMILY RECORD OF COBBS, OF ROBESON COUNTY, NORTH CAROLINA

## BEING THE SAME AS THE COBBS FAMILY, OF GOOCHLAND AND LOUISA COUNTIES, OF VIRGINIA

Richard Cobb of Oxford and Aberdeen, student of Christ Church, fought against the Spaniards in the Low Countries, married Sybil Sheets, in Holland, November 8, 1576. She bore him sixteen children.

Joseph Cobb, this son born at Amsterdam 1588, came to Virginia in 1613 and settled in Elizabeth City County. His wife and two sons, Joseph, born 1610 and Benjamin, born 1611, joined him there, 1621, coming over in the "Bonnie Bess."

Joseph Cobb, had two sons, Ambrose, born 1631, and Nicholas, born 1632. Both settled on Appomattox River. Ambrose lived where Petersburg is now.

Ambrose Cobb had two sons: Robert and Thomas, both settled in York County, Va., where Robert died 1682, leaving three sons and one daughter. Thomas afterwards moved to Goochland County.

Thomas Cobb left six sons: 1. John; 2. Ambrose; 3. Jessie Heritage: 4. Edmond; 5. Otho; 6. Samuel.

John Cobb left five sons: 1. Tobias, born 1721; 2. John, born 1723; 3. Thomas, born 1724; 4. Stephen, born 1727; 5. Jesse, born 1730. All left Virginia in search of cotton lands.

Jesse Cobb, born 1730, died 1805, married Elizabeth Heritage, 1771, and had five children: 1. Ann; 2. Susannah; 3. John; 4. Jesse; 5. Elizabeth. Removed from Goochland to Newburn, N. C., where he married and later went up the river and settled where Kinston is now.

John Cobb, born 1776, died 1834, of Kinston; married first, Ann Whitfield, and had: 1. William; 2. Elizabeth.

John Cobb, married second, Ann Byrant; married third, Ann Bryan Grist, who bore him 3. Harriet; 4. Jesse; 5. Richard Grist; 6. John Washington; 7. Frederick Henry.

William Downell Cobb, born 1805, died 1865, married Ann Spicer Collier, 1833, and had nine children: 1. John Probate; 2. Needham Bryan; 3. Elizabeth Green; 4. Bryan Whitfield;

5. William Henry; 6. Ann Whitfield; 7. Harriet Elizabeth; 8. Joseph George Willis; 9. Maria Caroline.

Needham Bryan Cobb, born 1830, died 1905, married first, Maria Louise Cobb. She bore him twelve children. Married second, Ann De Lisle Fennell. She bore him three children.

Collin Cobb, born 1862, married first, Mary Lynsey Battle. She bore him three children: 1. William Battle; 2. Collin; 3. Mary Louisa. Married second, Lucy Plummer Battle, who bore him: 4. Richard Battle (dead).

STEPHEN COBB, son of John, of Goochland, Va., settled in Tarsun, N. C., where he left sixteen sons and eight daughters.

Edward Cobb, youngest son of Stephen Cobb, settled on Otter Creek, Edge Combe County, N. C. Married and left five children:

1. Stephen; 2. Gray; 3. James; 4. Joel; 5. Edward.

Stephen Cobb, married first, Appie Mayo, who had five children:

1. Patsy, married Easton Cherry, and left six children.
2. Peter, married first, Miss Bayles, of Alabama; married second, Miss Best.
3. Elizabeth, married Johnathan Gay, and died childless.
4. Winnie, married Johnathan Gay, left two children, John and Elizabeth.
5. Gray, married Miss Wooten and went to Mississippi.

Stephen married second, Patsy Long, who had two children:

6. Edward, married Balcher, and left: John Gray.
7. James L. Cobb, married Mary Williams, and left children:
    a. Williams Edward Cobb, married Celia Spevey.
    b. Benjamin Joseph, who married Lelia Reese.
    c. James Thomas, married Linda Vines.
    d. Lucy Williams Cobbs, married Charles Spencer.
    e. Maria Louisa Cobb, married Needham Bryan Cobb.

OLD PRAYER BOOK—Dated 1783

Printed at Edinburg by assignees of Alexander Kincaid

Family Register.

Rebecca Gordon, born October 8, 1772.

Mary Gordon, born January 29, 1777.

Gray Cobb, born December 29 in the year of our Lord, 1770. Moved to Sampson County, February 19, 1805.

Gray Cobb and his wife, Rebecca Gordon, married November 26, in the year of our Lord, 1795. Issue:

1. Genetta Cobb, the daughter of Gray Cobb and Rebecca, his wife, was born in the year of our Lord, October 13, 1796.
2. Charlotte Cobb, born September 12, 1798.
3. Fanny Cobb, born 10 (date too worn to read.)
4. Willie Cobb, born May 14, 1804.
5. Sally Cobb, born May 24, 1807.
6. Gordon Holoworth Cobb, born January 12, 1809.
7. Gray Edward Cobb, born September 27, 1812.
8. Harriet Elizabeth Cobb, born January 1, 1815.

FLY LEAF—

Gray Cobb, March 26, 1801.

Keep always good before your eyes
With your whole Intent.
Commit no sin in any wise,
Keep his commandments.
(March 10, 1823)

TRACING—

Gray Cobb, married Rebecca (Gordon) Cobb.
Stephen Cobb, married Mary (Bethune) Cobb.
John W. Cobb, married Cordelia Owen.
William Stephen Cobb, married Martha May Harper. Issue:

1. Mary Harper Cobb, born December 28, 1902, married.
2. John Charles Cobb, born September 30, 1905.
3. William Stephen Cobb, born December 2, 1907.
4. Edward Gray Cobb, born January 14, 1910.
5. Frederick Cobb, born just before his father's death.

Martha May Harper, daughter of Charles Harper and Alice Harper, son of Gabriel S. Harper, (son of Charles Harper and Lucy Smither, of "Spring Hill", Albemarle County) and Sarah Thornton Anderson, daughter of Jane M. Lewis and Edmund Anderson, of "Locust Hill", Albemarle County.

END HARPER RECORD.

PENDLETON DISTRICT, S. C., BY RICHARD WRIGHT SIMPSON

## ANDERSON

John Jean Anderson came from Ireland to Philadelphia, 1735. 1735 they moved to Staunton, Virginia.

Had: 1. Robert Anderson; 2. James Anderson.

Robert Anderson, married Thompson, November 6, 1765, and later moved to South Carolina and settled in what was later "Pendleton District". He was an officer in the Revolution—rose to be Colonel. He was prominent in the formation of Pendleton and one of the judges who held the first court there, 1790. He was afterwards Brigadier-General of Militia.

James. Anderson, born December 10, 1771, married Agnes Craig, 1786 or '89, of Augusta County, Va. They removed to "Pendleton District." He was a captain in the Revolutionary War.

General Robert Anderson and Ann Thompson had five children:

1. Elizabeth Anderson, married Samuel Maverick.
2. Mary Anderson, married first, Capt. Robert Maxwell; married second, Mr. Corruth.
3. Jane Anderson, married Mr. Shaw, an Englishman.
4. Annie Anderson, married Dr. Wm. Hunter.
5. Robert Anderson, Jr., married Maria Thomas.

Captain Robert Maxwell, who married Mary Anderson, came from Ireland—was a prominent citizen and an officer in the Revolutionary Army. At the close of the war, he married and settled on Saluda River in old Pendleton District. 1797 he was shot from ambush and killed near his home, his grave marked by a monument in the family graveyard. He and his wife had two sons:

1. Capt. John Maxwell, married Elizabeth Earle.
2. Robert Anderson Maxwell, married Mary Prince Earle, daughter of Samuel Earle.

(This family intermarried largely with the Pickens family.)

# MAVERICK FAMILY

EMIGRANTS—

John and Samuel Maverick, came from London to Carolina before Charleston was built.

The son of one of these brothers, Samuel Maverick, born at Charleston, was a soldier in the Revolution, was taken prisoner and confined on the British man-of-war in New York. In handcuffs twelve months. On release he walked and begged food until he reached Charleston, S. C.

He married Lydia Turpin, daughter of Capt. Joseph and Mary Turpin, of Providence, Rhode Island.

*Note—*

Capt. Joseph and Mary Turpin had three children:

1. Joseph Turpin, who was the father of
   a. Capt. William Turpin, of Greenville, S. C.
   b. Catherine (Turpin) Weyman.
   c. Mary (Turpin) Footman.
2. Lydia Turpin.
3. William Turpin.

Catherine Weyman had: Mary, Robert and Edward Weyman.

Edward Weyman had: Joseph T. Weyman, married Mary Ann Maverick.

Samuel Maverick, born at Charleston, S. C., was the only child of Samuel and Lydia Turpin Maverick, who left descendants. He married Elizabeth Anderson, daughter of Gen. Robert Anderson of South Carolina and had: 1. Samuel Augustus Maverick; 2. Mary Elizabeth Maverick; 3. Lydia Ann Maverick.

Samuel Augustus Maverick, married Mary Adams of Alabama, and had:

a. Mary Elizabeth Maverick, married Joseph T. Weyman, and had:
   a. Eliza Houston Weyman.
   b. Augustus Maverick Weyman.
   c. Joseph B. Weyman, married Emily Maxwell, and had:
      1. Samuel T. Weyman, married Bennie Fontaine.
      2. Joey Weyman, married first, Mr. Houston; married second, Reuben Maury.

Mary Elizabeth Maverick, married second, Joseph Thompson, of Kentucky, and had:

a. Joseph Thompson, married first, ——; married second, —— Harden.

b. Samuel Maverick Thompson.

Lydia Ann Maverick, daughter of Samuel and Elizabeth Anderson Maverick, married William Van Wych, of New York, and left many descendants.

Capt. John Maxwell was a member of the South Carolina Legislature and member of the Secession Convention, 1860-1861. He and his wife, Elizabeth Earle Maxwell, had:

1. Dr. Robert Maxwell, married Lucy Sloan.
2. Samuel Maxwell, married Julia Keels.
3. Harriet Maxwell, married Dr. Baylis Earle.
4. Mary Maxwell, died unmarried.
5. Baylis Maxwell, unmarried.
6. Eliza Maxwell, married Dr. Thomas Lewis, son of Overton Lewis.
7. Dr. John Maxwell, married Mary Alexander, no issue.
8. Emily Maxwell, married Joe Weyman.
9. Martha Maxwell, married John Keels.
10. Annie Maxwell, married Major Ben Sloan.
11. Mirian Maxwell, unmarried.

Emily Maxwell and Joe Weyman had: a. Samuel Weyman, married Bennie Fontaine; b. Joey Weyman, married first, Bryan Houston; married second, Reuben Maury, died January 2, 1923.

Martha Maxwell and John Keels had: a. Fanny Keels, married Dr. Swandale; b. John Keels, unmarried; c. Sue Keels, married John J. Capers; d. Emily Keels, married Frank Capers.

Captain Robert Maxwell's widow, Mary Anderson Maxwell, married second, Corruth, and had:

a. Louisa Corruth, married Gen. Gilliam, of Greenville, S. C. No issue.

# FONTAINE

John de la Fontaine, born A. D. 1500, martyred 1563, had a son, James Fontaine (2), whose son, Rev. James Fontaine (3) (died 1666), Pastor of Vause and Royan, married first, Thompson; second, Marie Chaillon. His son, Rev. James Fontaine (4), born 1658, died January 29, 1721 in Dublin; married E. Bonssiguot and was ancestor of Virginia Fountaines and Maurys. Their daughter, Mary Ann Fontaine, born 1690 at Taunton, England, died in Virginia, 1755; married Matthew Maury in Dublin, 1716. He died 1752. 1718, emigrated to Virginia, where two of her brothers had come. One of them was Rev. Peter Fontaine, born at Taunton, England, came to Virginia 1716. Rector of Westover Parish, died 1757, married first, E. Fourrean; second, E. Wade. Children:

1. Peter Fontaine, born 1720, married E. Winston, (a daughter Mary, married first, Bowles Armistead; married second, Col. Lewis.)
2. Moses Fontaine, born 1742, married Ballard.
3. Sarah, born 1744.
4. Mary Ann, born 1746, married Isaac Winston.
5. Elizabeth, born 1747, married William Mills.
6. Joseph, born 1748.
7. Aaron, born 1754, married three times—once a Miss Terrell.
8. Abram, born 1756, married Sarah Ballard.

Fontaine Arms: Garland of roses; shield edged on outside with roses; elephant crest; elephant heads; black tusks upwards; couped neck; no dividing mark. Fully rigged ship on lower shield.

Aaron Fontaine and Miss Terrell had: (fifteen children and sixty-seven grandchildren)

1. Mary, married Cosby, and had seven children.
2. Elizabeth, married Bullock, had three children.
3. Matilda, married Praither, had seven children.
4. Martha, married Pope, had six children.
5. Sarah, married Floyd, had six children.
6. Maria, married Grymes, had four children.

7. America, married Vernon, had ten children.
8. Barbara, married first, Cosby, had two children. Married second, Saunders.
9. Ann, married Jacobs, had three children.
10. Emeline, married Dillon, had one child.
11. Peter, married ——, had three children.
12. James Terrell, had three children.
13. Wm. Maury, had five children.
14. Henry, had three children.
15. Aaron, had four children.

From this family descend: Armisteads, Alexanders, Seldons, Lees, Terrells.

Mary Ann Fontaine and Matthew Maury, had:

1. Rev. James Maury (1717-1769), married Mary Walker. (Record given.)
2. Mary Maury, born 1725, married Daniel Claiborne, son of Thomas Claiborne.
3. Abram Maury, born 1731, married Susannah Poindexter.

Daniel and Mary Claiborne, had: 1. Matthew, married Miss Harrison; 2. Mary, married Mr. de Butts; 3. Hannah, married Mr. Triplett; 4. Dorothea, married Henry Tatum, who had: a. Dr. Henry Augustus Tatum, married Miss Brooking; b. Mary Tatum, married Robert H. Branch; c. Dorothea Ann Tatum, married James McG. Boyd; d. Theophilus Tatum, married Anna Dunbar Edwards, widow of S. Puryear, and had among others, Miss Lou Tatum and William Henry Tatum.

W. H. Tatum married three times: first, Miss Armstrong, who left a son, Harry Tatum; second, Mary Pearman, who left a daughter, Annie Tatum, married Dr. M. L. Anderson. The third wife was Miss Walker, whose daughter, Lucy Tatum, married Carl Boschen.

Abram Maury, married Susannah Poindexter, had:

1. Matthew, born 1760, married F. Tabb.
2. Elizabeth, born 1762, married Wm. Dowsing.
3. Susan, born 1764, married Joel Parish.
4. Abram, Jr., born 1766, married Martha Worsham of Virginia, had nine children, of whom seven lived to be grown,

emigrated from Virginia 1788-9, died at Franklin, which town he laid out, 1825. His fourth child was Hon. Abram Poindexter Maury.

5. Mary, born 1768, married Metcalf de Graffenreid.
6. Philip, born 1770, married C. Cunningham.
7. Martha, born 1772, married Chapman White.

Hon. A. Poindexter Maury (1801-1848), of Williamson County, Tenn., was such a meditative child and bookworm, so different from the usual boy, his mother feared he did not have good sense. But his father said to her, "Never fear, my dear, Abraham is our smartest child."

At fourteen he was chosen to deliver a Fourth of July oration at Franklin, Tenn. At eighteen or nineteen he edited a paper in St. Louis for a year or two. Then he went to West Point for a year, came home, studied and practiced law for a time, went to Nashville and edited a political paper *The Republican*. He married Mary E. T. Claiborne (born 1806, married at nineteen, died 1852.) They had nine children. A year after his marriage he bought his deceased father's farm and made that his home. He was a Whig, served two terms in Congress and at various times in both legislative bodies in Tennessee.

"A pure honest man, of strict integrity, a poor farmer but a lover of books, systematic in reading—a chaste beautiful writer. He often lectured on library and political subjects, contributed both poetry and prose to the *Southern Literary Messenger* and was called the ablest writer of the Southwest.

Handsome and dignified, kind husband and father, honored and held in high respect by all. His children should feel the brightest heritage left them—the descent from one who was emphatically the noblest work of God—an *honest man*."

## WALLER FAMILY

### HAYDEN

*Domesday Book*—Burke's Peerage states that this family is derived from Alured De Waller of Newark County, Nottingham, who died 1183 and from whom lineally descended David De Waller, for thirty years Master of the Rolls to King Edward III. David died s. p. and was succeeded by his brother, Henry Waller of Hockerton, who dropped the "De". He married Alicia de Mortimer, their son Thomas purchased "Groombridge" in Kent, from Lord Clinton in 1360.

Thomas Waller died 1371, married Christina Chessunt. His son John Waller of "Groombridge", married Margaret, daughter and heiress of "Landsdale" of Landsdale, in Sussex County. Issue: Sir Richard Waller of Sheldhurst, sheriff of Kent. He served in France under Henry V and signalized himself at Agincourt in that he took prisoner in that battle, Charles Duke of Orleans, whom he brought back to England and kept prisoner at "Groombridge", near Speldhurst, Kent County. (M. S. at *Herald's* office.) He was a great benefactor to the church at Speldhurst where his arms still remain in stonework over the porch.

In these arms we find an addition to the former bearing of the family assigned by Henry V to him and his descendants, viz: a crest with the arms of France upon a shield hanging on the sinister side of a walnut tree with the motto: *Hic Fructus Virtutis.*

Sir Richard married Olivia Gulby, and had: 1. Richard, married daughter and heiress of Edmond Brudewell; 2. John, married Joan, daughter of William Whitenhall of Heckhurst, and dying 1517, left a son, William.

William Waller of "Groombridge" was High Sheriff of Kent, 1537, married Anne, daughter of Wm. Fallenmar of Esteney, Hants, died 1555, left two sons: 1. William, who succeeded him was ancestor of the Wallers of Castletown. 2. John Waller of Allentown, who was grandfather of Robert Waller, Esq. of Agmondesham, Bucks, who married Ann Hampden, daughter of Griffin Hampden and sister of the famous John Hampden. They had three daughters and five sons, of whom were:

1. Edmund Waller, the poet, and 2. John Waller, M. D., prominent citizen of Newport, Pagnel, Buckinghamshire, England, whose son, Col. John Waller settled in Virginia, 1635. He married Mary Key, or Keys, of Enfield, King William County, Va. He brought with him the seal of his family which became the property of his descendant, John Waller Holladay of "Prospect Hill", Spotsylvania County, Va. His son, Col. John Waller, gentleman of "Newport", Spotsylvania, born 1673, died 1754,

married Dorothy King, born 1675, died 1759. He was a member of the vestry and senior warden of St. George's Parish—one of the founders of Fredericksburg; High Sheriff of King and Queen, 1702; Justice of King William County; Burgess, 1714, 1720, 1722. When Spotsylvania was cut off from King William County he became its first clerk.

Children of John and Dorothy Waller:

A. John Waller of Pamunkey, married 1730, Agnes, daughter of Thomas Carr of Bear Castle.

B. Thomas (will ex. 1787), married Sarah or Elizabeth Dabney, had: Thomas; daughter married Joel Harris; Dorothy married Quarles; John married Mary Anne, etc.

C. William Waller, gentleman, born 1714, died January 10, 1760, married Ann Booker or Bouchier, whose mother was a Byrd.

D. Judge Benjamin Waller, married Martha Hall of North Carolina. A daughter married Henry Tazewell, had Littleton Waller Tazewell. Judge Waller made no will but record of births and deaths of his children are in the family Bible.

E. Edmund Waller, married Mary Pendleton of Caroline County, had: Rev. John Waller, noted Baptist minister.

F. *Mary Waller, only daughter of John and Dorothy Waller, born 1699, married Zachary Lewis II of King and Queen and Spotsylvania counties.

*Arms*—Sa three walnut leaves or between two bendlets ar.

*Crest*—On a mount vert a walnut tree p p r, on sinister side an escutcheon pendant, charged with the arms of France with labels of three points ar.

*Motto—Hic fructus virtutis.*

"BEL-AIR"—HOME OF ZACHARY LEWIS

*The Zachary Lewises of Wales*

# The Zachary Lewises of Wales

An old copy of Burke's *Heraldry* gives this Lewis family the following arms:

*Shield*—gules, three serpents mowed in triangle argent, within a border or.

*Crest*—a horse's head couped bridled ppr.

*Motto*—"Be wise as a serpent, harmless as a dove."

*Note:* The above crest is engraved on a very old silver spoon owned by John Overton Smith of Beaver Dam, Hanover County, Va. He is a direct descendant of Zachary Lewis of Virginia.

This same old *Heraldry* further states that the history of this ancient Lewis family is contained in *The Book of the House of the Golden Grove,* a Welsh record owned by the Earl of Cawdor, whose home in Wales is named the "House of the Golden Grove". This old record is kept in London. Some years ago one of the family genealogists, Miss Mary Greenhow of Richmond, (who is a direct descendant of Zachary Lewis I of Virginia) through a Mr. Leland who was doing research work for a Carnegie Foundation tried to look up this old record. He found it written mostly in Welsh and could not read it, so we are yet ignorant of what it tells of the earlier records of this family.

Burke's *Heraldry* further states these Zachary Lewises descend from Ednowain Lord of Thys Bradwin near Dolgelly Co. Mersoueth, founder of the XV noble tribe of North Wales and Cowys. He was sixth in descent from Rhodri Maur, King of Wales, who reigned A. D. 843, died 847. Rhodri Maur was son of "Cadwallender the Blessed", whose long line of descent traces to King David and to Aaron, the High Priest. (See Chart of Royal Lineage of Kings of England.)

Ednowain's descendants were the following noble families:

1. Lewis of Aber—Naut Cychan.
2. Loyds of Penniarth.
3. Loyds of Haut—y hynach.
4. Owens of lac y Berllan.
5. Griffiths of Garth and Cloddian Corhin.

(The above information is the research work of Miss Mary Greenhow.)

*Note:* A tradition found among several lines of the Zachary Lewises of Virginia that they are Huguenot French is not substantiated by the incidents they quote. For instance—a certain Pierre Lewis saved Henry of Navarre in a skirmish and was not only knighted but had conferred upon him the coat-of-arms won by Sir Richard Waller at the battle of Agincourt. (See Burke's *Peerage.*) Again—citing as an ancestor, Jean Lewis, a very distinguished officer who served with the Duke of Marlborough and who was later Earl Ligonier and Baron of Inniskillen (an Irish title). He died, aged 92, full of honors, but is said to have left no descendants.

The Welsh Peerage is said to show that these Lewises owned, 1692, in Wales estates named "Brecknock" and "Llangollen" in Brecknockshire.

All records of these Lewises in Virginia begin with Zachary Lewis I, emigrant to Virginia, 1692, a lawyer (we have mention of him as king's attorney, November 9, 1739) who took up lands in Virginia, lived for some time in Middlesex County, took up 450 acres of land in King William County, 1694, and in 1703 took out 500 acres of land in King and Queen County. (Patent in Virginia Library.) Name of wife not known. And we have full record of only two sons. An old letter says he had daughters, but we know nothing of them. The family of "John Lewis, the Planter", near Scottsville, Albemarle County, Va., claim a descent from Owen Lewis, who is supposed to be a nephew or perhaps a younger son of Zachary Lewis, the emigrant, but we have no record of this.

Zachary located on the high lands of "Dragon Swamp" in Middlesex County. His old home was inherited by his younger son, John Lewis, born 1704, who married Sarah Iverson and whose descendants yet live in their old homes in King William and King and Queen counties. I regret exceedingly my knowledge of this family is limited—that little will be given later under the head of the "Iverson Lewises", meanwhile we will return to the record of the older brother.

Zachary Lewis II was born January 1, 1702 in either King and

Queen or Middlesex, died January 20, 1765 in Spotsylvania County. (Spotsylvania was cut from King and Queen, King William and Essex, 1720.) He was married (Rev. Theodore Staige officiating) January 9, 1725 to Mary Waller (only daughter of Col. John Waller and Dorothea King). She was born January 30, 1699, died March 28, 1781, christened February 17, 1699 by Rev. John Moyroe. Zachary Lewis was a lawyer and a strict churchman. "On the division of his father's estate he gave his portion to be divided among his sisters, reserving only his riding horse and a violin; he settled in Spotsylvania and there acquired a large fortune." (This statement Mrs. Huldah Holladay, his granddaughter, received from her father, Zachary Lewis III).

Zachary Lewis II was in the House of Burgesses 1757-58-60-61. (*Virginia Colonial Register.*)

He had issue, ten children:

I. Ann Lewis, born November 30, 1726, baptized by Rev. Mr. Staige, December 29, 1726, died August 8, 1748, married December 26, 1747, Chancellor George Wythe. No issue.

*Note:* Record shows February 13, 1746, George Wythe qualified as attorney. He married first, Ann Lewis; second, Elizabeth Taliaferro, no issue by either marriage. He was a Signer of the Declaration of Independence, was an ardent patriot of the United States, was Professor of Law at William and Mary College. Later he lived in Richmond; and I have seen in the center of the pavement at a point on East Franklin Street a large sycamore which is said to have stood before his door. In its pleasant shade they say, were accustomed to gather many celebrities of that day, and many a mighty question was there debated.

II. Mary Lewis, born January 30, 1727, baptized by Rev. Mr. Staige, February 29, 1727, married Frank Meriwether, son of David and Ann Holmes Meriwether, and had issue:

a. Zachary Meriwether.

b. Nicholas Meriwether.

c. Mary Meriwether.

d. David Meriwether, who is mentioned in the widow's

estate of Zachary Lewis II, April 10, 1781. Deed Book, 1774-82.

This family moved from Virginia to South Carolina.

III. John Lewis, "the Honest Lawyer", born October 18, 1729, baptized by Rev. Rodham Kenner, November 28, 1729, died September 12, 1780. His colonial record was for Civil Service. At the meeting of the freeholders of Spotsylvania County, November 17, 1775, "John Lewis, attorney" was chosen one of the Committee of Safety. He was called the "Honest Lawyer" for his quixotic ideals of right and because he would not defend what he considered wrong. He was retained on the "Parson's Cause", after the first decision declared the case was established, he refused to act further. Later Patrick Henry by his eloquence swayed the decision of the jury against the established law. He married Ann Lewis, daughter of Col. Robert Lewis and Jane Meriwether of "Belvoir", Albemarle County. Issue: 1. John Z. Lewis; 2. Charles Lewis; 3. Nicholas Lewis; 4. Robert Lewis; 5. Mary Lewis, who married David Wood Meriwether. (See Lewises of "Belvoir".)

IV. Zachary Lewis, III, born May 6, 1731, baptized June 9, 1731 by Rev. Francis Pert, died July 21, 1803, was married by Rev. Robert Barrett, May 9, 1771 to Ann Terrell, daughter of Richmond and Ann Overton Terrell of Louisa County. She was born September 23, 1748, baptized by Rev. Robert Barrett, died November 30, 1820, aged 72 years.

V. Bettie Lewis, born October 6, 1732, baptized by Rev. William Dawson, December 16, 1732, married first, James Littlepage (his second wife), and had issue:

a. Mary Littlepage, married Robert S. Coleman, and left issue.

b. General Lewis Littlepage, born in Hanover County, December 19, 1762, died in Fredericksburg, July 19, 1802; educated at William and Mary College, where he entered, 1778. A full record of his brilliant European career given later as a "Memoriam".

Mrs. Bettie Lewis Littlepage married second, Major Lewis Holladay, son of Joseph Holladay and Betty Lewis Holladay, daughter of Harry Lewis of Spotsylvania, and had two children:

c. Waller Holladay of "Prospect Hill", married Huldah F. Lewis.

d. Nanny Holladay, married Rev. Hugh C. Boggs of "Livingstone". (Record given later.)

VI. Mourning Lewis, born April 1, 1734, baptized by Rev. Mr. Henry on April 6 and died April 19, (Easter) 1734. This name, "Mourning", came from the Waller family, also appears as a surname in Virginia and Kentucky, therefore is not used from some tragic association as tradition sometimes states. *Note:* Leanard James Mourning Waller, son of Edmond Waller, is mentioned in a codicil to John Waller's will dated August 15, 1754. Thomas Mourning served in Virginia Battalion under William Byrd, Hanover County.

VII. Lucy Lewis, born December 5, 1735, baptized by Rev. James Marye, January 2, 1736. Married Mr. Ford of Amelia County, and left several children, of whom I have no record.

VIII. Dorothea Lewis, born September 5, 1738, (died March 20, 1820), baptized by Rev. James Marye on "6 or 5 of ye same month," married April 13, 1762, Charles Smith, who was born July 22, 1729. Issue:

a. Christopher Smith, born March 21, 1763, died May 19, 1804, married Miss Anderson.

b. John Snelson Smith, born September 6, 1775, married (first cousin) Martha Bickerton Lewis.

c. Charles Smith, born November 18, 1778, died unmarried, October 17, 1815.

IX. Waller Lewis, born September 11, 1739 after 8 a. m., baptized by Rev. James Mayre thirtieth of same month, married Sarah Lewis of "Belvoir". (Issue given under "Belvoir" Lewises.)

X. Benjamin Lewis, born June 16, 1744, baptized by Rev. James Marye twenty-fourth same month, married Martha

Bickerton (daughter of Col. John Bickerton and Mary Todd Bickerton, Hanover County). Issue, six children. (*Cabells and Their Kin,* also tradition in family.)

a. Dr. Benjamin Lewis, died unmarried at "Walnut Grove", the home of his sister, Martha.

b. John W. Lewis, born 1775, died March 17, 1823, aged 48, buried in Episcopal Churchyard, Boydton, Va. Married Matilda Nelson (died 1838), lived at Oakland", Mecklenburg County. Issue:

   1. Martha B. Lewis, married Major Wallace B. Goor (pronounce "Your") during Civil War and moved to Arkansas. Issue:
      a. John Goor.
      b. Thomas Goor.
      c. Waring Goor.
      d. Wallace Goor.
      e. Raven Matthews Goor.
      f. Annie Goor.
   2. Benjamin Lewis, died unmarried near Boydton.
   3. Nancy Lewis, married Rev. Mr. Arthur of the Episcopal Church, Greenville, S. C.
   4. John Lewis, died in youth on his way home from Randolph-Macon College.
   5. Thomas Lewis, died unmarried. Practiced law from 1850 to 1860 at Boydton, later was in Confederate Army, then lived in New York.
   6. Caroline Matilda Lewis, died December 23, 1915, married Rev. Wm. H. Campbell. Issue:
      a. Caroline M. Campbell.
      b. Lucy Nelson Campbell.
      c. William Herbert Campbell.
      d. Mary Campbell.
      e. Nannie Arthur Campbell.
      f. Anne Bacon Campbell.
      g. Bertha Campbell.
      h. Virginia Campbell, married December 12, 1899,

John H. Lucas, (assistant cashier of bank, Charleston, S. C., 1925). Issue:

1. Wm. C. Lucas, born December 21, 1900. Graduate of United States Military Academy, 1923.
2. David Jennings Lucas, born October 28, 1902. Graduated "Citadel Class", 1924.
3. Matilda L. Lucas, born August 6, 1904, died 1906.
4. John Hume Lucas, born April 17, 1906.

i. Marian Campbell, died April 21, 1887, married A. Bacon Holmes, Jr. on April 7, 1886. Issue:

1. Marian Campbell Holmes, married June 21, 1921, Harold G. Guerard. Issue:
   a. Harold Goddin Guerard, born October 21, 1922.
   b. Russell Bogart Guerard, born October 29, 1923.

c. Nanny Lewis, daughter of Benjamin and Martha Bickerton Lewis, died 1828 in Mecklenburg County. She was first wife of Judge Thomas Tyler Bouldin. He was related to President Tyler, was elected member of Congress to succeed John Randolph of Roanoke. He fell dead on the floor of the House of Representatives in Washington while making a speech.
Issue, seven children:

1. Benjamin Bouldin, went to Kentucky.
2. Wood Bouldin, married first, Louisa Barksdale; second, Martha Daniel (daughter of Judge William Daniel of Lynchburg). He bought the estate of John Randolph of Roanoke in Charlotte County, Va., later moved to Richmond, where he practiced law, was at the time of his death at the head of the Virginia bar. (Issue given later.)
3. Thomas T. Bouldin, married first, Ellen Barksdale, who had one son; married second, Fanny Flournoy,

lived at the old Bouldin home in Charlotte County, and died there in the room in which he was born. Issue, ten children:

a. Thomas Tyler Bouldin, married Miss Harris, and had: Thomas, who died early, and Virginia, unmarried.

(Second marriage)

b. Fannie Lewis Bouldin, married Mr. Buford.

c. Mary Willis Bouldin, unmarried.

d. Henry Wood Bouldin, married first, Miss Cole; second, Miss Tabb.

e. Ellen Bouldin, unmarried.

f. Martha Cabell Bouldin, died.

g. Flournoy Bouldin, married Miss White.

h. Claiborne Bouldin, married May 10, 1904, Mary Crump. Issue, five children.

i. John Lewis Bouldin, married Miss Jones.

j. Annie V. Bouldin, married Mr. Daniel.

Claiborne Bouldin and Mary Crump, had issue:

1. Alice Goode Bouldin (named for her grandmother.)
2. Thomas Tyler Bouldin.
3. Mary Crump Bouldin.
4. Claiborne Bouldin.
5. Isabelle Bouldin.

4. Martha Bouldin, married Breckenridge Cabell, and lived in Lynchburg, Va. Issue:

a. John Cabell, unmarried.

b. Marion Cabell, unmarried.

c. Joan Cabell, married Mr. Morton.

d. Alice Cabell, married Mr. Withers, had two sons and three daughters. Some living in Campbell County.

e. —— Cabell, married and had issue: Mrs. Stuart and Mrs. Gen. Rush.

5. Joanna Bouldin, married Robert Carrington, went to Arkansas. Issue:
   a. John Carrington, went West.
   b. Thomas Carrington had a daughter, Priscilla, who was placed quite young in a Convent in Richmond.
6. Nanny Bouldin, married Claiborne Barksdale, and lived in Richmond. Issue:
   a. Robert Barksdale, unmarried.
   b. —— Barksdale, had several daughters unmarried.
   c. Claiborne Barksdale, married Priscilla Read. Issue:
      1. Mary Barksdale, married Mr. Gregory.
      2. Ann Barksdale, married Benjamin Mead.
      3. Elizabeth Barksdale, married Rev. ——.
      (This family all went to Kentucky.)
7. John Bouldin, moved to Kentucky.

d. Alice Lewis, daughter of Benjamin and Martha Bickerton Lewis, married Capt. Robert Jouett. Issue:
   1. Elsie Jouett, married Hon. James Wood Bouldin.

e. Martha Bickerton Lewis, married her first cousin, John Snelson Smith, lived at "Walnut Grove", near Bumpass Station, Hanover County. Here I called on her November, 1862. She was a beautiful old lady, though probably eighty years of age at the time. She died soon after I saw her.—S. T. L. A.

f. Elizabeth Ambler Lewis, died January 21, 1862, was the youngest daughter of Benjamin and Martha Bickerton Lewis. She married July 18, 1801, George Greenhow, who was sixth child of John Greenhow by his second wife, Elizabeth Tyler, who was born January 30, 1744 and died in Williamsburg, July 23, 1781. Was buried by the side of her husband (died August 29, 1787) in old Bruton churchyard. She was daughter of John Tyler, Marshall of Colony of Virginia. Issue, twelve children:
   1. George Greenhow, died infant in 1803.
   2. John Greenhow, died infant.
   3. Martha Ann Greenhow, died infant.
   4. Frances Elizabeth, born June 12, 1807, died January

19, 1892, married March 1, 1827, first, Thomas Williams, who was born September 14, 1798 in Monihan County, Ireland. He died June 10, 1828. She married second, 1848, John Nelson of Mecklenburg County, Va., no issue. Issue by first marriage:

a. Col. Thomas Greenhow Williams, born April 29, 1828, died January 22, 1885. He married July 12, 1853, Mary Christian Curtis of Hanover County, Va. He was a graduate of West Point Military Academy and served most of his life in the United States Army fighting Indians in Texas. He lived and died in San Antonio, Texas.
Two of his children were:

1. Frances Williams, married E. G. Gresham, Petersburg, Va.
2. Maria Williams, married John H. James of San Antonio, Texas.

5. Ann Willis Greenhow, born December 1, 1808, died December 21, 1866, married November 30, 1826, William Williams, who was born 1795, died December, 1866. He was brother to her sister's husband. Issue:

a. Sally Williams, born January 30, 1830, died June 23, 1852, married Edward Gallagher; two children died young.

6. Robert Lewis Greenhow, died young.
7. Samuel Crofton Greenhow, born February 18, 1814, died September 24, 1898, married September 24, 1839, Mary Tinsley Johnson( See Johnson and Meriwether line). She died August 19, 1877. Issue given later.
8. James Crofton Greenhow, born December 10, 1816, died September 24, 1862.
9. Martha Bickerton Greenhow, born September 3, 1820, died March 25, 1909, married December 19, 1848, Robert Henry Maury of Caroline County, Va. Issue:

a. George G. Maury, born 1850, died infant.
b. Ann Hooms Maury, born August 26, 1852, married January 31, 1878, Portiaux Robinson.
c. Allen Maury.
d. Robert Maury.
e. Gordon Woolfolk Maury.

10. Charles Greenhow, born July 31, 1822, died October 16, 1822.
11. Mary Jane Greenhow, born September 12, 1823, died March 31, 1909, married September, 1848, Dr. John G. Wayt. Issue:

a. George G. Wayt, born October 3, 1850, died April 7, 1876.
b. Twyman Wayt, died in infancy.

## GENERATIONS OF BOULDIN FAMILY

Supplied by Miss Mary T. Greenhow, who had it from Miss Ella Bouldin of Danville, Virginia.

1. Thomas Bouldin of Shelbourne, England, born 1523, had Thomas and John.
2. Thomas Bouldin of Warwick County, England.
3. Thomas Bouldin, born 1580, came to Virginia, 1610, married Mary ——.
4. William Bouldin of Pennsylvania, born 1620, died 1691, married Ann ——.
5. William Bouldin of Pennsylvania, born 1650, died 1717, married Elizabeth ——, had William, Elizabeth, Ann and John.
6. John Bouldin, born about 1680 in Pennsylvania, died 1711 in Maryland. He married Mary ——, and had Mary, William, John, Thomas.
7. Col. Thomas Bouldin, born 1706 in Pennsylvania, died 1783 in Virginia, married 1731, Nancy Clarke. They had James, Ehpraim, Thomas, William, Joseph, Wood, Richard, Mary Francemia.
8. Major Wood Bouldin, born 1742, married Joanna Tyler, who

died 1800. Had Mary, Thomas T., Rachel, Ann, Francemia, Martha, James W., Louis Contesse.

9. Thomas Tyler Bouldin, married Ann Lewis.
10. Wood Bouldin, married first, Miss Barksdale; second, Martha Daniel, in 1847. Issue, first marriage:
    a. Wood Bouldin, married Kate Easley, and had Elizabeth, Florence, Holt, Louise and Tyler.

    Issue, second marriage:

    b. Frank Bouldin, unmarried.
    c. Briscoe Bouldin, married first, Miss Ward; second, Miss Friend.
    d. Ellie Bouldin, unmarried.
    e. Ann Lewis Bouldin, married Mr. Overby.
    f. Mattie Daniel Bouldin, married Dr. Flournoy.
    g. Virginia Bouldin, unmarried.
    h. Alice Bouldin, married Baylor Green.
    i. Cornelia Bouldin, married Berryman Green.
    j. Charles Bouldin.
    k. William Bouldin.

Children of Samuel Crofton and Mary Tinsley Johnson Greenhow:

a. Mary Fleming Greenhow, born September 24, 1840, died March 20, 1922. Married first, September 24, 1863, Samuel Boyle Gassaway of Baltimore. Married second, Rev. Francis M. Baker. She was his third wife.
    1. Mary Greenhow Gassaway, born March 31, 1866, married June 16, 1891, James Adolphus Binford of Mecklenburg County. Issue: Mary Maury Binford, born October 21, 1892. Married October 4, 1910, Jesse Parsons of Petersburg. Issue: Ellen Heath Parsons, born January 30, 1918, and Mary Greenhow Parsons, born February 1, 1924.

b. Elizabeth Lewis Greenhow, born October 8, 1842, died August 20, 1907. Married December 22, 1864, Robert Henry Maury of Washington. He was killed April 27, 1870 by the falling floor of the State Capitol, Richmond.
    1. Greenhow Maury, born September 26, 1865, married Mary

Harvie, daughter of Dr. Lewis Harvie of Lynchburg. Five children.

2. Richmond Maury, born November 30, 1866, lives in Norfolk, Va. Married October 16, 1888, Mary Gordon of Smithfield, Va. Issue: Ellen Wilson Maury, born April 25, 1893, and Richmond Maury, Jr., born March 23, 1897.
3. Deane Maury, born January 12, 1869.

c. Mary Tinsley Greenhow, born January 4, 1845, was Founder of Home for Incurables, Richmond, Va.
d. George Greenhow, born July 30, 1847, died May 12, 1913, buried in Tallahasse, married first, Delia Roberts; second Octavia Chans of Florida. He left no descendants.
e. Samuel Greenhow, and
f. James Greenhow, twins, died at birth.
g. Fannie Nelson Greenhow, died infant.
h. Sally Williams Greenhow, born May 31, 1853, died July 21, 1923 from injuries received in a crowded street car which caught fire. She was knocked down and hurt in the crowd seeking escape from the yet moving car. Unmarried.
i. Lucy Greenhow, born January 8, 1856, married October 19, 1876, Andrew Langstaff Johnston, son of Peyton Johnston, formerly of Ireland and Ann Macon, his wife. Issue given.
j. Hallie Greenhow, married John Overton Smith. No issue.

Andrew Langstaff Johnston and Lucy Greenhow Johnston, had issue:

1. Mary Greenhow Johnston, born August 26, 1881.
2. Andrew L. Johnston, born May 24, 1887, married Phoebe Douglas Warwick. Issue:
   a. Andrew Langstaff Johnston III, born June 5, 1920.
   b. Warwick Douglas Johnston, born February 5, 1922.
   c. Peyton Macon Johnston, born April 26, 1923.
3. Samuel Greenhow Johnston, born May 24, 1887, married 1912, Ann Elizabeth White of Fredericksburg, Va. Issue:
   a. Greenhow Johnston, born August 12, 1922.
4. Lulie Greenhow Johnston, born January 21, 1892, married Major William ap Catesby Jones on September 24, 1918. Issue:

a. Catesby ap Catesby Jones, born July 17, 1919.
b. Lulie Greenhow Jones, born October 26, 1921.
c. Rosalie Fontaine Jones, born September 24, 1924, named for her father's mother, who was daughter of Col. Fontaine of Beaver Dam, Va.
(All this family live in Richmond, Va.)

## "PROSPECT HILL" HOLLADAYS

Waller Holladay, son of Betty Lewis Littlepage and Major Lewis Holladay, born August 17, 1776, baptized October 5, died August 27, 1860, married September 23, 1802, Huldah Lewis, born February 4, 1781, died October 25, 1863. They went at once to "Prospect Hill" where their long lives were spent and where all their many children were born. The present "Prospect Hill" house was built before 1812. They were a couple who stood for the highest in all things of truth and honor and Christianity, their influence being widespread. Their home was a center in the Lewis and Holladay connection, often including among its guests persons from foreign countries, as well as those of State and national distinction.

Waller Holladay was educated for the law but after inheriting means from Gen. Littlepage he ceased to practice law and devoted himself to management of his estate and to public duties. He did not have military record but served as County Assessor and Overseer of the Poor, 1798, also as Magistrate and was Member of Virginia Assembly, 1819-20 and of the State Convention, 1829-30 and Democratic Presidential Elector, 1836-40. (Family Bible record.)

Issue, thirteen children:

A. Dr. Lewis Littlepage Holladay, born August 7, 1803, died 1869, married first, November 8, 1827, Jean Thompson, daughter of Henry J. Thompson and Rebecca Welch of Chambersburg, Pennsylvania, and of "Pine Grove", Stafford County, Va. Issue:

1. Henry Thompson Holladay, born August 18, 1827, married first, December, 1853, Mary Jane Boggs, only daughter of Lewis Alexander Boggs, of Livingstone by his first

PROSPECT HILL, SPOTTSYLVANIA CO., VA., RESIDENCE OF MRS. H. F. HOLLADAY.

wife, Eliza Hart. Their only child, Mary Jane B. Holladay, died July 3, 1861. Henry T. Holladay married second, May 3, 1865, Frances Porter, and had:

a. Porter Holladay, died unmarried.

b. Dr. Lewis Littlepage Holladay, born December 25, 1868, married June 6, 1892, Sally Helen Price, born October 2, 1871. Issue:

   1. Louise Breckenridge, born October 28, 1898.

   2. Henry, and

   3. Lewis, twins, born 1902.

   4. James Porter, born 1904.

   5. Helen F., born 1907.

   6. Aubry Price, born 1913.

c. Mary Holladay, unmarried.

d. Helen Holladay, married Rev. Harvey Stover. Issue:

   1. Graham Stover.

   2. Frances Stover.

   3. Julia Stover.

   4. Grace White Stover.

   5. Harvey Stover.

e. Fanny Holladay, died young.

f. Nanny Holladay, married Dallas Shafer. Issue:

   1. Jean Shafer.

   2. Ann Shafer.

g. Henry Holladay, Jr., married Miss Warren, has six sons.

2. Dr. Waller Lewis Holladay, C. S. A., was son of Dr. L. L. and Jean Thompson Holladay. He was born March 23, 1830. Married first, Elizabeth Kelly Taliaferro, no issue. Married second, Mary Isabel Henderson, and had:

   a. William H. Holladay, married Affy Yerbey, and had:

      1. Percy Holladay, married Carry Holladay.

      2. Clayton Holladay, married 1925, Miss Walker.

   b. Lewis Littlepage Holladay (died June 6, 1925, aged nearly 62 years), married Mary Love Minor. Issue:

      1. Lewis L. Holladay, Jr., married Mildred Little.

2. Bessie, died young.
3. Frances Greenhow Holladay, married November 8, 1922, Robert Somerville, and has: Robert, born March 3, 1924 and Lewis L., born October 1926 and Mary Love.
4. James Scott Holladay, married October 18, 1923, Martha Trigg, and has: Barbara, born January 1924.
5. Margaret Holladay, adopted in 1934 by her uncle, Dr. James Minor.

c. Rev. James Minor Holladay, married ——, and
d. Henrietta Holladay, married first, Mr. Lee, no issue; married second, Mr. Peyton, no issue, were twins.
e. Elizabeth Holladay, married Mr. Jergenson, no issue.
f. Waller Lewis Holladay, married Miss Winston, has:
    1. Lewis Winston Holladay.
g. Alexander Holladay, died unmarried.

3. Prof. Lewis Littlepage Holladay of Hampden-Sydney College, born February 23, 1833, alumnus of Hampden-Sydney and of University of Virginia, married Nanny Morton of Prince Edward County. Issue:
    a. Mary Littlepage Holladay, married Rev. Mr. Lancaster, and has issue.
    b. Dr. Morton Holladay of Hampden-Sydney, married Genevieve Venable, and has issue.
4. John Zachary Holladay, died June 6, 1925, married Mary Dupuy, daughter of John Dupuy and Miss Daniel of North Carolina, descendant of Bartholemew Dupuy and his wife Susanne Lavillon, French Huguenots, who came to Virginia and settled on James River above Richmond. Issue:
    a. John Z. Holladay, Jr., married first, Alice Sampson, and had: Alice Holladay. He married second, Elizabeth Nicholas, and has Elizabeth Holladay and Waller Lewis Holladay.
    b. Lewis Littlepage Holladay, married Elizabeth Din-

widdie, daughter of Edgar Dinwiddie and Anna Bledsoe, and has:

1. Lewis L., Jr., born September 21, 1924.

c. Jean Thompson Holladay, married Webb Minor, and has:

1. Lucian Minor.
2. John Minor.
3. Mary Elizabeth Minor.

d. Rev. Dupuy Holladay, married November 15, 1910, Evelyn Glenn, daughter of John Glenn of Richmond. Issue:

1. Glenn Holladay, born 1911.
2. John Holladay, born 1917.
3. Evelyn Lavillon, born 1923.

f. Dr. Edwin Holladay of New York City.

g. Mary Dupuy Holladay, married John Nicholas. Issue:

1. Mary Nicholas.
2. John Nicholas, and
3. Robert Nicholas—twins.

5. Huldah Lewis Holladay, married George Peyton, had issue:

a. Willie H. Peyton, married Marian ——, has Huldah, and sons.

6. Rebecca Holladay, married Garnet Willis, has Henry Willis and Gordon Willis.

END OF ISSUE OF DR. L. L. HOLLADAY AND JEAN THOMPSON OF "BELLE FONTE", SPOTSYLVANIA COUNTY AND LATER OF "DUNLORA", ORANGE COUNTY, VA.

B. Rev. Albert Lewis Holladay, born April 17, 1805, died in Albemarle County, October 18, 1856, married October 30, 1836, Ann Yancy Minor, daughter of James and Catharine Thompkins Minor of Albemarle County. Rev. Albert Holladay was a brilliant scholar, 1827—took A. M. at the University of Virginia. After a professorship at Hampden-Sydney, he entered the Theological Seminary and later his wonderful facility in languages was of special value in Persia, where he spent nine years as missionary for the Presbyterian Church, preaching in Turkish and in the Syrian tongues; his special field being among the Nestorians in the valley of Lake Oroomiah. In 1846 the health of his family forced his return to the United States and, while pastor of Bethel and South Plains in the county of Albemarle, he died of fever which prevented his plan of accepting the presidency of Hampden-Sydney to which he had been elected. Issue:

1. Catherine Holladay, born 1838 in Persia, died infant.
2. Waller Holladay, born 1840 in Persia, C. S. A., Charlottesville Artillery, later 59th Infantry, later ordnance officer of Gen. Iverson's Brigade; after the War he taught at Norwood, Va., also had a select school in New York City; married Kate Emerson, his mother's niece. He died October 1, 1907. Issue:
   a. Kate Holladay, married Hawkins, and left a daughter.
   b. Nell Holladay, unmarried.
3. James Minor Holladay, C. S. A., born Oroomiah, Persia, June 23, 1841, a gallant Confederate soldier, who died in prison. Never married. A notice of him found in *University of Virginia Biographical Sketches,* page 249.
4. Albert Lewis Holladay, born in Persia, February 17, 1844, died February 1, 1915, married June 24, 1873, Nannie Eastham. He was educated at University of Virginia, member of Charlottesville Artillery (Capt. Carrington)—served through the War, lived and died near Charlottesville. Issue:
   a. William Holladay, married and has issue:
5. William Armstrong Holladay, C. S. A., born in Virginia, married October 20, 1886, Margaret Miller of Pulaski County. Too young for Army service, he served with the "Reserves". Issue:
   a. Albert Holladay, lives at Niagara, N. Y., married and has issue.
   b. William Holladay.
   c. Isabel Holladay, married her cousin, Mr. Miller, and has issue.

6. Alberta Wood Holladay, born in Virginia, died unmarried.

C. John Zachary Holladay, third son of Waller and Huldah F. Lewis Holladay, born December 13, 1806, died Scottsville, Va., October 12, 1842, married May 19, 1836, Julia Ann Minor, daughter of Dr. James and Mary Watson Minor of "Sunning Hill", Louisa County. He was educated by Miss Ann Boggs, a noted private teacher, later in the classical school of John Lewis of Llangollen, later studied law under Judge Henry St. George Tucker of Winchester. Of brilliant talents and promise his death was universally deplored as a loss to the State as well as to his relatives. He served, 1840-41, in the Virginia Legislature. Issue:

1. Mary Minor Holladay, born 1837, died 1922, married September 1855, Rt. Rev. James Allen Latané (1831-1902). Issue:
   a. Julia Latané, married Judge Claggett B. Jones, and had:
      1. Margaret Stuart Jones.
      2. Henry Latané Jones, married Janet Temple Varn, and had two daughters.
   b. Susan Latané.
   c. Henry Waring Latané (1859-1890), unmarried.
   d. Nannie Randolph Latané, married Rev. William D. Stevens. Issue:
      1. Henry Latané Stevens, married Marion Hayden, and has one son.
      2. Helen Kennedy Stevens.
      3. Marion M. Stevens, married Arthur Allen Eberly, and has two children.
      4. Paul Stevens, married Elizabeth Niles, has one daughter.
   e. Mary Minor Latané, married Rev. Samuel McLanahan. Issue:
      1. Allen McLanahan.
      2. Stewart Kennedy McLanahan, married Elizabeth Myrtle Kulling.
      3. John Davidson McLanahan.

4. Samuel McLanahan, M. D.
f. Lucy Temple Latané.
g. John Holladay Latané, married Elinor J. J. Cox (neé Junkin). Issue:
1. Elinor Latané.
h. Augusta Stuart Latané, died in infancy.
i. Edith Latané.
j. Samuel Peachy Latané, M. D. (1874-1910), married Elizabeth Love.
k. Lettice Latané, married Carroll Mason Sparrow.
l. James A. Latané, married Mary Douglas Dabney, and had:
1. Catherine Anne Latané.
2. James Allen Latané III.
2. Ann Elizabeth Holladay became, November 11, 1858, first wife of Dr. Wilson Cary Nicholas Randolph of Charlottesville. Issue:
a. Virginia Minor Randolph, married Judge George Shackelford, and had:
1. Virginius Randolph Shackelford, married Peachy Lyne (?), and had children.
2. Nannie Shackelford, married Rev. Carl Block.
3. Margaret Wilson Shackelford, married Mr. Walker.
4. George Scott Shackelford, married ——.
b. Wilson Cary Nicholas Randolph (died 1923), married Margaret Hager, and had:
1. John Hager Randolph, married.
c. Mary Buchanan Randolph (1864-1900).
d. Julia Randolph, married William Porterfield, and had:
1. William Porterfield.
2. Elizabeth Porterfield.
3. Virginia Porterfield, died in infancy.
4. John Porterfield, died as a boy.
5. Wilson Randolph Porterfield.
3. Sarah Watson Holladay, married April 19, 1860, Major

Thomas Henry Johnston, C. S. A., of Botetourt, County. Issue:

a. Thomas Henry Johnston, married first, Ann Johnston; second, Helen Johnston, and had by first marriage, three children:

1. John Johnston, killed in aviation, 1918.
2. T. Henry Johnston III, married Annis Quarles, and had two sons.
3. James Rawlings Johnston, died infant.

Issue by second marriage of Thomas Johnston:

4. Helen Johnston.
5. Andrew Johnston.
6. Walter Johnston.
7. Julia Johnston.

b. Leonora Johnston, married Robert L. Preston, and had:

1. Leonora Preston, married Mr. Nalle, and had one son.
2. Elliott Preston.

c. Julia Johnston, married John C. Gerndt.

D. Waller Lewis Holladay, born at "Prospect Hill", October 22, 1809, died December 11, 1873, married June 14, 1849, Emily Mansfield, who was born December 11, 1827, died July 3, 1866. She was daughter of John George Mansfield and Mary Buch (Streit) Mansfield and granddaughter of William and Catherine George Mansfield of Winchester, Va. Issue:

1. John Mansfield Holladay, born April 25, 1850, married September 2, 1874, Elizabeth Lee Wright, born March 18, 1855, daughter of Henry Wright and his wife, Susan Dick, daughter of Archibald Dick, of Caroline County, who was son of Rev. Archibald Dick, who served St. Margaret's Parish, Va., 1762-87. Issue:

a. Emily Gertrude Holladay, born August 22, 1875, married Mr. Charles Cowherd. No issue.
She made a home for many nieces and nephews.

b. Brian Holladay, born October 12, 1876, married, and has a daughter:

1. Grace Holladay.

c. Julia R. Holladay, born June 26, 1878, married Mr. Elam. No issue.

d. Mary Virginia Holladay, born September 18, 1880, married first, Philip Dew; second, Mr. Alexander. Issue:

1. Philip Dew.
2. Linton Dew.
3. Sally Dew.

e. Susan Elizabeth Holladay, born May 1, 1884.

2. Hon. Addison Lewis Holladay, born November 20, 1851, married January 17, 1877, Sally Binford Gwathmey, born April 18, 1855, only child of Charles Browne Gwathmey (son of R. Temple and Sally Browne Gwathmey) and his wife, Caroline Binford, daughter of James Marshall Binford and Mary A. Rutter Binford of Portsmouth, Virginia. Issue:

a. Caroline Holladay, born September 23, 1879.

3. Henry Milton Holladay, born July 10, 1855, unmarried.
4. Ann Elizabeth Holladay, born July 14, 1857, unmarried.
5. Mary Christian Holladay, born December 23, 1860, died unmarried, 1933.

E. Hon. Alexander Richmond Holladay was a twin and born at "Prospect Hill", September 18, 1811, died in Richmond, June 29, 1877, married September, 1837, Patsy Quarles Poindexter, daughter of Wm. Green Poindexter and Jane Quarles. He was a prominent lawyer in Spotsylvania County and Richmond, served in U. S. Congress, 1849-53, was President of Virginia Board of Public Works, 1857-61. He was sent on a special mission to the Court of St. James and also to that of Napoleon III. His brilliant mind and graceful dignity of person and of manner fitted him eminently for such service. (I remember him with admiration though I was only a child at the time.—S. T. L. A.)

His wife survived him many years. She was full of business energy to the last. When an old woman she developed an orange orchard in Florida and lived alone there. She, with her husband and children lived near "Prospect Hill" at "Cherry Grove" with her Aunt Patsy Quarles, later they lived at "Duncan Lodge", then on the suburbs of Richmond, opposite the Allen farm. Issue:

1. Alexander Quarles Holladay, C. S. A., born 1839, married April 17, 1861 at Bolling Island to Virginia Randolph Bolling, daughter of Thomas Bolling of Goochland County. He was educated at the University of Virginia and in Germany; served as lieutenant, C. S. A., 1861-5. He was member of the Senate from Richmond and was of the law firm with his father (Holladay, White and Holladay.) Issue:
   a. Mary Holladay.
   b. William Holladay.
   c. Julia Holladay.
   d. Randolph Holladay.
   e. Charles Holladay.
2. Frances A. Holladay, daughter of Hon. Alexander and Patsy Quarles Poindexter Holladay, married first, Samuel Baily, C. S. A.; second, Dr. William Walker. Issue:
   a. Hetty Baily.
   b. Rosa Baily.
   c. Guellma Walker, married Dr. Simpson. No issue.
3. William Waller Holladay, died 1860, age 17.
4. Jennie Lewis Holladay, married William Woods. No issue.
5. Rosa Holladay, married Charles Shafer, and had:
   a. William Shafer.
   b. Rosalie Shafer.
   c. Alan Shafer.
   d. Alice Shafer.
   e. Louis Shafer.
   f. Alexander Shafer.
   g. Claire Shafer.

F. Henry Addison Holladay, born at "Prospect Hill", September 18, 1811, was twin to Alexander R. Holladay, died June 18, 1872 at his home, "Woodside", near "Prospect Hill". He married, May 14, 1846, Mary Frances (Jenkins) Calvert, widow of Edward Calvert, who was brother of John Calvert, treasurer of Virginia, who was killed in the disaster at the Capitol in Richmond. Henry A. Holladay was educated by his uncle, John Lewis of Llangollen, whose classical school was widely known and patronized in its day, many of its alumni becoming distinguished in letters and in public life. Issue:

1. Edward Henry Holladay, born July 29, 1847, died February 26, 1865, while in Confederate Army, at Richmond.
2. Katherine Littlepage Holladay, born December 11, 1849, at "Prospect Hill", died Friday, July 13, 1923, married February 14, 1867, at "Woodside", Richard Moncure Conway, C. S. A., who was born in Falmouth, Va., December 9, 1840, died at Port Hope, Canada while United States Consul there, January 11, 1888. Issue: (ten children)
   a. Margaret Eleanor Conway, born December 4, 1868.
   b. John Moncure Conway, born June 5, 1870, died 1922, married Lilian Taliaferro, and left issue:
      1. Katharine Conway, married Madison Nicholson, and has a daughter.
   c. Edward Henry Conway, married Ann Keiningham. Issue:
      1. Edward H. Conway, married Rae Dickinson, has: a. Nancy Rae Conway.
      2. Ann Bernice Conway, married Holt Gandy.
      3. Constance Greenhow Conway.
   d. Mary Littlepage Conway, born April 2, 1873.
   e. Catharine Constance Conway, born June 17, 1874.
   f. Ellen Dana Conway, born March 28, 1876, died unmarried, 1933.
   g. Walker Peyton Conway, born January 26, 1878.
   h. Virginia Watson Conway, born September 29, 1879.
   i. Richard Eustace Conway, born January 2, 1883 (twin), married Mary Wallace Ashby, daughter of James Ashby, has:
      1. Mary Moncure Conway.

2. Katherine H. Conway.
3. Richard Eustace Conway.
4. James Ashby Conway.

j. Raleigh Travers Conway, born January 2, 1883 (twin), married Dolly Ashby, sister of Mary Wallace Ashby, has:

1. James Ashby Conway.
2. Raleigh Daniel Conway.
3. Dorothea Frances Conway.

3. Benjamin Lewis Holladay, born at "Woodside", November 1, 1855, son of Henry A. Holladay and Mary Calvert, married February 28, 1888, Mary Ida Jennings. Issue:

a. Mary Augusta Holladay, born August 3, 1879, married Paul Harris. Issue:

1. Ann O. Harris.
2. Henry Lewis Harris.
3. John Paul Harris.
4. Mary Frances Harris.
5. Victoria Harris.
6. Julia Harris.
7. William Overton Harris.

b. James Minor Halladay, born August 3, 1881, married Elinor Fitzhugh, and has:

1. James M. Holladay.
2. Wallace F. Holladay.
3. Elinor Stuart Holladay.

c. William Edward Holladay, born October 5, 1883, married Nancy Egleston, and has:

1. John E. Holladay.
2. William Edward Holladay.

d. Francis J. Holladay, born March 3, 1886, married Annie Davenport.

G. Ann Elizabeth Holladay, fourth child of Waller and Huldah F. Lewis Holladay, was born February 25, 1808, died December 1853. She was killed in a cyclone which wrecked her home in Mississippi. Her husband and her little girl, Jane Frances, were hurt. A nephew, George Poindexter, was killed and another nephew hurt. She was married at "Prospect Hill", May 23, 1833 to Dr. William Q. Poindexter, son of William Green Poindexter and Jane Quarles. Issue:

a. William Green Poindexter, born June 9, 1835, married Martha Morgan. (For issue, see Poindexters.)

b. Waller H. Poindexter, died unmarried.

c. Jane Frances, died young.

H. Huldah Lewis Holladay, was born at "Prospect Hill", April 24, 1814, never married. She was a woman of most practical turn of mind and was greatly interested in all political issues of her time. She lived many years.

I. Eliza Lewis Holladay, born October 12, 1816, died December 3, 1878, unmarried. She also was of remarkable characteristics—her quiet wit, her ready adaptation of quotations from books made her charming to young people as well as to old. In their youth she and Cousin Mary and Cousin Fannie all did exquisite fancy work of lacy collars and berthas which were the wonder of the younger generation.

J. Mary Waller Holladay, born September 22, 1818, died unmarried. Her long life was filled with active interests and wide sympathies. Her memory was a rich store house for information and interesting anecdotes. Her mind could concentrate itself even when in her old age, she became blind, to do the most exquisite patterns in knitting and even making a child's toy wagon by feeling. She often knit sentences in tidies and sent these original letters as gifts to friends.

K. Frances Eliza Holladay, born January 3, 1821, died unmarried. Her gentle disposition and her beauty drew all to her in admiration and love.

M. Virginia Watson Holladay, born August 29, 1829 at "Prospect Hill" and died there, May 2, 1888, unmarried, though the youngest of the thirteen children is given here as she fits in the group with these remarkable ladies. Her older brother is given later. Of pleasing beauty, sprightly mind and gentle manners, her company and her approval was sought by the younger cousins who admired and looked up to her. She was a flower wizard and her flower garden at "Prospect Hill" was a blaze of beauty. Box plants flourished under the hands of her older sisters and the green house brought a dream of the tropics in winter. All sorts of exotic plants flourished there—lemons in full fruit and oranges (then rare) besides a small nursery of old time plants ready to be planted out in the borders around the vegetable squares in the big old garden.

After the Confederate War labor conditions changed. But still Cousin Virginia's one square, devoted entirely to roses and annuals became a gathering place for all who loved successful floriculture. Such growth, such masses of bloom I never saw elsewhere.

L. James Minor Holladay, was born May 9, 1823, married January 22, 1861, his first and also second cousin, Lucy Daniel Lewis, daughter of John Lewis of Llangollen and Jean Daniel Lewis. While he might have claimed exemption in the War Between the States, he entered the service, was captured April 1, 1865 and was imprisoned for sometime at Point Lookout. Left after the war with the cares of a large old home and its inmates as his responsibility he made a gallant effort to meet the new conditions with old ideals. A christian gentleman whose standards yet live in the lives of the younger generation for all that is pure and high. Issue:

1. Louise Richmond Holladay, born at "Prospect Hill", July 15, 1862. Unmarried.
2. John Waller Holladay, born October 7, 1864, married Mary Caroline Harris. (Issue given below.)
3. James Minor Holladay, died infant.

John Waller and Mary Caroline Harris, daughter of Nelson and Victoria Harris of "Cherry Grove", were married and lived at "Prospect Hill". All their children were born there. Business conditions forced him to seek opportunities elsewhere and some years later he died in Georgia, where he held a responsible business position. Of delicate health always, he yet met the exigencies of life with the same quixotic ideals of duty and Christian fortitude which had been so conspicuous in his father. Like him his influence lives on in the lives of all who knew him. Issue:

a. Mary Caroline Holladay, married Percy Holladay, son of William Henderson and Affy Holladay. He was a soldier in the World War.
b. Lucy Nelson Holladay, married June 27, 1927, Alfred Boand.
c. Victoria Minor Holladay, married June 1923, Rev. John Alexander, and has:
   1. Victoria Alexander.
   2. Matilda Caroline Alexander.
d. Huldah F. Holladay, married Joseph B. Edens, and has:
   1. Huldah Edens.
   2. Joseph Edens.
e. Virginia Waller Holladay, missionary to Africa.
f. James Minor Holladay.

The two older girls now own "Prospect Hill", and the family gather there in the summer.

END OF RECORD OF "PROSPECT HILL" HOLLADAYS.

## BOGGSES OF "LIVINGSTONE"

Ann Holladay, daughter of Major Lewis and Betty Littlepage Holladay, (see page 359) was born at "Belle Fonte", the old Holladay homestead, in Spottsylvania, April 18, 1775, died at "Livingstone, January 26, 1846. She was married, December 29, 1796 by Rev. James Stevenson to Rev. Hugh Corran Boggs, who was born in County Donegal, Ireland, 1760, and died at "Livingstone", Spottsylvania County, September 17, 1828. He was son of Alexander and Margaret (Marshall) Boggs. After his mother's death his father came to Virginia and spent his last days with his son. He was buried at "Belle Fonte". Rev. Hugh Boggs served several parishes in Caroline, Spottsylvania and Orange counties. He was ordained by Rt. Rev. William D. White, Bishop of Pennsylvania, September 21, 1788. Issue:

A. Lewis Alexander Boggs, born December 27, 1811, died July 15, 1880. He married first, September 29, 1831, Eliza Hart, daughter of Malcolm and Mary Dick Hart, granddaughter of

Robert Hart of "Hartfield" and of Nicholas Dick. They had one child, (1) Mary Jane Boggs, who died July 3, 1861, married December 21, 1853, Henry Thompson Holladay, and their one child died young. Lewis A. Boggs married second, Mary Ann Lewis Scott, daughter of Dr. James Scott and Mildred Thomson. She left one daughter:

2. Eliza Hart Boggs, born March 3, 1839, died September 28, 1879, married May 1, 1861, Valentine Mason Johnson. (See Scotts.)

Lewis A. Boggs married third, May 5, 1841, Elizabeth Rawlings, who died July 6, 1875. She was daughter of Benjamin and Clara Lawrence Rawlings. Issue:

3. Clara Lawrence Boggs, born April 12, 1847, married February 6, 1872, James Lewis Rawlings, and had:
    a. Louise Livingstone Rawlings, second wife of Alfred R. Johnson. (See Scott record.)
4. Ann Holladay Boggs, born May 27, 1849. Unmarried.
5. Bettie Lewis Boggs, born May 11, 1851. Unmarried.
6. Hugh Livingstone Boggs, born June 12, 1853, married ——. Issue:
    a. Sadie Boggs.
    b. Livingstone Boggs.
7. Lewis A. Boggs, Jr., born August 21, 1856, married June 27, 1878 to Fanny Cleve Wallace, daughter of Gustavus Brown Wallace and Margaret Elizabeth, his wife. Issue:
    a. Lewis A. Boggs, III.
    b. Garlic Boggs.
    c. Clarence Boggs, married Miss Longfellow, and has:
        1. Francis Boggs.
    d. Margaret E. Boggs, married Mr. Hays, and has four children.
    e. Lawrence Littlepage Boggs, served in United States Navy, later in Army in France. Married, and has a daughter.
    f. Ann Wiley Boggs, married, 1919, J. E. Timberlake, and has:

1. Lewis Timberlake.
2. Ann Timberlake.
3. Betty Timberlake.
4. John Timberlake.

g. Frank Cleve Boggs, married Ira Jarrell, and has:

1. Lewis Boggs.

h. Byrd Wallace Boggs, killed in World War, just before the Armistice, 1918.

8. Rev. Waller Edward Boggs, born December 23, 1858, married December 6, 1883, Olive ——. He was a talented and distinguished minister of the Methodist E. Church. He died in Texas, where he lived many years. Issue:

a. Elizabeth Boggs.

b. Carl Boggs.

c. Charles Boggs.

## LITTLEPAGE

*Hayden's Virginia Genealogies* gives a broken account of the Littlepage family, traces it probably from Richard Littlepage of New Kent County, 1660, who took out land grants, 1663. He was sheriff of New Kent before 1674, died 1688, left a son, Richard Littlepage, who died 1717, married Frances ——. Issue:

A. Elizabeth Littlepage, born December 11, 1703.

B. Frances Littlepage, born 1705.

C. Alice Littlepage.

D. Richard Littlepage, married Oriana ——.

E. James Littlepage, born July 14, 1714, died 1768-9, married second, 1760, Elizabeth Lewis, and had:

1. Mary Littlepage, married Robert Coleman.
2. General Lewis Littlepage.

F. John Littlepage, twin to James Littlepage.

G. Judith Littlepage.

H. Susanna Littlepage.

*Clipping from Richmond Paper*

The Littlepages originated in Scotland. Sir William Littlepage came from Perth in Scotland to Kent, England when James I was king. Col. Edmund Littlepage was the first of this family in Virginia. He came from Kent and named the county in Virginia for the one he had left in England. New Kent was cut from York, 1654.

Issue of Col. Edmund Littlepage:

A. Col. James Littlepage.

B. Edmund Littlepage.

C. Richard Littlepage.

D. Susan Littlepage, married Col. Francis West, brother of Lord De la Ware.

E. Elizabeth Littlepage, married Edmund Rye Chamberlayne, and had:

  1. Thomas Chamberlain, who married a daughter of Wm. Byrd. Issue:

    a. Byrd Chamberlain, married Elizabeth Dandridge.

    b. Edward Chamberlain, married Agnes Dandridge.

    c. Thomas Chamberlain, unmarried.

F. Frances Littlepage, married Dr. Arnot.

G. Alice Littlepage, married Richard Squire Taylor.

H. Judith Littlepage, married Mr. Fauntleroy.

I. Ann Littlepage, married Col. Claiborne.

*Note.*—This account gives James Littlepage's first wife, Sarah Meriwether which is a mistake, since she married William Littlepage, and had Judith. It also gives Betty Lewis as James's second wife. Evidently both Hayden and this account mixed generations.

## MEMORIAL

General Lewis Littlepage was son of Betty Lewis, daughter of Zachary Lewis II and Mary Waller, who by her first marriage became second wife of James Littlepage.

He was a man of immense original fineness of mind and character and of a most attractive personality. He made a fine record at

William and Mary. The *Richmond Enquirer* of May 19, 1809 quotes from *The Freeman's Journal* of Philadelphia, which in publishing a translation of "XXII Ode 1st Book of Horace", done by Littlepage when fifteen years old, cites it as most creditable in comparison with Francis, the great English translator of Horace "when he was in full tide and maturity of his genius." This same paper declares less has been written of Littlepage than is his due.

At seventeen he became ambitious of a diplomatic career. Thus his uncle and guardian, Mr. Benjamin Lewis, requested Hon. John Jay appointed, September 27, 1779, representative of United States at Madrid, Spain, to receive young Littlepage as his protegé. Illness prevented his accompanying Mr. Jay to Europe, but he followed some months later, arriving in Madrid, November 1780.

A contemporary, Elkanah Watson tells of meeting him, tells of his fine manly figure and engaging appearance, of him as a prodigy of genius and acquirements though only a youth of eighteen years.

After eighteen months with Mr. Jay, restlessness prompted him to volunteer—applying to Charles III for permission to accompany the expedition against Fort Mahon and Gibraltar. Accordingly, as aide de camp to Duke de Crillon he participated in the siege of Mahon which surrendered to Spain. Again at Gibraltar, September 12, he was on board the "Pailla Piedras", one of the two largest decked batteries commanded by Prince of Nassau Sieghen. Littlepage wrote, "this battery was anchored nearest of the whole line to Gibraltar and was destroyed but was the only one that did not blow up, since we took the precaution of wetting our powder when the situation became desperate."

This ship burned to the water's edge, having lain fourteen hours under fire from Gibraltar, and sank September 14 at 1 a. m.

He was blown up on one of the floating batteries but saved and afterwards on board the Spanish Admiral's ship during one of the engagements he occupied himself on the quarter deck in sketching the various positions of both fleets, each vessel being faithfully drawn in the position it occupied in the battle line. (I have seen this picture which is still owned by the family at "Prospect

Hill".) Watson's Memoirs states that when dining with Littlepage at Dr. Franklin's at Passy he saw this same sketch and that at Versailles Littlepage attracted great attention.

On the return of the Spanish fleet to Cadiz he was sent with an officer bearing dispatches and was received with great distinction at the court of Madrid, giving there an ingenuous scientific view of the battle.

He was highly complimented for gallantry by the King, who also addressed an official letter of appreciation to the United States Congress and President. Hon. Robert R. Livingstone, September 27, 1782, telling of the disastrous issue of the siege of Gibraltar tells of the reputation acquired by Mr. Littlepage for gallant conduct there and at Mahon, the Prince de Nassau rendering public justice to his character at court.

At Cadiz, Littlepage met and formed a lasting and intimate friendship with Lafayette, who took him to Madrid and to Paris on public business and wished him to carry the treaty of 1783 to the United States Congress. This plan failed, however, and Littlepage was persuaded by the Prince of Nassau to go with him to Turkey as Captain in his regiment of "Royal Allemands". Returning from Constantinople he went with the Prince to the Diet of Grodno, where he met Stanislaus Augustus, King of Poland, who, eleven years later, April 25, 1795, at Grodno, laid down his crown and abdicated his throne.

Stanislaus then fifty-two years old was captivated with this youth of twenty-two and offered him permanent service at his court, granting him leave of absence for a year to go to the United States and arrange his affairs, also to get the consent of Congress for him to enter the services of Poland. He returned to Virginia, July 1785, and in November started on his return. En route he called at "Mount Vernon", and in a letter home told of General Washington's interest in his affairs and of his discussing and explaining to him military situations during the Revolution, also giving him letters to the Governor of Pennsylvania and to others on the route to New York.

At New York he applied through Mr. Jay to Congress for sanction to serve some years under the king of Poland, he wishing to retain his citizenship in the United States. This Mr. Jay failed to obtain before the adjournment of Congress, so Littlepage had to sail without the desired permission. *Elkanah Watson's Memoirs* states, "Littlepage established himself in Poland at Warsaw and became in effect Prime Minister. He went to St. Petersburg as Embassador from Poland acquitting himself with distinguished ability."

There were long years of silence during which the relatives in Virginia supposed Littlepage to be dead, but his stepfather, Major Lewis Holladay made another effort to get into communication with him and finally received a letter from which this extract is taken:

"March 1786 I was sworn into the service of the king of Poland's cabinet as his First Confidential Secretary with rank of Chamberlain. 1787 I was sent to negotiate a treaty with the Empress of Russia, which I affected. The same year I was secret and special Envoy to the Court of France to assist in the negotiations of the Grand Quadruple Alliance which failed. In 1788 I went to the camp of Prince Potempkin whom I had known intimately since the residence of the Empress at Kiew. I wished to join the Prince of Nassau already in sight of the Ottoman Fleet. But he obliged me to accompany him during his march through Tartary des Nogais. Upon the banks of the Liman I took command of a division of the flotilla under the orders of Prince of Nassau in the victory he gained July 1st (Russian style) over the Turkish fleet in the port of Oczacow. Some weeks later on the return of Capt. Pacha de Barna I was intrusted with a second flotilla."

*Note.*—Admiral John Paul Jones was in the naval service of Russia on the Black Sea and wrote flattering accounts to Thomas Jefferson in his frequent mention of association with Littlepage.

*Note.*—Mr. Jefferson wrote from Paris to the United States:

"Mr. Littlepage has returned from the Black Sea to Warsaw where he has been perfectly received by the King. I saw by the king's own hand and was pleased at the paternal expression towards him."

Letter resumed:

"1789 compelled to leave Warsaw I travelled in Italy. Shortly afterwards I was ordered to Madrid upon a highly political mission in which I completely succeeded. 1790 I was recalled from Spain and ordered to go by way of Berlin to Warsaw for the Revolution of May 3rd, 1791. 1792, 12,000 Russians invaded Poland. I was nominated Aid de Camp General to the King of Poland with rank of Major-General. He signed the Confederation of Fargowitz and April

1, 1793, sent me as special envoy to St. Petersburg to try to prevent the division of Poland. I was stopped by the Russian Government on the road—and the partition took place. 1794 Kosiusko Madalinksky began another Revolution in Poland. The garrison and inhabitants of Warsaw rose in arms against the Russians. To save the life of my unfortunate master and king I was obliged to take part with Poland and that dreadful battle ended with the slaughter of 10,000 Russians. The Empress Catherine never forgave me my conduct on this occasion. She was the more irritated on hearing I had consented to accept a Commander-in-Chief under the Revolution and on my having assisted in repelling Russian armies in the attempt to storm Warsaw. In short I had gone so far in the Revolution that I should have gone much further had I not been defeated with my friend Prince Joseph Poniatoski the king's nephew by the late King of Prussia, August 26, 1794. That event lost me all my popularity and was near to getting me hanged as I was regarded as the acting person, though upon my honor the Prince acted that day against my advice. The King of Prussia attacked us with three times our force and Kosiusko afforded us no support till we were beaten without redemption, although his left nor center were engaged all day except in cannonading.

"After this I took no further part in military affairs till the storming of Prague which cost the lives of 22,000 Polanders. The King of Poland was taken by the Russians to Grodno and I was separated from him by express orders of the Empress, it being hinted to me that nothing less than my former political services to Russia and my military services in the Turkish war would save me from the fate of the other chiefs of the Revolution. After the King's departure I set out for Vienna but was ordered from that metropolis which produced an altercation between me and the Austrian ministry but which ended to my satisfaction as Russia came forward and did me justice.

"The king of Prussia, Frederick William II afterwards allowed me to return to Warsaw where I remained till after the death of Empress Catherine II. I was then invited to Petersburg with the King of Poland, but refused unless reparation were made for the treatment I had recently undergone. The Emperor said all *that* regarded his mother; *he* had given no offense and would make no reparation. I might have gone to Russia but was prevented by the sudden death of my friend, my master and more than friend, Stanislaus Augustus, King of Poland, who expired February 12, 1798. A long correspondence then took place between the Emperor and myself which ended in his paying me in a noble manner the sum assigned me by the King of Poland as a reward for my long and dangerous service.

"I arrived in Hamburg last October. My intention was to go to France or England, but find myself strangely embroiled with both governments. I have settled affairs in France, but the Ministers of

England persist in believing me in a secret mission from Russia now at variance with England.

"God knows I am sick of European politics. I intended to spend the winter in Hamburg, but am driven from that sink of iniquity by a most atrocious plot against my life and fortune. The latter is in safety and if I should perish even here under the hospitable government of Denmark, I shall leave nine or ten thousand pounds sterling so disposed that my assassins cannot prevent it coming to my family. That sum is all I have saved from the wreck of my fortunes in Poland. In the Spring I shall proceed to America either by way of France or from here provided I escape the daggers and poison with which I am threatened.

"My duty and affection to my mother and kindest rememberance to all relatives and friends.

"Ever yours, my dear sir,

"Altoona, Jan. 9, 1801. "LEWIS LITTLEPAGE."

This letter is still extant and is quoted in *Hayden*.

Late in 1801 General Littlepage returned to his home in Spotsylvania, Virginia, hoping to find rest, but his health had suffered with exposure in camp, and the strain of diplomatic life at various courts. He died at his home in Fredericksburg, and was buried in the Masonic burial ground. The marble slab over his grave bears this inscription:

"Here lies the body of Lewis Littlepage who was born in the county of Hanover, Virginia, 19th December, 1762 and departed this life July 19, 1802, aged 39 years and 7 months. Honored for many years with the esteem and confidence of the unfortunate Stanislaus Augustus, King of Poland, holding under that monarch the most distinguished offices among which was that of embassador of Russia. He was Knight of St. Stanislaus, Chamberlain, confidential secretary, special envoy. Of talents military as well as civil, he served with credit as an officer of high rank in different armies. In private life he was charitable, generous and just and in various public offices he acted with uniform magnanimity, fidelity and honor."

The *Richmond Enquirer* further states:

"Lewis Littlepage was a man of immense original powers and was fraught with most striking anecdotes of men and of achievements, to the last moment of his life exhibiting the romantic and original cut of character which distinguished his earlier adventures. The friends of General Littlepage could not render us more acceptable service than laying before us the memoirs of the most eventful incidents of his romantic life."

He left the major part of his estate to his half-brother, Waller Holladay of "Prospect Hill", a large legacy to his stepfather, Major Lewis Holladay, whom he admired and loved; to his sister, Mrs. Robert S. Coleman, an annuity of one hundred dollars a year.

He charged his half-brother never to allow his interesting collection of papers to be published but to burn them, as they concerned also the fortunes of many prominent people in Europe and might cause trouble. And this was done despite regret at the loss of such valuable historic matter.

At "Prospect Hill", 1862, I was shown some court dress suits made of silk and other rich materials heavily embroidered and blazing with stars of various orders, also the military cloak which had been Stanislaus' and put by him on Littlepage when they parted; a gold key, his order as Chamberlain; a jewel set miniature of Stanislaus with S. A. R. in jewels, a gift from the king; insignia of the St. Stanislaus order set in rubies and bearing the motto: *"Incitat Procmiando"* worked in gold thread; there were two swords—a heavy Damascus blade and one with straight narrow Toledo blade in sheath ornamented with gold chasings. James Minor Holladay, bending this sword holding point and hilt together, showed me its wonderful quality, also a dent in one edge made by a Turkish assassin who under the role of dispatch bearer handed the papers to Littlepage with one hand and attempted to hew him down with a sword in the other hand. Littlepage throwing his sword up caught the blow and his guards dispatched the false dispatch bearer.

## SMITHS

Dorothea Lewis, daughter of Zachary Lewis II and Mary Waller, his wife, was born September 5, 1738, died March 20, 1820, married April 13, 1762, Charles Smith, who was born July 22, 1729, son of Christopher Smith and Miss Snelson, and had three sons: Christopher, John and Charles, who was born November 16, 1778, died October 17, 1815, unmarried.

Christopher Smith, born March 21, 1763, died May 19, 1804, married Katharine Anderson, and had issue: (two children)

A. Catharine Snelson Smith, married Frederick Harris of Fredericks Hall, Louisa County, Va., and had eight children:

1. Frederick Harris, unmarried.
2. Nat Harris of Fredericks Hall, married Ellen Goodwin. Issue:
    a. Flora Harris of Fredericks Hall, married Abner Harris, son of Hillary Harris and Miss Hobson of Powhatan County, and had:
        1. Frederick Harris.
        2. Ellen Harris.
        3. Flora Harris.
        4. ——.
    b. Frederick Harris III, married Bessie Dabney, and had:
        1. Beverly Dabney Harris, of Texas.
    c. Nat Harris, Jr., of Fredericks Hall, married Rosa Pettit, of Fluvanna County. Issue:
        1. Nat Harris, married Margaret Anderson.
        2. Pettit Harris.
        3. David Harris, killed in World War.
        4. Vara Harris, married Dr. Bickerton Phillips.
        5. Belle Ellen Harris, married Mr. Quin.
        6. Natalie Harris, married Mr. Hamlin.
    d. Ellen Harris, married Archie Overton, and has issue in Kentucky.
    e. Eliza Harris, married Mr. Woolfork, and has:
        1. David Woolfork.
        2. Tom Woolfork.
        3. Bessie Woolfork.
        4. Rosa Woolfork.
        5. Julia Woolfork.
        6. Flora Woolfork.
    f. Rosa Harris, unmarried.
    g. Waller Harris, married, left one child.
    h. John Harris, married, lives in Texas.
    i. Lee Harris, unmarried.
    j. David Harris, married.

3. Gen. David Harris of Woodville, Goochland County, married Miss Knight (an English woman), C. S. A. chief of Artillery for Gen. Beauregard, laid out the fortifications at Manassas and at Charleston, dying at the latter place in a yellow fever epidemic during the war. He was educated at West Point. Issue:
   a. David Harris, unmarried.
   b. Richard Harris, unmarried.
   c. Alexander Harris, married, and left issue.
   d. Fredrica Harris, married Page Morton, and had:
      1. Page Morton, married Dr. Kenneth McCoy, has:
         a. Henry McCoy.
         b. Eva McCoy.
   e. Rosa, died in childhood.
   f. Violet, married Judge Andrew Leake, and has issue.
   g. Lily, died in childhood.

   (e.–g.: Triplets who were named from the colors used to distinguish them.)
   h. Eva Harris, unmarried.
4. Mrs. Eliza Harris Overton, of Kentucky, left:
   a. Mrs. Green.
   b. Waller Overton, married Alice Pendleton, daughter of Dr. Wm. Pendleton and Katharine Harris.
   c. Archie Overton, married Ellen Harris, daughter of Nat and Ellen Goodwin Harris.
   d. Eliza Overton, unmarried.
   e. Julia Overton, married and left issue.
   f. Dabney Overton.
5. Juliana Harris, married Alexander Barrett, lived in Louisa, England and New York. Issue:
   a. Virgie Barrett, married Major Theodore Gibbs, of Newport, R. I. No issue.
   b. Alexander Barrett, Jr., married Miss Chinock of England, lives in New York.
6. Katharine Harris, married Dr. William Pendleton, and has:
   a. Alice Pendleton, married Waller Overton, and left issue in Kentucky.
   b. Juliana Pendleton, married first, Mr. Meredith, had

issue; married second, Capt. Wm. Pendleton, a gallant C. S. A. officer, who lost a leg in the service. They have issue.

c. Capt. Pendleton, married Miss Hunter, and left a son:

1. Professor Hunter Pendleton of Lexington, who married Miss White, daughter of Judge White of Charlottesville. They have issue.

7. Sally Harris, never married.

8. Charlotte Harris, married Joe K. Pendleton, and has:

a. Dr. Lewis Pendleton, married Ann Ferrell Kean, no issue. At their home is an old chair which belonged to Dorothea (Lewis) Smith.

b. Jane Pendleton, first wife of John Hunter, no issue.

c. Henry Pendleton, never married.

B. Nat Anderson Smith of Elleslie, Louisa County, son of Christopher and Katharine Anderson Smith, married Laura or Lavinia Callis, and had:

1. Charles Smith, married and had a daughter.

2. William Smith, died unmarried.

3. Laura Smith, married Dr. Garland.

4. Lucy Smith, married John Graves, and had among others, Richard Morris Graves who, 1863, married Susan (Kean) Boston, and had:

1. Richie Morris Graves, married John Peyton McGuire of Richmond, and had:

a. Richie McGuire.

b. John McGuire.

5. Catharine Smith.

END OF DESCENDANTS OF CHRISTOPHER AND KATHARINE ANDERSON SMITH.

John Snelson Smith, Sr. was second son of Dorothea Lewis and Charles Smith. He was born September 6, 1775, died July 12, 1837, married December 12, 1799, his first cousin, Martha Bickerton Lewis, daughter of Benjamin and Martha B. Lewis of Hanover County. She was born October 6, 1777, died April 10, 1863.

Issue: A. Dorothea, B. Benjamin, C. Martha, D. Christopher, E. Charles, F. Alice, G. Ann, H. John.

A. Dorothea Smith, born October 10, 1800, died August 20, 1855, married Edmund Swift, and had:
   1. John S. Swift, married Miss Winston, and had:
      a. William Swift.
      b. John Swift, Jr.
   2. Martha Swift, married Mr. Longan, and had:
      a. Martha Lewis Longan, married Andrew J. Phillips.
      b. Chastain Longan, died unmarried.
      c. William Longan, married Miss Andrews.
   3. Amanda Swift, married Thomas Longan, and had:
      a. Florence Longan, unmarried.
      b. Ella Longan, unmarried.
      c. Sally Longan, unmarried.
   4. William Z. Swift, married Eliza Thomas, had
      a. William Swift, unmarried.
      b. Dean Swift, unmarried.
      c. Ina Swift, married Gilbert Clendon.
      d. Cally Swift, married Mr. Bruner.
      e. Robinette Swift, unmarried.
      f. Annie Swift, unmarried.
   5. Ann Rebecca Swift, died unmarried.
   6. Dorothea Swift, twin to Ann, married George Duke, had:
      a. Emma Duke.
      b. Lewis Duke.
      c. Frank Duke.
      d. Nelly Duke.
      e. Leonora Duke.
      f. —— Duke, (daughter, name unknown.)

B. Benjamin Lewis Smith, born June 18, 1802, died March 28, 1875, married Ann N. Harris, daughter of Overton and Nancy (Hill) Harris, granddaughter of Zachary Lewis III and A. O. Terrell. Issue:
   1. John Overton Smith, born November 28, 1851, lived at Beaver Dam, Va. He married his cousin, Hally Greenhow, who died May 6, 1921. No issue.

C. Martha B. Smith, born August 6, 1804, died June 6, 1865, married William Cooke, and had:

1. John S. Cooke. (Record given below.)
2. William Cooke, married twice.
3. Annie Cooke, married her cousin, Benton Cooke, died without issue.

John Snelson Cooke, married first, December 18, 1856, Mary Matilda Moss, who died April 8, 1868. He married second, September 8, 1869, her first cousin, Anne E. Moss, daughter of Robert F. and Frances Ann Moss. She was born July 8, 1849. Issue:

a. Mary Cooke, born February 27, 1858, married George W. Hardin of Henderson, Ky., and had:
   1. Lilian Earle Hardin, born June 10, 1888.
   2. Kate Pearl Hardin, born April 17, 1890.
   3. Arthur G. Hardin, born 1894.
b. Mattie Coleman Cooke, born February 27, 1860, died October 10, 1873.
c. Laura Lee Cooke, born November 24, 1862, married W. T. Williamson. Issue:
   1. Mary Adelia Williamson, born October 8, 1893, married October 25, 1916, John Thomas Jackson, and had:
      a. Laura Elizabeth Jackson, born February 16, 1920.
      b. John Thomas Jackson III, born July 29, 1921.
   2. Cyrus Marion Williamson, born August 29, 1895, married December 3, 1917, Elizabeth Harris, and had:
      a. Cyrus M. Williamson, Jr., born June 8, 1922.

Children of second marriage:

d. John William Cooke, born July 30, 1870.
e. Helen Janette Cooke, born February 4, 1872, married October 24, 1903, Claud S. Bradshaw.
f. Robert Charles Cooke, born December 2, 1873, married August 25, 1909, Lucy Ann Townes, and had:
   1. Robert Charles Cooke, born May 27, 1910.
   2. Lucy Ann Cooke, born December 10, 1911.
   3. Frances Moss Cooke, born December 7, 1917.

g. Lula Moss Cooke, born December 9, 1875.
h. Annie Eliza Cooke, born October 2, 1878.
i. Francis Thomas Cooke, born April 19, 1881.
j. A. Wilfred Cooke, born June 6, 1884.
k. Julia Talmage Cooke, born September 23, 1888.
l. Temple Doswell Cooke, born September 29, 1891.

D. Christopher Snelson Smith, son of John Snelson Smith, Sr. and Martha B. Lewis, was born October 20, 1806, died November 7, 1846. Unmarried.

E. Charles Zachary Smith, born May 2, 1808, died August 5, 1866. Unmarried.

F. Alice Lewis Smith, born August 24, 1811, died November 21, 1841. Unmarried.

G. Ann Elizabeth Smith, born July 17, 1814, married Edward Hill, son of John Hill and Mary Waller Lewis and grandson of Zachary Lewis III. Issue:

1. Martha Bickerton Hill, married John William Philips, and had:
   a. John Philips, married Lannie Chewning, and had:
      1. Dr. Bickerton Philips, married Vara Harris.
      2. Hallie Philips, married Mr. McKinley.
2. Mary Waller Hill, died May 1820, unmarried.
3. John S. Hill, killed in a railroad accident.
4. Henry Addison Hill, died unmarried.
5. Benjamin Hill, married Edmonia Harris, and had:
   a. John S. Hill, married Eunice V. Whitehead.
   b. Rebecca Hill, married Hunter Philpotts, and has a daughter.
   c. Benjamin Lewis Hill, married Miss Mallory, and has:
      1. Lewis Hill.
   d. Virginia Hill, married John B. Chilton, has John and Mary.
6. Ann Elizabeth Hill, died unmarried.

H. John Snelson Smith, Jr., born July 29, 1817, Louisa County, Va., died at Brownwood, Texas, May 27, 1901, buried at Greenleaf Cemetery. He married at "Allen's Creek", Hanover County, Va., March 30, 1843, Paulina T. Doswell, daughter of Paul Thilman Doswell and his wife, Fanny Gwathmey. She was born May 27, 1822 in Hanover County and is buried beside her husband.

Issue of John S. Smith, Jr. and Paulina T. Doswell:

1. Richard Channing Moore Smith, born at "Allen's Creek", January 30, 1844, married at Acton, Indiana, June 3, 1875, Elizabeth Teague. He is a retired merchant and lives at McCordsville, Indiana. Issue:
   a. Theresa Smith, born May 2, 1876, died May 31, 1886.
   b. Eleanor Smith, born May 7, 1878, unmarried.
   c. Temple Doswell Smith, born March 31, 1882, married Ida Shafer, near Fortville, Indiana, May 1903. They have one child, Bernice Smith and live at Indianapolis.
2. Temple Doswell Smith, Sr. was born at "Walnut Hill" in Louisa County, August 22, 1846. He is president of the bank of Fredericksburg, Texas, where he and his family reside. He married Mary Alice Francis, January 19, 1876 at Indianapolis, Ind. Their only child, Estelle Francis Smith, born November 13, 1877 is a graduate of Wellsley College, Class 1900.
3. Fanny Gwathmey Smith, born at "Walnut Hill", July 14, 1848, married first, C. W. Turner of Savannah, Ga., August 16, 1880 at Waco, Texas. She married second, Anderson P. Jones at Brownwood, Texas, March 10, 1896. She died in Brownwood, March 29, 1899 and is buried by her first husband in Greenleaf Cemetery. She had no children.
4. Anna Lewis Smith, born at "Westfield", Louisa County, Va., September 18, 1849, unmarried.
5. Bickerton Smith, born at "Westfield", July 28, 1851, died unmarried at Brownwood, Texas, October 27, 1887.
6. Brooke Smith, born at "Westfield", March 13, 1853. He is president of the bank of Brooke Smith and Co., Brownwood, Texas. He married Julia L. Sparks, March 2, 1880, near Paris, Ky., and has issue:
   a. Flora T. Smith, died infant.
   b. Lola Doswell Smith, born July 29, 1882 at Brownwood, married first, Gardner Thomas; second, Elisha Lester. Issue:

1. Gardner Thomas, Jr., born September 17, 1903.
2. Lloyd Thomas, born September 7, 1906.

c. Norma Brooke Smith, born February 23, 1885, died December 30, 1910, married November 4, 1905, Glenn Hislip. Their one child died the day of his birth.

d. Brooke Smith, born December 10, 1887 at Brownwood, married April 6, 1909, Clara Blackburn, and has:

1. Norma Smith, born January 28, 1913.
2. Brooke Smith.

7. Alice Lewis Smith, born at "Westfield", July 1, 1855, married April 4, 1882 at Brownwood, Texas, John James Ramey of Trigg County, Ky. Issue:

a. Elizabeth Doswell Ramey, born at Brownwood, January 24, 1883, married on December 3, 1902, Clarence Yancy Early of Kentucky, who is connected with Walker-Smith & Co., a wholesale grocery house of Brownwood. Issue:

1. Clarence Fielding Early, born December 7, 1903.
2. Brooke Francis Early, born February 5, 1909.

b. Pauline Thelma Ramey, died infant.

c. Frank Bracken Ramey, born April 28, 1886, married at Waco, Texas, December 26, 1912, Louise Foster Greer, and has:

1. Virginia Lee Ramey, born at Brownwood, November 21, 1913.
2. Frank B. Ramey, Jr., born April 24, 1916.

*Note.*—The ancestry of this Smith family derived from ancient Virginia records.

Christopher Smith, merchant, owned various land grants. (Records in Hanover County.)

600 acres of land on Snelson's Branch of Hollowing's Creek deeded to Christopher, September 28, 1730.

400 acres granted to Charles Snelson by Wm. Snelson, his son and devisee, said deed recorded in Hanover County, September 28, 1730 deeded to Christopher Smith, merchant.

250 acres sold by Christopher Smith to Patterson Pulliam, on the north side of Pamunkey River—date May 6, 1730.

1,000 acres sold by Christopher Smith, gent. of St. Paul's Parish, Hanover County, Va. to James Rawlings of St. George's Parish on the north side of the North Anna River, Spottsylvania County, June 1, 1731. "Belair", "Ellengowan", "Brecknock", and Llangollen" were the farms of which this tract consisted.

Christopher Smith is supposed to have married Miss Snelson, daughter of Charles Snelson. They are supposed to have emigrated from England about the same time.

The original grant of "Belair" passed to the Lewises, who seem to have purchased it.

(Opinion of B. R. A. Scott, San Antonio, Texas.)

END OF SMITHS—DESCENDANTS OF DOROTHEA LEWIS AND CHARLES SMITH.

## "BELAIR" LEWISES

Zachary Lewis III was born May 6, 1731, died July 21, 1803. He had the following military record as given in records of Spottsylvania County, Va., *Colonial Register:*

"Among the officers who produced their commissions and took the oath and subscribed to the test as directed by law at court held for Spottsylvania County, May 4, 1756, was Zachary Lewis, Jr., gent., First Lieuenant of Foot in Spottsylvania County. Commission dated May 4, 1755.

"Among those taking said oath Zachary Lewis, gent., commissioned October 25, 1758, to be captain of said company.

"Zachary Lewis, gent., commission dated November 12, 1761, to be captain of a company of this county, took the oath April 5, 1762.

"Zachary Lewis, Jr., Esquire, commission dated April 30, 1764, to be Major of Militia, took oath August 7, 1764."

### COMMISSION

"ROBERT DINWIDDIE; His Majesty's Lieutenant-Governor and Commander-in-Chief, of the Colony and Dominion of Virginia.

To Mr. Zachary Lewis, Junr—

"By Virtue of the Power and Authority to me given as Commander of this Colony, I do hereby constitute and appoint you the said Zachary Lewis Captain of a Company of Foot in the County of Spottsylvania.

"You are therefore carefully and diligently to perform the Duty of a Captain in the said County by duly exercising and discipling the

Soldiers of your Company—and by seeing that they are provided with Arms and Ammunition as the Law requires. And I do hereby command them to obey you as their Captain. And you are to follow all such Orders and Directions from Time to Time, as you shall receive from me or any other, your commanding Officer, according to the Rules and Discipline of War.

"GIVEN under my Hand and the Seal of the Colony, at Williamsburg, the Seventeenth Day of February, in the 31st Year of his Majesty's Reign, Annoque Domini 1758.

"ROB. DINWIDDIE."

Col. George Washington's first regiment was raised 1756. His commission, dated December 13, 1752 as Major and Adjutant of Militia Horse and Foot in Counties of Princess Ann, Norfolk, Nansemond, Isle of Wight, South Hampton, Surry, Brunswick, Prince George, Dinwiddie, Chesterfield, Amelia, Cumberland. He took the oath September 4, 1753.

Zachary Lewis took part in the French and Indian War (1754-1768). He and George Washington were comrades and life-long friends. Among Zachary Lewis's effects were personal letters from Washington and from other distinguished men of Revolutionary times. By the carelessness of the guardian of Dr. Richmond Lewis's orphan children these souvenirs were lost and destroyed. (Mrs. Sarah Scott told me she remembered them but being very young and not realizing their value did not attempt to preserve them.)

Miss Jane E. T. Lewis of Missouri told me that Zachary Lewis made yearly visits to "Monticello", taking with him often his youngest son, Addison Lewis. Later Addison Lewis, his wife and Jane, then an infant, spent a day at "Monticello" as Mr. Jefferson's guests, and Mr. Jefferson in shaking the hand of the baby recalled that she was granddaughter of his two friends, Major Zachary Lewis and Col. Thomas Minor (Rev. Officer) both of Spottsylvania.

Zachary Lewis III was the fourth child of Zachary II and Mary Waller Lewis. He was born Thursday, May 6 about eleven or twelve of the clock in the night, one thousand seven hundred and thirty-one, baptized by Rev. Francis Pert, June 9, 1731, died July 21, 1803, married by Rev. Robert Barrett, May 8, 1771 to Ann O. Terrell. She was born September 3, 1748, baptized by Rev.

Barrett, and was daughter of Richmond Terrell and Ann Overton. They settled at "Belair", originally part of a grant to Christopher Smith, and by him sold to James Rawlings from whose hands it seems to have passed to this Zachary Lewis. His father, Zachary II lived near Spottsylvania Courthouse. By transfer of title the original deed to "Belair" passed to Zachary III and is now in the possession of his descendant, Mrs. Lucy Scott Griffith, Bronxville, New York.

Children of Zachary and Ann O. Lewis:

A. Ann O. Lewis, born April 23, 1772, baptized by Rev. Robert Barrett, June 6th of same year, married July 28, 1795, Dr. James Scott of Pennsylvania and Virginia. She died September 11, 1795—twenty-five minutes past 10 P. M.

B. Dr. Richmond Lewis, born March 14, 1774, baptized by Rev. James Stevenson, April 30, 1774, married October 28, 1802, Elizabeth Travers Daniel, daughter of Travers and Frances Moncure Daniel of "Crows Nest" in Stafford County. (Issue given.) Married second, Margaret Richardson (no issue). He died July 31, 1831. He read medicine under his cousin, Dr. William B. Lewis of Urbanna and later graduated from the Philadelphia School of Medicine. (His diploma is owned by S. T. L. S. Anderson.)

C. Cadwallader Lewis, born November 25, 1776, baptized December 28 by Rev. James Thomson, died February 4, 1797.

D. Mary Waller Lewis, born April 10, 1779, married May 23, 1798, John Hill and lived six miles from "Belair", home called "Hillsboro". Left issue.

E. Huldah Fontaine Lewis, born February 4, 1781, died October 25, 1863, baptized by Rev. William Douglass, married September 23, 1802, her first cousin, Waller Holladay of "Prospect Hill". (Issue given.)

F. John Lewis of "Llangollen", born at "Belair", February 25, 1784, baptized May 4, 1784 by Rev. Wm. Douglass, married 1808, Jean Daniel, daughter of Travers and Frances Moncure Daniel of "Crows Nest". He died August 15, 1858 in Frankfort, Ky. (Issue given.)

G. Eliza Lewis, born May 27, 1786, died September 1816, baptized by Rev. Wm. Douglass, July 10, 1786, married November 9, 1815, Walter Raleigh Daniel of "Crows Nest". Had issue, Lewis Daniel, died in childhood.

H. A son William, died infant.

I. Rev. Addison Murdock Lewis, born September 26, 1789, baptized by Rev. Hugh Boggs, married first, November 22, 1810, Sally Billingsley. Married second, March 28, 1821, Sarah Ann Minor. Rev. Samuel Wilson (Presbyterian minister of Fredericksburg) officiating. (Issue given.)

Issue of Dr. Richmond Lewis of "Bel-air" and "Brecknock" and his first wife, Elizabeth Travers Daniel, who was born October 18, 1778, married October 28, 1802. She died at Jennings Gap Hotel, Augusta County, on her way from the Red Sulphur Springs just after the death of her son, Alfred, where both had gone to seek health. Her grave for seventy years was in the garden of this old hotel. Her remains were finally removed to "Bel-air" and buried beside her husband, November, 1897. She was a woman of deep humility and piety, honored and beloved by all who knew her, and leaving a lasting impression for all that is highest in character and in education upon the younger generation who in turn have passed on these standards to their children. She and Dr. Lewis had many sorrows in the deaths of their older children just as they grew to maturity. This family was noted for personal beauty and for intellectuality.

1. Ann Overton Lewis, born July 27, 1803, died February 27, 1821, buried at "Bel-air".
2. Dr. Alfred Lewis, graduate of Baltimore Medical School, born March 8, 1805, died July 17, 1827 at Red Sulphur Springs, buried on Indian Creek on land owned by Benjamin Peek, a mile and a half from the Springs.
3. Jean Frances Moncure Lewis, born September 10, 1807, died January 14, 1823, buried at "Bel-air".
4. Huldah Lewis, born March 18, 1812, married January 5, 1832, John Thomson Scott, son of Dr. James Scott by his second marriage to Mildred Thomson, daughter of Waddy Thomson and Mary (Lewis) Cobbs.

Huldah and her husband died early; he on a search for health in Savannah, Ga., she later at the Fauquier White Sulphur Springs, October 5, 1836. Both are buried in the woods at "Brecknock" beneath a tree which had marked the gathering of the Literary Club of young people of "Bel-air", "Llangollen" and "Brecknock".

5. Sarah Travers Lewis, born November 7, 1813 at "Brecknock", married at "Prospect Hill", December 13, 1832, James McClure Scott, youngest child of Dr. James Scott by his second marriage to Mildred Thomson. Sarah Scott and her husband, James M. Scott, lived at "Bel-air" in Spottsylvania during the early years of their married life, later at "Little Whim" and "Pine Grove" in Stafford County and at "Kenmore" in Fredericksburg. Their latter years were spent at "Bel-air", where in 1882, they celebrated their golden wedding with the surviving ten of their fifteen children present. She died at the home of her daughter, near Rapidan, Va., December 18, 1891. He died at "Bel-air", July, 1893. Both are buried at "Bel-air".

   (Issue given under Scotts and Thomsons, Albemarle Lewis and Meriwether records.)

6. Zachary Travers Lewis, born August 7, 1816, died February 26, 1858, buried in Staunton, Va.

7. Mary Waller Lewis, born January 16, 1819, died January 31, aged two weeks. Buried at "Bel-air".

## HILL

Robert Hill, son of Col. Humphry Hill and Frances Baylor; his will dated February 8, 1774, probated March 13, 1775, his death probably February, 1775. He lived in King and Queen County, Virginia.

John Hill's brother, Samuel Hill, married Ann Lewis, daughter of Waller and Sarah Lewis. Their daughter, Dorothea Lewis Hill was second wife of Henry W. Meriwether of Kentucky, and had among other issue, Arthur Samuel Meriwether of Raymond, Illinois, who married Sally Baker. (See Meriwether record.)

Mary Waller Lewis, daughter of Zachary III, married John Hill, son of Robert Hill and Miss Garlic, and had:

A. Nanny Hill, married Overton Harris of Louisa County, and has:
   1. Mary Harris, died unmarried.
   2. Edmonia Harris, unmarried.
   3. Ann Overton Harris, married Benjamin Lewis Smith. (See Smith record.)
   4. Thomas Harris, married Rebecca Swift, and had:
      a. William Harris, married Miss Parish.
      b. Wortley Harris, married ——.
      c. Edmonia Virginia Harris, married Benjamin Hill. (See Smith record.)

## JOHN LEWIS OF "LLANGOLLEN"
## (1784-1858)

John Lewis and his wife, Jean Wood Daniel, lived at "Llangollen", Spotsylvania County, where for years he taught a classical school, having as pupils, boys, who later became prominent in professions and in statesmanship. Later he removed to the vicinity of Frankfort, Ky., where at his new home, named "Llangollen", he again opened a school of much usefulness. He was author of books on literary subjects, also of a novel, *Young Kate,* which depicts the dishonesty of the so-called land agents in defrauding the heirs of Revolutionary soldiers, under power of attorney, out of the land bounties granted as pay for service in that war. His books are yet to be found in big libraries and are still used by scholars for their valuable information and deductions.

Issue: (twelve children).

A. Frances Ann Lewis, born March 3, 1810, married William Mitchell of Virginia and later of Mississippi, had issue, Jane Mitchell and several sons.

B. Rev. Cadwallader Lewis, born November 5, 1811 in Spotsylvania County, studied under his father at "Llangollen" and completed his course at the University of Virginia. In 1831 he went to Kentucky, taught school at Covington and Georgetown. In 1834, he settled on a farm near Frankfort, where he lived until his death, April 22, 1882. In 1846 he became a Baptist minister and was widely known in Kentucky and in various Southern States as an eloquent and useful preacher, also as a writer of ability. After 1865 he occupied, for several years, the chair of Belles Lettres and Theology in Georgetown College. He was a thorough scholar and of varied and successful abilities. He married Elizabeth Henry Patterson of Appomattox Courthouse, Va., and left issue: (six children)

1. William Garret Lewis, married Louisa Taylor Wallace of Woodford County, Ky., and has:
   a. Frances Taylor Lewis.
   b. Elizabeth H. Lewis.
2. Dr. John Alexander Lewis, married Margaret Jane Scott of Franklin County, Ky., lived in Lexington, and had:
   a. John Cadwallader Lewis.
   b. Sydney Scott Lewis.
   c. Waller Lewis.
   d. Mary Lewis.
   e. Elizabeth Lewis.
   f. Jane Rebecca Lewis.
3. Norbonne Vivian Lewis.
4. Waller Holladay Lewis, C. S. A., died during siege of Port Hudson, La., married Miss Helm, lived at "Bel-air" Farm, Kentucky. No issue.
5. Mary Patteson Lewis, died unmarried.
6. Charles Cadwallader Lewis, married Letitia Barron of Davies County, Ky. Issue:
   a. Charles Cadwallader Lewis, Jr.
   b. Celia Boyd Lewis.
   c. Maud M'Farland Lewis.

C. Elizabeth Travers Lewis, born July 10, 1813 at Llangollen, Va., died unmarried.

D. George Wythe Lewis, born February 9, 1815, editor and publisher in Frankfort, married Mary Jane Todd of Frankfort, and had:

1. Joseph Bullock Lewis, married first, Emma Abbett; second, Keturah Thornton of Versailles, Ky.

   Issue by first marriage:

a. Margaret Lewis.
b. William Lewis.
c. George Lewis.

2. John Franklin Lewis, married Mary Sneed of Frankfort, and had:
   a. Sneed Lewis.
   b. John Lewis.
   c. William Herndon Lewis.
3. William Todd Lewis.
4. George Alexander Lewis, married. No issue.

E. Mary Overton Lewis, born November 7, 1816 at Llangollen, Va., died 1894, unmarried.

F. John Moncure Lewis, born May 11, 1820 at Llangollen, died in youth. He was of brilliant promise and a poet of genius.

G. Jean Wood Daniel Lewis, born September 22, 1822, married Dr. Alexander Augustus Patteson of Virginia, later of Sangamon County, Illinois. Issue:

1. Augusta Patteson, married John Parkinson of Sangamon County, and had:
   a. Ernest Parkinson.
   b. William Parkinson.
   c. Jean Parkinson.
   d. Mary Parkinson.
   e. John Parkinson.
2. Jean Francis Patteson, married Dr. Joseph Wilcox of Sangamon County. Issue:
   a. Dwight Wilcox.
   b. Augustus Wilcox.
   c. Annie Wilcox.
3. Alexander L. Patteson, married Ella Robinson of Sangamon County. Issue:
   a. Ella Patteson.
   b. Susan Patteson.
4. Susan Archer Patteson, married Hampton Gibson of Sangamon County. Issue:
   a. Robert Gibson.
   b. Marion Elizabeth Gibson, married Richard Smith.

H. Dr. Richmond Addison Lewis, born April 4, 1824 at Llangollen, Va., was a talented physician and professor in Richmond, Va. He married Margaretta G. Mitchell, and had:

1. John Moncure Lewis, married his first cousin, Lizzy H. Price of Franklin County, Ky., and has:
    a. Hugh Rodman Lewis, married Victoria Harris of "Cherry Grove", and had:
        1. Nelson Lewis, who died a youth.
    b. John Moncure Lewis.
    c. Richmond Addison Lewis, married, and has children.
    d. Margaretta Lewis, died in childhood.
    e. Dr. James Mitchell Lewis, married his first cousin, Effie Lewis, daughter of Rev. James Minor Lewis of Kentucky. No issue.
2. Waller Morton Lewis of Richmond, married Sophia Redding of Vicksburg, Miss., and had:
    a. Beach Lewis.
    b. Margaretta Lewis.
    c. Richmond Lewis.
    d. Waller Lewis.
    e. Gretchen Lewis, and others.
3. Richmond Lewis, Jr. of Richmond, married Leilia Curry of Richmond. Issue:
    a. Fanny Mitchell Lewis.

I. Lucy Daniel Lewis of Llangollen, Va., was born December 15, 1826, married her first cousin, James Minor Holladay, and had:

1. Louise Richmond Holladay, unmarried.
2. John Waller Holladay, married Mary Caroline Harris. (See "Prospect Hill" Holladays.)
3. James M. Holladay, Jr., died infant.

J. Susan Raleigh Lewis, born December 9, 1828, married Rev. John Gano Price of Kentucky, and had:

1. Elizabeth H. Price, married John Moncure Lewis.
2. Susan Gano Price, married Wm. B. Allison, and had:
    a. Annie Lewis Allison of Richmond, Va.
    b. Bessie Price Allison.

c. John Gano Allison, married Annie Watkins, and has:
1. Watkins Allison.
2. Elizabeth Allison.

3. John Gano Price, died unmarried.

K. Walter Raleigh Daniel Lewis, born at Llangollen, November 30, 1830, died unmarried.

L. Rev. James Minor Lewis, married Euphemia Miller Todd of Madison County, Miss. Issue:
1. Eugenia Lewis.
2. Effie Lewis.
3. Vivian Travers Lewis.

*Note.*—James Minor Lewis studied medicine, later became a Baptist minister and, 1884, located in Frankfort, Ky. Previously he had been pastor in Canton, Miss., in New Orleans, and in Jefferson, Texas.

END OF DESCENDANTS OF JOHN LEWIS OF LLANGOLLEN.

## REV. ADDISON MURDOCK LEWIS

A. M. Lewis was youngest son of Col. Zachary Lewis III of "Bel-air", Spotsylvania County, Va., and was born 1789, died in Huntsville, Missouri, August 26, 1857, aged 67 years, 11 months. He was an alumnus of William and Mary College and educated for the Episcopal Ministry, but became a Baptist. He was immersed by Rev. Absalom Waller, July 3, 1808. In his native State he was long known as an earnest minister and teacher, associated with many distinguished and literary men of his day; his influence was widely felt and acknowledged. He moved from his home in Spotsylvania, first to Georgetown, Ky. His family underwent the trials of real pioneer life in Missouri to which place he finally moved. His home was named for his father's home in Virginia, "Bel-air."

He was pastor of the church in Huntsville and trustee of Mt. Pleasant College. A fall had fractured his hip, but seated in a chair he preached with spirit and eloquence, spending his last days in faithful service. Believing the gospel should be without price, he never accepted a salary from any of his churches. He married first, December 1, 1810, Sally Billingsley, who was born 1793, died at "Salem", Va., January 18, 1820, aged 26 years and 6 months. She was daughter of Rev. John Billingsley of Spotsylvania. She was extremely pretty, tall, slender, dark-haired, delicate and graceful, reserved in manner, melancholy in temperament. He married second, March 1821, Sarah Ann Minor, who was fourth daughter and ninth child of Col. Thomas Minor of "Locust Grove", Spotsylvania County (an officer of the Revolution and War of 1812) and his wife, Elizabeth Taylor. Col. Minor was a man of note, a friend of Gen. LaFayette and of Gen. Washington.

Zachary Lewis III had been a college mate of Jefferson at William and Mary; their intimacy continued throughout their lives. Addison Lewis frequently accompanying his father on his yearly visits to "Monticello". Later, when in Charlottesville on business, Addison with his wife and baby spent a day there. Mr. Jefferson shaking hands with the baby, Jane E. T. Lewis, commented that she was the granddaughter of two of his old friends—Zachary Lewis and Col. Thomas Minor.

Issue by first marriage: (four children)

A. Sarah Lewis, born 1811, died 1816.

B. Virginia Ann, born May 30, 1813, died February 20, 1867, married James Duane Brown of Kentucky, and had:

   1. Sally Addison Brown, married Colby Taylor, and had:

      a. Rosalie Taylor, died young.

      b. Ernest Taylor, died young.

      c. Isadore Taylor, died young.

      d. Lewis Cadwallader Taylor, died young.

      e. Albert James Duane Brown Taylor, married and has issue.

C. John Llewellyn Lewis, M. D., born in Fredericksburg, Va., February 28, 1815, died in St. Louis, Missouri, February 15, 1889, married Mary Eliza Woolfolk of Kentucky, and had:

   1. Thomas Addison Lewis, lives in Colorado, married, and has:

      a. Hume Lewis.

      b. Lawrence Lewis.

2. Isabella Mildred Lewis, died January, 1901, married Oscar Stephens, and had a daughter.
3. Malcolm Duane Lewis, M. D. of Columbus, Mo., married, and has a daughter and two sons.
4. Charles Neville Lewis, M. D. of Fayette, Mo., married, and has four daughters and one son.
5. Annie Marshall Lewis, married Walter Scott and lives in New Rochelle, N. Y. Issue:
    a. Hugh Scott, married ——, and has a daughter.
    b. Frank Scott, married Nellie ——, and has:
        1. Walter Scott.
        2. —— Scott.
        3. Mary Ann Scott.
    c. Maizie Scott.

D. Joseph Addison Lewis, born at "Salem", October 18, 1818, died December 20, 1876, married Elizabeth McCoy of Missouri, and has:
1. Ellery Channing Lewis, born 1849, is a miner in Colorado, unmarried.
2. Nancy Lewis, born 1852, married Judson Berry, and has one son.
3. Josephine Lewis, born 1855.
4. Virginia Lewis, born 1858, died young.
5. Addie Brown Lewis, born 1861.
6. Thomas Addison Lewis, born 1863, miner in Colorado, unmarried.
7. Mary Elizabeth Lewis, born 1866, married Robert Fardwell, and has two sons.

Issue of second marriage of Rev. A. M. Lewis:

E. Thomas Minor Lewis, born at "Salem", January 19, 1822, died in Montana, September 17, 1903, aged 84 years. He was a farmer, Confederate soldier, and ranch man. He married 1844, Louisiana Cleveland Hughes, and had ten children. Issue:
1. Alice Minor Lewis, married J. C. Drake, no issue.

2. Overton Hughes Lewis of Montana, ranch man, inventor, married and has two sons and one daughter.
3. Florence Howard Lewis, married Wm. Brown, and has three sons and one daughter.
4. Ernest Cleveland Lewis, ranchman in Montana, married twice, and has three sons and two daughters.
5. Caroline Virginia Lewis, married Robert W. Hughes, ranchman, and has two sons.
6. Kate Richmond Lewis, music teacher, unmarried.
7. Addison Murdock Lewis, married, no issue.
8. Thomas Minor Lewis of Oklahoma, married, and has two sons; one is a musician, the other a farmer.
9. Joseph Swan Lewis, ranchman, unmarried.
10. Fannie Mary Lewis of Montana, unmarried.

F. Richmond Z. Lewis, born at "Salem", August 3, 1823, died December 28, 1845, unmarried.

G. Jane Elizabeth Taylor Lewis, born at "Salem", March 14, 1825, died in St. Louis, Mo., unmarried. She was a teacher of note, was of great mental ability and culture.

H. Waldo Lewis, M. D., born at "Salem", May 6, 1827, died September 4, 1864, married Sophie Shafer, and had:

1. Ellen Louis, married —— Sims, and has issue.
2. Ann Terrell Lewis, married Mr. Musick, and has issue.

I. Ann Terrell Lewis, born at "Salem", June 30, 1829, died at "Bel-air", Mo., October 17, 1853. Unmarried.

J. John Henry Lewis, born at his grandfather's home, "Locust Grove", September 30, 1831, died in Indiana, October 22, 1901, served as Captain 9th Cavalry U. S. Volunteers, 1860-65. He married Mary Susan Hicks of Fayette, Mo., and had:

1. Mary Lewis.
2. Frank Lewis, died 1890.
3. Ada Lewis.
4. Nannie Lewis, married Reno Alexander.
5. Robert Hunter Lewis, died July 6, 1893.

K. Sally Billingsley Lewis, was born at "Woodlawn" in Kentucky, June 22, 1834, died January 8, 1899, married Theodore Washington Dunica of St. Louis, who died 1874. Issue:

1. Sarah Lewis Dunica, married Henry J. Stewart of Detroit, and has three sons.
2. Eudora Dunica, married Phillip Winchester of Cleveland, Ohio, and has one daughter and one son.
3. Lillian Hopwood Dunica, teacher in St. Louis, unmarried.

L. Lucy Mary Lewis, born May 5, 1836 at "Woodlawn", Kentucky, married Gordon C. McGavoc, and lives near Franklin, Howard County, Mo. Issue:

1. John McGavoc.
2. Mary McGavoc.
3. Sally McGavoc.
4. Louise McGavoc, married Robert Woods.
5. Hugh McGavoc.
6. Robert McGavoc.

M. Huldah Fountain Lewis, born November 11, 1838 at "Woodlawn", died October 12, 1872, married, no issue.

Mrs. Sarah Ann Minor Lewis survived her husband twenty-nine years. She died in St. Louis, Mo in her 88th year, November 17, 1886. She had one son in the Union Army and one in the Confederate Army. She lived to thank God for peace. Her daughter, Jane, was her devoted nurse in the last five years of helplessness and blindness, and has left to the family a tribute to both her parents in a most interesting sketch.

END OF DESCENDANTS OF REV. ADDISON LEWIS AND ALSO THE END OF THE ZACHARY LEWIS LINE.

## OVERTONS

William, the emigrant, born in England, December 3, 1638, came to Virginia about 1669, married November 24, 1670, Mary Elizabeth Waters.

The will of Mrs. Mary E. Waters of St. Sepulcher's Parish, London, England, dated 1697, leaves to Elizabeth Waters, wife of Wm. Overton of Virginia, a few shillings; mentions also a son,

John Waters of Virginia, a son-in-law, Wm. Goodwin, brother-in-law Caleb Millett; a son, Thomas, residuary legatee and sole executor. (*Virginia Historical Magazine,* Vol. II.)

Issue:

1. Elizabeth Overton, born June 28, 1673 (probably Mary E.), married Robert Anderson. (See Andersons.)
2. William, born August 6, 1675, married Peggy Garland.
3. Temperance, born March 2, 1679, married Wm. Harris.
4. James, born August 14, 1688, married Elizabeth ——.
5. Barbara, born February 5, 1690, died October 30, 1766, age 75 years, married James Winston.
6. Samuel, born August 14, 1695.

James Winston came from Wales, 1702, settled in Hanover, where he had patented lands. He and Barbara Overton had: (a) John, born June 9, 1724, married February 3, 1746, Alice Bickerton; (b) James, married Anne Ferrell.

Robert Harris came to Virginia from Wales, 1650, married Mary, youngest child of Secretary William Claiborne and his wife, Elizabeth Butler. (See old Claiborne family records.) Only child of this marriage was William, who married Temperance Overton. Issue: Major Robert Harris, prominent citizen of Louisa County, married Mourning Gunn.

Children of James, died June 18, 1749, and Elizabeth Overton, died November 19, 1739: (See *Overtons* by Prof. Elmer Dickerson. Carr Bible.)

1. Mary Overton, married David Cosby (ancestors of Miss Mary Willis Minor of Washington City.
2. Barbara Overton, born April 20, 1720, was the second wife of John Carr of "Bear Castle". (See *Virginia Historical Magazine,* Vol. II, page 222; Vol. III, page 206, 208.)
3. James Overton, Jr., married Mary Waller, great-granddaughter of Edmond Waller, the poet. This James distinguished himself as a young officer in the Virginia Regiment at Braddock's defeat. He had three sons:

   a. Gen. Tom Overton of Tennessee, served as captain of cavalry in the Revolution and was a member of the Virginia Order of the Cincinnati. He was also a friend of Gen. Jackson, was his second in several duels, also served on his staff at the Battle of New Orleans. His descendants live in Louisiana.

b. Judge John Overton, President of Court of Appeals in Tennessee.

c. Waller Overton, whose son, Dabney, married Eliza Harris, and whose descendants live in Lexington, Newport, and in Frankfort, Ky.

4. John Overton, married Ann Booker Clough. Their son, Clough Overton was killed at the Battle of Blue Licks in Kentucky, 1782, fighting the Indians with Daniel Boone. This family moved to Kentucky in pioneer days and its representatives are scattered over the South and West.

5. Margaret Overton, married William Beckley.

6. William Overton, married Jemima Harris (daughter of Temperance O. and William Harris, son of Robert and Mary Claiborne Harris).

*7. Nancy Overton, married Richmond Terrell.

Children of William and Jemima Overton:

a. Elizabeth Overton, married her cousin, Samuel Overton, who raised the first company of volunteers after Braddock's defeat, July, 1755. He served for many years on the frontier against Indians. They had: (1) Samuel, (2) William, (3) James, (4) Mary.

b. Nancy Overton, married Capt. John Winston of Revolutionary Army, member of the Cincinnati. They had: (1) Horatio Gates Winston, (2) William Overton Winston, (3) Eliza, (4) Maria Winston.

c. Mary Overton, married Richard Morris. They had: (1) Dr. James Maury Morris, (2) William Morris, (3) Betsy Morris, married Ed. Garland, (4) Clara Morris, married Horatio Garland, (5) Maria Morris, married Dr. Frank Carr, (6) Patsy Morris, never married.

d. William Overton. (No record.)

e. Sally Overton, married Capt. John Syme (half nephew of Patrick Henry), and had Helen Syme, who married Ed. Garland (son of Ed. and Betsy Morris Garland).

f. James Overton, married Mildred ——.

g. John Overton, born January 20, 1755, died April 23, 1822. He served in the Revolutionary War from beginning to end; volunteered in the company commanded by Patrick Henry in the Spring of 1775, when he marched against Dunmore. At the close of the War he was captain of infantry in the Continental Line and a member of the Virginia Chapter of the Order of the Cincinnati. He married first, 1782, Susanna Garland, who died June 24, 1797, age thirty-one. He married second, May 1, 1799, Nancy Bacon, born 1760, died 1826.

RECORD COPIED FROM JOHN OVERTON'S BIBLE

John Overton and his first wife, Susanna Garland had six daughters:

1. Fannie Garland Overton, born January 26, 1784, married George W. Trueheart.
2. Elizabeth, born January 6, 1786, died unmarried.
3. Susan Grayson Overton, born February 1, 1788, died May 20, 1819, married John H. Steger.
4. Jemima Ann Overton, born November 15, 1789, died in Mississippi, 1863, married George Banks.
5. Martha Morris Overton, died young.
6. Sarah Meriwether Overton, born August 11, 1794, married Richmond Terrell.

John Overton and his second wife , Nancy Bacon, had:

7. John Bacon Overton, born June 14, 1800, died December 28, 1844.
8. William Overton, born October 9, 1801, died January 1, 1887.
9. Lucy Talman, born July 29, 1804, died November 1861, married Abner Nelson Harris (1795-1857), and had among others, Abner and Maria Louise.

Abner Nelson Harris, Jr. (1836-1899), married March 1, 1866, Martha Victoria Harris (1845-1920). They had:

a. Mary Caroline Harris, born December 31, 1866, married John Waller Holladay of "Prospect Hill", has five daughters and a son. (See Holladays.)

b. Abner Harris of "Cherry Grove".
c. Virginia Harris.
d. William Overton Harris, married Mary Todd, and has: (1) Mary Louise, (2) Victoria, (3) William, (4) Frederick, (5) Dick.
e. Frank Harris, married Frances Holland, has: Mrs. Frances Walker, (2) Virginia Harris, (3) Ann, died young.
f. Victoria Harris, married Hugh Lewis. Their son, Nelson, died young.
g. John Frederick Harris.
h. Lucy Talman Harris.

Maria Louise Harris, daughter of Abner Nelson Harris, Senior and Lucy Talman Harris, married Dr. Isaac Curd. Their son, Arthur Bryce Curd, married Julia Morris in Richmond, Va. They had: (1) William Curd, (2) Louise Curd, (3) Ann Curd, married October 22, 1935, Alfred Scott Anderson, Jr.

## GARLAND NOTE (BROCK)
(Supplied by Cousin Mary Greenhow)

The Garlands, came originally from Sussex, England. They moved to Wales, then to Virginia early in the eighteenth century. David settled in Richmond County. His brothers John and Edward located in that part of New Kent which is now Hanover.

Edward Garland, married Jane, daughter of Mr. Jennings, a large patentee of land, who died 1719 and whose wife was a Carr. Issue: (As given by Mrs. Emily Taylor)

A. Ann Garland, married first, John Thompson; second, Edward Sydnor. Issue:
    1. Susannah Thompson, married Thomas Tinsley.
    2. Edward Sydnor.
    3. Nanny Sydnor, married John Seabrooke.
    4. Elizabeth Sydnor, married Mr. Thompson.
    5. Mary Sydnor, married Mr. Mathews.
    6. Sarah Sydnor, married Allen Richardson.

B. Mary Garland, married Daniel Trueheart, son of Aaron Trueheart.

C. Edward Garland, Jr., whose son, David, lived in Lunenburg County, and had a son, Samuel.

D. Thomas Garland, married Frances Herndon, and had:

1. Edward Garland, married Elizabeth Morris.
2. Susannah Garland, married 1782, John Overton.

*Note.*—William Jennings, emigrant soldier, came to America via the West Indies. He married Mary Fulton of Hanover County. They lived at "Jennings' Ordinary". Their children were:

A. John Jennings, married Temperance Thompson.
B. Robert Jennings, married Miss Chiles.
C. William Jennings, married Miss Dickerson.
D. James Jennings, married Miss Granshaw.
E. Joseph Jennings, married Anna Billups.
F. Agnes Jennings, married Mr. Dickerson.
G. Sarah Jennings, married Mr. Foulks.
H. Elizabeth Jennings, married Mr. Walton.
I. Mary Jennings, married Mr. Foulks.
J. Anna Jennings, married Mr. Thompson, and moved to Pittsylvania County. (A descendant of this marriage is Mrs. Martha Ann Farmer of Mt. Airy, Va.)

END OF OVERTON RECORD

## TYRELLS

Sir Hugh Tyrrell of Great Thornton, Essex, was son of Sir Edward Tyrrell, governor of Carisbrook Castle during its successful defense against the French, 1377. He married Jane, daughter and heiress of Sir James Flambert; their son,

Sir James Tyrrell, knighted before Ardes, 1380, married first, Margaret, daughter of Sir Wm. Heron of Heron Hall, Essex; married second, Elizabeth, daughter of Sir John Flambert, son

Sir Walter Tyrrell of Heron, son

Sir John Tyrrell of Heron, sheriff of Essex, 1423, treasurer to household of Henry VI, was at Agincourt, was of retinue of Sir Walter Hungerford, Speaker in House of Commons, died 1437, married Margaret or Alice or Eleanor (daughter of Sir Wm. Coggeshall and his wife, Mary, daughter of Sir John Hawkwood, a celebrated soldier of fortune in time of Edward III). Son

Sir Thomas Tyrrell of Heron, sheriff of Essex and Harts, 1460, chamberlain of Exchequer, died 1476, married Ann, daughter of Sir John Marney of Essex, son

Sir Thomas Tyrrell of Okendon, died before 1490, held one-third manor of Springfield, Essex. Married Elizabeth, daughter and heiress of Sir Humphrey Le Brun and his wife, who was daughter of Robert d'Arcy of Malden.

Ancient Heraldic Arms and Crest of Tyrrells:

*Arms*—argent within a bordure engrailed, gules, two chevrons, azure. *Crest*—a peacock's tail issuing from mouth of a boar's head, couped, erect. *Supporters*—two tigers, regardant. *Motto*—*Sans Dieu Rien* or *Sans criante.*

## TERRELLS OR TYRELLS OF AMERICA

Taken from the genealogy of Richmond and William Tyrrell, brothers who settled in Virginia in the Seventeenth Century. Published in England 1910, compiled by Joseph H. Terrell of "Castleknock", Queen's Road, Twickenham, England.

Royal Descent is given in two lines from Edward I and his wife, Eleanor of Castile. Their daughter, Joan, married first, Gilbert de Clare. She married second, Rolph de Monthermer. These two lines of descent joined in the tenth generation.

| | | | |
|---|---|---|---|
| I. | Eleanor de Clare, daughter by the first marriage, married Hugh Despencer, Earl of Gloucester. | I. | Sir Thomas Monthermer, son by the second marriage, married Margaret, daughter of first Lord Tiptoft. |
| II. | Isabel Despencer, married Richard Fitzalen, fifth Earl of Arundel. | II. | Margaret Monthermer, married Sir John de Montacute. |
| III. | Philippa Fitzalen, married Sir Richard Serjeaux. | III. | Sir Simon Montacute, m. Elizabeth Broughton. |
| IV. | Elizabeth Serjeaux, married Sir William Marney. | IV. | Thomas Montagu, married Christian Bassett. |
| V. | Sir John Marney, married Agnes Throckmorton. | V. | John Montagu, married Alice Halcot. |
| VI. | Anna Marney, married Sir Thomas Tyrrell of Heron. | VI. | William Montagu, married Mary Butline. |

VII. Sir Thomas Tyrrell, married Elizabeth le Brun.

VIII. William Tyrrell, married Elizabeth Bodley.

IX. Humphrey Tyrrell of Thornton, married Jane Ingle.

X. George Tyrrell, married Eleanor or Elizabeth Montagu.

VII. Richard Montagu, married Agnes Knotting.

VIII. Thomas Montagu, married Agnes Dudley.

IX. Sir Edward Montagu, Chief Justice, married Helen Roper.

X. Eleanor or Elizabeth Montagu, married George Tyrrell.

XI. William Tyrrell of Reading, married a daughter of —— Richmond of Stewley, Bucks.

Robert Tyrrell of Reading was the son of William Tyrrell and Miss Richmond. He was Guardian 1616, St. Giles Ward 1623. He married Jane, daughter of Robert Baldwin, June 29, 1617. Issue:

A. Mary Tyrrell.

B. John Tyrrell, never left England.

C. Robert Tyrrell of London, born November 14, 1619, came to Virginia but returned to England.

D. Richmond Tyrrell of New Kent County, Va., 1656.

E. William Tyrrell of New Kent County, Va., married Martha.

Richmond Tyrrell came to Virginia about 1656, bought lands, also had a grant of 640 acres in New Kent on the west side of the York River, November 28, 1658 and took another grant of land on Chickahominy River in New Kent, February 8, 1670. His son, Richmond Tyrrell II, had a son, Richmond Tyrrell III, who married Nancy Overton. Issue:

1. Richmond Tyrrell.
2. James Tyrrell, died unmarried.
3. William Tyrrell, married Patsy Winston.
4. Richard Tyrrell, married Lucy Maria Carr (great-grandfather of Dr. Staige Davis.)
5. Samuel Tyrrell, died unmarried.
6. Elizabeth Tyrrell, married Frederick Harris.

7. Mary O. Tyrrell, married Garrett Minor of "Sunning Hill".
8. Barbara Tyrrell, married Aaron Fontaine; daughter Betsy, married Forts Cosby, 1796.
*9. Ann O. Tyrrell, married Zachary Lewis III of "Bel-air".
10. Rebecca Tyrrell, married Nicholas Hunter Meriwether.
11. A daughter, married Patrick Belchers of Hanover, went to Kentucky.

Mary O. Tyrell and Garrett Minor of "Sunning Hill", had issue:

1. Patsy, married first, Robert Quarles; second, Hall.
2. Ann, born December 14, 1771, died 1820, married July 27, 1791, Thomas Meriwether; second, John Brockman.
3. Rebecca, married John Quarles.
4. Elizabeth, died 1861, married 1799, John Stapleton Crutchfield (1775-1818).
5. Garrett Minor of Fredericksburg, married Eliza McWilliams.
6. Sally, died 1849, married David Watson of Green Springs.
7. Mary, married Garland Anderson.
8. Peter, married Lucy Walker Gilmer.
9. Dr. James, married Polly Watson.
10. Louisa, married Elijah Hutchinson.
    Mary Louise Hutchinson, married Chiles Barker.
11. Samuel O., married Lydia Laurie Lewis.

Ann Minor and Thomas Meriwether, had:

1. Richard T., born in Louisa County, May 11, 1792, died December 7, 1840, Madrid Bend, Tenn., married Elizabeth Rivers.
2. Garrett, born in Louisa, April 25, 1794, died September 26, 1851 at his home, "Cabin Row", Christian County, Ky., married September 28, 1819 at "Woodlawn", Orange County, Mary Ann Minor (daughter of Dabney and Lucy Herndon Minor).
3. Peter, named for his Uncle Peter of "Sunning Hill", married Mary Walker Meriwether (no surviving issue); married second, Mrs. Frances Tapp, neé Gamble (no issue). They adopted her relative, George Geiger, who was killed at

Gettysburg. She died December 24, 1883, buried at "Cismont".

4. Mary M., married John Walton Barker. She is buried at her home, "Cloverlands", Montgomery County, Tenn. Her half-sister, Virginia Brockman Fowkes, lies beside her.
5. Thomas, died 1838, unmarried.
6. Frances, scalded to death at three years of age 1804.

Second marriage of Ann Minor and John Brockman, had:

7. Virginia, married Joseph Fowlkes.
8. Francis Brockman, married Margaret McDougal.
9. Emmet.
10. Hugh.
11. Charles James, M. D., married Margaret Terrell Cobbs at "Music Hall", Va. She was daughter of Samuel and Mary Noel Cobbs, was raised at "Music Hall" by James Hunter Terrell. Dr. Charles Brockman was associated in practice with Dr. Gerrard, at whose home in Kentucky he died. Issue:
    a. James Hunter Brockman.
    b. Garrett Meriwether Brockman.

Garrett Minor, married Eliza McWilliams. Issue:

1. Dorothea, married Dr. Wm. Bankhead of Orange County. Issue, a son and several daughters.
2. Mary, born 1810, married Thomas R. Roots, lieutenant in United States and Confederate Navies. She lived later at Bowling Green, Mo. with her son-in-law, Judge N. P. Minor. Her daughter, Lizzie was Peter Minor's second wife. Mrs. Roots died, December, 1890 at "Hinton", the residence of N. P. Minor, near Louisiana, Mo.
3. Ann French, died 1859, married Judge Waller of Cape Gerardeau, Mo.
4. Wm. Garrett, married Ann, sister of Thomas Roots.
5. George Buckner Minor, U. S. and C. S. A. Navies, married Ann Chew of Fredericksburg, died 1872-3.
6. James L., married Mrs. Sydney Smith, had Sallie, married Hambleton Gamble.

7. Andrew Jackson Minor, appointed to West Point by Gen A. Jackson, but dismissed for not tying his shoes. Married Mary Bouldin.
8. Robert Dabney Minor, C. S. Navy, married Landonia Randolph of Fauquier. Issue: (a) Mary, married John B. Lightfoot, (b) Landonia, married William Sparrow Dashields, (c) Ann Elizabeth, (d) Robert.

Mary Minor and Garland Anderson moved from Louisa to northern Kentucky. They had:

1. Mary O. Anderson.
2. Franklin Anderson.
3. Eliza Anderson.
4. Louisa Anderson.
5. Robert Semple Anderson of Gallatin, Tenn.
6. Peter Anderson of Montgomery County, Tenn., was father of: (a) Jack and (b) Minor Anderson.
7. Ellen Anderson of Nashville, "a lovely woman", married Hough.

From lineage of Meriwethers and Minors—by Minor Meriwether, Sally Minor and David Watson of "Bracketts", Green Springs, Louisa County, had issue:

1. James Watson, married Susan Morris, had one daughter, who married a Taylor.
2. Henry Paulett Watson, married Pauline Wills, moved to Christian County, Kentucky, had one daughter, Vivian, who married Mr. Robertson and lives at Demopolis, Ala.
3. Lewis Watson, married Magruder, and had eight children.
4. Shelton Watson, a guide in Arkansas, died unmarried.
5. George Watson, married Miss Duke, and had three children.
6. Thomas Watson, youngest, and in 1887, only living child of Sally and David Watson, married Miss Morris, twin sister of Mary W. Morris (wife of Dr. James Hunter Minor of "Music Hall"). Thomas lived at "Bracketts", died there, February 1895. His daughter, Ellen Morris Watson, married 1876, Thomas Barker Fergeson, son of Nanny Barker and Robert Fergeson.

Dr. James Minor and Pollie Watson (daughter of David Watson, Sr.), had issue:

1. Maria Minor, married Benjamin Magruder, and had:
   a. Henry Minor Magruder, married Sally (daughter of Franklin and Lucy Ann Gilmer Minor.)
2. Julia Anna Minor, married John Z. Holladay. She was last of the family to own "Sunning Hill". She had saved plank for a set of furniture and took it with her from place to place when refugeeing from the Yankees. As Thomas Watson said, "She displayed a regard for family trees." Three daughters were:
   a. Mary Minor Holladay, married Rev. James Allen Latine. There were eleven children. Thomas Watson remarked, "Eleven is the line of precedent". Old Garrett Minor, Mr. Watson, Mary Latine, Mary Barker, also Samuel O. Minor, had eleven children.
   b. Nanny Holladay, married Dr. Wilson Randolph of Charlottesville.
   c. Sally Watson Holladay, married Henry Johnston of Botetourt County.
3. Virginia Minor, married James H. Rawlings, one surviving child, Rev. James Minor Rawlings, married Helen Watson of Charlottesville, daughter of Judge Egbert Watson.

Elizabeth Minor and Col. Stapleton Crutchfield, had:

1. Sarah Elizabeth Crutchfield (1816-1884), married John James Young (?) (1814-1901).
   a. Susan Smith Young (1840-1905), married 1863, Charles de Lysle La Laude de Ferrière.
      1. Louise La Laude, married William Hoyt.

*Note.*—John A. G. Davis (died 1840, married Mary Jane Terrell, daughter of Richard and Martha Carr Terrell. Issue:

1. Eugene Davis.
2. Dr. John Staige Davis.
3. Rev. Dabney Cary Davis.
4. Rev. Richard Davis.
5. Caryetta Davis, married Robert C. Saunders of Bedford.
6. Lucy Davis.

END OF THE DESCENDANTS OF RICHMOND TERRELL.

## WILLIAM TERRELL

William Terrell of Hanover, died (1727) and Susan Elizabeth Mary Waters, said to be daughter of Earl Waters, had issue: (eight children)

A. William.

B. Timothy, married Elizabeth, daughter of John Foster, and had: (1) Eliza, (2) Mary, (3) Ann, (4) Joseph, (5) Joel, (6) Robert (1697-1786), married first, Mary Foster; married second, Judith Towles of Orange County, had: (a) Robert, (b) William, (c) Mary, (d) Sarah, (e) Ann, (f) John, married Elizabeth Towles, had Oliver and Susan Mallory, (g) Edward (1724-1784), Orange County, Va., married a daughter of Henry Willis, and had John Terrell of Missouri (1763-1830).

C. Joel, died 1758, had: (a) Major Henry Terrell, married Ann Dabney, (b) Joel Terrell.

D. John.

E. David, 1757, married Agatha Chiles, and had David (1729-1805), who had Edward, born 1753.

F. Henry, died 1764, married first, Ann Chiles, daughter of Micajah Chiles and his wife, who was daughter of Joel Terrell; married second, Sarah, daughter of Col. John Woodson and his wife, who was a Miss Pleasants. Issue first marriage: (1) Henry, born March 29, 1735, Caroline County, married Mary, daughter of Capt. Wm. Tyler, had John Terrell of Spottsylvania, died 1811. (2) Thomas (1736-1804), married Rebecca Peters, had Joseph, born 1777, married Sally Terrell, issue, Joseph (1812-1873), married Mary Anderson. (3) Elizabeth, married Zachary Moormau. (4) Ann, born 1740.

Henry Terrell, married second, Sarah Woodson, issue: (1) Ursula, born 1742. (2) Charles, born 1748, married Nan Tyler. (3) Judith, born 1750, married George Tyler. (4) Abigail, born 1751, married Capt. Wm. Durette of Caroline County. (5) George, born 1753.

*Note.*—Wm. Durette, married second, Mrs. Sarah Tilghman Connor, and one child of this marriage, Abigail, married George Tyler, son of George and Judith Terrell Tyler.

Issue of Abigail and Captain Durette: (1) Richard, married Kitty Tyler (first cousin). (2) Henry, married Mary Cammack. (3) Woodson, married Nancy Cammack. (4) Sally, married Lewis Terrell, son of Charles and Nan Tyler Terrell. (5) Pleasants, married Elizabeth Cunningham. (6) Tarleton, married Dorothy Tompkins. (7) Benjamin, died. (8) Judith, married Paul Connor. (9) Mildred, married 1813, Thomas Woolfolk (son of Samuel and Agatha Crutchfield Woolfolk of Caroline County), issue: (a) Mary Eliza Woolfolk, married 1839, John Llewellyn Lewis (see Zachary Lewis line), (b) William Samuel, (c) Ann Maria, (d) Thomas Addison Woolfolk. All died young.

G. James Terrell (son of William and Mary Waters Terrell).

H. Ann Terrell, died 1734, married David Lewis (1685-1779) of "Birdwood", Albemarle County, Va. He was son of John Lewis of Hanover.

Ann and David Lewis of "Birdwood", had:

William T. (1718-1802), married 1738, Sally Martin, moved to Surry County, N. C., lived in sight of Pilot Mountain. At beginning of the Revolution, applied to Governor Caswell of North Carolina for commissions for *all* his sons. 1781-3-6-8 he represented Surry County as member of General Assembly. Emigrated 1793 to Nashville. Had eleven children.

Susannah, born 1720, married Alexander Mackey.

Hannah, born 1722, married James Hickman.

Sarah, married Abraham Musick.

David, married Rebecca Stovall; second, Elizabeth Lockhart.

John, married Sarah Taliaferro; second, Susan Clarkson.

Joel, married first, Mary Trueman; second, Mrs. Gordon; third, Lucy Daniels.

Anna, married Joel Terrell; second, Stephen Willis (no issue).

(See *Lewis Family* by Wm. Terrell Lewis.)

Anna Lewis and her cousin, Joel Terrell, Jr. had among others, Richmond Terrell, married Cecilia Derracate of Virginia and Joel Terrell, married Martha Williams.

END THE DESCENDANTS OF WILLIAM TERRELL.

# POINDEXTER FAMILY

Extract from *Evening Post* of St. Helier, Jersey Island, October 31, 1910.

The tradition in the Poindexter family is that its founder in America came to Virginia in consequence of the Revocation of the Edict of Nantes.

The American Poindexters descend directly from the Grainville branch of the family in Jersey Island, owners for many centuries of the Manor House of Grainville. They have been land owners in Jersey since 1250 and residents since the earliest Norman times. In 1424, John Poingdestre (hence Poindexter) was civil governor of Jersey. His son, John Poindexter served in the same high office in 1447, and his grandson, another John in 1467. For five successive generations the head of the Poingdestre family in Jersey sat as Jurat of the Royal court of the Island until 1831. The Poingdestres were loyalists in the Cromwellian Wars. Some of them went to France and fought under Henry of Navarre.

*Virginia Historical Magazine and Biography,* Vols. 19 and 20. Vol. 19, No. 2, page 215.

## POINGDESTRE FAMILY

A gentle family of Jersey Island.

An Armorial of Jersey—and account Heraldick and Antiquarian—of the chief familie arms of this island yet used by these families.

### POINGDESTRE.

*Arms*—Per fesse argent—and or in chief a dexter hand clenched ppr. Cupped of the second in base a mullet of the first.

*Crest*—a Squiers helmet ppr.

Two mottos used by different branches of the family: first, *Nemo me impune lacessit;* second, *Dextra fidic pigmus.*

*Note.*—Mr. Mark Anthony Sower quotes a passage from Talbot's *Etymologis.* Under the head "Poindexter".

"This name does not signify" the right hand "but an old Norman name" "Signifying" "Spur the Steed" analogous to "Hotspur" coming from two old words from (the Latin *Purgo*) "fut to Spur". The second word—a steed or courser in French Destrier, Italian Destriere. Explanation curious and speculative.

On an outer wall of a house at Mont au Pectre formerly owned by the Poingdestres is the following sculptured arms. On a fesse between two roses—a mullet. Crest, a dexter arm clenched.

Poindexter Arms (America) Crest—Right hand mailed fist. Motto—*Nemo me impune lacessit.* (No one injuries me with impunity).

JERSEY ISLAND RECORDS

1250—Geoffery and Raul Poingdestre mentioned as land owners.

1424—John Poingdestre was Bailie of the Island of Jersey.

1452—His son, John Poingdestre was Bailie of Jersey.

1469—John Poingdestre III, grandson of John I occupied this post.

1485—John Poingdestre was Lieutenant Bailie, as was also his descendant—

1669—John Poingdestre.

This family for some generations owned the fief of Grainville in St. Saviors Parish, and has always held a high social position. An eminent member of it was John Poingdestre, born 1609, son of Edward Poingdestre. He was Fellow of Exeter College, Oxford, and one of the first to partake of the benefits of the Jersey scholarships. He had every quality to adorn private and public life and exercised them. He was one of the soundest Greek scholars of his day—and an adept in the penmanship of that language, and prepared for private use, texts of several Greek poets. He held official appointment under Lord Digby, Secretary of State to Charles I. He was deputed by Sir Charles Carteret to go to France to discuss the state of affairs with Charles II. He went into voluntary exile when the Royalists were expelled from the island, until the Restoration when he was made Lieutenant Bailie under Sir Edward Carteret—1669. He was buried in the church of St. Savior. His portrait was preserved at Grainville. He retained until his death, his seat as Jurat.

For five generations the head of this family sat as Jurat of the Royal Court of the island. The last one died 1831.

The eldest branch of this family represented by Edward Gibbs

Poingdestre of Grainville Manor. A Junior branch represented by Rev. George Poindexter.

Jersey Island Notes continued.

1309—Peter Poingdestre of the Parish of St. Savior.

1367 to 1389—John Poingdestre, one of the twelve jurats of the Royal Court of Jersey.

1419—John Poingdestre and Johanna, his wife, bought from St. Helier, widow of Pierre des Augres, the Fief de Moutier (or Mottier); this fief afterwards called Fief es Poingdestre, is situated in the Parish of St. John.

1450—John Poingdestre, one of the first Jurats of the Royal Court—probably the one who became Bailie of Jersey—that is President of the Royal Court—and of the States of Jersey (the highest civil officer).

John Poingdestre, Bailie of Jersey, 1452-1462-1464-1476.

1462-1500—John Poingdestre (son of John Poingdestre the Bailie), was, in 1462, Major of St. Saviors; also in 1462, was Lieutenant Bailie 1485-1486-1492. He was probably father of George Poingdestre—Siegneur of the Fief es Poingdestre.

## PEDIGREE OF POINGDESTRE OF GRAINVILLE

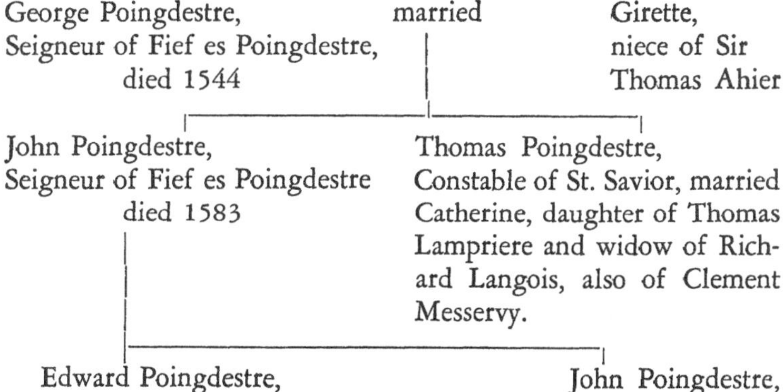

George Poingdestre, Seigneur of Fief es Poingdestre, died 1544 married Girette, niece of Sir Thomas Ahier

John Poingdestre, Seigneur of Fief es Poingdestre died 1583

Thomas Poingdestre, Constable of St. Savior, married Catherine, daughter of Thomas Lampriere and widow of Richard Langois, also of Clement Messervy.

Edward Poingdestre,

John Poingdestre,

Seigneur of Fief es Poingdestre, married first, Margaret, dau. of Clement Messervy; married second, Pauline, daughter of Guyon Ahier.

m. Perroline, dau. of Peter Laell.

Issue by second marriage:

John Poingdestre, b. 1609. M. A. Fellow of Exeter College, Oxford; Lieutenant Bailie of Jersey. Married Ann, dau. and co-heiress of Laurens Hamptonne, Viscount of Jersey.

Thomas, b. 1613, Rector of St. Savior m. Mary, dau. and co-heiress of James Ripon

Edward

Mary, married Richard Ansley

Issue by first marriage:

Thomas Poingdestre, b. 1581, Seigneur Fief es Poingdestre, married Elizabeth, dau. —— Efford.

Philip Poingdestre, Seigneur Fief es Poingdestre, m. Sarah, dau. Rev. John Pinel.

Jacob, m. and had John, Thomas and Mary, who married G. Nicolle.

George settled in Va.

Rachel

Edward Poingdestre, Seigneur Fief es Poingdestre, m. Susan, dau. and co-heiress of Peter Poingdestre.

Philip

Sarah

*Virginia Historical Magazine,* Vol. 19.

THE POINDEXTERS OF VIRGINIA.

George Poindexter (Emigrant) settled at the Middle Plantation (Williamsburg) in the seventeenth century. Destruction of the records of New Kent and James City counties and almost total destruction of those of Hanover prevent a connected genealogy of various branches of Poindexters, but such official and private papers as we can find, furnish what record we can find of them.

Members of this family settled before the Revolution in half a dozen different counties of Virginia and this name now has representatives throughout the United States from the Atlantic to the Pacific.

The original name as given in the Jersey Island records as Poingdestre and Poindestre—is Poindexter in America.

Fortunately the name of George Poindexter is preserved in the Jersey Record, entitled: "An Armorial of Jersey Heraldic and Antiquarian", of its chief families and their arms. A further record in this book states he came to America.

The Virginia Poindexters acquired most of their lands by purchase and not by land grants.

March 16, 1675.

George Poindexter and George Thompson acquired 350 acres in Gloucester County.

September 27, 1739.

John Poindexter purchases 1,000 acres in Hanover County.

July 20, 1738.

John Poindexter purchases 400 acres in Hanover County.

February 12, 1742.

400 acres in Goochland County acquired by Philip Poindexter.

September 10, 1755.

Philip Poindexter acquired 400 acres in Lunenburg County, on Meherren River and Juniper Creek.

August 16, 1756.

John Poindexter purchased 400 acres in Louisa County.

George Poindexter acquired land in Middle Plantation, January 8, 1667.

April 1673, certificate given George Poindexter for persons imported, one of whom was Susannah Poindexter.

York County Records No. 4, Virginia State Library—Middleton Parish—Peter Efford agrees with George Poindexter about a farm, etc., April 1, 1664.

July 1689, John Poindexter and wife, Katharine, convey land

to John Layton, a part of which had been given John by his father, George Poindexter.

At the close of the 17th century the Poindexters moved from York County to Kent County, the immigrant still living, 1688 (St. Peter's Vestry Book, May 4, 1689), names of three children are George II, John, married Katharine, and Elizabeth.

George Poindexter II, died 1716 (*William and Mary Quarterly,* Vol. II, page 207), married Susannah, daughter of Benskin Marston, had George and John.

George Benskin Poindexter, married first, July 17, 1760, Frances Lightfoot. He married second, March 20, 1777, Sarah Parke (New Kent County). He himself entered the following births on the register, May 18, 1790, stating that he was then in his fifty-fifth year.

Issue by first marriage:

1. Edwin, born July 10, 1762.
2. Robert, born February 23, 1765.
3. George, born March 29, 1767.
4. James, born January 7, 1770.
5. Lightfoot, born October 20, 1772.
6. Armistead, born May 14, 1775.

Issue by the second marriage:

7. Susannah, born May 3, 1778.
8. Parke, born March 12, 1779, married Eliza Jones Archer.
9. Frances, born September 17, 1781.

Parke and Eliza Archer Poindexter had six children:

A. Sarah Parke Poindexter, born December 6, 1818, married June 2, 1836, Richard W. Flournoy, and had:

1. Eliza Flournoy, married Dr. Alex.
2. Samuel Flournoy, senator, West Virginia.
3. Richard W. Flournoy.
4. Ellen Flournoy, married McCarthy Thornton.

B. Frances Poindexter, born August 26, 1820, married, May 15, 1839, Robert C. Anderson, and had:

1. Robert Anderson.
2. Margaret Anderson.

3. Eliza. Parke Anderson.
4. Henning Anderson.
5. Harry Anderson.

C. Eliza Claiborne Poindexter, born April 25, 1822, married April 25, 1843, Thomas F. Perkins, and had:
1. William Merry Perkins.
2. Mildred Perkins, second wife of Judge Thomas Dew. Issue given.
3. Parke P. Perkins, married Major William Bentley, had a daughter, Sarah.

D. George W., died young.

E. Robert, died young.

F. Parke Poindexter, born September 5, 1826, died October 27, 1863 from wounds received April 24, at Suffolk, Va. Was Lieutenant-Colonel C. S. A. of Fourteenth Virginia Regiment, which he and Major Clay Drewry clothed and presented to the State. His only child, Parke Poindexter, married November 27, 1890, Willis B. Smith. They have: Frances Smith and Mary Sterling Smith.

Mildred Perkins and Judge Thomas Dew had:

a. Lucy, died young.

b. Dr. Thomas Welch Dew, married 1907, Alice Dew, and has:
1. Thomas R., died young.
2. Robert W. Dew.
3. Joseph Dew.
4. Alice Dew.
5. Juliet Dew.
6. William, died young.
7. Thomas Dew.

c. Minnie Dew, married John Boyd Washington, and has:
1. Dr. Thomas Boyd Washington, married.
2. Katharine Washington, married Mr. Vaughan, has a son and a daughter.

d. Parke Dew, married Gray Brokenborough, and has:
   1. Mildred Brokenborough.
   2. Maxwell Brokenborough.

e. Kate Dew, married Judge Robert Waller, and has:
   1. Nannie Waller.
   2. Robert Waller.

END OF DESCENDANTS OF GEORGE BENSKIN POINDEXTER.

## JOHN POINDEXTER

John, another son of George Poindexter II, married Christian ——. He lived near Gold Mine Creek, owned large estates, was prominent in church and county affairs, vestryman in Frederickville Parish 1732, was one of the first Justices of Louisa County, Virginia, December 13, 1742. His will was dated January 10, 1753, and was proved May 22, 1753. Christian's will was dated June 25, 1778, and was proved June 14, 1779. She mentions three daughters, also her grandson, William, Jr.

Issue: (five sons and three daughters)

I. Thomas Poindexter, born in Louisa, Justice of Louisa 1766, died in Franklin County, Ky. His will was dated July 15, 1796. He married Lucy Jones of Culpeper County, Va., daughter of Gabriel Jones, Captain in the Navy during the Revolution.

II. John Poindexter left Louisa 1790, and moved to Bedford, later to Campbell County. He was father of Ann G. Poindexter, who married Robert Cobbs, and of Mary Poindexter who married Charles Slaughter.

III. William Poindexter.

IV. Richard Poindexter died before 1778, had two children who are mentioned in his mother's will—Christian and Feby.

V. Joseph Poindexter, born 1736, died June 29, 1826, was a captain in the Revolution. He married, February 10, 1768, Elizabeth Jane Kennerly, who died February 5, 1828, aged

82 years. They moved 1790 to Bedford, later to Campbell County.

VI. Frances Anderson.
VII. Ann Slaughter.
VIII. Sally Triton.
} Daughters mentioned in Christian's will.

Thomas and Lucy Poindexter, had issue:

A. Rev. John Poindexter, clerk of Louisa, 1766 to September 28, 1819, which was the day of his death. He was for thirty years a prominent county and court official, having a large record as writer of wills and deeds, was of a decided character, of strong and vigorous intellect. In 1792 he was ordaine;d minister of the Baptist church and served actively for twenty-five years. He married first, Ann Green, daughter of Col. William Green, and had a son, William Green Poindexter, who married Jane Quarles. The Rev. John married second, Miss Elizabeth Johnson, descended from Ann Meriwether and Thomas Johnson of Colonial service. The Rev. John married third, 1813, Margaret Maer of North Carolina, who had one daughter, Mrs. Frances E. Thompson.

B. James Poindexter died in Louisa 1843, was Justice of Peace, member of Baptist church. He married first, Miss Wyatt. No issue. He married second, Miss West, and had a son, James West Poindexter, who married Miss W. of Charlottesville, and left a son, Charles, who was a druggist.

C. Thomas Poindexter, born May 25, 1760, died in Louisa, April 10, 1843, married March 28, 1790, Sally Ragland, born June 6, 1769, died February 10, 1857. Issue given later.

D. Richard Jones Poindexter, Baptist minister, moved to North Carolina. His son, Elder Abram M. Poindexter, born September 22, 1809 in Bertie County, N. C., became a distinguished Baptist minister, died in Orange County, Va., and left two grandchildren, Abram P. Taylor and Dr. James Boyce Taylor.

E. Gabriel Poindexter, born May 8, 1758, died August 28, 1831 in Floyd County, Indiana, married in Virginia, Mary Swift.

A great-grandson is Charles E. Poindexter of Jeffersonville, Indiana.

F. George Poindexter, born 1779 at Louisa, lived for a time at Milton, Albemarle, moved to Mississippi while it was yet a territory. He was Aide to Jackson at Battle of New Orleans, was Attorney-General of Mississippi, Governor of Mississippi 1819-21, U. S. Senator 1831-5, died September 5, 1853 at Jackson, Mississippi.

G. Lucy Jones Poindexter.

H. Robert Poindexter, moved to Kentucky.

I. Elizabeth Poindexter, married Christopher Carmack and moved to Franklin County, Ky.

J. Mollie Cosby, whose heirs are mentioned in the will of Thomas Poindexter, Sr.—Garland Cosby, Stith Cosby, Nicholas Cosby, and Francis Cosby.

## DESCENDANTS OF REV. JOHN POINDEXTER

1. William Green Poindexter (son of the first marriage), married Jane Quarles of "Cherry Grove", Spotsylvania County, Va. Her mother was Frances Vivian.

   Issue: (seven children)

   a. Dr. William Quarles Poindexter married first, Ann E. Holladay and moved to Mississippi. He married second, Ellen Lynch.

      Issue by first marriage:

      1. William Green Poindexter, married 1863, Martha Morgan.
      2. Waller Poindexter, died unmarried.
      3. Jane Frances Lewis Poindexter, died young.

      Issue by second marriage:

      4. Sedley Poindexter, died unmarried.
      5. Henry Poindexter, died unmarried.
      6. An infant.

b. John Green Poindexter, married Miss Poindexter. They had:
   1. Charles R. Poindexter, married Molly Streator.
   2. Junius Poindexter, unmarried.
   3. Helen Poindexter, unmarried.
   4. John Green Poindexter, unmarried.
   5. Frances Ann Poindexter, married A. B. Carrol. They had:
      a. A. B. Carrol, has children in Liberty, Miss.
      b. William Holmes Carrol, has Charles and Nolan.
   6. Mary Poindexter, married Mr. Pruden of Tennessee.

c. Patsy Quarles Poindexter, married Hon. Alexander Holladay of Richmond, Va. (See Holladay record.)

d. Sarah Poindexter, married Mr. Johnson, and had four children:
   1. William H. Johnson, married first, Harriet Perkins; married second, Lou McGehee.
   2. George Johnson (hurt in the storm), married Miss Foster.
   3. Helen Johnson.
   4. Vivian Johnson, married.

e. James Nicholas Poindexter, born November, 1810, at "Cherry Grove", married and had George, who was killed in the storm, and Molly. He married second, Margaret Jane Perkins, and had six children, who are given later.

f. Frances Poindexter, died young.

g. Henry Pleasants Poindexter, unmarried.

William Green and Martha Morgan Poindexter, had issue: eight children, died young then:

a. Aida Poindexter, married T. H. Baird, had one daughter, Elizabeth.

b. William Green Poindexter, married Pauline Scott, and has:
   1. William Green Poindexter.
   2. Lewis Scott Poindexter, and
   3. Mildred Poindexter, twins.

c. Ann Elizabeth Poindexter, married Clive Metcalf, and had:
  1. Martha Metcalf, married.
  2. Albert Metcalf, married Ruth ——.
  3. Ann Metcalf, married Mr. Clark.

d. Sally Morgan Poindexter, died 1926, married Dr. Clement Jordan, and had:
  1. Clement Jordan, married.
  2. Robert Jordan.
  3. Sally Jordan.

James Nicholas Poindexter and his second wife, Margaret Jane Perkins had:

1. Frances Quarles Poindexter, married Gordon G. Sims, and had:
   a. Alice P. Sims, married Mr. Stiles, and had:
      1. E. P. Stiles.
      2. J. G. Stiles.
   b. Hallie P. Sims, married S. A. Eggleston, had:
      1. Hallie Eggleston.
      2. Frances Eggleston.
      3. Sarah Eggleston.
2. Alice Poindexter, married John M. Chilton, and had:
   a. St. John Chilton.
   b. Courtnaye Chilton.
3. Mary Ann Poindexter, married William Britton, and had:
   a. Herbert Britton.
   b. Mamie Britton.
   c. William Britton, married Ellen Ward of Memphis, and had:
      1. William Britton.
      2. George Britton.
      3. A daughter.
4. Herbert Poindexter, died.
5. Margaret Jane Poindexter, died.
6. Hallie Perkins Poindexter, married W. B. Ricks, and had:
   a. W. B. Ricks.

b. Ben S. Ricks.
c. Herbert P. Ricks, married Miss Smith, and had three children:
    1. Hallie Ricks.
    2. Carol Ricks.
    3. Vivian Q. Ricks, married Louise Powell, and has three children:
        a. Sarah Ricks.
        b. Frances Ricks.
        c. John Ricks, married Marie Reed, and has two children:
            1. John P. Ricks.
            2. Catharine Ricks.
d. John P. Ricks.
e. f. g. Three children, who died young.

Rev. John Poindexter and Elizabeth Johnson, who was his second wife. Issue:

1. Nicholas Poindexter went to Kentucky. One of his descendants is George Gilmer Poindexter.
2. John Poindexter went to Kentucky.
3. Thomas, married Miss Frances Schooler, sister of Rice Schooler of Caroline County.
4. Andrew Poindexter, died.
5. Waller Poindexter, married Miss Talley of Goochland County, and went to Kentucky.
6. Lucy Jones Poindexter.
7. Mary Poindexter, married Garrett Quarles.

Thomas Poindexter was a lawyer in New Orleans, was heir to "Aunt Quarles" of Virginia and Tennessee. He died in New Orleans and is buried at Woodville, Miss. His wife, Frances Schooler Poindexter, was killed in the storm in Mississippi. They had three children:

a. William Rice Poindexter had an institute for young ladies in Macon, Miss. He married first, Martha Barnett, "a lovely lady." He married second, Addie S. Brother.

b. Mildred Poindexter taught music in her brother's school. She had a scar from the storm.
c. Dr. John Poindexter moved to Arkansas.

Children of William Rice Poindexter:

1. Thomas Poindexter, died infant.
2. Frances Poindexter.
3. John Quarles Poindexter, married Georgia Lucinda Richards, and had:
    a. Mattie Poindexter.
    b. Orrin Poindexter.
    c. Barnett Poindexter.
    d. Ethel Poindexter, married W. G. Mullen, has William, Andrew and John Mullen.
4. Willie Matt Poindexter, died young.
5. Rice Schooler Poindexter.
6. Edwin Poe Poindexter.
7. Weenonah Van Hice Poindexter, child of second marriage.

THIS ENDS THE RECORD OF DESCENDANTS OF REV. JOHN POINDEXTER.

## THOMAS POINDEXTER

Son of Thomas and Lucy Jones Poindexter, was a farmer of strong and vigorous intellect. In 1790, he married Sally Ragland. Issue:

1. Lucy J. Poindexter, born July 21, 1791, died November 30, 1827, unmarried.
2. Polly Poindexter, born February 11, 1793, died November 22, 1820, married January 15, 1818, Colin Johnson, who was born December 7, 1786.
3. Patsy Poindexter, born October 25, 1794, died April 3, 1875, married Garland Lilly. Whence Thomas Lilly of Louisa.
4. Dr. William Ragland Poindexter, born March 9, 1796, died July 20, 1822 at Woodville, Miss.
5. Thomas Poindexter, born April 19, 1798, died February 7, 1851, married Eliza Burton. Three children lived at his old home, "Waverly", near Belleview in Bedford. They were:

Mrs. Sally West, Mrs. Maggie Moore, and Jenny Poindexter, unmarried.

6. Sally R. Poindexter, born December 27, 1799, died February 10, 1837, married Nathaniel Perkins.
7. James L. Poindexter, born July 1, 1801, died June 29, 1853, married M. A. Callaway.
8. Anna Lipscomb Poindexter, born July 5, 1803, died November 22, 1836, married January 9, 1822, William Smelt Winston, who was born October 12, 1796.
9. George Poindexter, born March 8, 1805, died May 12, 1837.
10. Louisa Poindexter, born February 12, 1807, died August 29, 1840, unmarried.
11. Henry Poindexter, born August 1, 1812, died January 4, 1843.
12. Samuel Ragland Poindexter, born September 13, 1818, died March 23, 1853 at Vicksburg.
13. John Jones Poindexter, born August 19, 1816, died July 12, 1837.
14. Edward Poindexter, born July 7, 1814, died April 15, 1851. He was greatly respected in Louisa for his sense, character, and management.

THIS ENDS THE RECORD OF THE DESCENDANTS OF THOMAS POINDEXTER.

## CAPT. JOSEPH POINDEXTER

Capt. Joseph, son of John and Christian Poindexter, married Elizabeth Jane Kennerly, daughter of James Kennerly. Issue:

A. Samuel Poindexter, married first, 1790, Ann Poindexter Slaughter, daughter of Reuben and Bettie Poindexter Slaughter. This Reuben was probably a son of Col. Francis and Ann Lightfoot Slaughter. Samuel married second, Sarah Garth of Albemarle County. He married third, Martha Otey, daughter of James Otey of Kentucky, no issue.

Issue by first marriage:

1. Dabney Poindexter, born November 17, 1791, died

September 27, 1848, married Mary Elizabeth Watts, daughter of James Watts.

2. James Poindexter, married Susan Shelton.
3. John Poindexter, married Miss Robinson.
4. Caroline Poindexter, married Mr. White.

Issue by second marriage:

5. Garland Poindexter, married Julia Bingham.
6. Willis Poindexter, married Emily Slaughter.
7. Samuel Poindexter, married Ann Tucker, September 4, 1844.

B. James Poindexter, born November 6, 1765, married December 4, 1794, Mary Thomson, born May 21, 1770, daughter of Waddy and Mary Lewis Cobbs Thomson.

C. Joseph Poindexter, married Mrs. Harrison.

D. William Poindexter, died 1834, married 1798, Judith Thomson, who was also a daughter of Waddy and Mary L. C. Thomson. (See Thomson record for seven children.)

E. Reuben Poindexter.

F. Thomas Kennerly Poindexter, married Mrs. Mary Rall Kennerly, moved to South Carolina and left descendants.

G. John Poindexter, married Miss Chilton.

H. Louis Poindexter, married Ann Smith.

I. Ann Poindexter, married John Chilton of Amherst County.

J. Elizabeth Poindexter, married Raleigh Chilton.

K. Richard Poindexter, married Miss Ford, moved West.

Issue of Dabney and Mary E. Watts Poindexter:

a. David Durrett Poindexter, born September 11, 1820, married November 8, 1849, Ann Poindexter.

b. Sarah W. Poindexter, born February 5, 1822, married October 4, 1843, William Gills.

c. Richard W. Poindexter, born October 8, 1823, married first, 1849, Mary Elizabeth Durrett; married second, 1865, Mary Ellen Lee, daughter of John Calhoun and Catharine Newell Lee. Issue given below.

d. Caroline E. Poindexter, born October 6, 1825, married March 8, 1844, Asa Gills.
e. James W. Poindexter, born November 3, 1827, married January 5, 1858, Sophia Nicholls.
f. Samuel Thomas Poindexter, born August 30, 1829, died 1904, married October 31, 1876, Benjie James Hughes, had one child, Walker Watts Poindexter of Lynchburg.
g. Pauline Ann Poindexter, born May 3, 1832, married October 4, 1849, Joseph Hardy.
h. Frances Susan Poindexter, born May 17, 1835, married Joseph Rucker.
i. Mary Eliza Poindexter, born June 3, 1838, married Charles Hardy.
j. William Dabney Poindexter, born November 29, 1843, married Mary Jeter.

Children of Richard Poindexter by his first marriage:

1. Elizabeth Mildred Poindexter, married Edward Gills.
2. Hugh Davis Poindexter, married Frances Poindexter.
3. Elijah Poindexter, never married.

Children by his second marriage:

4. Cora Lee Poindexter, married Richard Haden Penn.
5. Lula Bell Poindexter, married Glenmore Torch Browne of Georgia.
6. Mary Richard Poindexter, married Charles Lewis Watts.
7. Richard Newell Poindexter, married Daisy Byrd Long of Alabama.
8. John Samuel Poindexter, married Eller Sharp of Tennessee.
9. Dabney Thomas Poindexter.

Issue of Samuel and Anna Maria Tucker Poindexter:

a. Sarah Ann Poindexter, born February 21, 1845.
b. Mary Elizabeth Poindexter, born October 28, 1851, married July 9, 1874, John H. Isbell of Appomattox, and had:
    1. Aubrey Tucker Isbell, married Emma Conway of Texas, and has a daughter, Elizabeth.
    2. Cleora Isbell, married Fauntleroy Lambert of Staunton, Virginia.

c. Rosa Ellen Poindexter, born June 27, 1854.

d. Virginia Tucker Poindexter, born September 5, 1855, married James Woodson Jones, and has:

   1. Edna Earle Jones.
   2. Reginal Fairfax Jones, U. S. Navy, Pacific Fleet.
   3. John Dillard Jones.

e. William Samuel Poindexter, born July 27, 1858, died October 15, 1897. He married first, Alma Imogen Phelps on October 7, 1884. He married second, November 17, 1895, Lula Barksdale. Issue given below.

f. —— Poindexter, born July 16, 1861.

g. Robert Lee Poindexter, born July 25, 1865, married Effie Woolwine of Pearisburg, Va. They had:

   1. William Donwreath Poindexter.
   2. Robert Lee Poindexter, Jr.

Children of William Samuel Poindexter by his first marriage:

1. William Samuel Poindexter, born November 17, 1885.
2. Jefferson Ward Poindexter, born September 7, 1887.
3. Ernest Lee Poindexter.
4. Carl Tucker Poindexter, born June 7, 1890.
5. Frank Poindexter.
6. Alma Terrell Poindexter, born July 28, 1893.
7. Frederick Augustus Poindexter, born September 17, 1894.
8. Barksdale Poindexter, born October 6, 1896 (son of second marriage.)

Children of James Poindexter and Mary Thomson, married: 1794:

1. Lewis Thomson Poindexter, born August 30, 1795.
2. Edwin Waddy Poindexter, born June 23, 1797.
3. Josephus Poindexter, born February 19, 1798.
4. James Poindexter, died infant.
5. Robert Warner Poindexter, born June 14, 1801, died February 3, 1871.

6. Albert Gallatin Poindexter, born March 12, 1803, died June 9, 1833.
7. Mary Elizabeth Poindexter, born November 16, 1805, married Mr. Gamewell.
8. Nicholas Meriwether Poindexter, born September 24, 1807.
9. Hartland Poindexter, born May 27, 1811.
10. James Monroe Poindexter, born August 25, 1815.

Further record supplied by Mrs. Irene M. Poindexter of Long Beach, California.

Robert Warner Poindexter married three times: first, Margaret Caldwell, born 1806, died 1845; second, Isabella Rintoul, born January 30, 1821, died May 5, 1852; third, Mary Wotring, born June 20, 1824, married 1860. She had no children.

Children by first marriage:

a. Theodore Poindexter (1827-1854), married Ann Liggett Wetherill.
b. Orlando Poindexter, died young.
c. Charles Poindexter, died young.
d. Cordelia Poindexter, born December 20, 1835, married 1861, Alexander Quail.
e. Helene Poindexter, married 1866, Erskin Carson.
f. Francis Herron Poindexter (1842-1898), married 1865, Anna B. Moody, and had a son, Theodore Poindexter.

Children by second marriage:

g. Chalmers Poindexter (1847-1906).
h. Robert Warner Poindexter, Jr., born June 29, 1849, died November 4, 1927. Married first Amy Robsart Marston; second, Madeline R. Wade.

Robert Warner Poindexter had by his first marriage a son, Charles, who married Cornelia Richert. The children of the second marriage were:

1. Romaine Le Moyne Poindexter, born 1889.
2. Robert Wade Poindexter, born 1887, married February 5, 1916, Irene Mersereau. They have:
    a. John Daniel Poindexter, born 1916.
    b. Romaine Le Moyne Poindexter, born 1919.
    c. Robert Warner Poindexter, born 1923.

d. William Mersereau Poindexter, born June 16, 1925.

END OF THE RECORD OF CAPT. JOSEPH POINDEXTER, SENIOR OF BEDFORD COUNTY, VIRGINIA.

List of Revolutionary soldiers—State Library, Virginia:

POINDEXTERS—Gabriel, Jacob, John, Jonathan, Capt. Joseph, Bedford County Militia, Level (or Love), Richard C.

## GREEN FAMILY

Robert Green, son of William Green, an Englishman, born 1695, emigrated 1710 from Ireland to Virginia with his uncle, Wm. Duff, settled in Culpeper, had large grants of land also in Essex, Spotsylvania and Orange. Member of Virginia House of Burgesses 1736, one of first vestrymen of St. Mark's Parish. Married Eleanor Dunn, a Scotchwoman, had seven sons:

A. William, married Miss Coleman of Caroline County. Issue:
   1. William, Jr., married Eliza, daughter of his uncle Duff. She moved to Kentucky after his death.
   2. Ellen, married Peter Mayre.
   3. Betsy, married H. Camp.
   4. Mary, married George Thomas.
   5. Millie, married Streniger.
   6. Nancy, married John Poindexter.
   7. Frances W., married Levy Strother, moved to Kentucky.

B. Robert, married Pattie Ball of Northumberland. Issue:
   1. William, married Miss Blackwell, moved to Kentucky.
   2. Armistead, married Frances, daughter of Capt. Henry Pendleton of Culpeper County.
   3. Samuel B., married Miss Blackwell of Port Royal, Va.
   4. Ellen, married Aaron Lane of Culpeper.
   5. Anne, married Dr. Joel Gustin of Pennsylvania.

C. Duff, married first, Miss Thomas; second, Annie Willis, who died 1820, Danville, Va. Her tombstone is yet to be seen at Old Reed Fort.

She was daughter of Col. Henry Willis and his third wife, Mildred Washington. Her grandson, Judge John Green, married Sally Fry, granddaughter of Dr. Thomas Walker and his wife, Mildred Thornton Meriwether Walker of "Castle Hill", Albemarle County, Va. Children of Duff Green given in *Green's Culpeper*:

1. Bettie, married her cousin, William Green.
2. Willis, married Sarah Reed, moved to Kentucky.
3. William, married Marshall, moved to Kentucky.
4. Ellen, married John Smith, moved to Kentucky. Issue: John, Henry, Willis.

D. John—House of Burgesses 1769, Col. in Revolution, married Susannah Blackwell. Issue:

1. William—Capt. U. S. Navy, lost his life in brig *Defiance,* married Lucy Williams.
2. John, killed in duel.
3. Robert, married Frances Edmonds.
4. Moses, married Fannie Richards.
5. Thomas, married first, Miss Miller; second, Lucy Peyton, moved to Christian County, Ky.

E. Nicholas, married Elizabeth Price, daughter of Argola Price of Orange County. Issue:

1. Robert, died unmarried.
2. John, married Jennie Hawkins.
3. William, moved to Tennessee.
4. Nicholas.
5. Mary, married Stephen.
6. Lucy.
7. Eleanor, married Rankin.
8. Joice, married Willis Ballance, went to Kentucky.

F. James, married Elizabeth Jones. Issue:

1. Gabriel, married, went to Kentucky.
2. James, married Betsy Jones.
3. Jones, married Miss Neville, went to Kentucky.

4. Robert, married Miss Edmonds, had: a. Wm., b. James, c. Thomas, d. Fannie, e. Ellen, f. Eliza, g. ——, married Cross.
5. John, married Miss Catlett, went to Kentucky.
6. Dolly, married Nimrod Farrow.
7. Elizabeth, married Rev. R. W. Peacock, moved to England.
8. Lucy, married Noah R. Glascock, moved to Missouri.
9. Polly, married Catlett.

G. Moses, married Mary Blackwell, sister of his brother John's wife. Issue:

1. Sarah, died unmarried.
2. Elizabeth, married Gen. James Williams.

## IVERSON LEWISES

### JOHN LEWIS

John Lewis, son of Zachary Lewis I, was born 1704, and inherited the old Lewis homestead in King and Queen County where he lived and died. Like his brother, Zachary II, he was an eminent lawyer.

General tradition says he married Sarah Iverson and the name, Iverson is so persistant in every line of his descendants that this seems circumstantial evidence. Hon. John C. Underwood of Kentucky states in his *Rogers History* that Sarah Iverson was John Lewis's mother and that his wife was Katherine Booker. But the name, Iverson, is unknown in the descendants of Zachary Lewis II, who hold the tradition that she was the wife of John Lewis. Neither does Iverson appear in the family of John Lewis, the Planter, of Scottsville, Albemarle County, who however, retained the Zachary, and through their ancestor, Owen Lewis, claim relationship to the Welsh family of Zachary Lewis.

Zachary Lewis had daughters, but my efforts to trace them have failed. Some old letters from Rev. Iverson Lewis and his sons, Dr. William and Dr. John Lewis mention various ladies, but the ceremonious manners of that day simply presume them already well known to Dr. Richmond Lewis.

Mr. Samuel Rogers Twyman, of Buckingham County has kindly

given me a partial record of the Lewis and Rogers line—a list of the children of John Lewis and of Rev. Iverson, as found in a record furnished him by a cousin, Gen. John C. Underwood, of Kentucky.

Unfortunately I did not see the copy of the Richmond paper in 1927 in which this Lewis line was given and for further record rely upon the meager list given in *The Genealogy of Lewis Families* by Wm. Terrell Lewis, and in *The History of Albemarle.*

John Lewis, born 1704, married Sarah Iverson (or Katherine Booker). Issue:

I. Sarah Lewis, born 1729, married Rev. Edward Byrne, of King and Queen County. She died in Burke County, Ga. Issue:

  A. Ann Byrne, married Augustus Harris.

  B. (A daughter), married Moses Walker, of Brunswick County, Va.

  C. Thomas Byrne.

  D. Lewis Byrne.

  E. Richard Byrne.

II. William Lewis, born 1732, married 1759, Hannah Underwood, daughter of Thomas William Underwood, of Hanover County. They resided in Goochland County, and had issue:

III. Katherine Lewis, born 1733, married Mr. Richards, and had:

  A. Elizabeth Richards, married Mr. Watts.

  B. Nancy Ann Richards, married Mr. Dunn, and had:

    1. Thomas Iverson Dunn.

IV. Christopher Lewis, born 1735, married in South Carolina, a relative of Gen. Wade Hampton. Issue:

  A. Sarah Iverson Lewis, married Mr. Oliver, of Louisiana.

  B. John Christopher Lewis, married Miss Wardlaw, of Abbeville, South Carolina. Issue:

    1. Mrs. Scott, of Augusta, Ga.

    2. Mrs. ——, of Barnville, S. C.

    3. Oscar Lewis, m. Miss Boyston in Louisiana.

4. Andrew W. Lewis.
5. David Lewis, railroad agent, Augusta, Ga.
6. —— Lewis, a mechanic.

V. Ann Iverson Lewis (probably Sarah Ann), born 1737, died January 1816, married 1757-8, Giles Rogers (born 1719, died 1794), who was son of John Rogers and Mary Byrd, daughter of William Byrd I, of "Westover". Ann Lewis and G. Rogers moved from King and Queen to Albemarle County, where they lived to raise a large family and died in the Buck Mountain section.

Descendants—Walkers, Rogers, Twymans, Buckners, Eddins, Kinsolvings, and others.

VI. Rev. Iverson Lewis, born March 4, 1741, died January 5, 1815 in King and Queen County. He was educated in the established church of his day but was immersed 1770, and became a Baptist preacher. He married three times—first, Frances Byrd; second, Martha Clopton; third, Catherine Byrd of the King and Queen family of that name. He had a number of children by each of these marriages.

VII. Robert Lewis, born 1744 (no authentic record.)

REV. IVERSON LEWIS lived at the family residence in King and Queen. He was educated in the Established Church of his day but when quite young became interested in the preaching of Rev. John Waller, a noted Baptist minister. In 1772 he went on a visit to relatives in Mathews County and having lately, through earnest searching of the Scripture, obtained a hope of salvation zealously realized the necessity of vital religion wherever he went. His conversation made much impression and the rumor arose that a new preacher had come. This drew a crowd to the house where he was staying, to hear him preach. He had not preached before this and felt alarm, but relying upon divine aid addressed the people. God opened their hearts and they received His doctrine. Mr. Lewis not long after this became a Baptist preacher, and though forty miles off, visited this Mathews church once a month for some years. Pettsworth Church (sometimes called Ware's), and Abington in Guinea Peninsula, Gloucester, originated in his preaching.

Rev. Iverson Lewis is said to have had the "gift of exhortation." "He was so mild, so gentle and so dignified, with so much heavenly simplicity that all were struck with him as a man and as a Christian and were at once disarmed of their enmity to religion and felt a reverence for his character." (Semple's *History of Baptists in Virginia.*)

Issue of Rev. Iverson Lewis and his first wife, Frances Byrd:

A. Ann Lewis, married Jonathon Brooks, of Caswell County, North Carolina. Issue:
   1. Rev. Iverson L. Brooks, of Abbeville, S. C.
   2. George Brooks.
   3. Thomas Brooks.
   4. William L. Brooks.
   5. John L. Brooks.

B. Dr. William B. Lewis, graduate of William and Mary College, Virginia, member of Medical College, Edinboro, Scotland. He received a diploma in literature and medicine signed by twenty-four professors—among them some of the most distinguished names known to the literary world—such as Ferguson, Blair, Robertson, Dugald, Steward, Greenfield, Playfair, Dalzel, Hume, etc.

   After returning home he practised with great reputation at the head of the medical profession for four years in Eastern Virginia and died through exposure; never married. (Dr. Richmond Lewis was a student under direction of this cousin before going to the medical college in Philadelphia.)

C. Frances Lewis, married Solomon Graves, of North Carolina. Issue: (seven children)
   1. William B. Graves, of Randolph County, Ga.
   2. John D. Graves, of Texas.
   3. Frances L. Graves, married Dr. W. P. Graham.
   4. Soloman Graves.
   5. Iverson L. Graves.
   6. Gen. B. Graves, of Randolph County, Ga.
   7. Sydney Graves, died young.

D. Joanna Lewis, married James Dickey, and had issue: (seven children)

1. William Dickey.
2. Ann Dickey, married McGrasley, of Nelson County, Va.
3. Frances Dickey, married John W. Watkins, of King and Queen County, Va.
4. Jonathan Dickey, married Miss Daniel, of Middlesex.
5. Ann Dickey, married Col. Mason, of Middlesex.
6. Marion Dickey, unmarried.
7. Elizabeth Dickey, unmarried.

E. Dr. John Lewis, son of Rev. Iverson Lewis, and his first wife, Frances Byrd; died of yellow fever on shipboard a few days after leaving Norfolk for Europe. Never married.

Issue of Rev. Iverson Lewis by second marriage to Martha Clopton:

F. Dr. Zachary Lewis was for some years a demonstrator of anatomy in the Medical College of Philadelphia, later practiced medicine in King and Queen County.

He often visited "Prospect Hill", was "a great genealogist and seemed well acquainted not only with the Lewis family but almost all the families you mentioned. I was amused to hear him tell Mr. Holladay, 'the Lewises are as good a family as I have ever known'." Fanny Holladay laughed and replied, "Dr. I think mother entertains the same opinion." (From an old letter.)

He married first, Miss Skison, daughter of Rev. Mr. Skison, (of the Episcopal Church.) Issue:

1. Dr. John J. Lewis, married Miss Hill.
2. Dr. William B. Lewis, of Pittsylvania County, married a daughter of E. Winston Henry and granddaughter of Patrick Henry.

G. Sarah Iverson Lewis, married Thomas G. Crittendon.

H. Martha Churchill Lewis, married first, George Shackleford. No issue. Married second, Rev. Richard Claybrook, and had:

1. William L. Claybrook, lawyer of Lancaster County, Va.

2. Zachary L. Claybrook.
3. Frances Elizabeth Claybrook, married Samuel Fauntleroy, M. D.

I. Iverson Lewis, Jr., volunteered in a cavalry company in the War of 1812. Died in the service of his country.

Issue of Rev. Iverson Lewis by third wife, Catharine Byrd:

J. Catharine Lewis, died unmarried.

K. Mary Lewis, married Mr. Backhouse, of Gloucester County, Virginia. Issue:

1. John W. Backhouse.

Issue of Giles Rogers and Ann Iverson Lewis, daughter of John Lewis and Sarah Iverson:

A. Achilles Rogers, died 1820, married his cousin, Mary George, lived on Ivy Creek, Albemarle County.

B. Ann Rogers, married Robert Davis.

C. Rachel Rogers.

D. Frances Rogers, married April 1782, Samuel Twyman (five sons and three daughters.

E. Lucy Rogers, married Jonathan Barksdale, and died 1831. One son, seven daughters.

F. Parmenas Rogers inherited the home. Was magistrate 1807, sheriff 1834. Married first, Miss Baber; married second, Elizabeth Ferguson.
Issue: (fifteen children)

William, Joseph, Ralph, George, Parmenas, Permelia, Giles, Frances, Orville, Catharine, Thomas, Ann, Jonathan, Elizabeth, married Nathan Barksdale, Dr. James B. Rogers, died 1863, married Margaret Wood, daughter of David Wood and Mildred Lewis, daughter of Nicholas and Mary Walker Lewis, and had issue:

a. Martha Rogers, married Dr. Alfred Wood, and had:
    a. Chas. H. Wood.
    b. James Wood.
    c. Alfred Wood.

b. Dr. W. G. Rogers, of Charlottesville, married Marion

Wood, daughter of Ben. Wood and Jane Anderson. (See Wood note.)

Issue of Lucy Rogers and Jonathan Barksdale:

1. Nancy Barksdale, married Col. George W. Kinsolving, vestryman in the Episcopal church. She died 1856.
   a. Ovid Alexander Kinsolving (Episcopal minister). He had three sons who were ministers.
      1. George Herbert Kinsolving, Bishop of Western Texas.
      2. Arthur B. Kinsolving, rector in Brooklyn, N. Y.
      3. Lucian Lee Kinsolving, Bishop of Brazil.
   b. Virginia Kinsolving, married William Abney.
   c. Vienna Kinsolving, married William C. Fretwell.
   d. Veturia Kinsolving, married Thomas Clark.
   e. Volusia Kinsolving.
   f. Verona Kinsolving.
   g. Verbelina Kinsolving.
   h. Vermelia Kinsolving.
2. Lucy Barksdale, married Richard Rothwell.
3. Ralph Barksdale.
4. Nathan Barksdale, married Elizabeth, daughter of Parmenas Rogers. Issue:
   a. Ralph Barksdale.
   b. Lucy Barksdale.
   c. Mary Barksdale.
   d. George Barksdale.
5. William G. Barksdale, married Elmira Wood, daughter of John Wood.

## TWYMAN

George Twyman I, emigrant from England, came to Middlesex County, Va. Married Catherine Montague, and had:

George Twyman II, who married 1724, Agatha Buford, and had:

George Twyman III, who married 1754, Mary Walker. They lived in Albemarle County, and had:

Samuel Twyman, who married April 1782, Fannie Rogers. They lived in Orange County, Va., near Stanardsville. He died 1822 or 1823. She died 1837-8.

Issue of Samuel Twyman and Fannie Rogers: (eight children)

A. John Twyman, born 1785, died 1854, married 1809, Margaret Wayt and moved to Barren County, Ky. Issue:
   1. William Twyman, married and had:
      a. Fannie Twyman.
      b. Mary Twyman.
   2. Fannie Twyman.
   3. Mary Twyman.

B. Elijah Twyman (1788-1835), married 1812, Mary Bell, moved to Kentucky. Issue:
   1. Thomas Bell Twyman.
   2. Iverson Lewis Twyman.
   3. Robert B. Twyman.
   4. Samuel Walker Twyman.
   5. Ishmael Ready Twyman.
   6. Wm. Bell Twyman.
   7. Paschal R. Twyman.
   8. Mordicai E. Twyman.
   9. Frances J. Twyman.
   10. Mary E. Twyman.
   11. Henry C. Twyman.
   12. Catherine A. Twyman.

C. Judith Twyman (1790-1845), married Benjamin White, and had issue.

D. Nancy Twyman (1793-1867), married Anthony Thornton, and had issue:
   1. Dr. George Thornton, died unmarried.
   2. Jackson Thornton.
   3. Fannie Thornton, married Frank Walker, of Madison County. Issue:
      a. Iverson Walker.
      b. George Walker.
      c. Lavinia Walker, of Wolftown, Madison County. She owns a china cream pitcher that belonged to grandmother Ann (Lewis) Rogers.

d. Amelia Walker, married Dr. Buckner, and had:

1. Addie Buckner, married Thos. Eddins, and had:

a. Clara Eddins.

b. Nettie Eddins

E. Fannie Twyman, born 1795, married her first cousin, Jonathan Rogers and moved to Elizabethtown, Ky. Issue:

1. Frances Rogers, married Mr. Conway.

2. Fettene Rogers, married Mr. Bowles.

F. Paschal Twyman (1798-1883), married 1822, Patsy Malone, and moved to Roanoke, Mo. in 1844.

G. Mordecai Twyman, son of Samuel Twyman and Fannie Rogers, born 1801, married 1835, Ellen Duke, moved to Missouri. Issue:

1. Francis Twyman, married Emily Webster. No issue.

2. Samuel Twyman, married Linda Damerson. Nine children.

3. Paschal Twyman, married Rebecca Waterfield. Issue:

a. Charlie Twyman.

b. Willie Twyman.

c. Alice Twyman.

4. Lizzie Twyman.

5. Mariah Twyman, married James Jackson.

6. John Twyman, married his brother Paschal's widow, Rebecca (Waterfield) Twyman.

H. Iverson Lewis Twyman, M. D., born May 2, 1810, died April 18, 1864 at his home, "Westfield", Buckinghom County, Va. Graduated in medicine at University of Pennsylvania in 1832, was devoted to his profession, took many medical journals, also wrote articles for them. He married Lavinia Horsley, November 8, 1838. She died 1844 and their two children died in infancy. He married second, 1848, Martha Elizabeth Austin, daughter of Archibald Austin, lawyer, member of Legislature, also member of U. S. Congress.

Issue by second marriage:

1. Iverson Lewis Twyman (1849-1921), married 1884, Antonia Spiller, and had:

a. Julia Twyman, born 1886.
b. Pattie Austin Twyman, died young.
c. Iverson Lewis Twyman, born September 6, 1889, married Edith Moffett, and had:
    1. Jeane Aby Twyman.
d. James Spiller Twyman, born 1892.
e. Marshall Gordon Twyman, born 1893.

2. Grace Rogers Twyman, died infant.
3. Augusta Giles Twyman (1852-1920).
4. Fannie Austin Twyman, born 1854.
5. John Austin Twyman, born 1856, Superintendent of Schools in Buckingham for many years.
6. Samuel Rogers Twyman, born 1858.
7. Mabel Booker Twyman (1861-1896).

END OF IVERSON LEWIS RECORD.

## ROGERS

John Rogers of King William County and his wife, Mary Byrd, daughter of William Byrd of "Westover", had three children:

I. Giles Rogers, married Ann Iverson Lewis.

II. Anna, married John Clark; their children were Gen. George Rogers Clark, William Clark, and Jonathan Clark.

III. Byrd Rogers, married first, Mary and second, Martha Trice. A son of this marriage was John Rogers, a sagacious and successful farmer; he had the best tilled farm in the county, lived near Keswick, married Susan Goodman. He died 1838. Issue: John, Thornton, Mary, and Janetta Rogers.

A. John Rogers (died 1841), married Agnes Sampson, and had two sons: Thornton and William Rogers. Mrs. Agnes S. Rogers married second, Mr. Edward Thurman. Their children were:

1. Agnes Thurman, married Mr. Winchester, had Agnes.
2. John Thurman, married Mildred Scott of "Bel-air".
3. Frank Thurman, married Mamie Rice, had Frank, Winchester, and Robert.

4. Robert Thurman, died unmarried at "Bel-air".
5. Edward, married. No issue.
6. Clara Thurman, married James B. Green, who, though blind, taught law at the University of Virginia.
7. Hamilton Thurman, married and has a daughter and a son.

B. Thornton Rogers had a classical school at Keswick, died 1834, married Margaret Hart, daughter of Andrew Hart and Elizabeth Bickley of "Sunny Bank", North Garden, Va. Their children were:

1. Adeline Rogers, married Rev. E. L. Cochrane.
2. Dr. A. Hamilton Rogers.
3. Susan Rogers, married Rev. Joseph Baxter.
4. Oscar Rogers.
5. William Rogers.
6. Julia Rogers, married Keating Nelson.
7. Celia Rogers, married Rev. James M. Wilson.
8. John Rogers.

Celia Rogers and Rev. James Wilson had:

a. Thornton Wilson, married Fannie Owen, had Owen, Thornton, Sallie, Harriet, Baxter, Archer, and Frank.
b. Oscar Wilson, died unmarried.
c. Elizabeth Wilson, married Richard Edgar Timberlake, had four daughters: Celia Mason, Josephine, Elizabeth, and Nannie, who married Lee Dillon and has Josephine Dillon and Annie Lee Dillon.

Celia Mason Timberlake was an accomplished and lovely lady. She married Mr. Hansell Watt of Thomasville, Georgia and had three children: James Watt, Elizabeth Mason, and Margaret Rogers. Useful and much beloved, her life reached out to touch and to help many. She died in July 1929.

C. Mary, daughter of John and Susan G. Rogers, married Richard Sampson, who died 1862, aged 92 years. They had a son, Rev. Francis S. Sampson, Professor in Union Theological Seminary.

D. Janetta Rogers, married J. Price Sampson, had: Edward,

Thornton, Elizabeth, Margaret, married Micajah Clark, and Mrs. Mantaprise.

*Note.*—Robert, brother of Richard and John Price Sampson, had a son, Stephen Sampson, who married first, Ann Lyndsay; second, Sarah Campell. Issue:

1. Eugene Sampson, married Maggie Lewis.
2. Joe Sampson, married and had Eudora.
3. Sally, unmarried.
4. Willie Sampson, kept store at Ivy, died unmarried.
5. Dora Sampson, married Mr. Shackleford, had Dr. Robert, and Mary.

## FOWKE
### (HAYDEN)

Roger Fowke of Gunston Hall, Staffordshire, England, third son of Fowke of Gunston Hall and Brerewood, married 1600, Mary ——.

Their son, Col. Gerard Fowke, born in England, died in Virginia 1669, married Ann (daughter or widow of Col. Chandler of Port Tobacco, Md.). Col. Fowke was gentleman of the bed chamber to Charles I and Colonel in the Royal army, was of fiery temper by heredity and transmitted that trait to his descendants, had frequent suits with his neighbors about land lines, etc.

He and his cousin, Capt. George Mason, who emigrated with him and Capt. Brent and Mr. Lord were indited for having injured and affronted Wahonganoche, King of the Potomac Indians, and again for permitting a "murtherer of the English" delivered bound into his hand by said King to escape. Col. Fowke was ordered to pay to the publique 10,000 lbs. of tobacco, also he with the three above named gentlemen were declared "incapable of bearing any office, civil or military, in this country."

This indignation soon blew over however, as after a special committee of investigation, Col. Fowke and the others were admitted to the Virginia House of Burgesses, September 11, 1663.

Col. Fowke's son, Gerard Fowke, married first, Miss Lomax (no issue); married second, Sarah Burdett, and their daughter Frances, (born February 2, 1691, died November 8, 1744) married Dr. Gustavus Brown.

## BROWN

Dr. Gustavus Brown of Port Tobacco, Charles County, Maryland was the first of this family to settle in America.

On the fly-leaf of a Bible still preserved in the family is found written:

"This Bible originally belonged to Jane Mitchelson, my mother, who was daughter to George Mitchelson, grandson of the house of Middleton, near Dalkieth and Isabel Elfoston, daughter of Soloms, seven miles to the west of Edinburgh.

"I came into Maryland in May, anno 1708 and anno 1710, married Frances Fowke, daughter of Gerard Fowke in Nanjemy, of which marriage the following children were born":

1. Gustavus, died infant.

*2. Frances, born July 29, 1713, married June 18, 1741, Rev. John Moncure.

3. Sarah, born 1715, married 1738, Rev. James Scott.

4. Mary, born 1717, married first, Mathew Hopkins; second, Thelkeld.

5. Christian, born 1720, married John Graham, no issue.

6. Gustavus, died infant.

7. Elizabeth, born 1723, married Dr. Michael Wallace.

8. Richard, born 1725, married first, Helen Bailey; second. Mrs. Key; third, Mrs. Hawkins.

9. Gustavus R., died infant.

10. Jean, born 1728, married Rev. Isaac Campbell.

11. Cecilia, born 1730, married Dr. John Key; second, Major Thomas Bond.

12. Ann, born 1732, married first, Rev. Samuel Claggett; second, Robert Horner; third, Samuel Hanson.

By his second marriage to Margaret (Black) Boyd:

13. Gustavus Richard, born 1747, married 1769, Peggy Graham.

14. Margaret, born 1749, died 1787, married after 1762, Hon. Thomas Stone of Maryland.

The "Nine Misses Brown" are well known in Virginia genealogy.

# MONCURE

## (Taken partly from Hayden)

Rev. John Moncure, the first of the name known in Virginia, was born probably in the parish of Kinoff, shire Mearns, Scotland, about 1709, died in Virginia, March 1764, married June 18, 1741, Frances Brown, daughter of Dr. Gustavus and Frances Fowke Brown. He and his wife are buried under the chancel of Aquia Church, Stafford, Va.

Extract from a letter written 1820 by Jean Moncure:

"I was only ten years old when I lost my father. He was a Scotchman, descended from a French ancestor who fled among the first protestants, who left France in consequence of the persecution that took place soon after the Reformation. He had an excellent education and had made considerable progress in the study of medicine when an invitation to seek an establishment in Virginia induced him to cross the Atlantic. His first engagement was in Northumberland County, where he lived two years in a gentleman's family as a private tutor. During that time, although teaching others, he was closely engaged in the study of divinity and at the commencement of the third year from his arrival returned to Great Britain and was ordained a minister of the Established Church; came back to Virginia and engaged as curate to Rev. Alexander Scott, who at that time was minister of Overwharton Parish in Stafford County."

This minister died soon after. Mr. Moncure succeeded him in the parish, and became the first minister of "Aquia", where his name with those of his vestry may still be seen painted on one of the panels of the gallery. He preached also at "Potomac Church" and at "Pohick".

Issue of Rev. John Moncure and Frances Brown:

I. John Moncure, died infant.

*II. Frances Moncure, born at "Dipple", September 20, 1745, married October 7, 1762, Travers Daniel. Issue given in Daniel record.

III. John Moncure, born 1746, married 1770, Anne Conway.

IV. Anne Moncure, born 1748, married 1775, Walker Conway.

V. Jean Moncure, born at "Clermont", on the Potomac, 1753, died 1823, married Gen. James Wood, a distinguished officer of the Revolution, and Governor of Virginia, 1796-9.

Jean Wood, in her sphere, was quite as distinguished as

was her husband. "Her manners were peculiarly dignified and graceful, her politeness was genuine and unaffected. She possessed uncommon fluency, had a ready and brilliant wit, and a rich imagination. These qualities fitted her to shine in the most brilliant circles, and made her society attractive to both the aged and the young." She was gifted with poetic and musical talents. Some of her poems are preserved in *The Southern Literary Messenger,* and she left in manuscript, a volume of unpublished poems and sketches. She founded, and, till her death, was president of a society for the assistance of widows and children—"The Female Humane Society of Richmond", incorporated by the Legislature, 1811. Her grave is in the Robinson Cemetery in Byrd Park, Richmond. Her only child died young.

John Moncure, Jr. inherited "Clermont" from his father. He and his wife, Anne Conway Moncure, are buried at "Dipple", Stafford County. Issue: John, William, Agnes, Edwin, Anne.

John Moncure III, married 1792, Alice Peachy Gaskins. He was justice of Stafford County 1796, sheriff 1798, vestryman of Aquia. Issue: (nine children)

1. John Moncure IV, married 1818, Esther Vowles; married second, 1834, Frances Daniel.
2. Alice P. Moncure, died.
3. Frances Moncure, married John Hull. No issue.
4. Thomas G. Moncure, married 1822, Clarissa Hooe; married second, Mary Bell Haxall. Issue:
   a. Alice Moncure, married Wm. Perkins.
   b. Mary Bell Moncure, married first, Mr. Hall; second, Mr. Dobbin. No issue.
5. Hannah H. Moncure, married 1844, Michael Wallace. No issue.
6. Hon. Wm. Augustus Moncure, 1828, married Lucy Ann Gatewood, great-granddaughter of Col. Wm. Byrd of "Westover".
7. Richard Cassius Lee Moncure, married 1825, Mary B. W. Conway.

8. Edwin Moncure, died.
9. Henry Moncure, died.

John and Esther Vowles Moncure had seven children:

a. Mary Robinson Moncure, married 1845, Wm. Armistead Nelson, M. D. Issue: (six children)
   1. Fan Nelson, married James Lyon, and had:
      a. Mary Lyon, married Arthur Hall, and has: Frances, Alice, Arthur, James.
      b. Chas. Edward Lyon, married Helen Gill, and has: Helen and Charles.
      c. Fannie Lyon, married Aubry Pearre, and has: Fanny, Anne, Aubry, Elizabeth, Sarah.
      d. James Lyon, married Catherine Munnichuy, and has: James and Courtney.
      e. Moncure Lyon, married Constance Bentley, and has: Constance, Fannie, Mary, Rob, Moncure, Sam.
   2. Lucy Nelson, married Charles Towson, and has:
      a. Mary Nelson Towson, married Ralph Dorrity, and has: Lucy Dorrity.
      b. Agnes Towson, married W. B. Shelton, and has: Charles Ashby Shelton.
      c. Charles Ashby Towson, killed in World War in France, 1918.
   3. Armistead Nelson, married Henrietta Payne, and has:
      a. Ada Nelson, married Rev. Dwight Chapin, and has: Dwight and Louis.
      b. Mary Nelson, married Conway Allen. (Page 478.)
      c. Wm. Armistead Nelson.
      d. Blanche Nelson, married Charles Blanford of England.
      e. Page Nelson.
      f. Florence Nelson.
      g. Paul Nelson.
      h. Etta Nelson.
   4. Esther Nelson, married Edward Waller, and had:
      a. Mary Page Waller, married W. K. Goolrick, and has: Jane Goolrick and Wm. Kinloch Goolrick.

b. Edward Waller, married Alice Hoge, and has: Edward Waller III.

c. John Waller, married Marie Koiner, and has: John Waller, Jr.

5. Agnes Nelson, married R. P. Miller, and has:

a. Mary Miller.

b. Rudolph Miller.

c. Matilda Miller.

6 Alice P. Nelson, married Thomas Waller, and has:

a. Alice Waller.

b. Mary Waller.

c. Emily Waller, married Capt. Louis Bourne, U. S. M. C., and has: Emily Bourne.

b. John Moncure, son of John and Esther Vowles Moncure, died.

c. Esther Moncure, died.

d. William E. Moncure, married 1853, Georgiana Carey Bankhead. They lived at "Somerset".

Issue: (eight children)

1. Rev. John Moncure, married 1884, Lalla Vance, has: Eliza Moncure, artist.

2. William B. Moncure.

3. Robert Minor Moncure, married Miss Hunt, and has:

a. Hunt Moncure.

b. John Moncure, married Lucile Derrick.

c. Edwin Moncure.

4. Mary Moncure.

5. Georgiana Moncure.

6. Lewis Benger Moncure.

7. Dorothea Moncure, married E. N. Reese, no issue.

8. Richard T. Moncure, married first, ——, had Robert. He married second, Katherine W. McKenzie of Canada. No issue.

e. George Vowles Moncure, married 1849, Mary Ashby, and had:

1. Turner Moncure, married Kate ——, and has four children.

2. John Moncure.

3. George Moncure, married Elizabeth Ford, and has:
   a. George Moncure, married Louise Scott.
   b. Margaret Moncure.
   c. Nannie Moncure, married first, Mr. Portner. Married second, ——.
   d. Turner Moncure, M. D.
   e. Mary Moncure, married Mr. Lewis.
4. Robert S. Moncure, married Elizabeth Dexter.
   a. Robert.
   b. Catherine.
5. James Moncure, married Maria Grey, and has:
   a. Maria Moncure, married Mr. Dunn.
6. Bettie Moncure, married Wallace Moncure.
7. Richard and Walter Moncure (twins), died young.

f. Fanny Moncure, married 1850, James Green Ashby, and had:
1. John Moncure Ashby, married Minnie DuVal, and has:
   a. Charles Ashby.
2. Charles Ashby, died young.
3. Jim Ashby, married Mary Moncure, lived at "Woodburn". Issue: (eight children)
   a. Fan Ashby, married James Boxley, and has: James Boxley, Jr., Richard Boxley, Fenton Boxley, Frances Boxley.
   b. Richard Ashby, married ——.
   c. Virginia Ashby, married Ernest Yourtee, has: John Ashby Yourtee, Mary R. Yourtee.
   d. Mary Wallace, married Richard Conway, has: Mary M. Conway, Katharine Conway, Richard Conway, James A. Conway.
   e. Nannie Ashby, married Fred Blackburn, has five children: Nancy Blackburn, Wm. F. Blackburn, Mary Frances Blackburn, Turner A. Blackburn, Dorothea Blackburn.
   f. Dolly Ashby, married Raleigh Conway, has: James Conway, Dan Conway, Dorothea Frances Conway.
   g. James Ashby, married first, Virginia Percival, and had: James Ashby, Jr. Married second, Genivieve Leary, has: Mary Lou Ashby, Richard L. Ashby.

h. John Moncure Ashby, married Laura Bowman, has: Douglas Ashby, John Ashby, another son.

g. Powhatan Moncure, married Dorothea F. Ashby, has:

1. Dr. Powhatan Moncure, married Lelia Carter, has: Mildred Moncure, Powhatan Moncure, Dorothy Moncure, Jack Moncure (girl).
2. Fanny Moncure, married Samuel Taylor of Clarke. Issue: Gertrude Taylor, married Dr. Jim Smith of Richmond. Dora Taylor, Sam Taylor, Lida Taylor, Hugh Taylor, Annie Taylor.
3. Ashby Moncure, married Mabel Stump, no issue.
4. Harry Moncure, died young.
5. Frank D. Moncure, married Hallie E. Chichester on December 5, 1912, and has: Mary Lewis Moncure, Frank D. Moncure, Jr., McCarty C. Moncure.
6. Dorothea Moncure, married Wm. J. Morton, has: Bruce Morton, M. D., Dorothea Morton, Wm. Jackson Morton, Powhatan Morton, Caroline Morton, married ——.
7. Alice Bell Moncure, married first, Judge Howe Wallace; second, Mr. Beverly, no issue.

h. Rev. Walter Raleigh Moncure, son of John IV by second marriage, married 1868, Mary Moncure. Issue:

1. Fanny Moncure.
2. Mary Moncure.
3. Sally Moncure.
4. R. C. L. Moncure.
5. John Moncure.
6. Emily Moncure.
7. Alice Moncure.

## "GLENCAIRN"

Hon. R. C. L. Moncure, LL. D., son of John III, was a man of great simplicity of manner, of the strictest honor and truth—beloved, respected, and trusted by all. President of Supreme Court of Appeals of Virginia 1852-64; vestryman of St. George's

Parish, Fredericksburg, for forty years and over. He married Mary B. W. Conway. Issue: (fourteen children)

I. Hon. John C. (Honest John) Moncure, Judge of Louisiana Court of Appeals, married Fannie Tomlin, and had:
   A. Conway Moncure, married Effie Jones.
   B. Fanny Dulaney Moncure, and others who died.

II. Catharine Moncure, died young.

III. Mary Moncure, died young.

IV. Alice Moncure, married 1852, Rev. Henry Paynter, and has:
   A. Annie B. Paynter, elocutionist, married Hiram Tucker.
   B. Mary Paynter, authoress, married Wm. P. Parker.
   C. Susanne Paynter.
   D. Henry Paynter, born 1868, Chicago.

V. R. C. L. Moncure of "Stony Hill", married first, 1851, Virginia Buchanan. Married second, ——. Issue:
   A. Mary Moncure, married James Ashby.
   B. R. C. L. Moncure, married first, Nannie Waller; second, Miss Meredith. Issue:
      1. Dick Moncure, married Warrie Sneed, and had eight children.
      2. Lewis Moncure, married Lilian Berry.
      3. Virginia Buchanan Moncure, died unmarried.
      4. Caroline Moncure, married Wiley Long.
      5. Ellen Moncure, daughter by second marriage.
   C. M. Wallace Moncure, married Bet Moncure.
   D. Willie Moncure, married Emma Edrington, no issue.
   E. Henry Moncure.
   F. Virgie Moncure, married Christian Growth.
   G. Harriet Moncure, daughter by second marriage, married Howell Drake.

VI. Anna Moncure, married John M. Hull, C. S. A.

VII. Thomas Moncure, married Jean Charlotte Washington, and had:
   A. Temple Moncure, married ——, and has:
      1. Audré Moncure, married Mr. Emil Bachschmidt, and had:

a. Eugenia Bachschmidt.

b. Paul Bachschmidt.

c. Temple Bachschmidt.

d. Emil Bachschmidt.

B. Eugenia Moncure, married first, Mr. Brown; second, Geo. K. Bradfield. No issue.

C. R. C. L. Moncure, died young.

D. Paul Hull Moncure, married Bessie ——, no issue.

VIII. Marguerite E. Moncure, married Thomas J. Moncure, and had:

A. Judge Robinson Moncure.

B. Mary Moncure.

C. R. C. L. (Pickle Dick) Moncure, married May Wallace.

D. Wm. Moncure, married Carrie Pemberton.

IX. Fannie Moncure, died 1862, was first wife of Thomas J. Moncure. No issue.

X. Dr. Walker Peyton Moncure, C. S. A., married 1869, Mary Hughes. Issue given later.

XI. Agnes R. Moncure, married Dan McC. Chichester.

XII. Harriet Eustace Moncure, died 1929, married Thomas Wallace, no issue.

XIII. William Eustace Moncure, married Mary Campbell Knox.

XIV. Mary Moncure, married Rev. Walter R. D. Moncure. (See page 466.)

Issue of Dr. Walker Peyton Moncure and Mary Hughes:

A. Ada Moncure, married first, J. Powell; second, Vernon Ford, had four daughters.

B. Alfred Moncure, married Jennie McCartney, and had:

1. Charles Moncure.
2. Nelson Moncure.
3. Virginia Moncure.

C. R. C. L. Moncure, married Irene Winship, and had:

1. Winship Moncure.
2. R. C. L. Moncure.

D. Walker Peyton Moncure, married Anna Pollack, and had:
   1. Hughes Moncure.
   2. Walker P. Moncure.

E. Anna Moncure, married Wm. Draper Brinkloe, and had:
   1. Frances Rodney Brinkloe.
   2. Anna M. Brinkloe.
   3. Mary Peyton Brinkloe.
   4. Wm. Draper Brinkloe.

F. Thomas Hughes Moncure, married Marguerite B. —— in France.

G. Delia Moncure, married Charles McCartney, and has: Frank McCartney.

H. Hallie W. Moncure, married Franklin P. Sagendorf, has:
   1. Peyton Sagendorf.
   2. Franklin Sagendorf.
   3. Jack Sagendorf.
   4. Joanna Sagendorf.

I. Thomas McCartney Moncure, married Esther ——, no issue.

J. Frank P. Moncure, married Frances de Lashmutt of Washington, D. C., has:
   1. William B. Moncure.
   2. Grace de Lashmutt Moncure.
   3. Thomas McCartney Moncure.

Issue of Agnes Moncure and Dan Chichester:

A. Mary Elliot Chichester, married Dr. Lewis.

B. Judge R. H. L. Chichester, married Belle Wallace, and had:
   1. Dan Chichester.
   2. Mary W. Chichester, married ——.
   3. Henry Chichester, married Van. Massie.

C. Dan McC. Chichester, died young.

D. John Conway Chichester, married —— Fitzhugh.

E. Frank Chichester, married Lena Harrison.

F. Harriet E. Chichester, married Frank D. Moncure.

G. Cassius Chichester.

H. Peyton Chichester.

Issue of Wm. Eustace Moncure and Mary C. Knox:

A. Thomas Moncure, died 1881.

B. Frances Moncure.

C. Virginia Moncure, died 1881.

D. R. C. L. Moncure.

E. Mary C. Moncure, married Houston K. Sweatser.

F. Ann Somerville Moncure, died 1882.

G. Wm. Eustace Moncure, died 1912.

H. Margaret Moncure, married Henry Kellam, has Shirley Kellam.

I. Robert Moncure, married Eliza Brannin, has Robert Moncure.

J. Alice G. Moncure, married Robert C. Moore, has Robert Moore, Jr.

Issue of Hon. William Augustus Moncure, son of John III and Lucy Ann Gatewood. Ten children.

a. John James Moncure, married Julia, and then Ann Decherd.

b. Wm. Cassius Moncure, C. S. A., married Allenia Cottrell.

c. Thomas J. Moncure, C. S. A., married 1859, Fanny, and 1867, Marguerite E. Moncure (sisters). (See page 468.)

d. Anna G. Moncure, married Daniel Norment, and had:

   1. Walter Norment, married his first cousin, Ann Moncure.
   2. Lee Norment.
   3. Mary Norment.
   4. Fannie Norment, married E. C. Moncure, Jr.

e. St. Leger Landon Moncure, married Lucy G. Olliver, and had:

   1. Belle Moncure.
   2. Elizabeth Moncure.
   3. Anna Moncure.
   4. Philip Moncure.
   5. Alice Moncure.
   6. Byrd Moncure.
   7. Grace Moncure.
   8. Olander Moncure.

f. Eustace Moncure, married Fanny Irby, and had:
   1. Anna Moncure, married Phil Gravatt, and had William M. Gravatt.
   2. Eustace C. Moncure, married Fannie Norment, had Fanny Moncure.
   3. William Augustus Moncure—lawyer, Richmond, Va.
   4. Maria Moncure.
   5. Lucy Moncure.
   6. Irby Moncure.
   7. Richard Moncure.
g. Mary Alice Moncure, married Samuel Burke, and had:
   1. Moncure Burke, who adopted Moncure, the son of his sister.
   2. Rubynetta Burke, married ——.
h. Rubynetta Moncure, married Wm. Glasscock. No issue.
i. Cassandra Moncure, married Wm. Henry Lyne, and had:
   1. Hiram Lyne.
   2. Cassie Lyne.
   3. Wm. Henry Lyne, Jr.
j. Richard T. Moncure, married Anna Gaskins.

THIS ENDS THE RECORD OF JOHN MONCURE III.

## "WINDSOR FOREST"

William Moncure, son of John II, married Sarah E. Henry, and had:

1. Henry Wood Moncure, married 1824, Catherine Carey Ambler, and had:
   a. Sarah Ann E. Moncure, married Pierre P. J. Pecquet Comte de Bellet, C. S. A., of Paris, France, had:
      1. Catherine.
      2. Louise.
      3. Ella Brooke.
      4. Henry.
      5. Marie.

b. John James Moncure.
c. Wm. Carey Moncure, died young.
d. Catherine Moncure, married M. Peter Francis N. Pecquet, had:
  1. Louise Pecquet.
  2. Ida Carey Pecquet, married Alfred H. Platt; married second, James Phillips. Issue:
    a. Nemours William.
    b. Alfreda Holt.
    c. Ida.
    d. Uriah Burr.
    e. Delphine Pillow.
  3. Wm. J. J. Pecquet, married Annis Ledoux, had:
    a. Alfred Pecquet.
    b. Nemours Pecquet.
  4. Nemours Francois Pecquet, married Troemie Chauff.
  5. Richard Carey Pecquet.
e. Charles Moncure, married Catherine Doyle, had:
  1. Catherine Moncure, married E. B. Smith.
f. Henry Wood Moncure, Jr., married 1860, Julia Trent Warwick. Issue:
  1. Henry W. Moncure, married Sallie Henderson; second, Marian S. Waller, who had:
    a. Ann Moncure.
    b. Marion Moncure.
  2. Sarah E. Moncure, married —— Shacklette, has:
    a. Warwick Shacklette.
  3. Robert ("Cappy") Moncure, married Agnes Waller, had:
    a. Julia Moncure, married Corey Wood.
    b. Roberta Moncure, married Harry A. Gills.
    c. Ellen Moncure, married Capt. Gilchrist, has: a son.
    d. Ann E. Moncure.

e. Agnes Moncure, married Neville Hall, has: Neville, Jr. and Jim Hall.

f. Henry Moncure, married Kitty Bigby, has: Kitsy, "Cappy" and Henry Moncure.

g. Richard Carey Moncure, C. S. A., died of yellow fever.

h. Marshall Moncure, married Elizabeth Wynne, had: 1. Henry; 2. Ambler Moncure.

i. James Dunlap Moncure, C. S. A., married Anna Patterson McCaw.

j. John J. Moncure, C. S. A., married Mary Edith Fairfax.

2. John James Moncure, M. D., son of William Moncure and Sarah E. Henry, died unmarried.

3. Robinson Moncure, unmarried.

4. Charles Prosser Moncure, married Ann Lewis Daniel—"Horseshoe", Rapidan, Va.—had issue:

a. Peter V. D. Moncure.

b. William Moncure, married Belle Chapman, had:

1. Vivienne Moncure, married Wm. Allen Butler of New York.

c. Dr. Charles Moncure.

d. Lucy Randolph Moncure, married Mr. Grymes.

5. Edwin Moncure, died young.

6. Sarah Elizabeth Moncure, married Paul Hull, had:

a. John Hull, killed in battle.

b. Richard Hull, C. S. A.

7. Travers D. Moncure, married Susan B. Carter, and had:

a. Travers Moncure, married Bessie Douglas.

b. Julian Moncure, killed in battle.

c. John Moncure.

d. Hecter Moncure, unmarried.

e. Josephine Moncure.

f. Agatha Moncure.

## ROBINSON

Agnes Moncure, daughter of John II, married John Robinson. Issue: (ten children)

1. Moncure Robinson, married 1835, Charlotte Randolph Taylor, had:
   a. John M. Robinson, married Champe Conway.
   b. Edmund Robinson, married Augusta Jay.
   c. Agnes Robinson, married Charles Chauncey.
   d. Dr. Beverly Robinson.
   e. Charlotte Meigs Robinson.
   f. Moncure Robinson, married Lydia Biddle.
   g. Nat Robinson.
   h. Frances Brown, married Algernon Sydney Biddle.
2. Conway Robinson, married Mary Susan Selden Leigh, had:
   a. Leigh Robinson, married Alice Morson, no issue.
   b. Elizabeth Robinson, unmarried.
   c. Carey Robinson, killed in battle, unmarried.
   d. William Robinson, unmarried.
   e. Conway Robinson, unmarried.
   f. Susan Leigh Robinson, unmarried.
   g. Agnes Conway Robinson, unmarried.
3. Edwin Robinson, married Frances Brown, had:
   a. Henry Robinson, C. S. A.
   b. Frances Robinson, married Capt. John Milledge.
   c. Alice Robinson, married Charles Carpenter, had:
      1. Alice Carpenter.
      2. Charles Carpenter.
      3. Catherine Carpenter.
      4. Edwin Carpenter, twin.
      5. Moncure Carpenter, twin to Edwin.
4. Anna Jane Robinson, married Col. John Sheilds, had:
   a. Alfred Sheilds, married Eliza Clarke.
   b. Phoebe Sheilds, married Dr. R. H. Randolph.
   c. Cary Sheilds.
   d. Agnes Sheilds.
   e. Nannie Sheilds.
   f. Cornelia Sheilds.

5. Eustace Robinson, graduate of West Point.
6. Octavia Robinson, married Richard Barton Haxall, had:
   a. Agnes Haxall, married Lewis W. Carter, had Shirley Carter.
   b. Philip Haxall, married Mary Triplett.
   c. Harriet Haxall, married Rev. Henry Wise, had Obediah Wise.
   d. Mary Parke Haxall, married Alex. Cameron of Scotland.
   e. Charlotte Haxall, married Capt. R. E. Lee, son of General Lee.
   f. Rosalie Haxall, married Powell Noland (seven children). She died 1935.
   g. Barton Haxall.
7. Alfred Robinson, died young.
8. Margaret Robinson—interested in Tredeger School, Richmond, Va.
9. Moore Robinson.
10. Cornelia Robinson, married James B. Cunningham.

END ROBINSON RECORD.

Edwin Moncure, son of John II, married 1808, Eleanor Edrington. Issue:

1. William Moncure, moved to Mississippi, had a son, Edwin.
2. John Moncure, M. D., had a son in C. S. A.
3. Agatha Ann Moncure, married George Glasscock.

Ann Moncure, daughter of John II, married first, Thomas Gaskins; second, Richard Gaskins. Issue:

1. Hannah Gaskins, married Rev. David T. Ball. No issue.
2. Elizabeth Gaskins.
3. Sarah Gaskins, married Rev. J. B. Jeter. No issue.
4. William Gaskins, son by second marriage.

END OF RECORD OF DESCENDANTS OF JOHN MONCURE THE SECOND.

## CONWAY

Ann, daughter of Rev. John Moncure, born 1748, married 1775, Walker Conway, son of George Conway and Ann Heath. Issue:

A. George Conway, killed accidentally.

B. Agatha Ann Conway, born 1778, married Richard Gaskins. (See foregoing.)

C. John Moncure Conway—vestryman of Aquia 1815-25—born November 23, 1779, died May 24, 1864, married December 29, 1802, Catherine Storke Peyton, who was born July 20, 1786, died April 10, 1865. She was daughter of Dr. Valentine and Mary Butler Washington Peyton. Thirteen children.

   1. Dr. Valentine Yelverton Conway, born 1803, died 1882, married December 22, 1824, Mary Catherine Henry.
   2. Walker Peyton Conway, born 1805, married 1829, Margaret E. Daniel.
   3. Mary B. W. Conway, married R. C. L. Moncure, of "Glencairn".
   4. Agatha Ann Conway, married Dr. Maurice Emanuel, of Mississippi. Issue:
      a. Mary Emanuel.
      b. Lelia Emanuel.
      c. Maurice Emanuel.
      d. John Emanuel.
      e. Jenny Emanuel.
   5. Eliza Jane V. Conway, died young.
   6. Marguerite Catherine, died young.
   7. John M. Conway, married Elizabeth Fitzhugh, and had:
      a. Edmonia Conway, married Lawrence, and had:
         1. Edmo Lawrence, married Mr. Wahlen.
         2. Catherine Lawrence, died young.
   8. William Edwin Conway, fell from a window and was killed, 1820.
   9. George W. Conway, died young.
   10. Judge Eustace Conway, married Maria Tomlin.

11. Frances Lucy Conway, married Lieut. Harrison Brockenbrough Barnes, C. S. A.
12. Henry Rowzee Conway, was first elected clerk of Stafford, 1852 to 1863. Married Elizabeth Griffin Chinn, and had:
    a. Lucy Conway, died unmarried. (1855-1875)
    b. John Conway, died unmarried.
    c. Edwin, died infant.
    d. Charles Conway, 1856-1926, unmarried.
13. Harriet Eustace Conway, died 1846.

Frances Lucy Conway, married Lieutenant Harrison Barnes, and had:

a. Kate Barnes, married J. W. Brannin.
b. Newman Barnes.
c. Lucy Ball Barnes, married Rev. James T. Smith, and had:
    1. Lucian Smith.
    2. Fanny Smith.
    3. Elizabeth Smith.
    4. Harrison Smith.
    5. Charles Smith.
    6. Katherine Smith, married Campbell, and had:
        a. James Wilbur Campbell, married ——.
        b. Frances Campbell.
        c. Eliza Campbell, married Robert K. Moncure, and has one son.

Dr. Valentine Yelverton Conway graduated from the University of Pennsylvania 1832—Surveyor-General of Florida, delegate from Richmond and Lancaster counties 1837, assistant Surgeon-General in C. S. A. His wife, Mary Catherine Washington Henry, was daughter of Edward Hugh and Elizabeth W. Peyton Henry. Issue: (fourteen children)

a. John Conway, died young.
b. Elizabeth Conway was second wife of W. P. Harrison, had: Cora and Lee, both died young.
c. Catherine Cora Conway was first wife of W. P. Harrison, had:
    1. Valentine Harrison, died young.

2. Mary Harrison, married ——, has Mary.

d. Mary V. Conway, unmarried.

e. Edward Henry Conway, married Sarah J. Strother, had:

1. Valentine Conway.
2. —— Conway, married Dr. Maphis of the University of Virginia.

f. Valentine P. Conway, died young.

g. Margaret J. Conway, died young.

h. Agatha A. Conway, died young.

i. Walker P. Conway, died young.

j. Ella H. Conway, married A. E. Bloxton, had:

1. Estelle Bloxton, married Frank Eustace, no issue.
2. Conway Bloxton, married second, Erma Sparks, had:
   a. Erma Bloxton, twin.
   b. Charles Bloxton, twin to Erma.
   c. Mary Bloxton.
3. Belle Bloxton, married Ernest Jones, has:
   a. Roland Jones.
   b. Ella Jones.
4. Lucy Bloxton, married Sydney Stevens, has issue.
5. Walter Bloxton, married ——, has three children.

k. Florida Virginia, married J. G. Allen, had issue:

1. Geraldine Allen, married —— Moore.
2. Florida Allen, married Wm. Towson.
3. Conway Allen, married Mary M. Nelson.
4. Martha W. Allen, unmarried.
5. Walter Allen, married ——.
6. Elizabeth Allen, married ——.

l. Patrick Henry Conway, married M. H. Hall (author), had:

1. Genevieve Conway.
2. Arthur Conway.
3. Bernard Conway.

m. John M. Conway, died unmarried.

"TRAVERS NECK"

*A Tract of Land Between the Creeks.*
*The Site of the Family Home "Crow's Nest."*

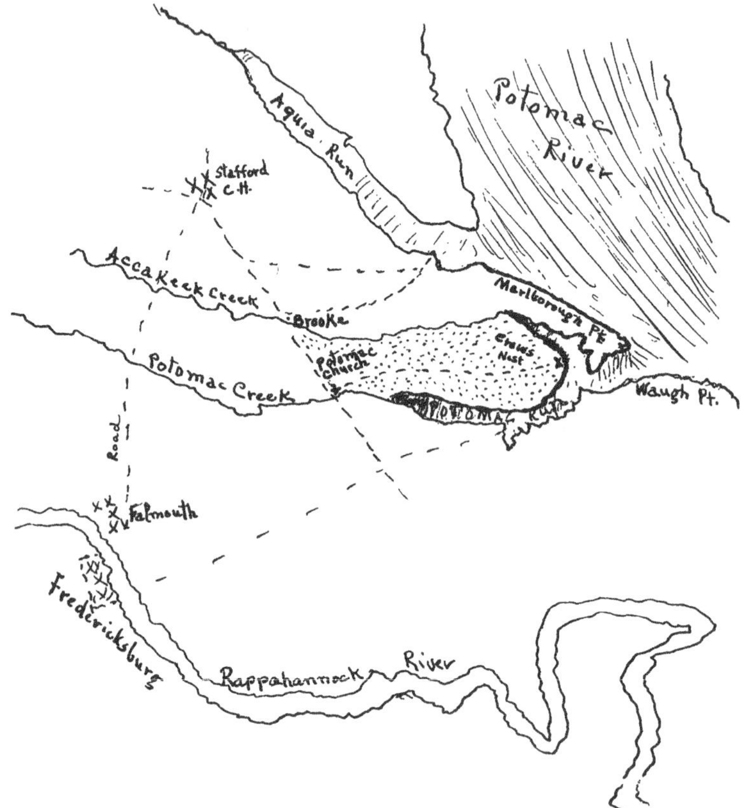


*Looking from "Crow's Nest" across the Run to the Potomac, an old letter describes the view as beautiful—says the Marlborough hills look like islands floating in the sea.*

n. William W. Conway, born December 29, 1849, married December 28, 1871, Laura D. Clark, and had:

1. Eva Conway, married George S. Derrick, has:
   a. Mary Lucile Derrick, married first, John Moncure.
2. Mary W. Conway, married Charles McGregor, has:
   a. Alfred Henry McGregor.
   b. Eugene Everard McGregor, married Marjorie Allen, has:
      William Allen McGregor.

## GASKINS OR GASCOIGNE

Agatha Ann, daughter of Ann Moncure and Walker Conway, born 1778, married Richard Gaskins, and had:

1. Thomas Gaskins, married daughter of Richard Henry Lee Gaskins.
2. Richard Gaskins, married first, ——; second, Gatewood; third, widow of his half brother, William.
3. John Gaskins, married a Spanish lady.
4. Henry Gaskins, unmarried.
5. Ann Gaskins, unmarried.
6. Betty Gaskins, unmarried.
7. Mary Gaskins, unmarried.

END OF RECORD OF ANN MONCURE AND WALKER CONWAY.

## TRAVERS

*Arms*—A chevron between three escallops and a chevron between three boars' heads.

Trace to an ancestor on the Battle Abbey Roll—Hayden.

Raleigh Travers (in Virginia before 1653), was a Burgess a hundred years before the Revolution. He and Col. Gerard Fowke were on a committee of six, who, under Sir William Berkeley, built a new State House in James City County. This new State House was burned in 1676.

From this Raleigh Travers and his wife, Elizabeth, descend two brothers: Giles, who died a bachelor, leaving his property to his brother Raleigh, who married before 1707, Hannah Ball, born about 1683, daughter of Col. Joseph Ball and Elizabeth Romney Ball. Children:

I. Raleigh Travers, died unmarried, will probated October 14, 1749, Stafford County.

II. Elizabeth Travers, married Sir John Cooke, Bart, of Ireland and Virginia, and had Travers Cooke and Hannah Cooke.

*III. Sarah Travers, died 1789, married July 15, 1736, Peter Daniel, of Falmouth, and had Hannah, *Elizabeth, and Travers Daniel.

A. Travers Cooke, vestryman of Stafford 1752, married February 26, 1754, Mary, daughter of Mottram Doniphan, and had:

1. Col. John Cooke of "West Farms", born 1755, vestryman of Aquia 1815-23. He married Mary T., daughter of George Mason of "Gunston Hall". They had eight children.

Issue of Col. John and Mary Cooke:

a. John Cooke, whose daughter, Million, married October 9, 1817, Hon. John W. Green.

b. Gen. George M. Cooke, married 1817, Agatha Eliza Eustace, and had John and George.

c. Sarah Cooke, married Cary Selden; second, Dr. Robert O. Grayson.

d. Elizabeth Cooke.

e. Harriet Cooke.

f. Mildred Cooke.

g. Hannah Cooke.

h. Nancy Cooke.

B. Hannah B. Cooke, daughter of Elizabeth and Sir John Cooke, married 1751, John Brown. They had:

1. Mary Brown, married John W. Green.

2. Raleigh Travers Brown, married Million Waugh, and had:

a. John Brown, married first, Mary Elizabeth Hedgeman; second, E. Morton.

b. Dr. William Brown, married and had: Mary Green Brown.

c. Raleigh T. Brown, married Hannah Ball Daniel. She married second, John Hedgeman.

Lt.-Gov. John Mayre, of Fredericksburg, married one of this family of Browns. The Greens, Wisharts and Browns, of Fredericksburg, are also of this family.

## BALL FAMILY
### (HAYDEN)

Col. William Ball, of ye county of Lancaster, England, born 1615, died at "Millenbeck", Lancaster County, Va., November 1680. Married in London 1638, Hannah Atherold. Issue:

A. Hannah, born 1650, married Mr. Fox.

B. Col. William (1641-1694), married first, Miss Williamson; second, Miss Harris; third, Margaret Downman.

C. Col. Joseph of "Epping Forest", England, born May 24, 1649, died at "Epping Forest", Virginia, will probated Lancaster County, Va., July 11, 1711. He married in England, Elizabeth Romney. Issue:

a. Hannah, married Raleigh Travers.

b. Elizabeth, married Rev. John Carnegie.

c. Esther, married Raleigh Chinn.

d. Ann, married Edwin Conway.

e. Joseph, born March 11, 1689, died January 10, 1760, married December 3, 1709, Frances Ravenscroft, and had:

1. Charles, 2. Hetty Band, 3. Frances, who married Raleigh Downman.

Col. Joseph Ball, Sr., married second, Mrs. Mary Johnson (née Montague), who had, it is said, a daughter Elizabeth Johnson. They had one child, (f) Mary, second wife of Augustine Washington and mother of General George Washington.

Issue of Frances Ball and Raleigh Downman: (Downman Bible)

1. 2. Margaret and Sarah—infants.

3. Joseph, married Olivia Payne.

4. Frances R., married Col. James Ball, of "Bewdley", son of Col. James, son of James, son of William, son of William.
5. Millian, died of measles.
6. Raleigh Wm., married first, Pricilla Chinn; second Cordelia Gilman; third, Lucy Campbell; fourth, Eliza Currie. Issue: 1. Margaret, 2. Joseph, 3. Fidelia, 4. Amelia, 5. Sarah, 6. Raleigh Wm., 7. John B, 8. Pricilla, 9. Thomas R., 10. Henry C., 11. Robert, 12. Frances, 13. Elizabeth, 14. Joseph H., 15. Daughter, 16. Millian.

Issue of Joseph Ball and Olivia Payne:

1. Raleigh Wm.; 2. Olivia, married first, B. Chinn; second, Joseph Ball; 3. Frances, married Montague; 4. Sarah; 5. Margaret, married Wm. B. Mitchell; 6. Joseph, married Priscilla Downman; 7, 8. Twins—William and Judith; 9. George Wm.; 10. Hugh Richard; 11. Harriet Jane; 12. James Wilmot Payne.

*Downman Note:*

Margaret Ball and Raleigh Downman, Lancaster County, Va. 1. William, born 1717, married June 12, 1747, Ellen Ball Chichester had Raleigh; 2. Raleigh, born 1719, died March 18, 1781, married October 23, 1750, Frances Ball; 3. Charles; 4. Christopher; 5. Elisha.

Wm. Downman, sheriff of Richmond County, 1722-3, had: 1. Eliza, married Smith of Austin, Texas; 2. Mildred, married Thomas Ball. (Hayden does not recognize of what line); 3. Elizabeth, married Major Stokeley Towles.

## DANIEL

James Daniel, born 1680, was vestryman in Middlesex Parish 1724. He succeeded Wm. Daniel, who took up lands in Middlesex County 1669 and, who mentions in his will a son, James. (Hayden) This James married Mary or Margaret Vivian, daughter of John Vivian, constable of Middlesex 1681, sheriff 1719. Issue:

I. Rachel Daniel, born 1704, married 1722, Thomas Amis.

*II. Peter Daniel, born 1706, married Sarah Travers.

III. Charles Daniel, born 1708, married 1732, Jane Mickleboro.
IV. William Daniel, married Elizabeth (Watkins) Woodson, who by her first marriage had: Jacob, Joel and Susannah Woodson.
V. James Daniel, married 1753, Mary Killingham.
VI. John Daniel, married Elizabeth Morton.
VII. Pheobe Daniel.
VIII. Vivian Daniel, married Elizabeth Vivian.
IX. Susannah (?) Daniel, married Henry Mickleborough.

William and Elizabeth Woodson Daniel had:

A. William Daniel, married Pattie Allen.
B. Benjamin Daniel, died young.
C. Hezekiah Daniel, died young.
D. William Pride Daniel, married Anne Goode.
E. John Daniel, married Lucy Hecking.
F. Judith Daniel, married Joseph Fuqua.
G. Mary Daniel, married John Fuqua.
H. Betty Daniel, married Mr. Nelson.
I. Sallie Daniel, married Mr. Womack.
J. Rhoda Daniel, married Ambrose Nelson.

William and Pattie Allen Daniel, married 1765, had:

1. Pattie Archer Daniel, married Henry Coleman.
2. Hon. William Daniel, born 1770, married first, Margaret Baldwin; married second, Pauline Cabell (widow of Hector Cabell.) Issue:
    a. Mary Cornelia Brisco Daniel, married 1825, Mayo Cabell.
    b. Hon. William Daniel, married first, Sarah Warwick; second, Elizabeth Cabell:
        1. Hon. Major John Warwick Daniel, C. S. A., born September 5, 1842. Distinguished lawyer, orator and U. S. Senator. Married 1869, Julia Elizabeth Murrell.
        2. Sarah A. Daniel, married 1868, Major Don P. Halsey, C. S. A.

3. Elizabeth Daniel, married Elliot Coleman.
4. Obedience Allen Daniel, married Lilian Thomas.
5. Fanny Daniel, married William Talley.
6. Mary W. Daniel, married first, Henry Woodson; second, Benj. Fuqua.
7. Lucy Woodson Daniel, married William Miller.

William Pride and Anne Goode Daniel, had:

1. Samuel Daniel, married Martha Friend.
2. John Daniel of "Hickory Grove", Charlotte County, married first, Miss Spencer; second, Frances, daughter of Capt. John Dupuy and his wife, Polly Watkins. Issue:
   a. Julia Daniel.
   b. William Daniel, married Bettie McGehee.
   c. Robert Daniel, married Agnes Anderson.
   d. Kate Daniel, married Sam Clarke.
   e. Joel Daniel, married first, Alice Harper; married second, Elizabeth Dupuy. He had by his first marriage, one daughter:
      1. Sadie Daniel, who was raised at "Locust Hill". She married Nathan B. Topping, had:
         a. Nat Topping, died unmarried.
         b. Harper Topping, died in France during World War from exposure on trip through Russia after leaving Roumania.
         c. Ruth Topping.

      Children by second marriage:

      2. Joel Daniel.
      3. Lena Daniel, married Samuel Anderson, lawyer, Richmond, had:
         a. Pauline Anderson, married ——.
         b. Dr. Sam. Anderson, married ——.
         c. Lavillon Anderson.
         d. Bessie Anderson.
      4. Robert Daniel.
      5. Lavillon Daniel.
3. William Pride Daniel, married first, Miss Mosely; second, Miss Hill.

4. Mary Daniel, married Mr. Goode.
5. Hezekiah Daniel, married Mary Le Fevre, daughter of Benjamin and Susan Dupuy Watkins, had among others, Jennie, who married William H. Ward, Tazewell Courthouse, son of Wm. Ward of Wythe.
6. —— Daniel, married Major Fuqua.

## PETER DANIEL

Peter Daniel settled in Northumberland County, later in Stafford. He was vestryman of Aquia church 1757, justice of Stafford 1744, later presiding justice, member of Stafford Committee 1744. He married July 15, 1736, Sarah Travers of "Crows Nest". Hannah, Elizabeth and Travers were the children.

A. Hannah Ball Daniel, born September 9, 1737, died 1829, married first, Gibson Foote; married second, Geo. Hedgeman; married third, Mr. Hardy, had:
   1. John Hedgeman, married Catharine Grayson, and had:
      a. John Grayson Hedgeman, married Hannah B. Daniel, two of whose children were:
         1. John Hedgeman, married and left a son, Travers.
         2. Mary Hedgeman, married James Brown, and had:
            a. John Brown.
            b. Mary Brown.
            c. Lily Brown, married Mr. Cooke.

*B. Travers Daniel, born May 26, 1741, lived at "Crows Nest" on the Potomac. Justice of Stafford 1765. The Richmond *Enquirer* of 1824 has this notice:

> "Died June 28, 1824, Travers Daniel, Sr., Esq., descended from an ancestor who was in the Royal Army and who came to Virginia."

He married, October 7, 1762, Frances Moncure, born September 20, 1745. Issue: (eleven children)

   1. Travers Daniel, Justice Stafford, 1788, married July 1791, Mildred Stone, daughter of Governor Stone, of Maryland.

2. Dr. John Moncure Daniel, Senior, hospital surgeon, U. S. A. Married first, Jean Nivin; second, Margaret Stone; third, Maria Vowles.
3. Sarah T. Daniel, married Col. Charles Hay, U. S. A.; married second, Col. Richard Adams.
4. Peter Daniel, died young.
5. Frances B. Daniel, married Samuel Greenhow, of Richmond, no issue.

*6. Elizabeth Travers Daniel, married Dr. Richmond Lewis. (Zachary Lewis record.)

7. Hannah B. Daniel, born December 29, 1780, married first, Travers Brown; second, John Grayson Hedgeman.
8. Anne Moncure Daniel, died young.
9. Walter Raleigh Daniel, born 1783, died September 11, 1818, married Elizabeth Lewis, sister of Dr. Richmond Lewis. (Zachary Lewis record.)
10. Hon. Peter V. Daniel, married first, Lucy Randolph; second, Elizabeth Harris.
11. Jean Wood Daniel, married John Lewis of "Llangollen." (Zachary Lewis record.)

Travers and Mildred Stone Daniel had issue:

a. Frances Daniel, was the second wife of John Moncure, of "Woodburn". They had one son:
    1. Rev. Walter Moncure.
b. Emily Daniel, married Gustavus Brown Wallace, and had:
    1. Mildred Wallace, married Mr. Nalle.
    2. Dr. Gustavus Wallace, married Dora Green, and had:
        a. Emily Wallace, married Mr. Peden.
        b. May Wallace, married R. C. L. Moncure ("Pickle Dick").
        c. Gustavus B. Wallace, lawyer, Fredericksburg.
c. Samuel Greenhow Daniel, married first, Mrs. Margaret Richardson Lewis. He married second, Maria Henderson.

    Issue by second marriage:

    1. Samuel Daniel, married Miss Fitzhugh, and had one daughter.

2. William Daniel, married Lizzie Lane, and had Helen Daniel.
3. Henry Daniel, married.
4. Peter Daniel, married Marion McDowell, and has a daughter, Vivian.

Dr. John M. Daniel and Margaret Stone, had issue:

a. Hon. Raleigh T. Daniel of Richmond, married Susan Tabb, and had:
   1. Raleigh T. Daniel, Jr., C. S. A.
   2. Augusta Daniel, teacher in Richmond, died unmarried.
   3. Elizabeth Daniel, married Major James West Pegram, who was a brother of Gen. William Pegram.
   4. Charlotte Daniel, died unmarried.

b. Jean Daniel, married William Crane.

c. John Daniel, married first, Eliza Mitchell. (See Mitchell note.) He married second, Euphemia Tolson.

d. Mary Daniel, married Rev. Bride, no issue.

e. Margaret Eleanor Daniel, married Walker Peyton Conway.

Dr. John M. Daniel and his third wife, Maria Vowles, had:

f. Thomas Cushing Daniel, married 1835, Eliza Bronaugh, sister of "Aunt Maggie". These were devoted friends of the "Bel-air" family. Mollie Scott died while on a visit to them in Richmond. Pet died at the same time. Issue:
   1. Maria (Pet) Daniel, born 1835.
   2. John Daniel.
   3. Nannie Daniel, married Mr. Brooke.
   4. John W. Daniel, married Betty Fitzhugh.

g. Dr. John Henry Daniel, married Fenton Brooke, and had:
   1. John Daniel.
   2. Brooke Daniel.
   3. Thomas Cushing Daniel.

Margaret E. and Walker Peyton Conway, had issue:

1. Walker P. Conway, lawyer, died early.
2. Moncure D. Conway, writer of prominence, married Ellen Dana, and had:
   a. Eustace Conway, married 1901, Maud Allis, no issue.

b. Mildred Conway, married 1895, Philip Sawyer, and has:
   1. Mildred Sawyer.
   2. Eleanor Sawyer.

3. Mildred, married Prof. Francis March, LL. D. Issue given below.
4. Richard M. Conway, C. S. A., married Kate Holladay. (Zachary Lewis record.)
5. Peter Vivian Daniel Conway, banker, Fredericksburg, married first, Mary Porter; married second, Letitia Stansbury, no issue.

Issue by first marriage: Mary Vivian Conway and three other daughters, Susan, Kate, and Elizabeth, who all died young.

Mildred and Prof. March had:

a. Prof. Francis March, married September 4, 1889, Alice Grey Youngman, had:
   1. Katharine March, married Stanley Thomas.
   2. Francis Andrew March, married.
   3. Robert Y. March.

b. Gen. Peyton Conway March, of World War, married July 4, 1891, Mrs. Josephine Smith Cunningham. He married second, September 1923, Cora Virginia McEntee.
   Issue by first marriage:
   1. Mildred March, born October 4, 1893, married November 28, 1917, John Millikan, and has John Millikin, Jr.
   2. Josephine Mary, married June 8, 1918, Joseph May Swing, and has Joseph, and another.
   3. Peyton March, twin of Josephine, died.
   4. Peyton March, born January 1, 1897, killed in aviation, 1918.
   5. Vivian March, born October 29, 1899, married 1918, Paul Frank.
   6. Lewis Alden March, born May 10, 1904.

c. Thomas Stone March, married June 20, 1893, Jennie Baldridge Bridge, and had:
   1. Francis Andrew March, born June 6, 1895.
   2. Judith March, born August 1, 1899.

d. Alden March, married Hattie ——.

e. Moncure March, married first, Regina Ankers, and had Joseph and another. He married second, Katharine Marie O'Connell.

f. John Lewis March, unmarried.

g. Mildred March, unmarried.

h. Margaret, died February 1923, unmarried.

Hon. Peter V. Daniel, son of Travers and Frances Moncure Daniel, was a prominent lawyer, in Virginia Legislature 1809-10, member of Privy Council 1812-30, Lieutenant-Governor of Virginia, President of Council, and Attorney-General United States. He declined the appointment as Judge of U. S. District Court 1836. He was Associate Justice of Supreme Court 1840. He married first, Lucy Randolph; second, Elizabeth Harris. Issue:

a. Elizabeth R. Daniel.

b. Peter V. Daniel, married Mary Robinson.

c. Ann Lewis Daniel, married Charles Prosser Moncure. (See Moncure record.)

d. Mary Campbell Daniel.

e. Travers Daniel, married Flora Bradford.

*Mitchell Note.*

From family papers owned by Mrs. Frances Ann Lewis Mitchell of Virginia, but living in Bryan, Texas, August 13, 1888, which was the date of a letter to her nephew from which these notes were taken.

In Scotland, James Mitchell died February 26, 1804 in his ninety-first year after forty-eight years in the marriage state, says an old letter written by Jean to her son.

Jean Gillan Mitchell, his wife, died sometime whilst the war of 1812 stopped communication with England.

Their son, James Mitchell of Elgin Scotland, came to America, landed at Philadelphia 1792, when the yellow fever was prevailing there as an epidemic. He was put in the hospital and recovered. He married his first wife, Ann Smith, January 4, 1794. She had four children of whom Eliza, wife of Dr. John M. Daniel, was the youngest.

Mrs. Ann (Smith) Mitchell died December 8, 1803.

James Mitchell married his second wife, Jane Wells, August 5, 1804. She died April 10, 1827, aged fifty years, and leaving children. James died May 4, 1822, aged about fifty-five years. These children were: William, Margaretta, Mrs. Reed, Mrs. Morton.

END OF DANIEL RECORD.

Louisa divided from Hanover 1742, was named for daughter of George II. First court of Louisa County, December 13—24, 1742:

Presiding Justice: Col. Robert Lewis of "Belvoir",

Commission of Justices: Christopher Clarke, Ambrose Joshua Smith, Abram Venable, Charles Barrett, Richard Johnson, Thomas Meriwether, Robert Harris, John Carr, Joseph Bickley, Joseph Fox, John Starke, Joseph Shelton, John Poindexter.

Upper part of Louisa County added to Albemarle 1761. Commission of Justices abolished about 1868 by the Underwood Administration in Virginia, County Judges replacing the Presiding Justices.

## COLONIAL RECORD
## OF
## C. H. ANDERSON, SR. AND JAMES MCCLURE SCOTT, SR.

I. Nicholas Martian, born 1591, died 1657, married ——, had a large family. Frenchman naturalized in England, came to Virginia 1620; Burgess from James City County 1630-2, Justice of York County 1635-7, Burgess of York 1623, Kyskicake 1632, Isle of Kent and Kyskicake 1632. His home was the present site of Yorktown, this land was inherited by his descendants, the Nelsons. His daughter, Elizabeth Martian, married Col. George Reade. (See Royal lineage.)

II. Col. George Reade, born in England 1600, died in Virginia 1671, came to Virginia 1637. Burgess of James City County 1649, Burgess York and Gloucester 1658, member of Council 1656-7, holding office of Burgess for York and Gloucester at his death 1671, was Colonel of Militia. His daughter, Mildred Reade, married

III. Col. Augustine Warner II, born ye 3rd June, 1642, died

ye 19th June, 1681; Burgess 1674, Speaker of House of Burgesses 1672-1677, Burgess 1676, Member of King's Council 1676-1677, Col. Gloucester Militia 1680. He was son of

IV. Capt. Augustine Warner I, of Virginia and England, died 1674, came to Virginia before 1630; Justice and Burgess from York County 1652, Burgess for Gloucester County 1656, 1658-9, 1674. Mary, his wife, born May 15, 1614, died August 11, 1660.

### "WARNER HALL" LEWISES

V. Major John Lewis, son of Robert Lewis the emigrant, 1635. Member of Virginia House of Burgesses, held rank as Major; married Isabella Warner 1666. His son.

VI. Col. John Lewis, born ye 30th November, 1669, died ye 14th November, 1725, was one of "His Majesty's Honourable Council", married Elizabeth, daughter Mildred Reade and Col. Augustine Warner. She was born ye 24th November, 1673, died ye 6th day of February 1719/20. "The Tender Mother of 14 children" (epitaph). Their son

VII. Col. Robert Lewis of "Belvoir", Albemarle County, baptized May 4, 1702, died 1766. Burgess for Louisa County 1744-6, first county Lieutenant for Louisa, first Presiding Judge for same; married Jane Meriwether, born ——. She and her brother David were children of

VIII. Nicholas Meriwether II, born October 26, 1667, died 1744 in Albemarle, then part of Goochland. Burgess for Hanover County 1723-6-7-8, Sheriff of New Kent 1702, Burgess of New Kent 1710-14, Major for New Kent 1690, 1705-7-8, 1716-18-19, Justice for New Kent 1722, Colonel for New Kent 1723-4-8-9-33; married Elizabeth Crawford. (St. Paul's Parish Register.) He was son of

IX. Nicholas Meriwether I, emigrant, born in Wales 1631, died in Virginia, December 19, 1678; was first clerk of Surrey County, April 22, 1655. Elizabeth Woodhouse, his wife, survived him.

Here the record of James T. Scott branches off. Record of C. H. Anderson continues as follows:

Two children of Nicholas II and Elizabeth C. Meriwether:

Jane Meriwether, married Col. Robert Lewis, of "Belvoir". (See VII.) Their son, William Lewis, of "Locust Hill", died 1781, married 1769, Lucy Meriwether (born February 4, 1752, died September 8, 1837). They had:

1. Jane Lewis, married Edmund Anderson,
2. Meriwether Lewis, of Lewis and Clark Expedition.
3. Reuben Lewis, married Mildred Dabney, no issue.

David Meriwether, born 1690, died December 25, 1744-5; Major for New Kent County 1723-4-8-9-33. Married Anne Holmes, died March 11, 1736. Their son, Thomas, (1714-1756) married Elizabeth Thornton (daughter of Col. Francis Thornton and Mary Taliaferro), and their daughter, Lucy Meriwether, married William Lewis, of "Locust Hill".

William Lewis served in the Revolution against Lord Dunmore, 1775, in Col. Meredith's command. Lieutenant in battalion of Minutemen from Amherst and Albemarle—changed to Continental Line with same rank. His is the third signature to the Declaration of Independence of Albemarle County.

*Land Book* at Richmond, Va., Vol. 3, page 499, states: "The heirs of Lieutenant Wm. Lewis are allowed land bounties for seven and a half years and one month."

There is a D. A. R. marker at his grave, "Cloverfields", near Keswick, Va. His daughter, Jane Meriwether Lewis, born March 31, 1770, married 1785, Edmund Anderson, born April 1, 1763, died April 19, 1810. Their son

Dr. Meriwether L. Anderson, born June 23, 1805, died March 5, 1862, married June 16, 1831, Lucy S. Harper, born December 8, 1811, died December 4, 1885. Dr. Anderson was a member of the Virginia Legislature at time of his death. He had served as surgeon in Charlottesville hospitals 1861. His second son

Charles Harper Anderson, born June 28, 1848, died February 13, 1920, was a Justice of Peace in Albemarle for years, served on a commission from Albemarle in care of the Confederate wounded around Fredericksburg. Copy of the certificate:

CHARLOTTESVILLE, VA., *May 8, /64.*

"This will certify that Mr. Harper Anderson visits the Army as a member of the Albemarle Committee for the relief of wounded soldiers from Albemarle County, appointed by authority of the county Court of said county.

"Given under my hand this 8th day of May 1864.

"ROBERT R. PRENTIS,
"Chairman of Albemarle Military Committee."

Charles Harper Anderson, married February 15, 1872, Sarah T. L. Scott, born March 31, 1847, died February 6, 1926, who was descended from Jane Meriwether and Col. Robert Lewis, of "Belvoir", inheriting through them the same Colonial Records thus:

Mary Lewis (daughter of Robert and Jane Lewis, of "Belvoir"), died 1813. Married first, Samuel Cobbs, and had issue. Married second, Waddy Thomson (died 1803), of Louisa and Albemarle, and had five daughters.

X. He was Justice of Louisa County 1768, 1774. Member of Louisa Committee of Safety 1775 (Revolutionary Record), Commissioner of Louisa County 1764 (*Virginia Historical Magazine*). Their daughter, Mildred Thompson, born September 22, 1775, died October 9, 1824, married December 9, 1807, Dr. James Scott, born February 17, 1760, died April 14, 1822. Their youngest son was

James McClure Scott, born August 17, 1811, died July 7, 1893, "Bel-air", Spotsylvania, Va., married December 13, 1832, Sarah Travers Lewis, born November 7, 1813, died December 18, 1891. Their daughter

Sarah Travers Lewis Scott, born March 31, 1847, died February 6, 1926, married February 15, 1872, Charles Harper Anderson (1848-1920), of "Locust Hill". Had issue:

1. Dr. Meriwether L. Anderson, 2. Mrs. Sarah Travers Gordon, 3. Charles Harper Anderson, 4. Rev. Alfred Scott Anderson, 5. Jane Lewis Anderson, died young, 6. William S. Anderson, died infant, 7. Mrs. Lucy B. Ward, 8. Rev. Alden Scott Anderson.

*Extract from "Anderson Family" by Edward L. Anderson.*

Robert Anderson II, born 1673, died 1716, aged 53 years, Vestryman St. Peter's Parish, New Kent 1702, Vestryman St. Paul's Parish 1705, served as captain for New Kent 1705 to

1713 (14), Justice for New Kent 1714, died February 22, 1716, married Mary Overton, died 1734. (*Vestry Book,* St. Paul's Parish.)

(St. Peter's *Register*)

Robert Anderson I, died 1712, aged 72 years. Grantee 727 acres in New Kent. Vestryman St. Peter's Parish 1686, St. Paul's Parish 1704-12. Married Cecilia Massie.

(Genealogical Records of New York City, Philadelphia and Virginia)

Colonial Record of Elizabeth Thornton, wife of Thomas Meriwether.

She was daughter of

XI. Col. Francis Thornton of "Snow Creek", born January 4, 1682. Burgess of Spotsylvania 1723 to 1726, Justice for Caroline County 1723, married Mary Taliaferro, daughter of

XII. Col. John Taliaferro of "Snow Creek", born 1637, died May 3, 1744. Settled at "Snow Creek 1707; Burgess for Spotsylvania 1720, Vestryman of St. George's Parish 1725; married Mary Catlett. He was son of

XIII. John Taliaferro, died 1720. 1692, he was a lieutenant, commanding company of Rangers against Indians. 1695, Justice of Essex County. 1699, Sheriff. He married before 1683, Sarah Smith, daughter of Col. Lawrence Smith. (*Virginia Historical Magazine,* Vol. I, No. 2, P. C.)

XIV. Major Lawrence Smith of Gloucester County, Va. bore arms of Smith of Totten, Devon, England. Came to Virginia early in the seventeenth century, died 1700. The Governor of Virginia placed Major Smith, 1676, in charge of forts on the Rappahannock and Potomac in defense against the Indians, he had also legal jurisdiction over this section. The Governor recommended him to be made a King's Councillor but he died before taking his seat. He married Mary ——. Her daughter, Sarah, married Lieut.-Col. Taliaferro, the Ranger.

# COLONIAL RECORD
## OF
## MRS. SARAH TRAVERS (LEWIS) SCOTT OF "BEL-AIR"

I. Col. Gerard Fowke, born in England, died in Maryland, 1669. Settled first in Virginia, built "Gunston Hall", named for his ancestral home in Staffordshire England; later sold it to his cousin, George Mason, and moved to Port Tobacco, Md. Married Ann Chandler, widow or daughter of Mr. Chandler of Port Tobacco, Maryland. He was Colonel in army of Charles I of England, Burgess from Westmoreland County, Va. 1663, Lieutenant-Colonel of Westmoreland Troop 1660, Burgess of Charles County, Md. 1664-9, Justice of same 1667-9. (Spotsylvania record and family register used by Hayden.) His son

II. Gerard Fowke, born 1662, will probated January 20, 1734, Charles County, Md.; married second, Sarah Burdett and their daughter, Frances Fowke, born February 2, 1691, died November 8, 1744, married 1711, Dr. Gustavus Brown, born Dalkieth, Scotland, 1689, died 1762 in Maryland. Frances Brown, their daughter, born at "Riches Hill", Md., July 29, 1713, married June 18, 1741, Rev. John Moncure, rector of Overwharton Parish, Va., born in Kincaide, Scotland, died March 10, 1764 at his home, "Clermont", Stafford County. He came to Virginia 1733. Their daughter, Frances Moncure, born September 20, 1745, died ——, married October 7, 1762. (Hayden, *Church and County Records*.)

III. Travers Daniel, born May 26, 1741, died June 28, 1824 at "Crow's Nest", his home in Stafford. Justice of Stafford County 1765, succeeded his father as Presiding Justice. Their daughter, Elizabeth Travers Daniel, born October 18, 1778; died August 8, 1827, married October 28, 1802.

IV. Dr. Richmond Lewis, born March 4, 1774, died July 31, 1831. Hayden states: served in War of 1812 as surgeon.

Travers Daniel was son of

V. Peter Daniel, born September 29, 1706, married 1736, Sarah Travers, died 1788. Presiding Justice for Stafford 1744, retaining this office till his death, October 14, 1765. He and his son, Travers, also of the Stafford Commission of Justices, addressed and signed a protest against the Stamp Act, addressing it to Hon.

Francis Fauquier, "Governor of His Majesty's Ancient Colony of Virginia." Peter Daniel was a zealous advocate of the Freedom of the Colonies. He was a member of the Committee of Safety for Stafford 1774, as was his son, Travers 1775. His wife was daughter of Raleigh Travers II and Hannah Ball, (eldest daughter of Col. Joseph Ball and his first wife, Elizabeth Romney, and half sister of Mary Ball, mother of George Washington.)

VI. Raleigh Travers I, died before 1674; Justice for Lancaster County 1656, Burgess for Lancaster County 1660-1-2-3-4-5-6-9-70. Married before 1644, Elizabeth ——.

## COLONIAL RECORD
### OF
### DR. RICHMOND LEWIS, Surgeon U. S. A., 1812.

Spotsylvania County and Family records used by Hayden.

I. Zachary Lewis II, settled in Spotsylvania, born January 1, 1702, died June 20, 1765. Burgess from Spotsylvania 1756-7-8-9, married June 9, 1725, Mary Waller, born January 20, 1699, died March 28, 1781. She was daughter of

II. Col. John Waller (1670-1754), married Dorothy King (1675-1759), first clerk of Spotsylvania County, 1722-42.

III. Zachary Lewis III, son of Zachary and Mary Waller, was born May 6, 1731, died July 20, 1803, served in Spotsylvania Foot Co. His commission as lieutenant dated 1755; as captain, May 8, 1762; as major, 1764; his commission issued at the same time with George Washington's. (Spotsylvania record.) They served together in the French and Indian War and in parting exchanged swords. This sword is owned by Dr. John Lewis, of Lexington, Ky. Zachary Lewis' powder horn is owned by John Moncure Lewis, of Richmond. He married May 8, 1771, Ann Overton Terrell, born November 3, 1748, died November 30, 1820. Their son

IV. Dr. Richmond Lewis, married Elizabeth Travers Daniel. Their daughter, Sarah Travers Lewis, married James McClure Scott. Their daughter, Sarah Travers Lewis Scott, married Charles Harper Anderson.

*Copy*

ROBERT DINWIDDIE; His Majesty's Lieutenant-Governor and Commander in Chief of the Colony and Dominion of Virginia.

TO MR. ZACHARY LEWIS, JUN.

By Virtue of the Power and Authority to me given as Commander of this colony I do hereby constitute and appoint you, the said Zachary Lewis, Captain of a company of Foot in the County of Spotsylvania. You are therefore carefully and diligently to perform the duty of a Captain in the said County by duly exercising the Soldiers of your Company and by seeing that they are provided with arms and ammunition as the Law requires.

And I do hereby command them to obey you as their Captain. And you are to follow all such Orders and Directions from Time to Time as you shall receive from me or any other of your commanding Officers, according to the Rules and Discipline of War.

Given under my hand and the Seal of the Colony at Williamsburg the seventeenth day of February in the 31st Year of His Majesty's Reign, Annoque Domini 1758.

ROB DINWIDDIE.

FORT MANDAN, 1,609 MILES ABOVE THE ENTRANCE OF THE MISSOURI, *March 31, 1805.*

DEAR MOTHER:

I arrived at this place on the 27th of October last with the party under my command, destined to the Pacific Ocean, by way of the Missouri and Columbia rivers. The near approach of winter, the low state of the water, and the known scarcity of timber which exists on the Missouri for many hundred miles above the Mandans, together with many other considerations equally important determined my friend and companion, Capt. Clark and myself to fortify ourselves and remain for the winter in the neighborhood of the Mandans, Minetares and Ahwahhanways who are the most friendly and well disposed savages that we have yet met with. Accordingly we sought and found a convenient situation for our purpose a few miles below the villages of these people on the North side of the river in an extensive and well watered bottom, where we commenced the erection of our houses on the 2nd of November, and completed them so far as to put ourselves under shelter on the 21st of the same month, by which time the season wore the aspect of winter.

Having completed our fortifications early in December, we called it Fort Mandan in honor of our friendly neighbors. So far we have experienced more difficulty from the navigation of the Missouri than danger from the savages. The difficulties which oppose themselves to the navigation of this immense river, arise from the rapidity of its current, its falling banks and sand bars, and timber, which remains wholly or partially concealed in its bed, usually called by the navigators of the Missouri and Mississippi, Sawyers or planters. One of these difficulties the navigator never ceases to contend with from the entrance of the Missouri to this place, and in innumerable instances most of these obstructions are at the same instant combined to oppose his progress or threaten his destruction, to these we may also add a fifth and not much less inconsiderable difficulty, the turbid quality of the water, which renders it impossible to discover any obstruction even to the depth of a single inch. Such is the velocity of the current at all seasons of the year from the entrance of the Missouri to the mouth of the great river Platte that it is impossible to resist its force by means of oars or poles in the main channels of the river, the eddies therefore which generally exist one side or the other of the river, are sought by the navigator; but these are almost universally encumbered with concealed timber, or within the reach of the falling banks, but notwithstanding are usually preferable to that of passing along the edges of the sand bars over which the water, though shallow, runs with such violence that if your vessel happens to touch the sand, or is by any accident turned side ways to the current, it is driven on the bar and over set in an instant—generally destroyed—and always attended with the loss of the cargo. The base of the river banks being composed of fine light sand is easily removed by the water, it happens that when this capricious and violent current sets against its banks, which are usually covered with heavy timber, it quickly undermines them, sometimes to the depth of 40 or 50 feet and several miles in length, the banks being unable to support themselves longer tumble into the river with tremendous force, destroying everything within their reach. The timber thus precipitated into the water with large masses of earth about their roots are seen drifting with the stream, the points above the water with the roots firmly fixed in the quick sands which forms the bed of the river, where they remain for many years, forming an irregular, though dangerous *chevaux de frise* to oppose the navigator.

This immense river so far as we have yet ascended, waters one of the fairest portions of the globe, nor do I believe that there is in the universe a similar extent of country equally fertile, well watered and intersected by such a number of navigable streams.

The country as high up this river as the Mouth of the river Platte, a distance of 630 miles, is generally well timbered. At some little distance above this river the open or prairie country commences. With respect to this open country, I have been agreeably disappointed, from previous information I had been led to believe that it was barren, sterile and sandy, but on the contrary found it fertile in the extreme, the soil being from one to twenty feet in depth, consisting of a fine black loam intermingled with a sufficient quantity of sand only to induce a luxuriant growth of grass and other vegetable productions, particularly such as are not liable to be much injured or wholly destroyed by the ravages of the fire. It is also generally level yet well watered, in short, there can exist no other objection to it except that of the want of timber, which is truly a very serious one. This want of timber is by no means attributable to a deficiency in the soil to produce it, but owes its *orrigine* to the *ravages* of the fires which the natives kindle in these plains at all seasons of the year. This country on both sides of the river, except some of its bottom lands for an immense distance is one continuous open plain in which no timber is to be seen except a few detached and scattered copse, and clumps of trees which from their moist situations on the steep declivities of hills are sheltered from effects of fire.

The general aspect of the country is level so far as the perception of the spectator will enable him to determine, but from the rapidity of the Missouri it must be considerably elevated as it passes to the N. West, it is broken only on the borders of the water courses.

Game is very abundant and seems to increase as we progress. Our prospect of starving is therefore consequently small. On the lower portion of the Missouri from its junction with the Mississippi to the entrance of the Osage River, we met with some deer, bear and turkies, from there to the Kancey river the deer were more abundant. A great number of black bear, some turkies, geese, swan and ducks, from thence to the mouth of the great river Platte, an immense quantity of deer, some bear, elk, turkies, geese, swan and ducks, from thence to this river Souise some deer, a great number of elk. The bear disappeared almost entirely, some turkies, geese, swans and ducks to the mouth of White River, vast herds of buffalo, elk and some deer and a greater quantity of turkies than we had before seen, a circumstance I did not much expect in a country so destitute of timber. From thence to Fort Mandan, the buffalo, elk and deer increase in quantity with the addition of *cabri,* as they are usually called by the French *engages* but which is a creature about the size of a small deer. Its flesh is deliciously flavored.

The ice in the Missouri has now nearly disappeared. I shall set out on my voyage in the course of a few days. I can see no material obstruction to our progress and feel the most perfect confidence that we shall reach the Pacific Ocean this summer. For myself, individually, I enjoy better health than I have since I commenced my voyage.

The party now are in fine health and excellent spirits, are attached to the enterprise and anxious to proceed—not a whisper of discontent or murmur to be heard among them, but all act in unison and with the most perfect harmony. With such men I feel every confidence necessary to insure success.

The party with Capt. Clark and myself consists of thirty-one white persons, one negro and two Indians. The Indians in this neighborhood assure us that the Missouri is navigable nearly to its source, and that from a navigable part of the river at a distance not exceeding half a day's march there is a large river running from South to North along the western base of the Rock Mountains, but as their war excursions have never extended far beyond this point they can give no account of the discharge or source of this river. We believe this stream to be the principal South fork of the Columbia river, and if so, we shall probably find but little difficulty in passing to the Ocean.

We have subsisted this winter on meat principally with which our guns have furnished us an ample supply and have by that means reserved a sufficient stock of the provisions which we brought with us from Illinois to guard us against accidental want during the voyage of the present year. You may expect me in Albemarle about the last of next September—twelve months.

I request that you will give yourself no uneasiness with respect to my fate, for I assure you that I feel myself as perfectly safe as I should do in Albemarle, and the only difference between three or four thousand miles and 130 is that I cannot have the pleasure of seeing you as often as I did while at Washington.

I must request of you before I conclude this letter, to send John Marks to the college at Williamsburg as *soon* as it shall be thought that his education has been sufficiently advanced to fit him for that seminary, for you may rest assured that as you regard his future prosperity you had better make a sacrifice of his property than suffer his education to be neglected or remain incomplete.

Give my love to my brothers and sisters and all my neighbors and friends and rest assured yourself of the most devoted filial affection of

Yours,

Mrs. Lucy Marks. MERIWETHER LEWIS.

---

The address on the outside of this large foolscap paper, space being left free for this purpose, extends across the middle of the sheet which is folder and written on elsewhere.

MRS. LUCY MARKS,
Charlottesville,
*Mail* Virginia.

## MERIWETHER LEWIS

The old adage, "the boy is father to the man" seems peculiarly true of Meriwether Lewis. The characteristics shown in his childhood were the very same which in manhood gained for him the confidence and admiration of those who entrusted to him the command and arrangement of a great expedition, and later a political position calling for statesmanship to meet complex conditions in his office as Governor of Louisiana.

These characteristics were courage, resourcefulness, faithfulness, devotion, executive ability, a high sense of duty for himself and others, to all these was added a charm of mind, manner and person which drew all hearts to him.

At eight years of age he habitually hunted alone at night with his dog as his only companion in the mountains and dark woods. And once when on a visit to "Cloverfields", the Meriwether home near Keswick, returning from a hunt he crossed a lot in which was a vicious bull. As it rushed at him he coolly raised his gun and shot it dead.

On one of his boyhood journeys with friends, the camp was thrown into a panic by a false alarm of an Indian attack. He alone had the thought to throw water on the camp fire, thus enabling the darkness to restore confidence.

As a school boy he returned to Virginia from Georgia where he and his younger brother, Reuben had lived with his mother and stepfather, Capt. John Marks. His filial respect is shown in affectionate letters to them both, full of details of his school life, news from the various relations, and finally combining with these messages from Reuben who later came also to school in Virginia. Their studies were pursued under noted teachers—Parson Waddell (the blind parson so celebrated in Wirt's book, *The British Spy*) and Parson Maury. And Reuben, at least, was taught by the celebrated teacher, Rev. Mr. Robertson.

At an age when most boys are still at school, seventeen or eighteen, Meriwether Lewis took charge of his patrimony "Locust Hill", which he inherited under the primogeniture law. But the breaking out of the "Whiskey Rebellion" aroused the desire for a wider field of action and shaped his future, for at the end of this volunteer service he entered the United States regular army. Letters to his mother during the campaign were full of patriotic enthusiasm, enjoyment of camp life and a comforting assurance to her of his determination to resist all its temptations.

In later life her expostulations on his roving propensities were met with the laughing charge that he had inherited this disposition from her.

The death of Capt. Marks in Georgia brought out a protective aspect towards his mother whose mainstay he at once became—

helping in the settlement of his stepfather's estate in Georgia, going to Kentucky to establish the interests of his half brother and sister in land claims due their father, finally going in his carriage (which carriage is said to have been built at Monticello by Mr. Jefferson's mechanics and afterwards to have been General Clark's coach at St. Louis) to bring his mother back to "Locust Hill", where the remainder of her long life was spent and where she is buried. She inherited "Locust Hill" from her son, Meriwether at his death.

While Meriwether Lewis was Jefferson's private secretary at Washington, the latter recognized in him qualities peculiarly fitted to command the expedition to explore the Mississippi and Columbia Rivers. Mrs. Marks was much grieved at his departure from Washington without coming to see her, but his letters cheered her—telling of his duty, the occasion for prompt departure, assurance of the safety of his journey, encouraging her with the promise of seeing her again in two years, saying the only drawback to him in being so far away was in not seeing her occasionally as when in the "White House" at Washington. He advises regarding the schooling of his half brother, John Marks, and insists that his own means be used if John's proved insufficient for a course at William and Mary College. This attitude of council and direction was felt to be wise and loving and was honored and followed by the household at home.

Captain Lewis when chosen by Mr. Jefferson for the command of the proposed expedition took special courses of study at Philadelphia and at Lancaster, Penna. under scientific professors that he might be enabled to report in a scientific manner information gained on his journey of exploration.

Congress voted a sum of money to defray expenses, also open letters of credit were given Capt. Lewis for paying persons employed and for expenses in case the party should have to return by sea.

Originally he was empowered in case of his illness or death on the way to appoint as his successor any one of the party he judged competent to command and fitted to carry on the work. This emergency however, he forestalled by asking the appointment of Capt. Clark for this purpose.

President Jefferson's *Biography of Meriwether Lewis* states that Captain Lewis proposed William Clark as a competent person to accompany him in order to guard against any accident which might befall himself that might prevent the success of the undertaking. This proposition being approved Clark was duly commissioned a Captain in rank.

*Lewis and Clark Expedition,* 1814 Edition states that Capt. Lewis having received requisite instructions left Washington and being joined by Captain Clark at Louisville, Ky. went on to St. Louis, arriving there December 1803.

The passage of the party was here delayed, since the Spanish Governor of this city had not been advised that Spain had ceded Louisiana to France and that France had sold it to the United States. They wintered at the mouth of Wood river opposite the mouth of the Missouri, and from this point began their journey May 14, 1804.

While interest in the fur trade was a great incentive to the furtherance of this expedition Mr. Jefferson's far-sightedness prompted him to give Lewis a much wider range of instruction and these were faithfully followed and reported in Lewis's diary in London, England, also in the 1814 edition of the Lewis and Clark Exploration of the Missouri across the Rocky Mountains to the Columbia and to the Pacific.

The discovery of the Pacific Coast added two States to our country. They were not a part of Louisiana and an exploring party coming down from the British possessions were on the eve of laying claim to that country for England.

This expedition originating with Jefferson and executed by Captain Lewis with Captain Clark's efficient assistance opened up seventeen States for trade, for settlement and for marvelous development—a fact which is scarcely noticed in the histories of the United States.

Sergeant Floyd was the only man who died on the expedition. And now regarding the matter of Captain Lewis' death—his family always maintained that he was murdered. Subsequent events establishing their belief, and that Mr. Jefferson's theory of suicide was expressed before this evidence came out.

I wrote widely to the scattered branches of the family trying to get more definite evidence but always met tradition with invariably the same story.

The Historical Society of Tennessee had much research on this point and much tradition on both theories—suicide and murder.

I have been told the tradition of the vicinity where his death occured is murder, and that Grinder, the owner of the house where he died, was suspected but there was lack of evidence to support the charge. I have heard the Grinders assert Captain Lewis's sisters visited them. This can not be true. His only full sister, Mrs. Jane M. Anderson, so far as known, never left Virginia, spending her whole life within the radius of a few counties in that State. The half sister, Mrs. Mary (Marks) Moore lived in Georgia, in her old age with her numerous family emigrated to Alabama and Texas. She died in Texas. She believed firmly her brother was murdered and transmitted this belief to her descendants. She would not have visited a family she suspected of complicity in his death.

Lewis County, named for Meriwether Lewis, was taken from Maury, Lawrence and Hickman counties 1843. In the center of this county, a lonely spot on the old Natchez trail stands a monument erected 1848 by the Legislature of Tennessee. On one face of it is inscribed "He was born at 'Locust Hill', Virginia, August 18, 1774, died October 11, 1809, aged 35 years." On the other face, "An officer of the regular army, Commander of the Expedition to Oregon 1803-6, Governor of Louisiana. His melancholy death occured where stands this monument under which his mortal remains lie."

The old "Locust Hill" house was burned 1837-8 when many valuable and interesting things belonging to Meriwether Lewis were lost. This house was of three periods of construction—the original part being one room with a small hall and a stairway to the upper hall and to the half story chamber adjoining. The next addition was of two stories the rooms lower pitched and on a lower level, and at the end of this addition was the usual shed of one story. The primitive house was of logs, very comfortable and filled with things of value, among other things much table silver. It was the gathering place of a wide circle of relatives and of many distinguished people.

Mrs. Marks was a woman with mind and characteristics similar to those she transmitted to her son, Meriwether. Her portrait shows a fragile figure, a refined face and a masterful eye.

I saw the copy of Peale's portrait of Meriwether Lewis from Philadelphia at the Exhibition in St. Louis. This portrait was taken from life, it has brown hair and blue or hazel eyes, I forget which.

The St. Memin portrait owned by Dr. M. L. Anderson of Richmond is beautifully handsome but does not give the coloring.

"Locust Hill", burned just after Mrs. Mark's death, was rebuilt by her grandson, Dr. M. L. Anderson, Sr. It stands on an elevated plateau and commands a magnificient view of the circle of mountain ranges more or less distant—some a mile, some twenty or thirty miles.

## MEMORANDA OF JEFFERSON'S INSTRUCTIONS TO LEWIS

1. Geography of country traversed.
2. Take celestial observations.
3. Explore Missouri and tributaries especially its Southern branches to see if there was any communication with the Columbia, Oregon or Colorado that would allow commerce by water from ocean to ocean.
4. Careful location, marking route of party by instruments and scientific observations that the way might be readily recognized by others later.
5. All points of portage.
6. Indians—number, nations, extent of possessions, relation between tribes, language, traditions, monuments, agriculture, fishing, hunting, arts, employments, food, clothing, domestic accommodations, diseases, remedies, morals, physical condition, laws, customs, disposition, articles of commerce—all needed in order to civilize, instruct and understand them.
7. Observe soil and face of country, growths and vegetation, particularly those not found in the United States.
8. Any tradition or any remains of extinct species.
9. Mineral productions of all sorts, particularly metals, limestone, coal, saltpetre, saline and mineral waters and their temperature, volcanic appearances.
10. Climate—rain, cloudy days, lightnings, hail, snow, ice, frost and wind at various seasons.

## COPY OF ROYAL GRANT TO "BEL-AIR"

GEORGE the Second, by the grace of God of Great Britain, France and Ireland, King defender of the faith, To all to whom these presents shall come Greeting—WHEREAS our Roial father of blessed memory on the humble petition of the general assembly of our Colony and Dominion of Virginia was graciously pleased to grant unto each of our subjects which should go to settle in the County of Spotsylvania before the first day of May, which should be in the year of our Lord, One Thousand Seven Hundred and Twenty-Eight, the liberty of taking up any quantity of land not exceeding one thousand acres free and discharged of the duty of purchasing rights for the same, WE have given, granted and confirmed, and by these presents for us our heirs and successors do give grant and confirm unto Christopher Smith of Hanover County, One Certain tract or parcel of land containing One Thousand acres lying and being on the North side of the North Anna in Saint George's parish in Spotsylvania County aforesaid, and bounded as ffolloweth (to-wit) BEGINNING at ffour hickorys Corner of Mr. Moore's land running along his line North thirty-five East five hundred and forty poles to John Holladay's Corner hickory on the north East side a small branch. Thence North fforty-seven West Two hundred and eighty-six poles to two small white oaks of Mr. Rowland Thomas'—Thence along his line South Thirty West Six hundred and ffour poles to a small maple, small white oak and small gum on the North side of the North Anna—Thence down the same by the water courses to the Beginning, WITH ALL woods, underwoods, swamps, marshes, lowgrounds, meadows, ffeedings, and his due share of all veins, mines and quarries, as well discovered as not discovered within the bounds aforesaid, and being part of the said quantity of One Thousand acres of Land, and the Rivers Waters and water courses therein contained together with the privileges of hunting, hawking, ffishing, ffowling and all other profits, rights and hereditaments whatsoever to the same or any part thereof belonging, or in anywise appertaining TO HAVE, HOLD, possess and enjoy the same said tract and parcel of land and other the before granted premises and every part thereof with their and every of their appurtenances unto the said Christopher Smith and to his heirs and assigns forever to the only use and behoof of him the said Christopher Smith, his heirs and assigns forever TO BE HELD of us our heirs and successors, as of our Manor of Greenwich in the County of Kent in Free and common socage and not in catite or by Knight Service. YIELDING AND PAYING after the said Ffirst day of May, One Thousand Seven Hundred and Twenty-Eight, unto us our heirs and successors for every ffifty acres of land and so proportionally for a less or greater quantity than ffifty acres the ffee rent of one shilling yearly to be paid upon the feast of Saint Michael the Arch Angel and also Cultivating and Improving Three

Acres part of every ffifty of the tract above mentioned within three years after the date of these presents PROVIDED always that if Three years of the said Ffee rent shall at any time be in arrear and unpaid or if the said Christopher Smith his heirs or assigns do not within the space of three years next coming after the date of these presents Cultivate and Improve three acres part of every ffifty of the tract above mentioned, then the Estate hereby granted shall cease and be utterly determined, and thereafter it shall and may be lawful to and for us our heirs and successors to grant the same land and premises * * * any part thereof * * * such other person or persons as we our heirs or successors shall think ffitt.

IN WITNESS, whereof we have caused, these our letters patent to be made Witness our trusty and well beloved William Gooch, Lieut.-Governor and commander-in-chief of our said Colony and Dominion at Williamsburgh under the seal of our said Colony the Twenty-Eighth Day of September, One Thousand Seven Hundred and Twenty-Eight in the second year of our reign

WILLIAM GOOCH.

(Seal)

# Notes

# Notes

# Notes

# Bibliography


"A Glimpse of an Old Dutch Town"—*Harper's Monthly Magazine,* March, 1881.

*Americans of Gentle Birth* by H. D. Pitman.

*Anderson Family* by E. L. Anderson.

*A Royal Lineage* by A. R. Watson.

Battle Abbey Roll.

*Biography of Meriwether Lewis* by Thomas Jefferson.

Brown Family Bible.

*Burke's Heraldry.*

*Burke's Landed Gentry.*

*Burke's Peerage.*

*Cabells and Their Kin* by Alexander Brown.

Carr Family Bible.

*Century Dictionary of Proper Names.*

*Colonial Register.*

*Descendants of James W. Thomas and Eliza A. Johnston* by John L. Thomas.

Dowman Family Bible.

*Early Settlers* by Saunders.

*Evening Post* of St. Helier, Jersey Island.

Family Letters.

Family Bibles.

Francis Lewis Chart 1755 by M. C. Hood.

Genealogical Records of New York City.

Genealogical Records of Philadelphia, Pa.

*Genealogy of the Lewis Family* by William Terrel Lewis.

*Gordon Family Prayer Book 1783*—Cobb.

*Green's History of Culpeper Co.*

*Hayden's Virginia Genealogy.*

*Henning's Statutes at Large.*

*History of Albemarle County, Virginia* by Wood.

*History of the Baptists in Virginia* by Semple.

*History of Old Pendleton District South Carolina* by R. W. Simpson.
*Howe's History of Virginia.*
Holladay Family Bible.
*Hume's History of England.*
*Lewis Family* by William T. Lewis.
Lewises of Wales, family Bible.
*Lewises and Kindred Families* by J. M. McAllister and Mrs. Lula Tandy.
*List of Revolutionary Soldiers* in Virginia State Library.
*Mitchell Family Papers.*
*New York Tribune,* 1904.
*Notable Families of America* by Watson.
*Old Churches and Families of Virginia*—Meade.
*Overton Family* by Dickinson.
Richmond Newspapers.
St. Paul's Vestry Book (Hanover and New Kent Counties.)
St. Peter's Parish Register.
St. Peter's Parish Vestry Book.
Slaughter Family Bible.
*Some Prominent Virginia Families* by Du Bellet.
*Southern Literary Messenger.*
*The Revolutionary Patriot.*
*Tyler's Quarterly Magazine.*
*The Meriwethers* by L. H. A. Minor.
*Virginia Gazette.*
Virginia County Records.
Virginia Land Office Books.
William W. Harper Papers.
*Willis Family* by Byrd C. Willis.
*Wood Family,* Records of Mrs. Susan Hunter Bull.

# Index

## B

D

F

## G

H

I

J

L

M

P

## Q

R

T

Y



Z

# ERRATA

Page 19, line 21—Maryland Official Records do not record a "Gov. Fuller."

Pages 20, 144, 145, 217, 282, 356, 430, 491—for "emigrant" read immigrant.

Page 26, line 12—Maryland Official Records do not record a "Gov. Bowles."

Page 38, line 3—The Mary Washington Monument was erected by the women of the United States, see *Mother of Washington and Her Times* pages 353-357, by Mrs. Roger Pryor.

Page 106, line 8—for "Faros" read Jaros.

Page 134, line 17—for "Fayetteville Co." read Fayette Co.

Page 185, line 13—for "Barwin Co." read Baldwin Co.

Pages 214, 215, 241, 414, 427, 430, 493, 494—for "Virginia Historical Magazine" read *Virginia Magazine of History and Biography.*

Page 350, lines 2, 11, 22—for "Groombridge" read Groomsbridge.

Page 337, lines 3, 4, 5—for "Thraives" read Thraves.

Page 481, line 5—for "Mayre" read Marye.

CPSIA information can be obtained
at www.ICGtesting.com
Printed in the USA
BVHW042150280422
635565BV00014B/190

9 780806 310725